Little Monster

12

Robico

CONTENTS

STORY

When Shizuku Mizutani does a favor for problem child Haru Yoshida, who sat next to her in school, he develops a huge crush on her. Attracted to his innocence, she eventually falls for him, too. As the couple repeatedly fail to find themselves on the same page, they move on to their second year of high school. After that, Haru confesses his love, and the two finally become an official couple. However, Shizuku inexplicably begins to feel jealous of Haru. They get into an argument, and the next day, Haru goes AWOL for two weeks… When Haru returns, Shizuku somehow manages to begin the reconciliation process, but when he tells her he wants to know how she feels, she is at a loss for how to respond, and ends up attacking him with cruel words. But in response, Haru…?!

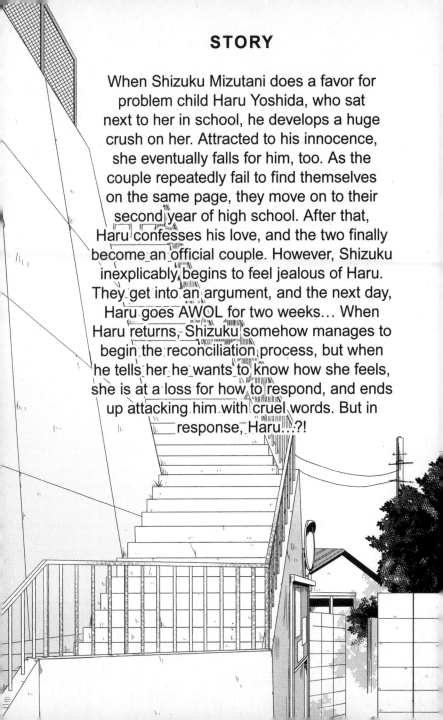

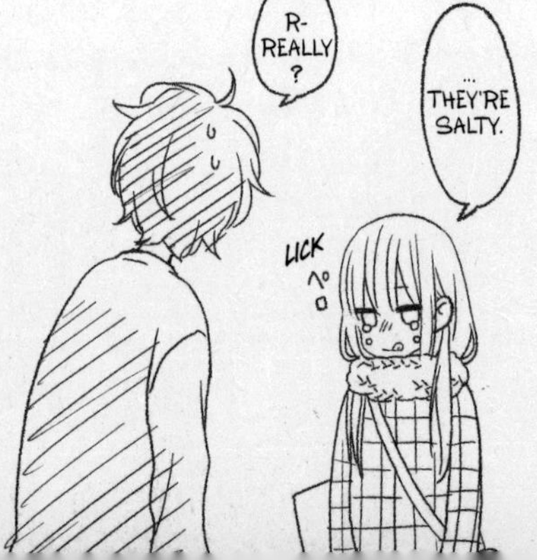
...THEY'RE SALTY.
LICK
ペロ
R-REALLY?

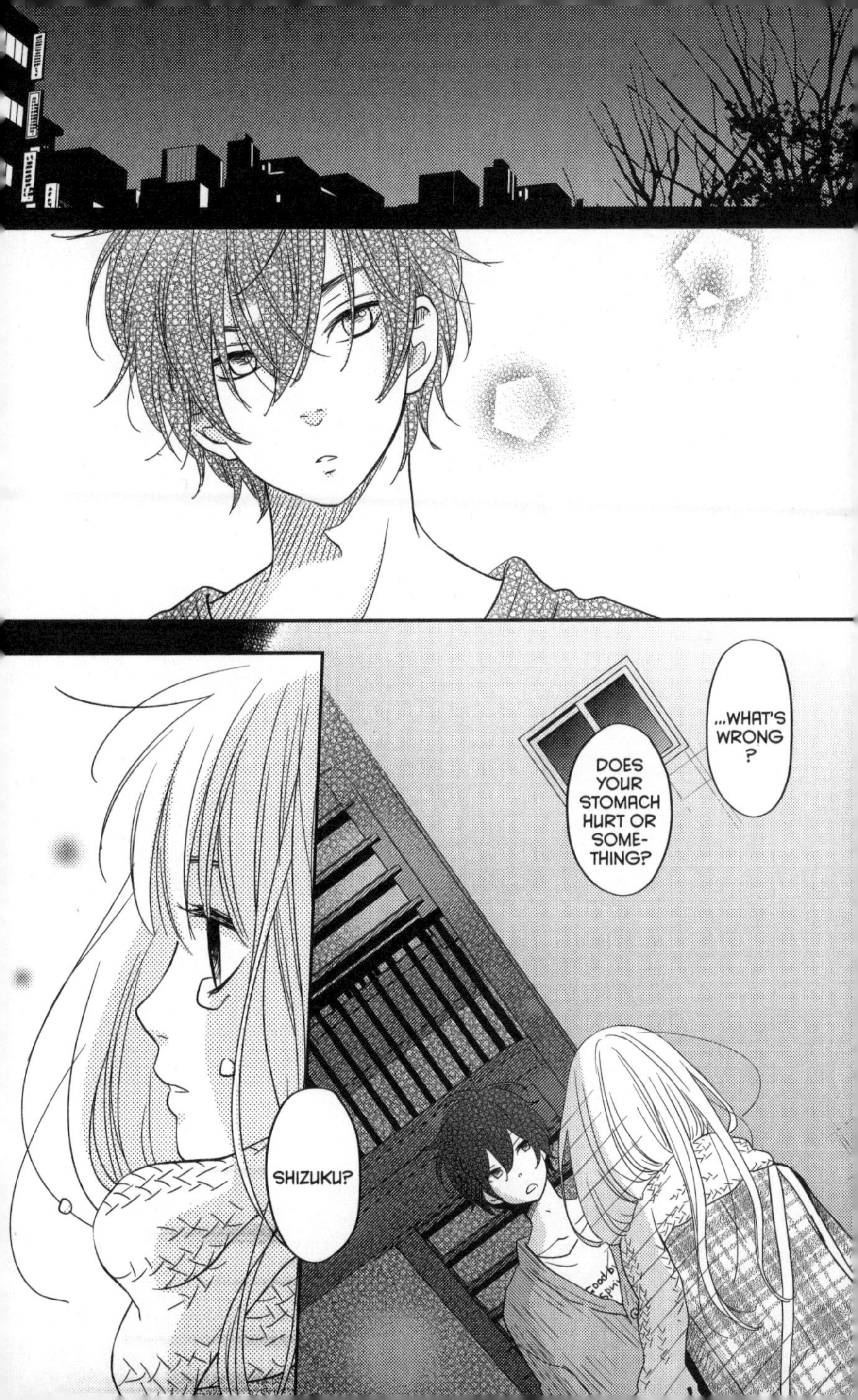
...WHAT'S WRONG?
DOES YOUR STOMACH HURT OR SOME-THING?
SHIZUKU?

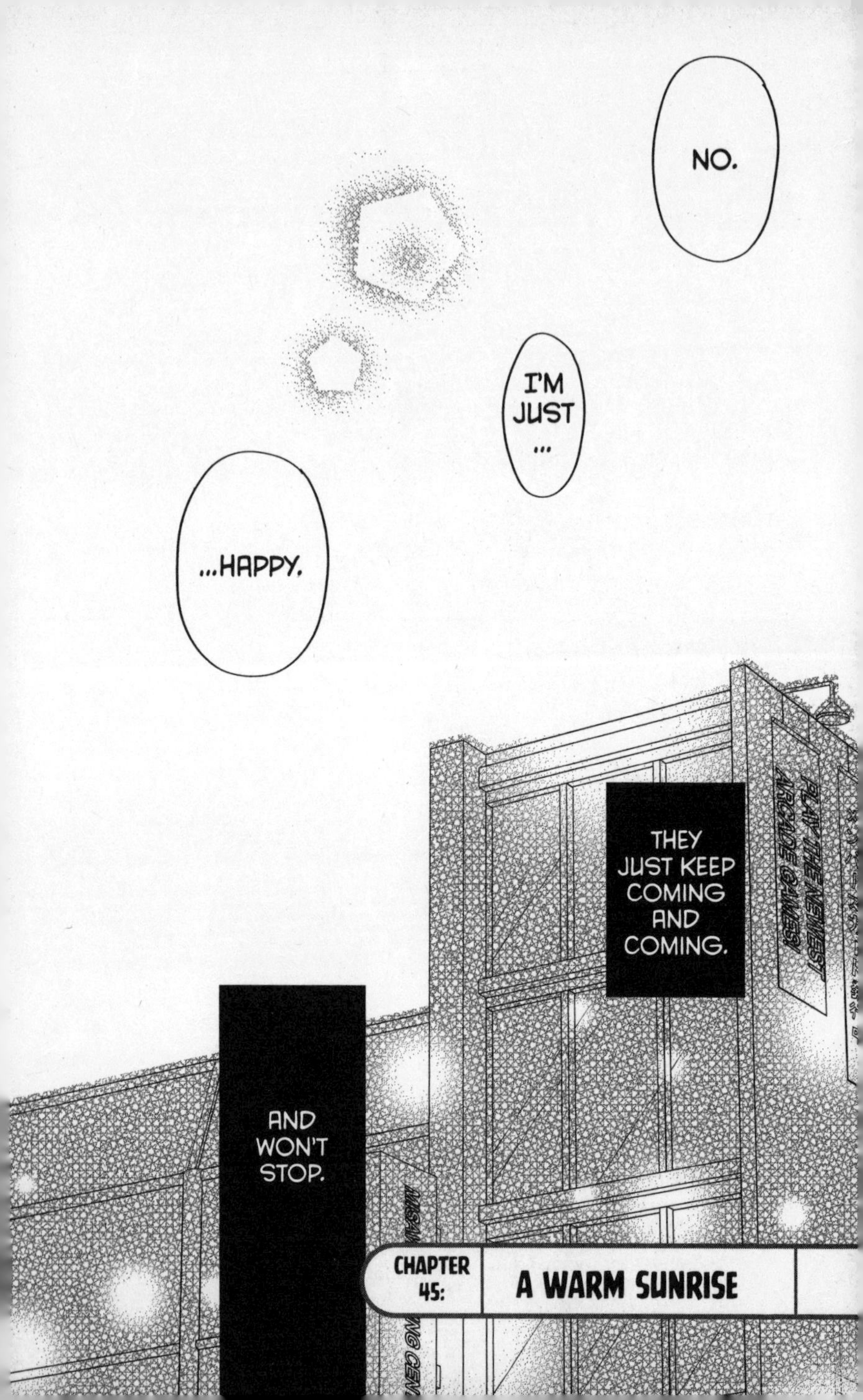
NO.
I'M JUST ...
...HAPPY.
THEY JUST KEEP COMING AND COMING.
PLAY THE NEWEST ARCADE GAMES!
AND WON'T STOP.
CHAPTER 45:
A WARM SUNRISE

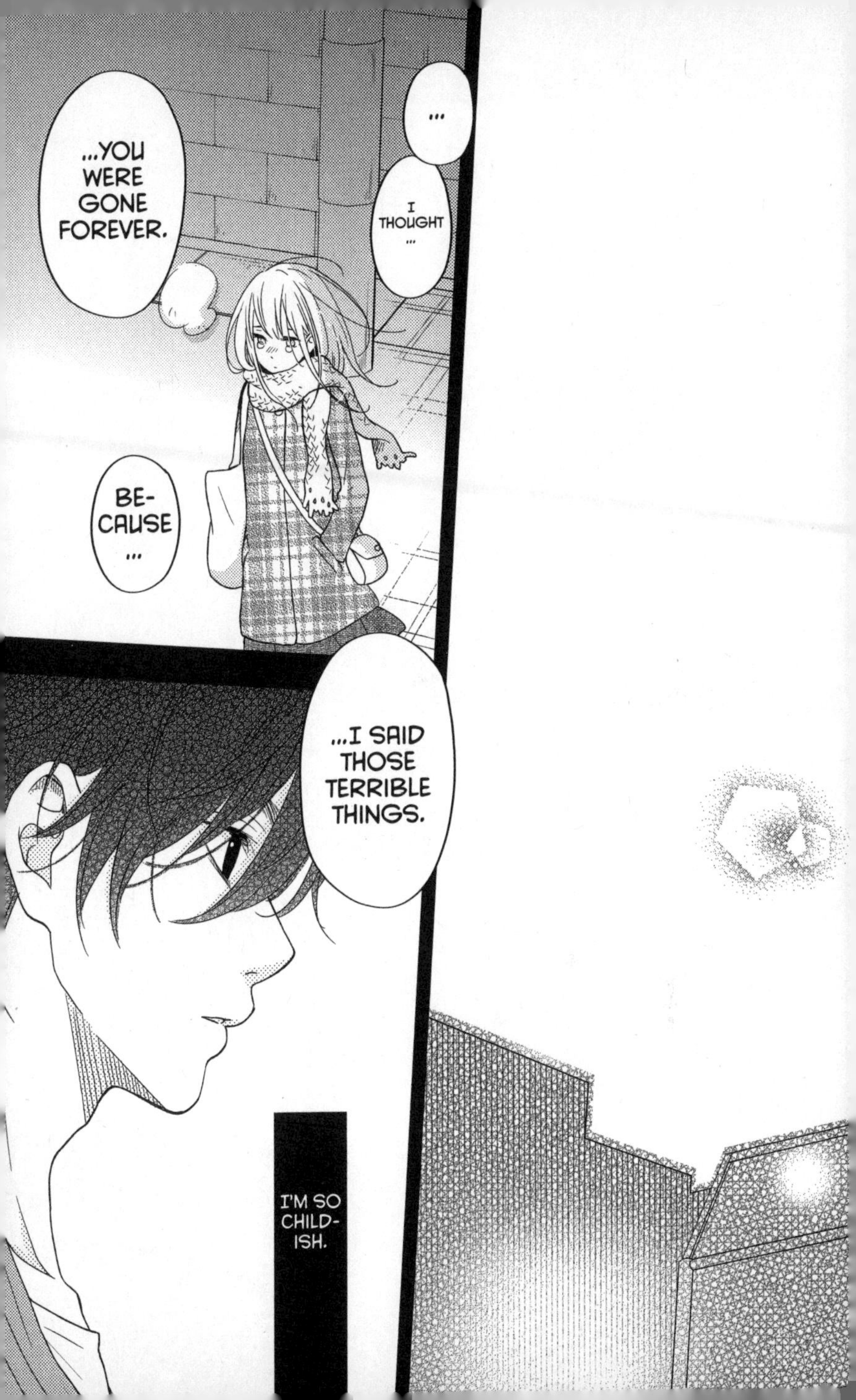
...
I THOUGHT ...
...YOU WERE GONE FOREVER.
BE-CAUSE ...
...I SAID THOSE TERRIBLE THINGS.
I'M SO CHILD-ISH.

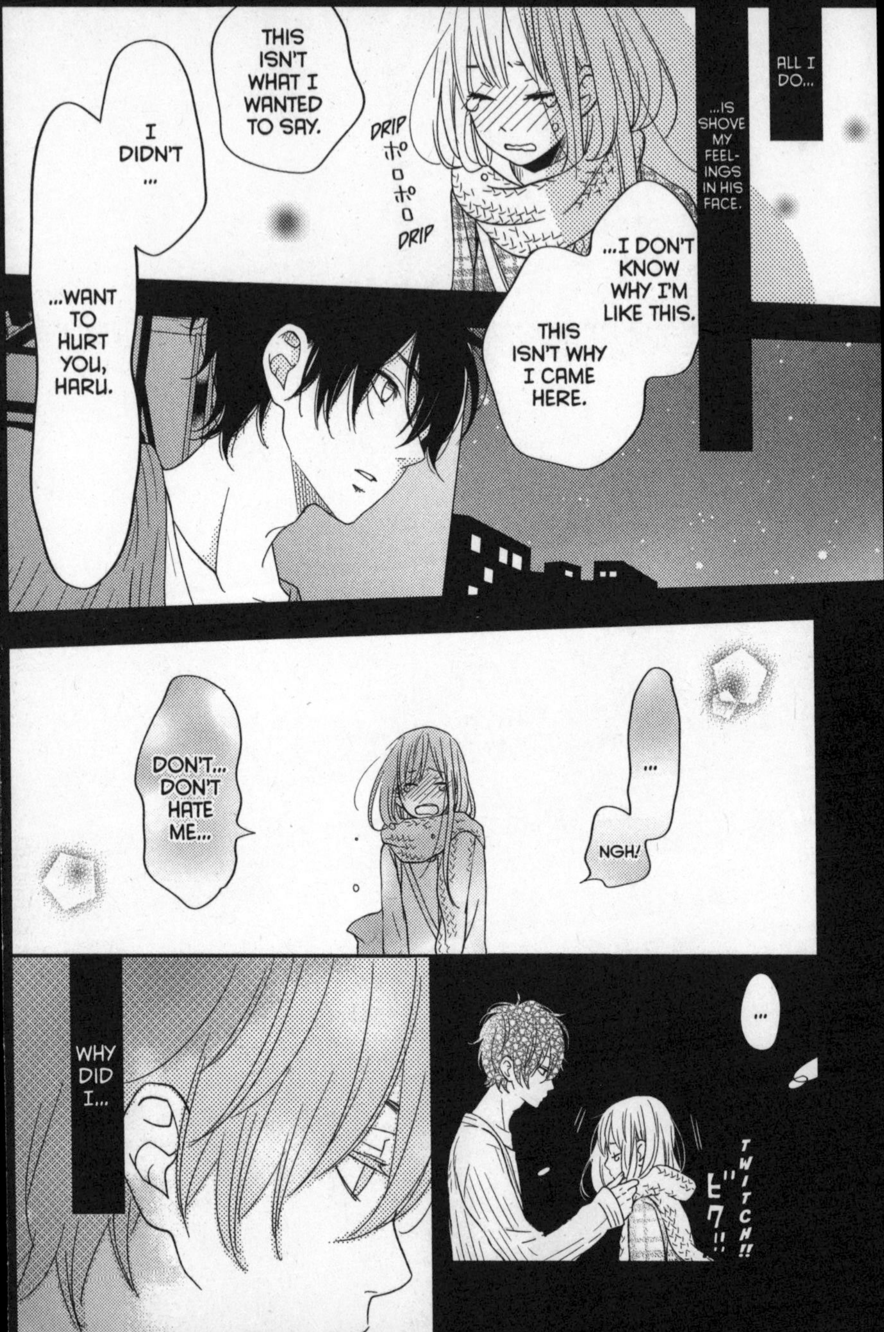
ALL I DO...
...IS SHOVE MY FEEL-INGS IN HIS FACE.
THIS ISN'T WHAT I WANTED TO SAY.
DRIP
ポロポロ
DRIP
...I DON'T KNOW WHY I'M LIKE THIS.
THIS ISN'T WHY I CAME HERE.
I DIDN'T ...
...WANT TO HURT YOU, HARU.
...
NGH!
DON'T... DON'T HATE ME...
...
ビク!!
TWITCH!!
WHY DID I...

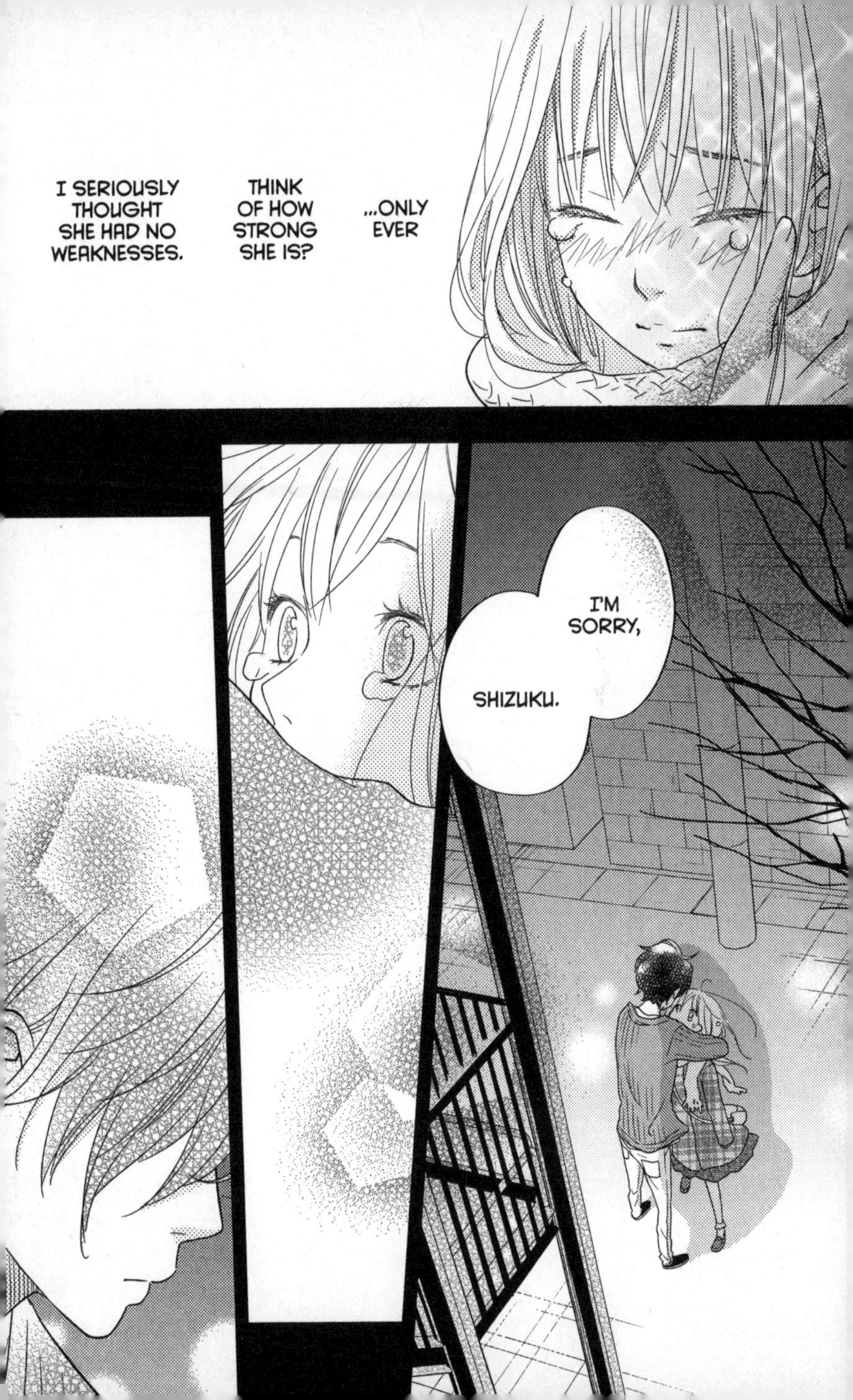
...ONLY EVER
THINK OF HOW STRONG SHE IS?
I SERIOUSLY THOUGHT SHE HAD NO WEAKNESSES.
I'M SORRY,
SHIZUKU.

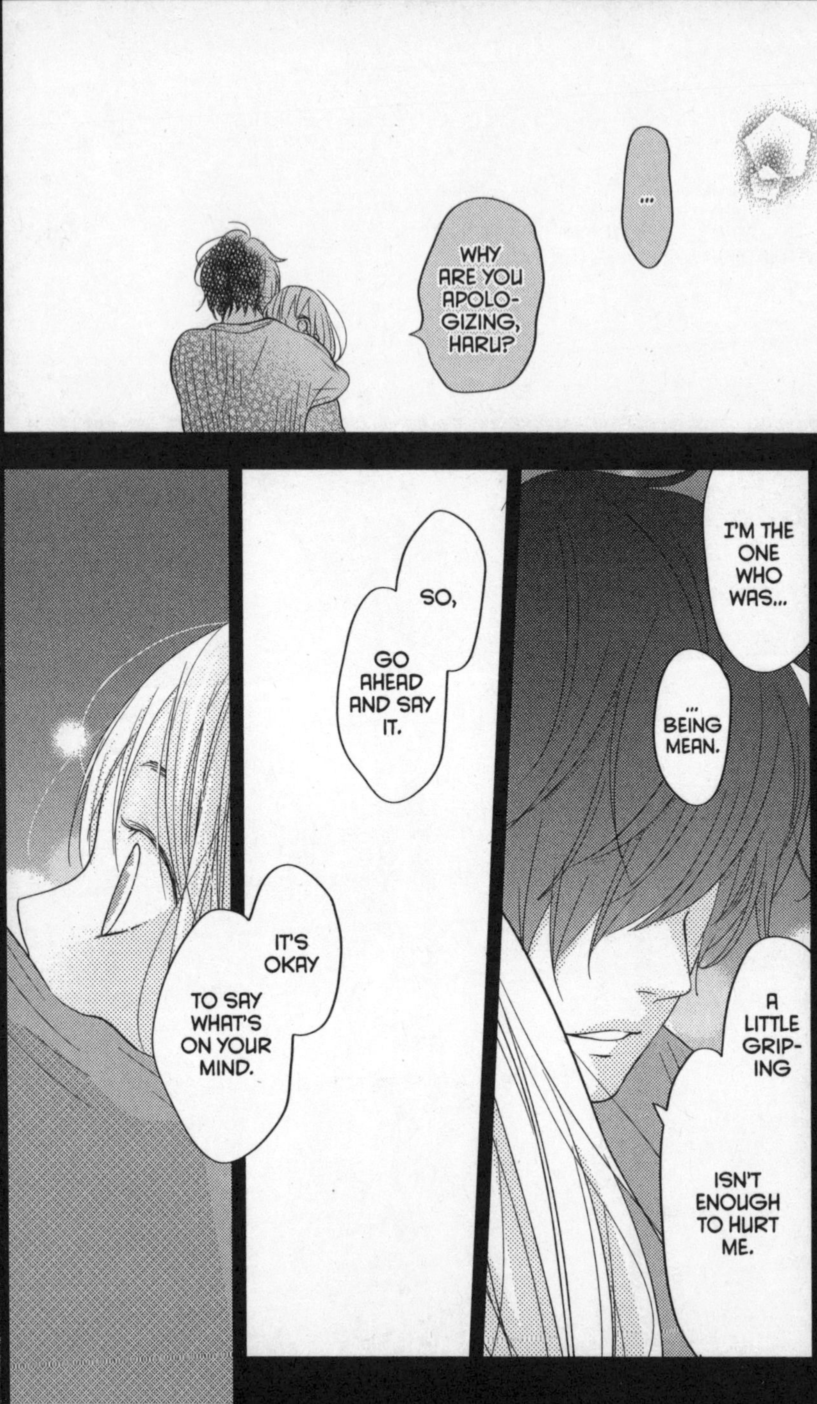
...
WHY ARE YOU APOLOGIZING, HARU?
I'M THE ONE WHO WAS...
... BEING MEAN.
A LITTLE GRIPING
ISN'T ENOUGH TO HURT ME.
SO,
GO AHEAD AND SAY IT.
IT'S OKAY
TO SAY WHAT'S ON YOUR MIND.

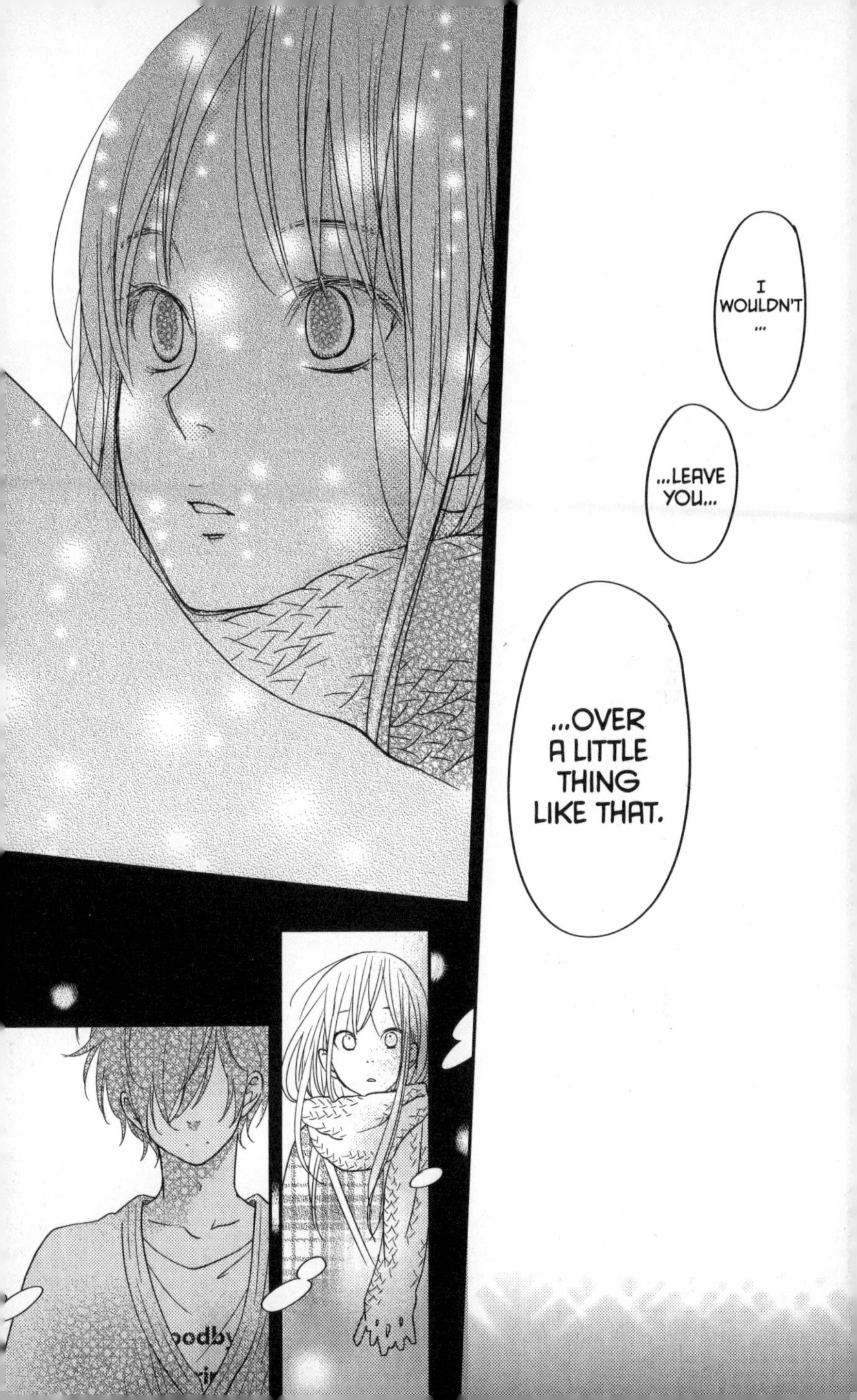
I WOULDN'T ...
...LEAVE YOU...
...OVER A LITTLE THING LIKE THAT.

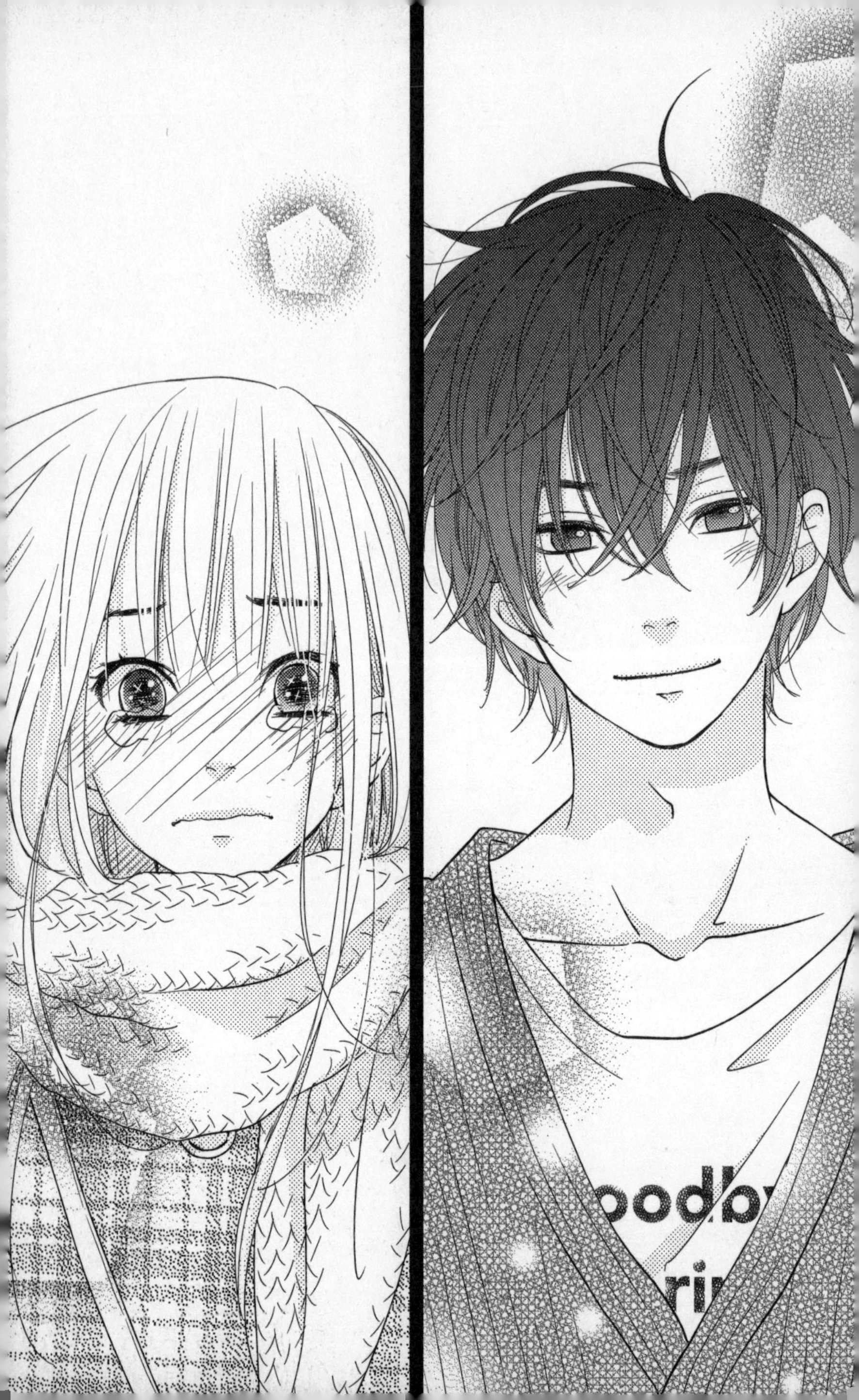

HARU.

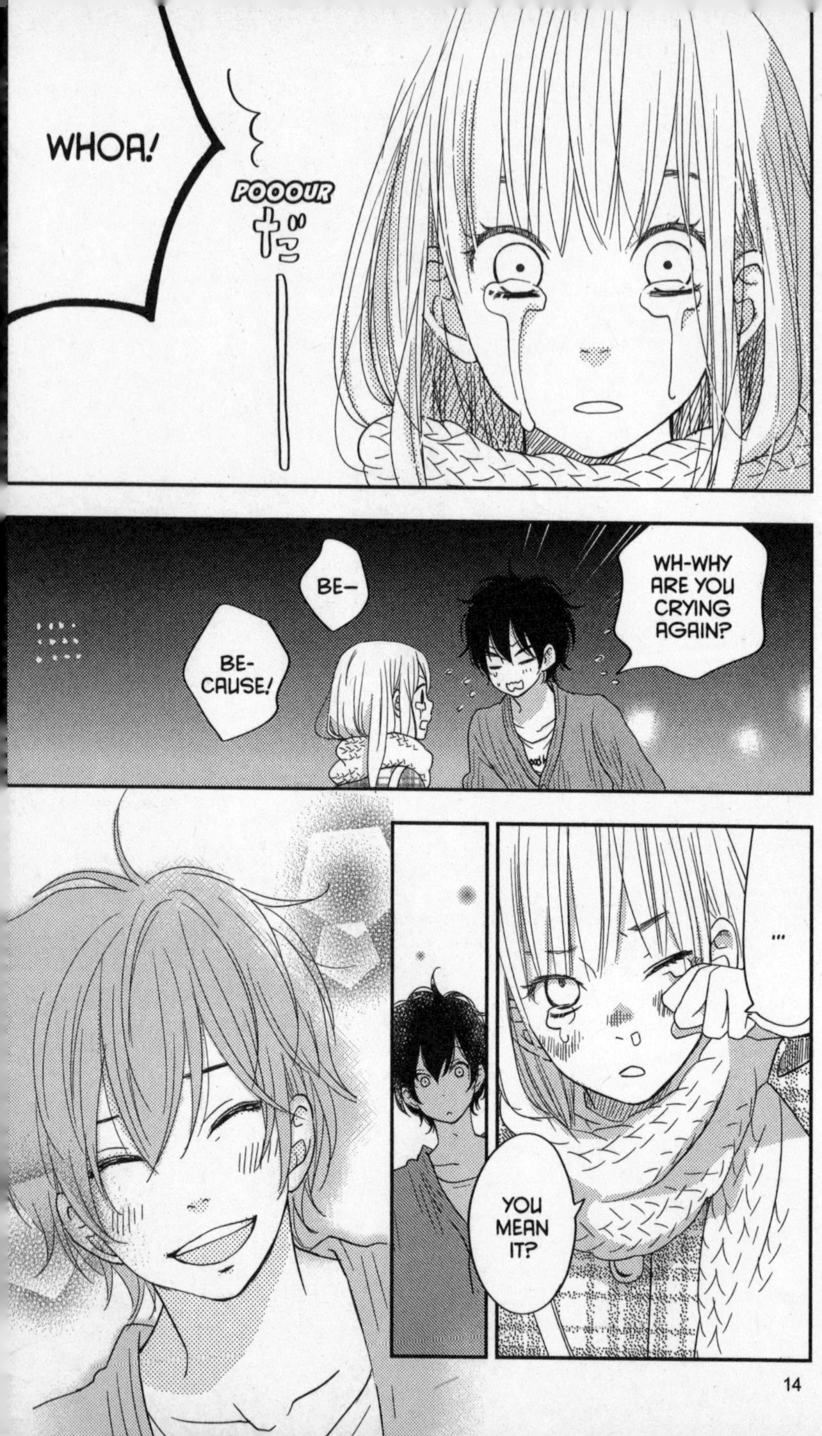
POOOUR
WHOA!
WH-WHY ARE YOU CRYING AGAIN?
BE-
BE-CAUSE!
...
YOU MEAN IT?

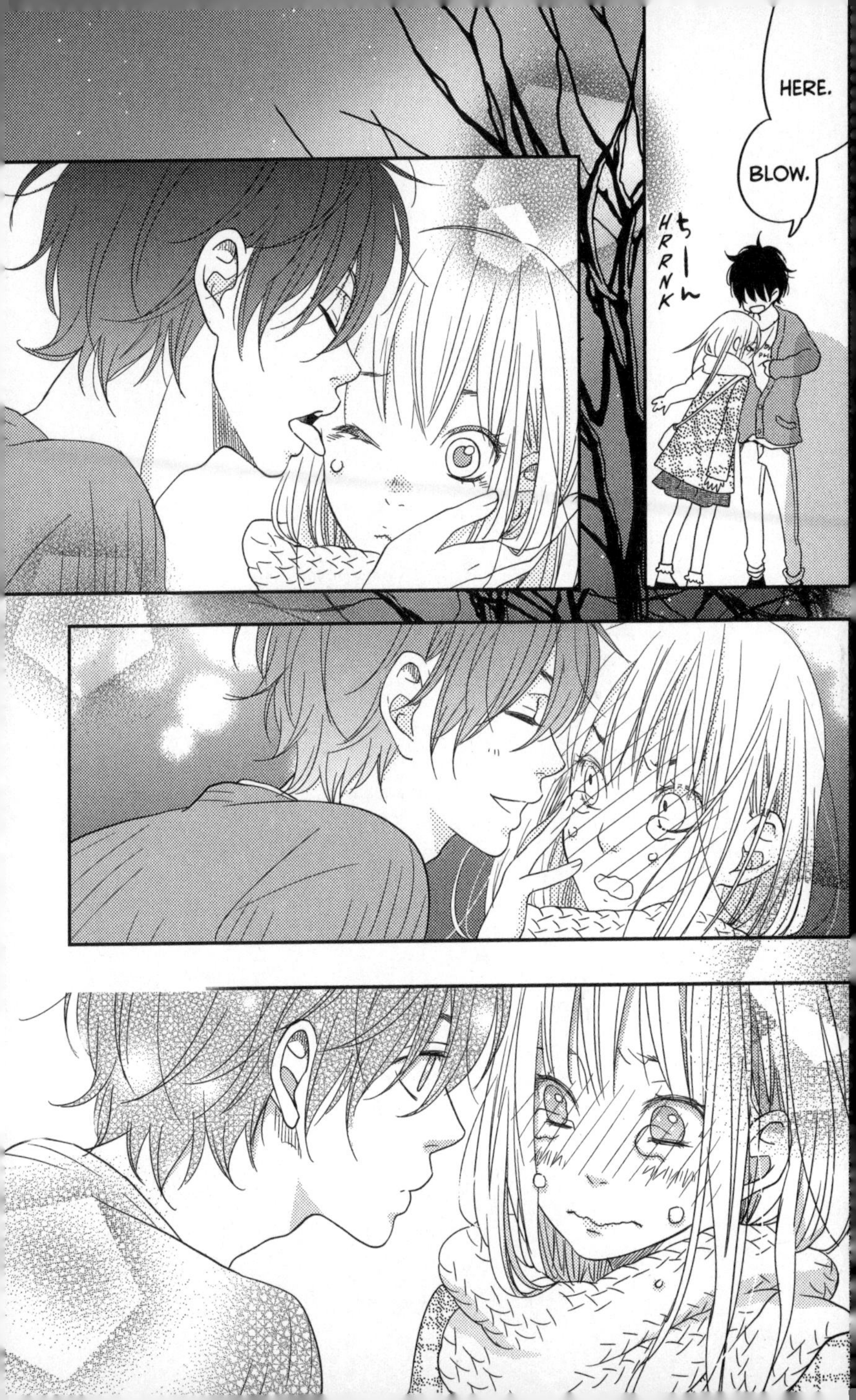
HERE.
BLOW.
HRRNK
ちーん

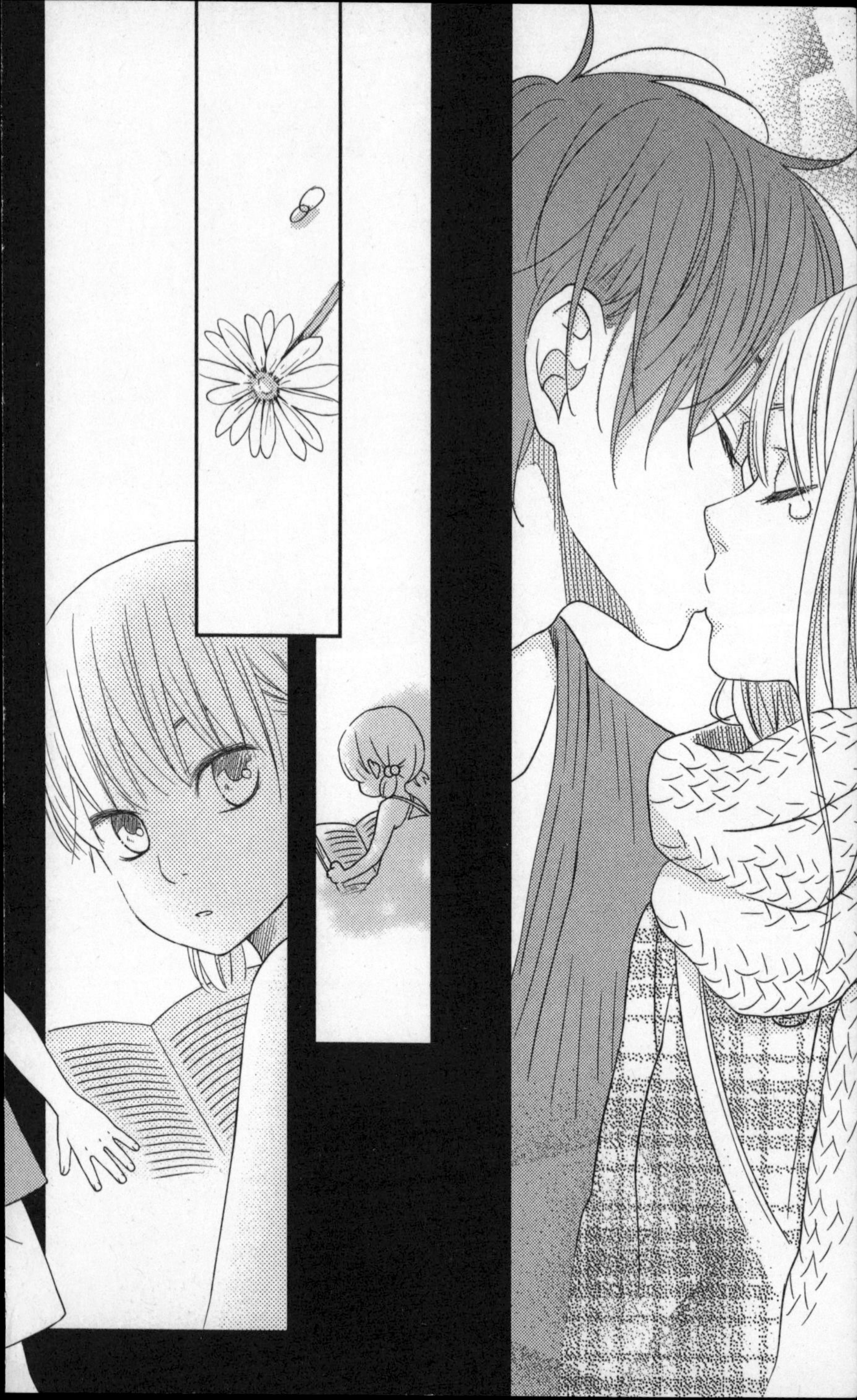

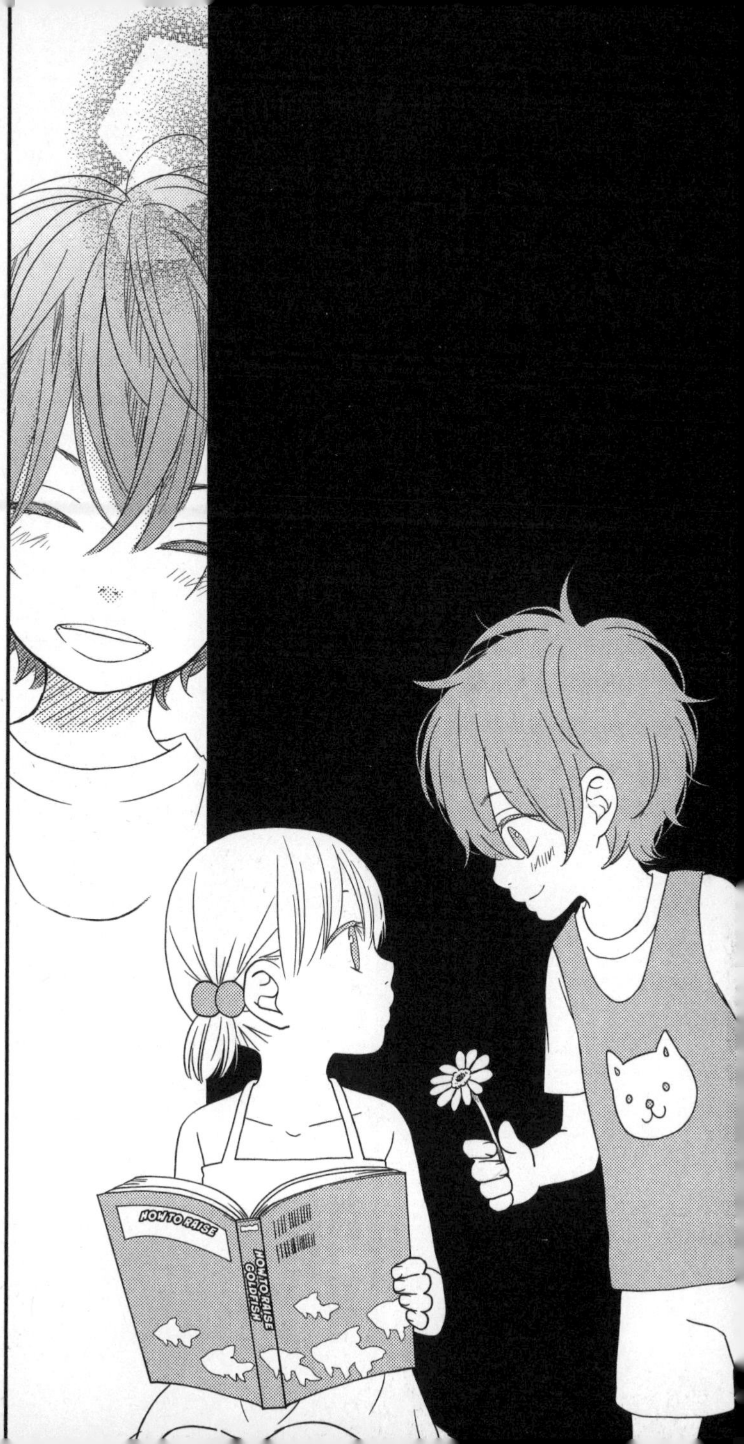
HOW TO RAISE
HOW TO RAISE GOLDFISH

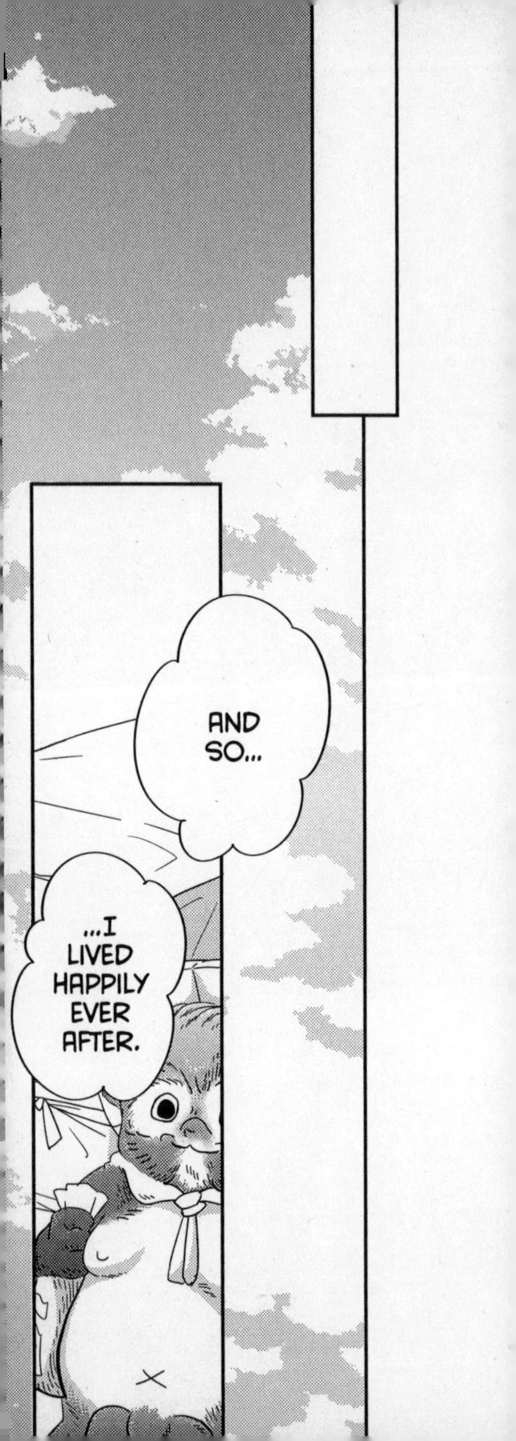
AND SO...
...I LIVED HAPPILY EVER AFTER.

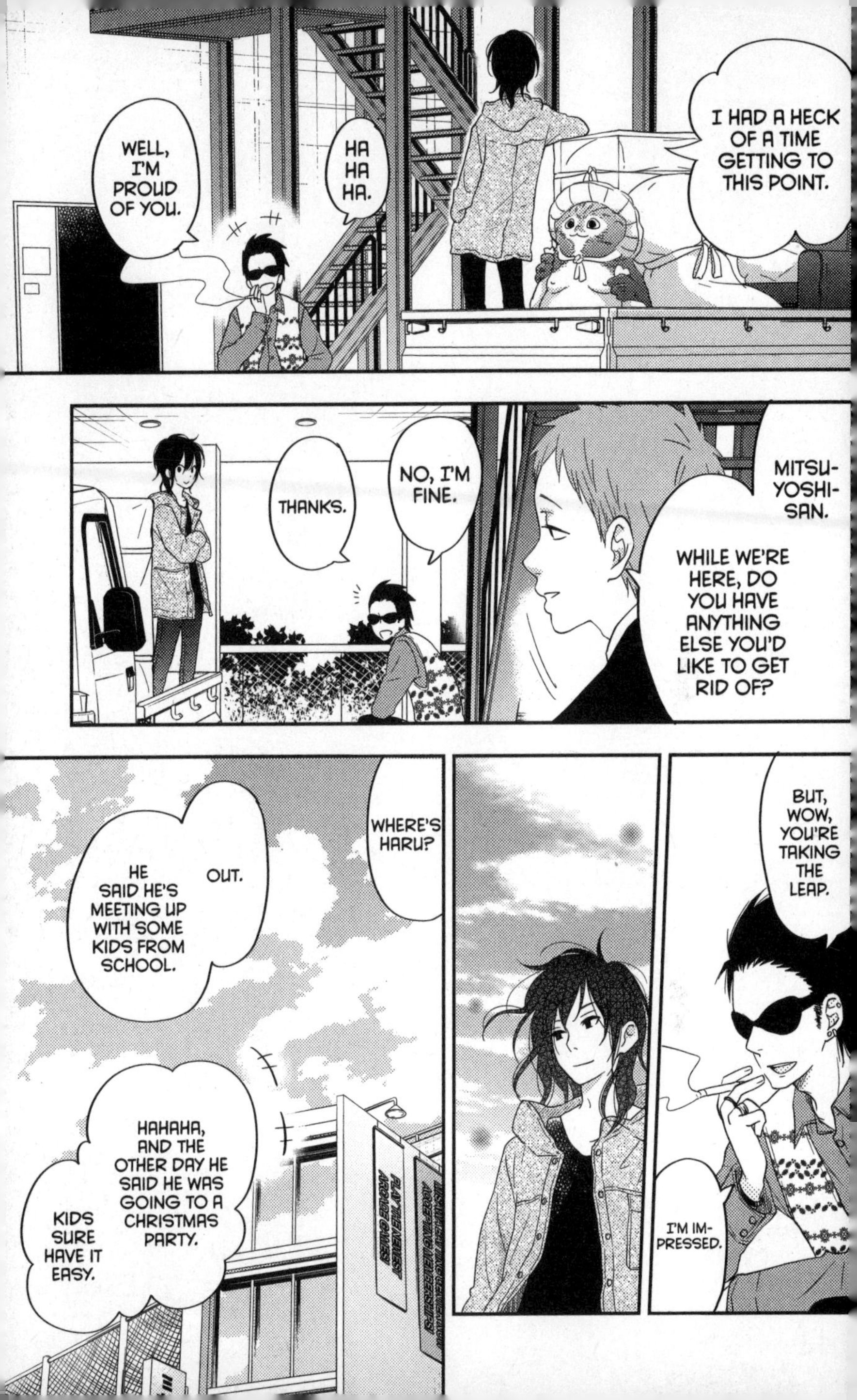
I HAD A HECK OF A TIME GETTING TO THIS POINT.
HA HA HA.
WELL, I'M PROUD OF YOU.
MITSU-YOSHI-SAN.
WHILE WE'RE HERE, DO YOU HAVE ANYTHING ELSE YOU'D LIKE TO GET RID OF?
NO, I'M FINE.
THANKS.
BUT, WOW, YOU'RE TAKING THE LEAP.
I'M IM-PRESSED.
WHERE'S HARU?
OUT.
HE SAID HE'S MEETING UP WITH SOME KIDS FROM SCHOOL.
HAHAHA, AND THE OTHER DAY HE SAID HE WAS GOING TO A CHRISTMAS PARTY.
KIDS SURE HAVE IT EASY.

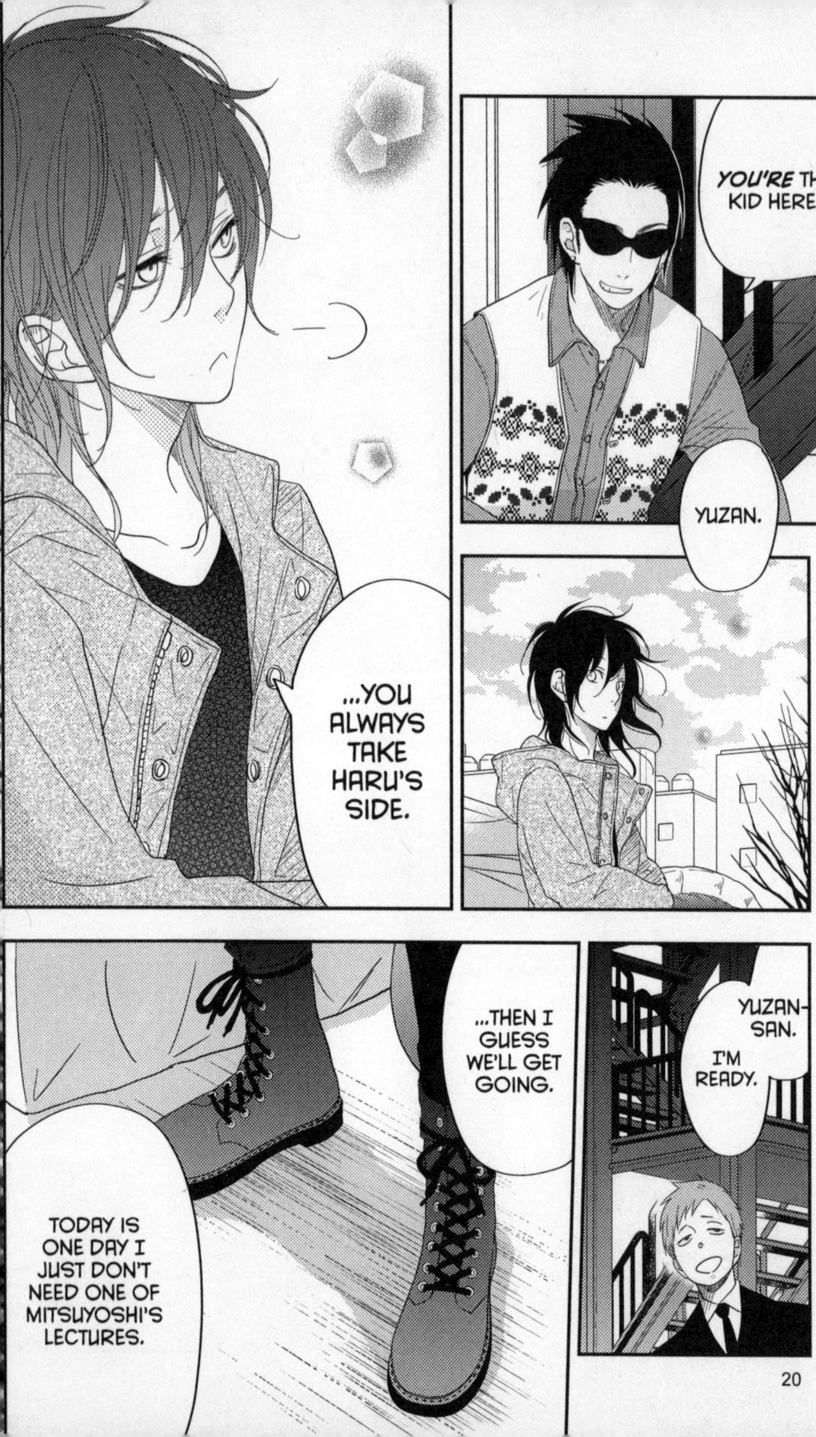
YOU'RE THE KID HERE,
YUZAN.
...YOU ALWAYS TAKE HARU'S SIDE.
YUZAN-SAN.
I'M READY.
...THEN I GUESS WE'LL GET GOING.
TODAY IS ONE DAY I JUST DON'T NEED ONE OF MITSUYOSHI'S LECTURES.

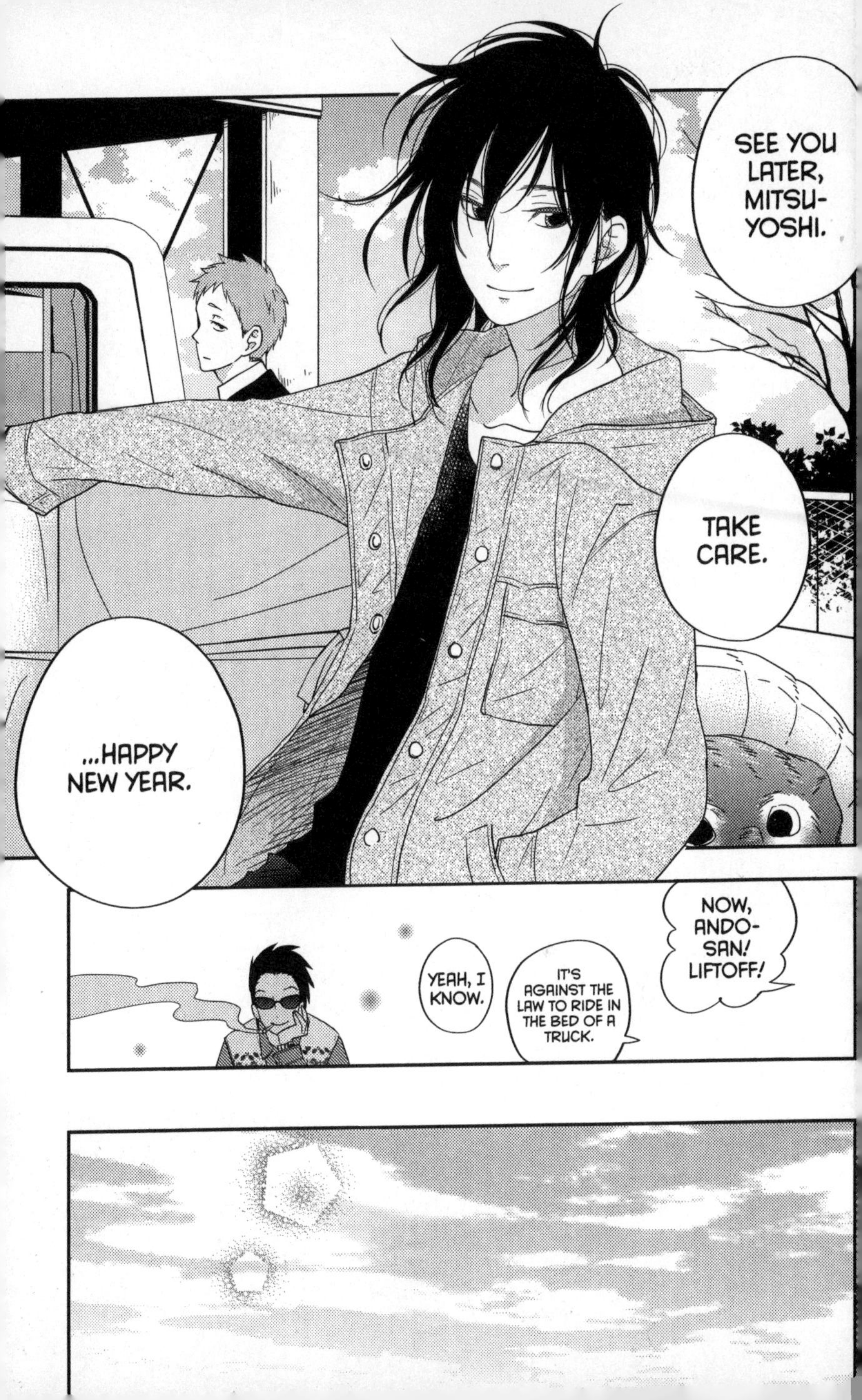
SEE YOU LATER, MITSU-YOSHI.
TAKE CARE.
...HAPPY NEW YEAR.
NOW, ANDO-SAN! LIFTOFF!
IT'S AGAINST THE LAW TO RIDE IN THE BED OF A TRUCK.
YEAH, I KNOW.

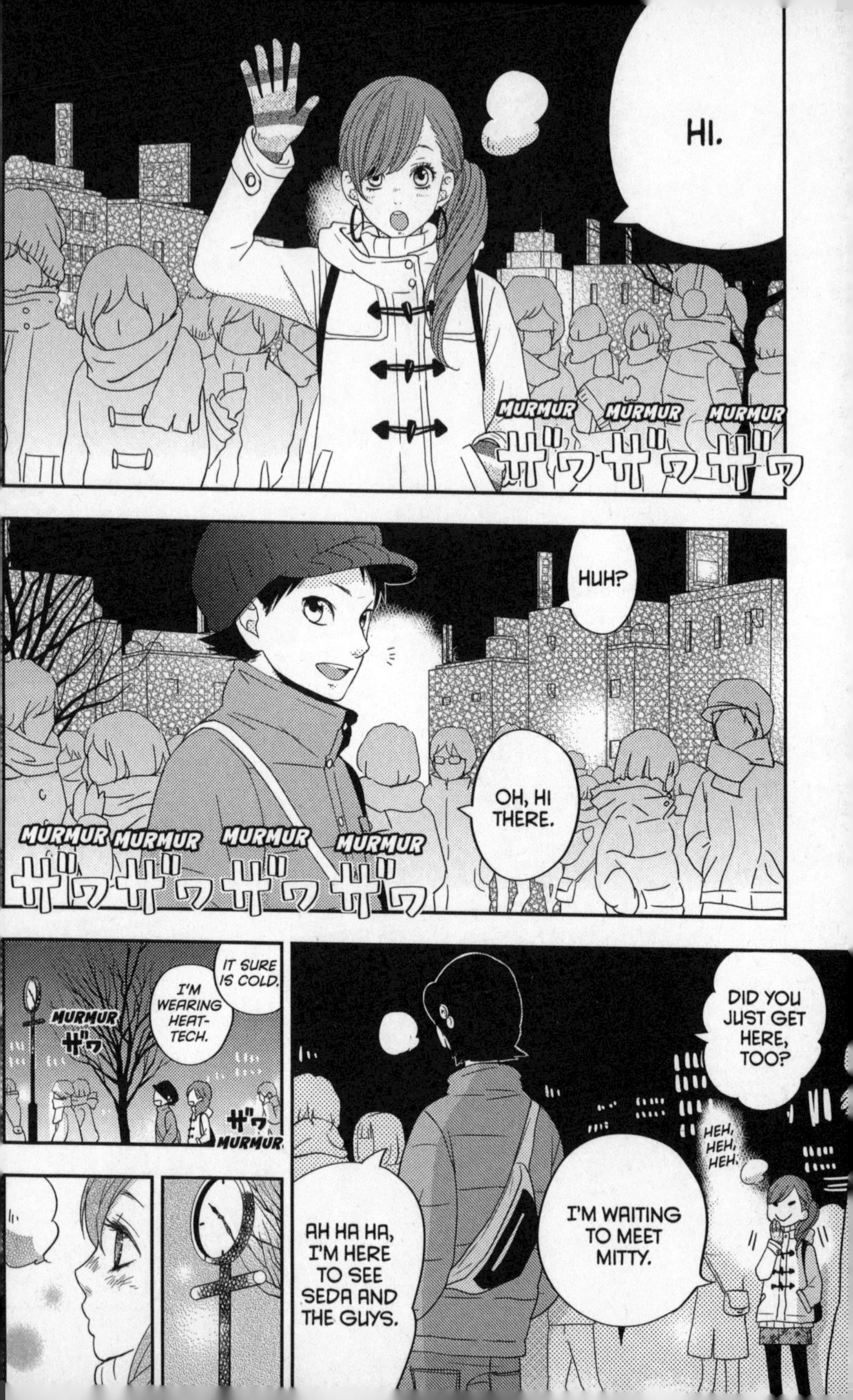
HI.
MURMUR MURMUR MURMUR
ザワザワザワ
HUH?
OH, HI THERE.
MURMUR MURMUR MURMUR MURMUR
ザワザワザワザワ
DID YOU JUST GET HERE, TOO?
HEH, HEH, HEH.
I'M WAITING TO MEET MITTY.
AH HA HA, I'M HERE TO SEE SEDA AND THE GUYS.
IT SURE IS COLD.
I'M WEARING HEAT-TECH.
MURMUR
ザワ
ザワ
MURMUR

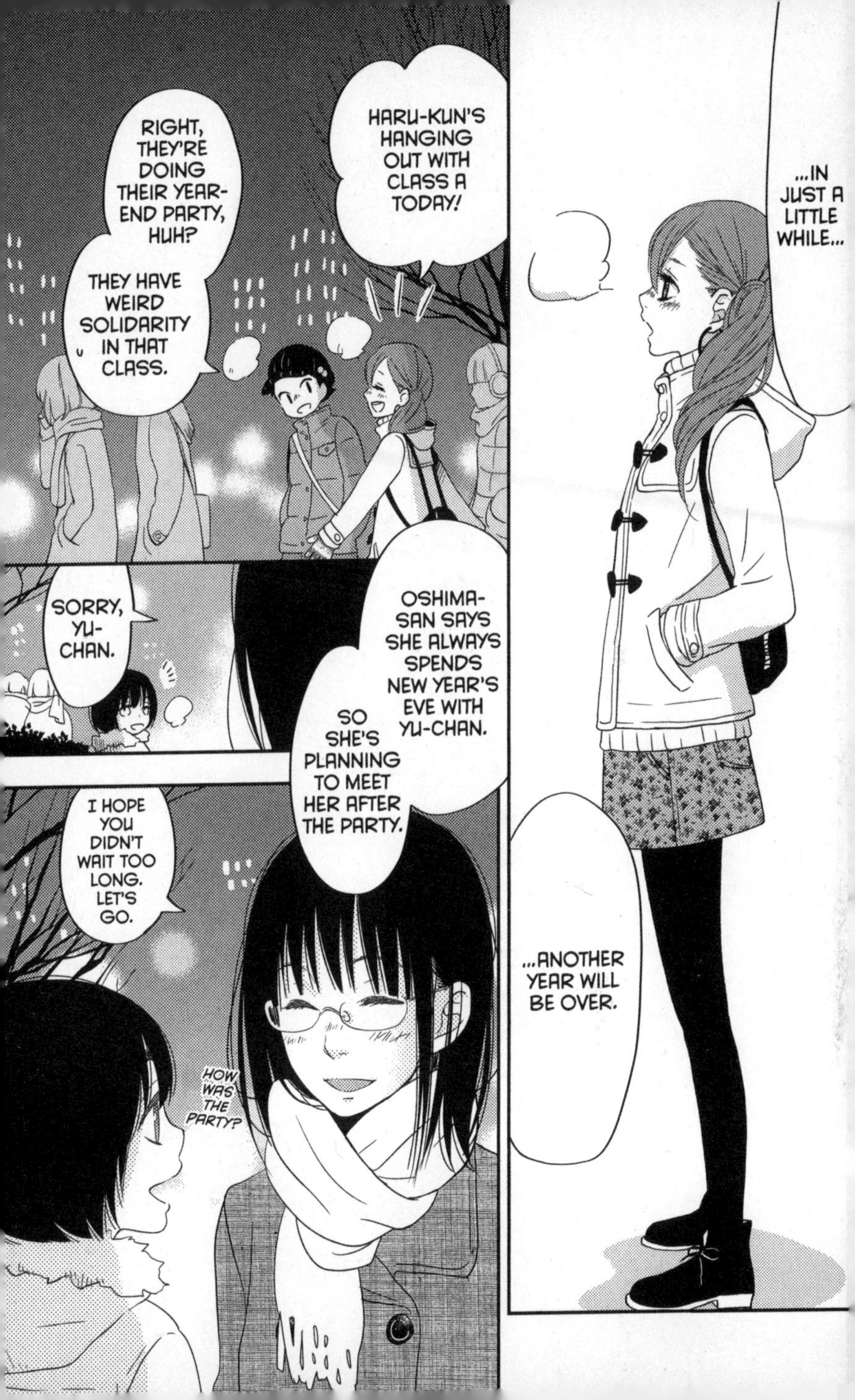
...IN JUST A LITTLE WHILE...
...ANOTHER YEAR WILL BE OVER.
HARU-KUN'S HANGING OUT WITH CLASS A TODAY!
RIGHT, THEY'RE DOING THEIR YEAR-END PARTY, HUH?
THEY HAVE WEIRD SOLIDARITY IN THAT CLASS.
OSHIMA-SAN SAYS SHE ALWAYS SPENDS NEW YEAR'S EVE WITH YU-CHAN.
SORRY, YU-CHAN.
SO SHE'S PLANNING TO MEET HER AFTER THE PARTY.
I HOPE YOU DIDN'T WAIT TOO LONG. LET'S GO.
HOW WAS THE PARTY?

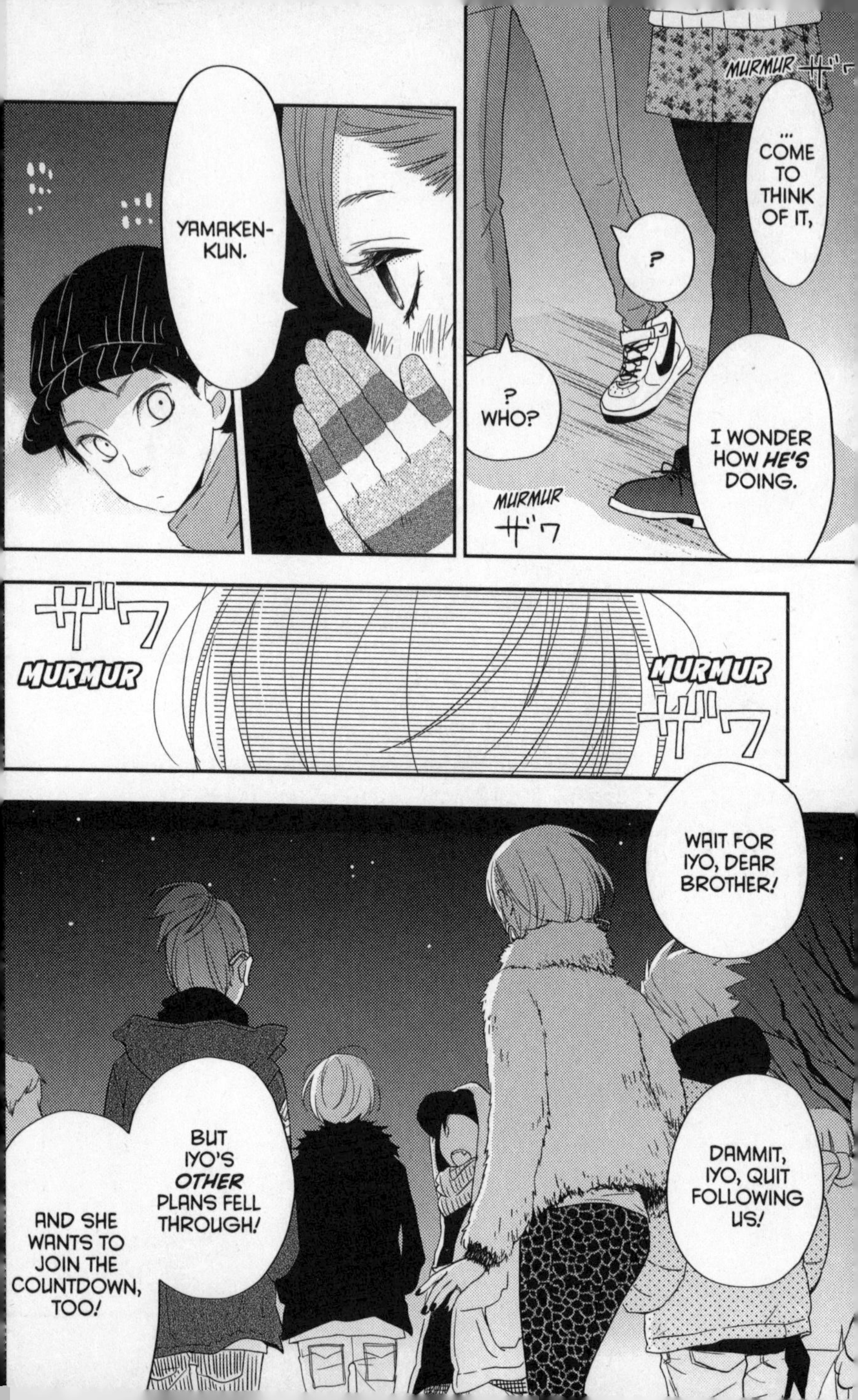
MURMUR ザワ
... COME TO THINK OF IT,
?
I WONDER HOW HE'S DOING.
? WHO?
MURMUR ザワ
YAMAKEN-KUN.
MURMUR ザワ
MURMUR ザワ
WAIT FOR IYO, DEAR BROTHER!
DAMMIT, IYO, QUIT FOLLOWING US!
BUT IYO'S OTHER PLANS FELL THROUGH!
AND SHE WANTS TO JOIN THE COUNTDOWN, TOO!

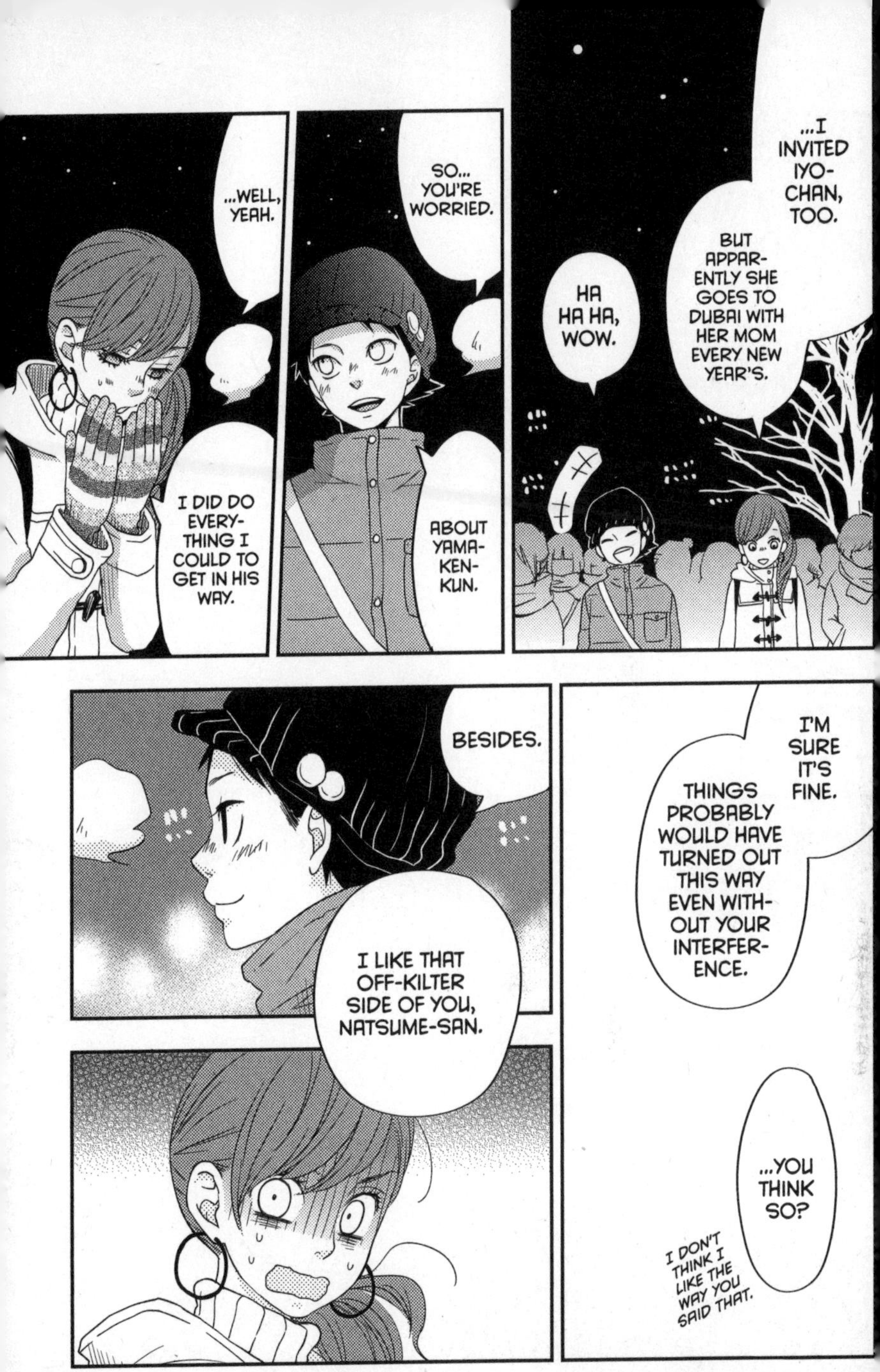

...I INVITED IYO-CHAN, TOO.
BUT APPARENTLY SHE GOES TO DUBAI WITH HER MOM EVERY NEW YEAR'S.
HA HA HA, WOW.
SO... YOU'RE WORRIED.
ABOUT YAMA-KEN-KUN.
...WELL, YEAH.
I DID DO EVERYTHING I COULD TO GET IN HIS WAY.
I'M SURE IT'S FINE.
THINGS PROBABLY WOULD HAVE TURNED OUT THIS WAY EVEN WITHOUT YOUR INTERFERENCE.
...YOU THINK SO?
I DON'T THINK I LIKE THE WAY YOU SAID THAT.
BESIDES.
I LIKE THAT OFF-KILTER SIDE OF YOU, NATSUME-SAN.

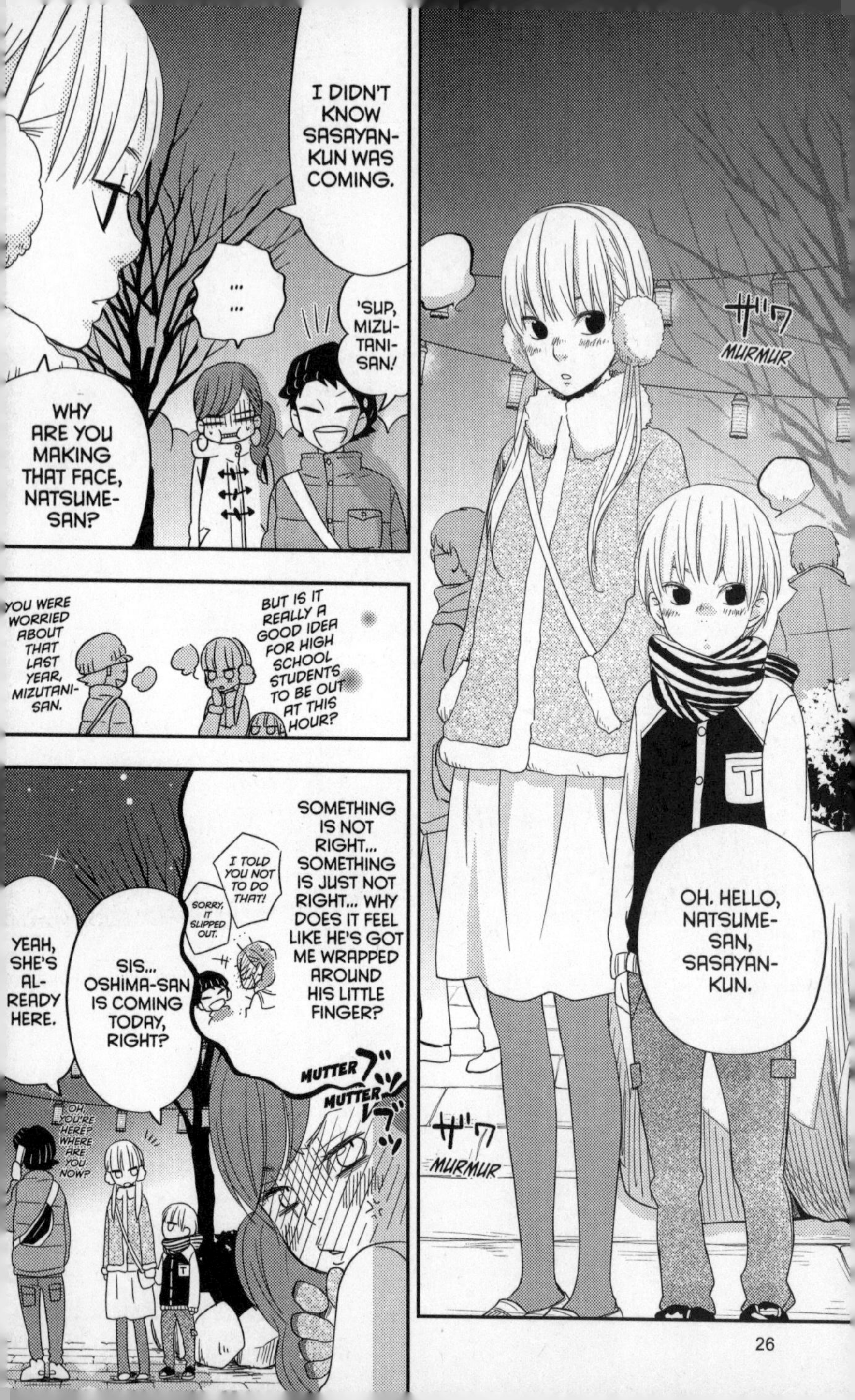
ザワ
MURMUR
OH. HELLO, NATSUME-SAN, SASAYAN-KUN.
ザワ
MURMUR
I DIDN'T KNOW SASAYAN-KUN WAS COMING.
'SUP, MIZUTANI-SAN!
... ...
WHY ARE YOU MAKING THAT FACE, NATSUME-SAN?
BUT IS IT REALLY A GOOD IDEA FOR HIGH SCHOOL STUDENTS TO BE OUT AT THIS HOUR?
YOU WERE WORRIED ABOUT THAT LAST YEAR, MIZUTANI-SAN.
SOMETHING IS NOT RIGHT... SOMETHING IS JUST NOT RIGHT... WHY DOES IT FEEL LIKE HE'S GOT ME WRAPPED AROUND HIS LITTLE FINGER?
I TOLD YOU NOT TO DO THAT!
SORRY, IT SLIPPED OUT.
SIS... OSHIMA-SAN IS COMING TODAY, RIGHT?
YEAH, SHE'S AL-READY HERE.
MUTTER
MUTTER
OH, YOU'RE HERE? WHERE ARE YOU NOW?

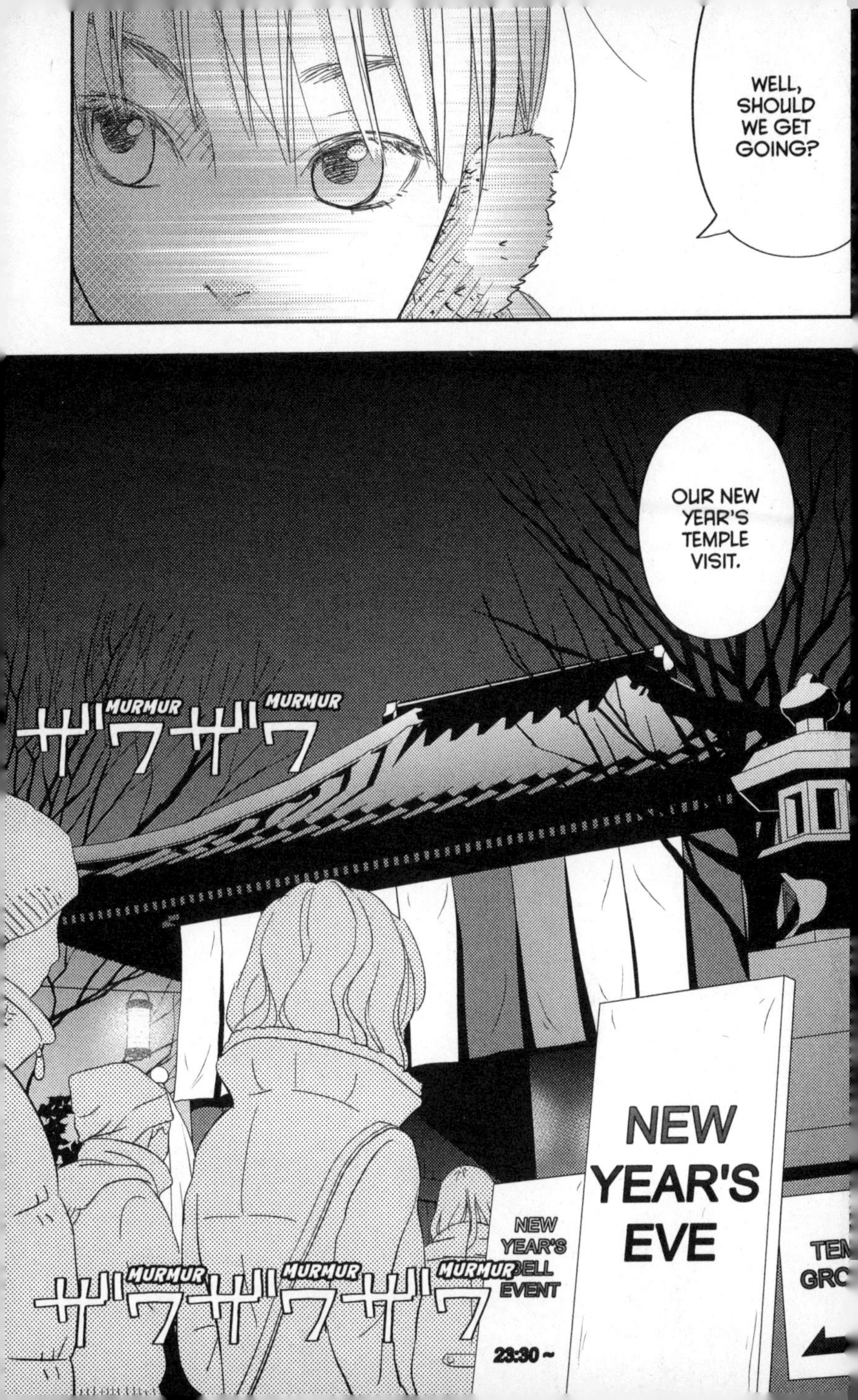
WELL, SHOULD WE GET GOING?
OUR NEW YEAR'S TEMPLE VISIT.
ザワザワ
MURMUR MURMUR
NEW YEAR'S EVE
NEW YEAR'S BELL EVENT
23:30 ~
ザワザワザワ
MURMUR MURMUR MURMUR

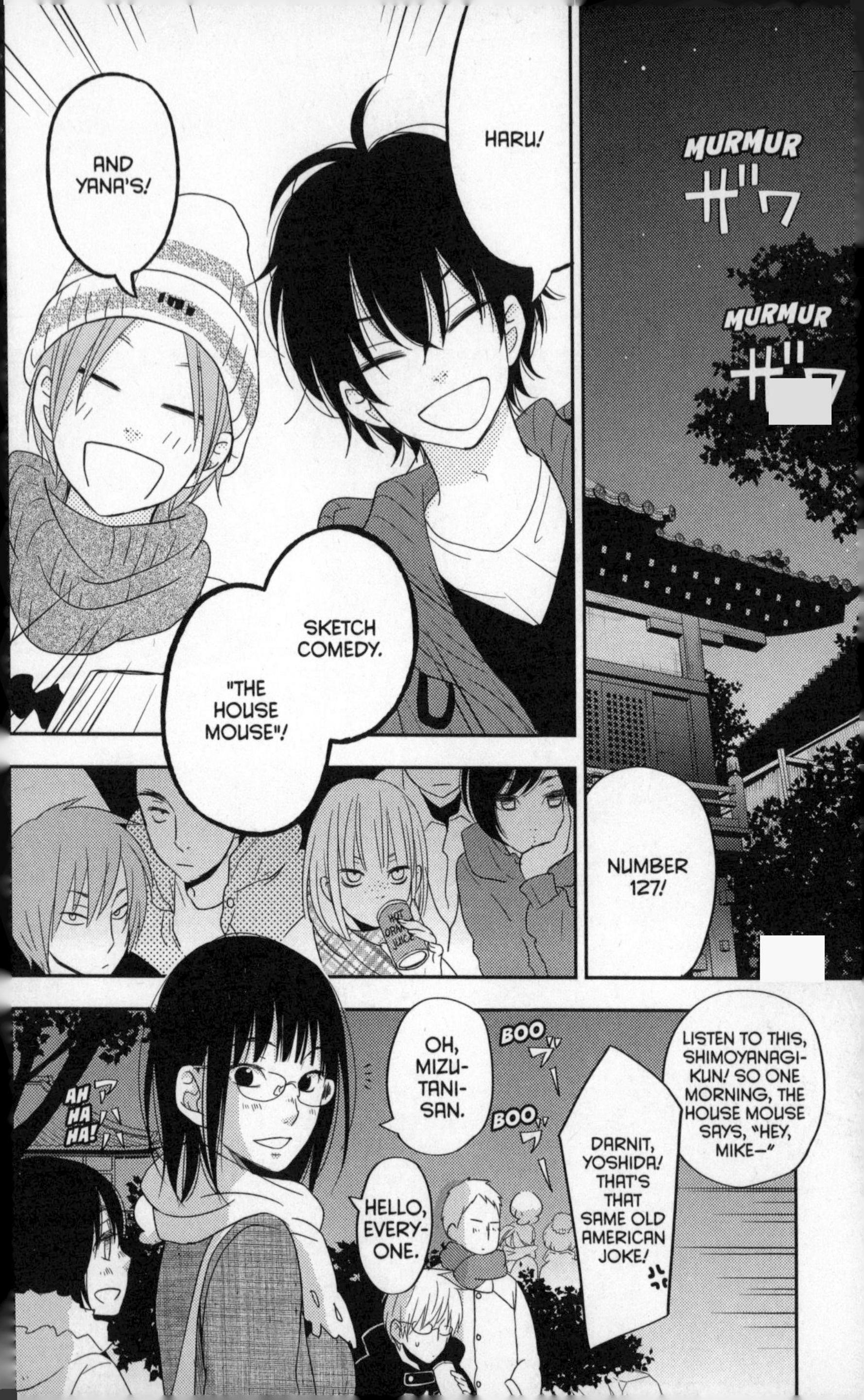
MURMUR
ザワ
MURMUR
NUMBER 127!
HARU!
AND YANA'S!
SKETCH COMEDY.
"THE HOUSE MOUSE"!
LISTEN TO THIS, SHIMOYANAGI-KUN! SO ONE MORNING, THE HOUSE MOUSE SAYS, "HEY, MIKE–"
DARNIT, YOSHIDA! THAT'S THAT SAME OLD AMERICAN JOKE!
BOO
BOO
OH, MIZU-TANI-SAN.
HELLO, EVERY-ONE.
AH HA HA!

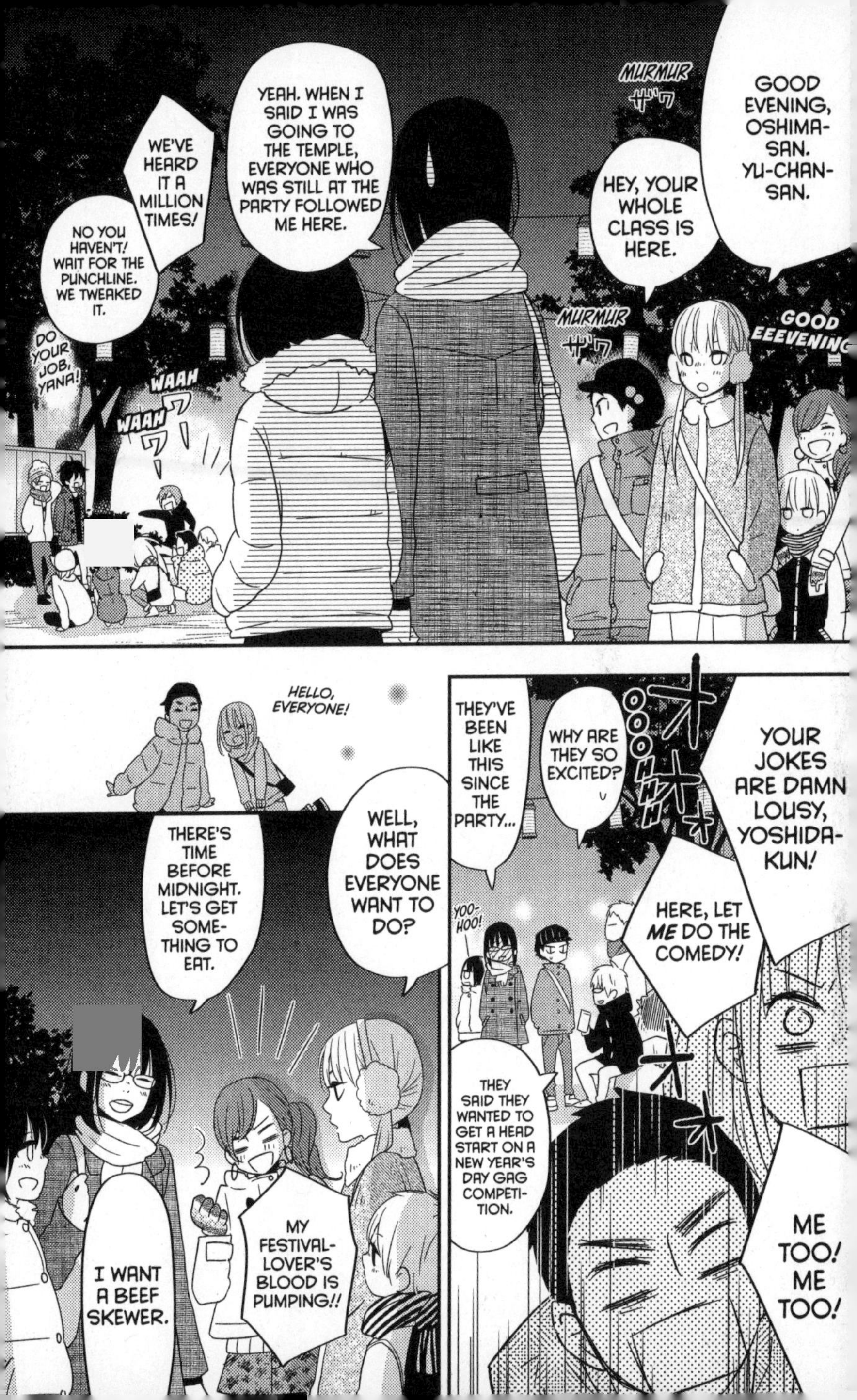
GOOD EVENING, OSHIMA-SAN. YU-CHAN-SAN.
MURMUR ザワ
HEY, YOUR WHOLE CLASS IS HERE.
GOOD EEEVENING
MURMUR ザワ
YEAH. WHEN I SAID I WAS GOING TO THE TEMPLE, EVERYONE WHO WAS STILL AT THE PARTY FOLLOWED ME HERE.
WE'VE HEARD IT A MILLION TIMES!
NO YOU HAVEN'T! WAIT FOR THE PUNCHLINE. WE TWEAKED IT.
DO YOUR JOB, YANA!
WAAH ワ
WAAH ワ
YOUR JOKES ARE DAMN LOUSY, YOSHIDA-KUN!
OOOHHHH オオオ
WHY ARE THEY SO EXCITED?
THEY'VE BEEN LIKE THIS SINCE THE PARTY...
HERE, LET ME DO THE COMEDY!
YOO-HOO!
THEY SAID THEY WANTED TO GET A HEAD START ON A NEW YEAR'S DAY GAG COMPETITION.
ME TOO! ME TOO!
HELLO, EVERYONE!
WELL, WHAT DOES EVERYONE WANT TO DO?
THERE'S TIME BEFORE MIDNIGHT. LET'S GET SOMETHING TO EAT.
MY FESTIVAL-LOVER'S BLOOD IS PUMPING!!
I WANT A BEEF SKEWER.

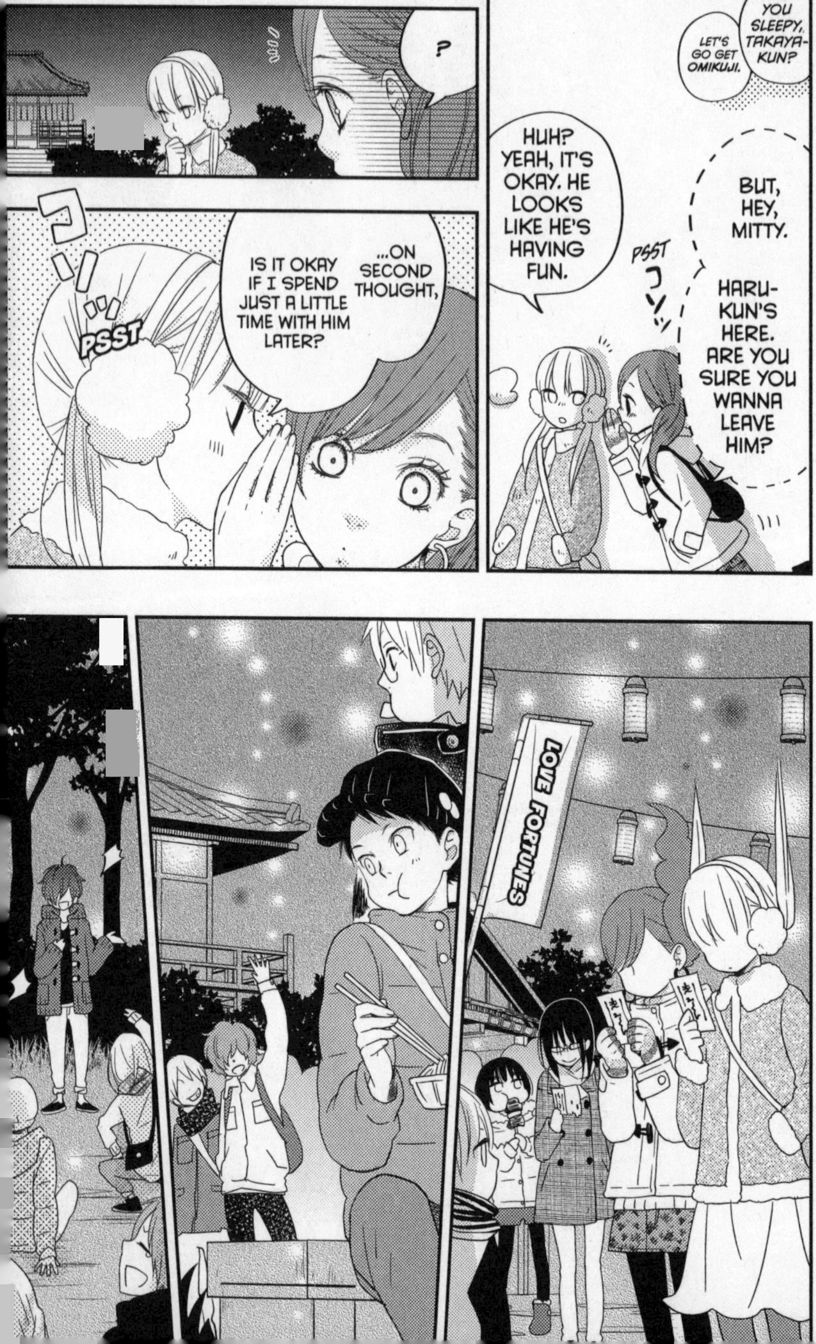
ARE YOU SLEEPY, TAKAYA-KUN?
LET'S GO GET OMIKUJI.
BUT, HEY, MITTY. HARU-KUN'S HERE. ARE YOU SURE YOU WANNA LEAVE HIM?
PSST
HUH? YEAH, IT'S OKAY. HE LOOKS LIKE HE'S HAVING FUN.
?
...ON SECOND THOUGHT,
IS IT OKAY IF I SPEND JUST A LITTLE TIME WITH HIM LATER?
PSST
LOVE FORTUNES

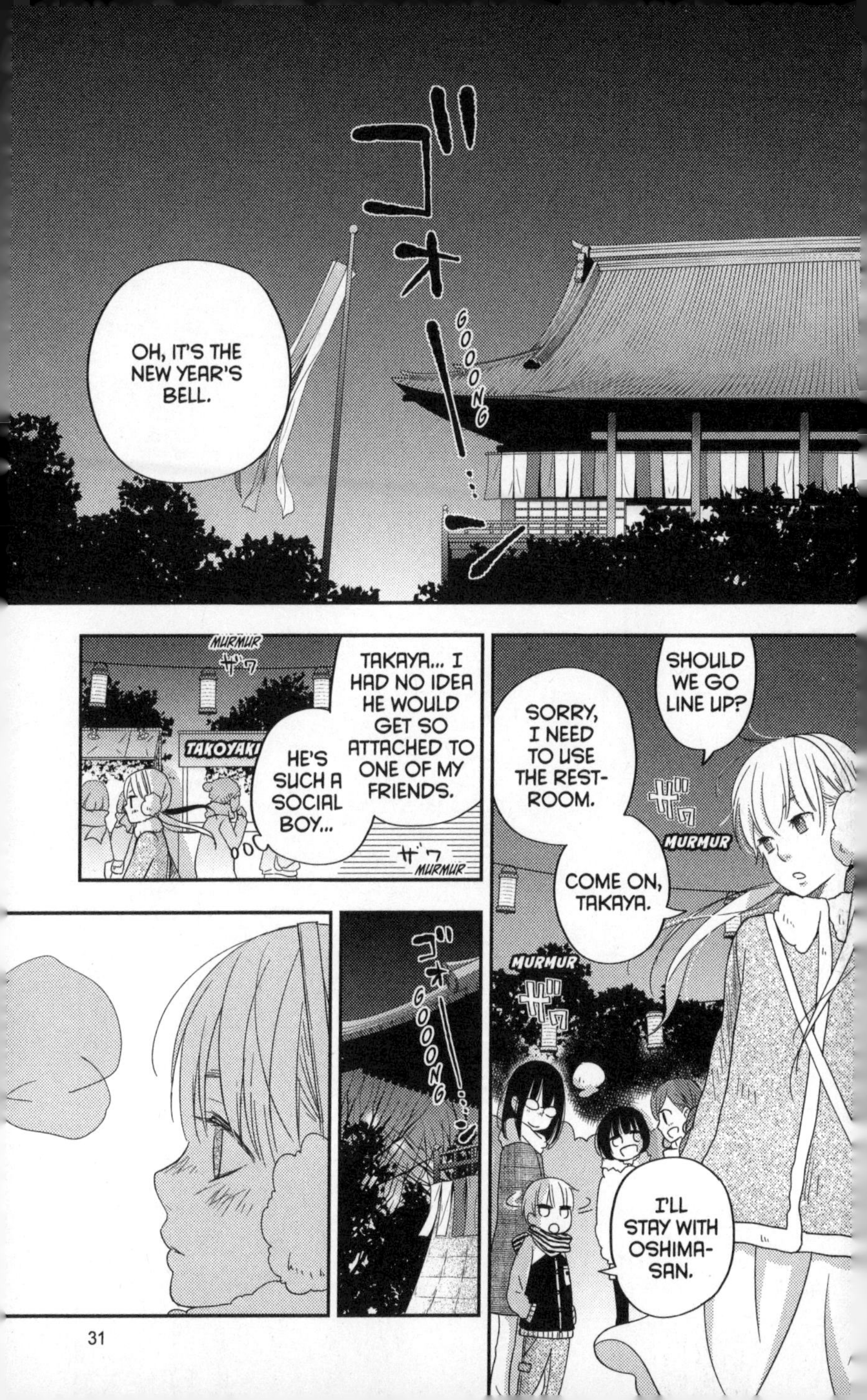
GOOOONG
OH, IT'S THE NEW YEAR'S BELL.
SHOULD WE GO LINE UP?
SORRY, I NEED TO USE THE REST-ROOM.
MURMUR
COME ON, TAKAYA.
MURMUR
I'LL STAY WITH OSHIMA-SAN.
MURMUR
TAKOYAKI
TAKAYA... I HAD NO IDEA HE WOULD GET SO ATTACHED TO ONE OF MY FRIENDS.
HE'S SUCH A SOCIAL BOY...
MURMUR
GOOOONG

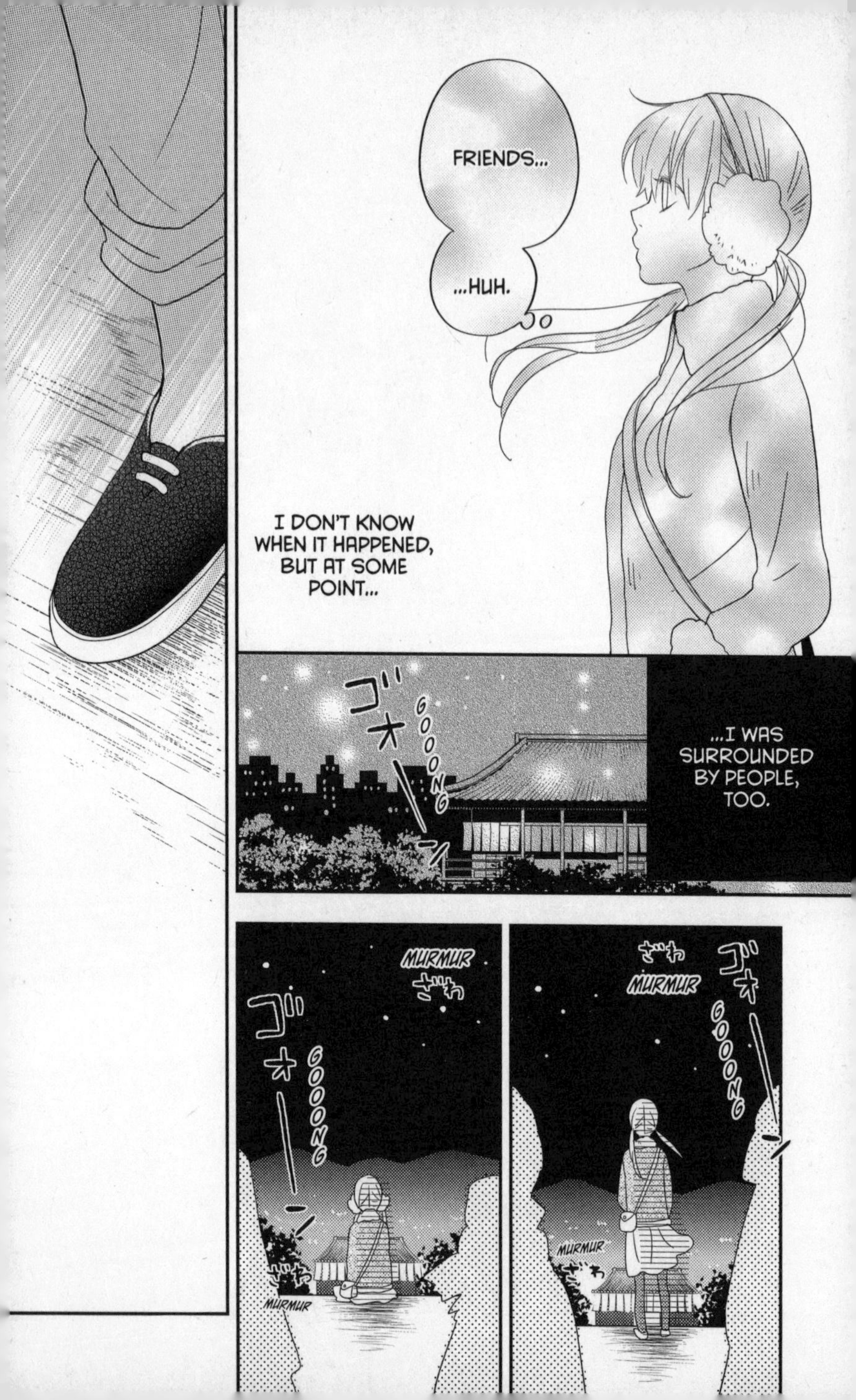
FRIENDS...
...HUH.
I DON'T KNOW WHEN IT HAPPENED, BUT AT SOME POINT...
...I WAS SURROUNDED BY PEOPLE, TOO.
ゴオーン
GOOOONG
ざわ
MURMUR
ゴオー
GOOOONG
MURMUR
ざわ
MURMUR
ざわ
ゴオー
GOOOONG
ざわ
MURMUR

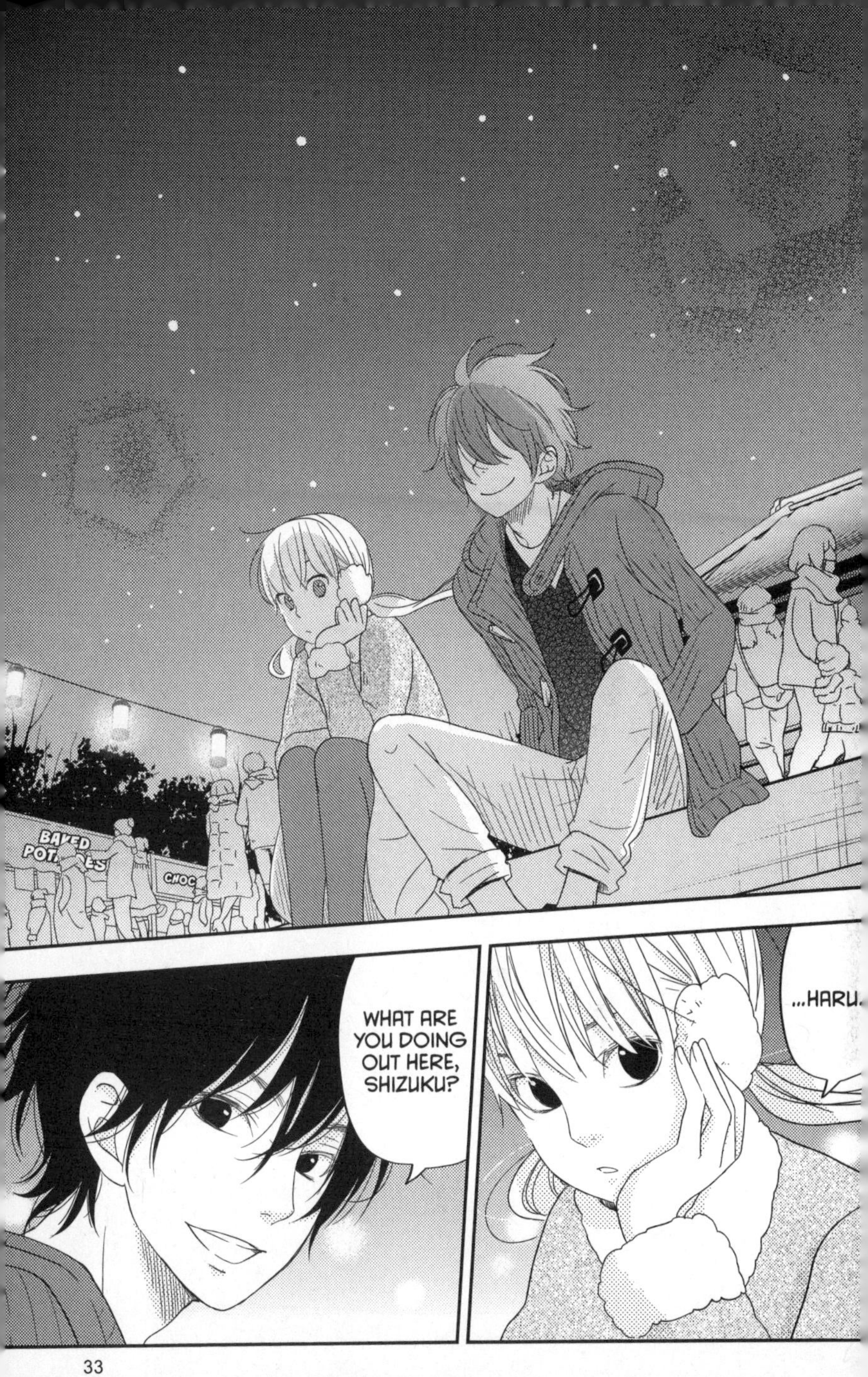
BAKED
...HARU.
WHAT ARE YOU DOING OUT HERE, SHIZUKU?

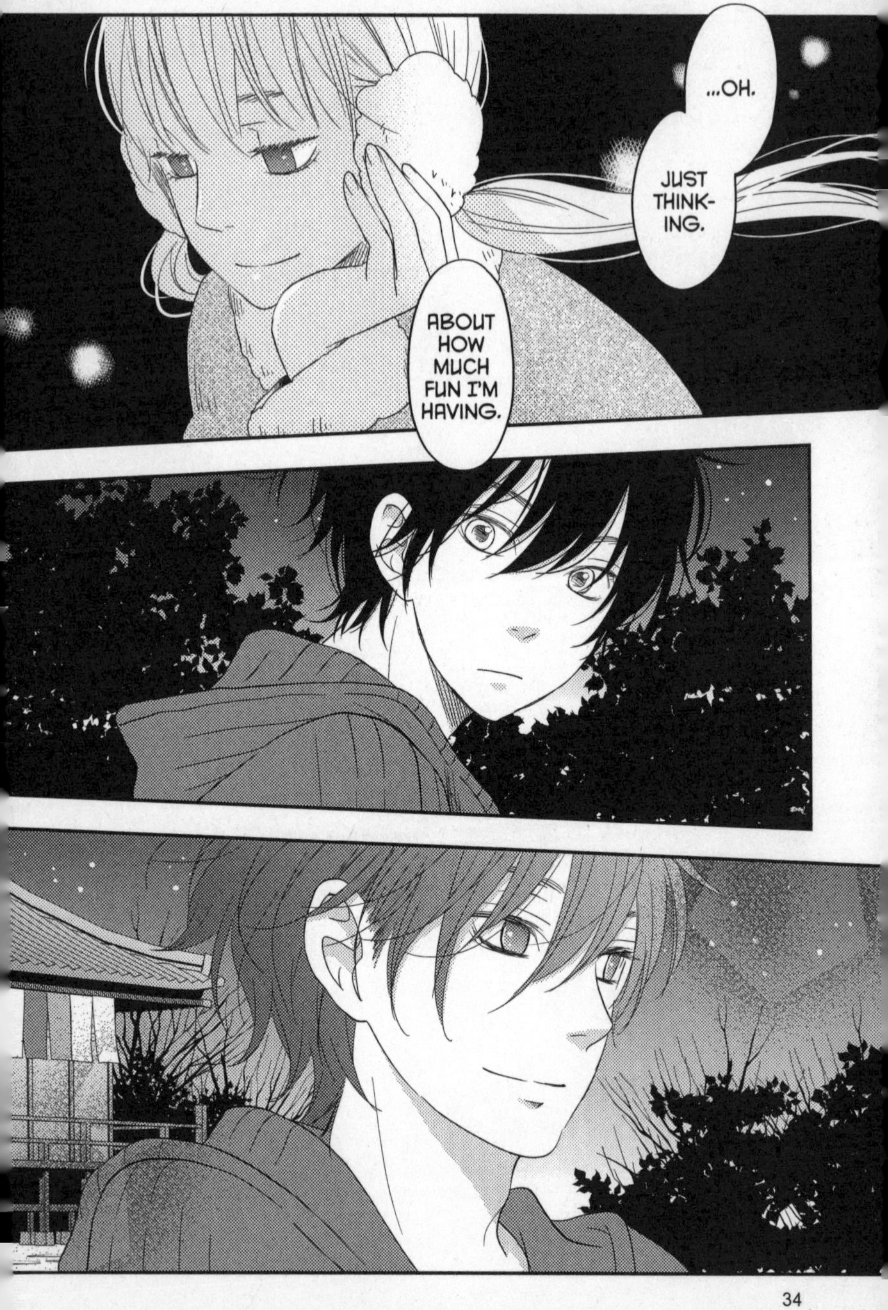
...OH.
JUST THINKING.
ABOUT HOW MUCH FUN I'M HAVING.

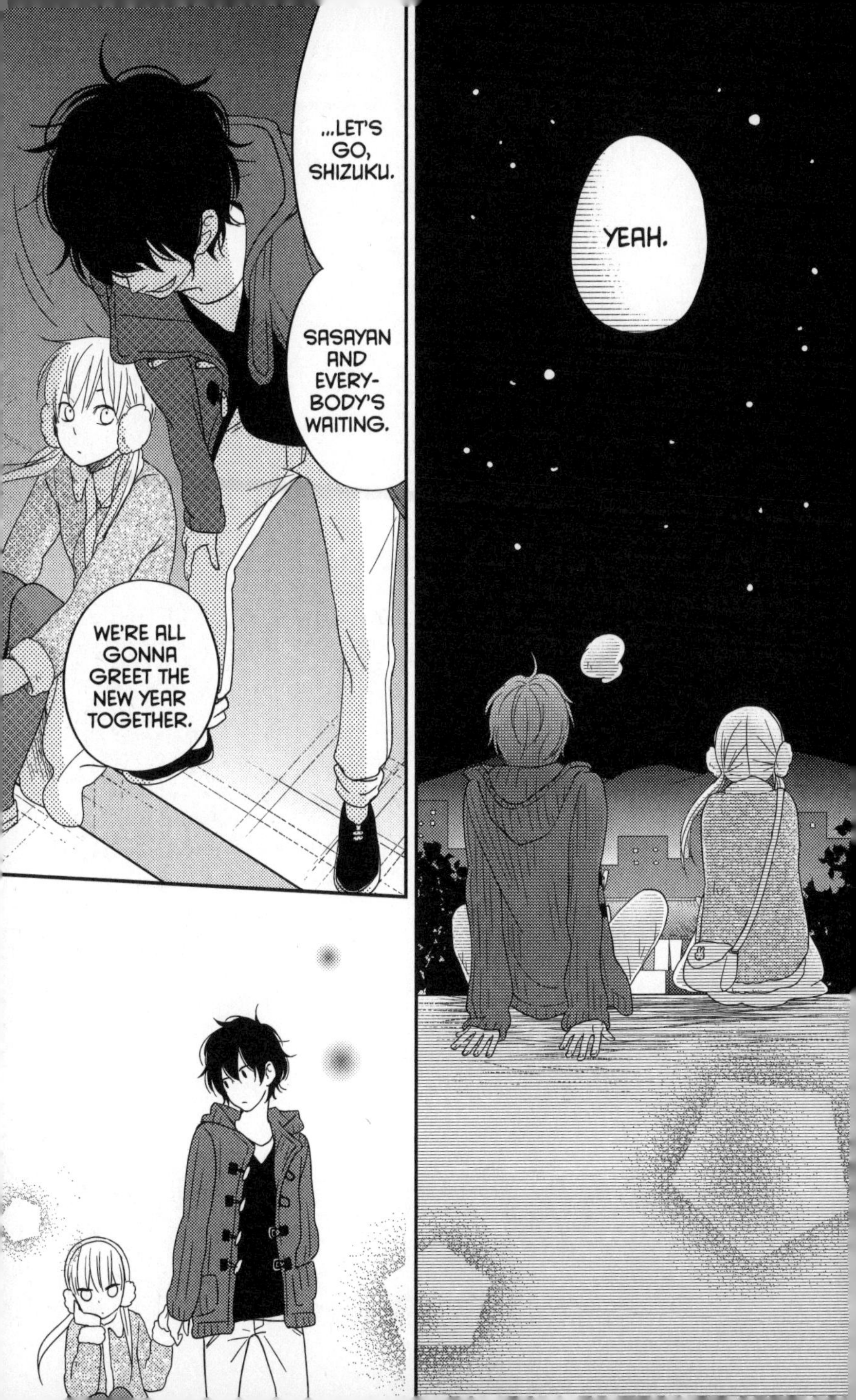
YEAH.
...LET'S GO, SHIZUKU.
SASAYAN AND EVERY-BODY'S WAITING.
WE'RE ALL GONNA GREET THE NEW YEAR TOGETHER.

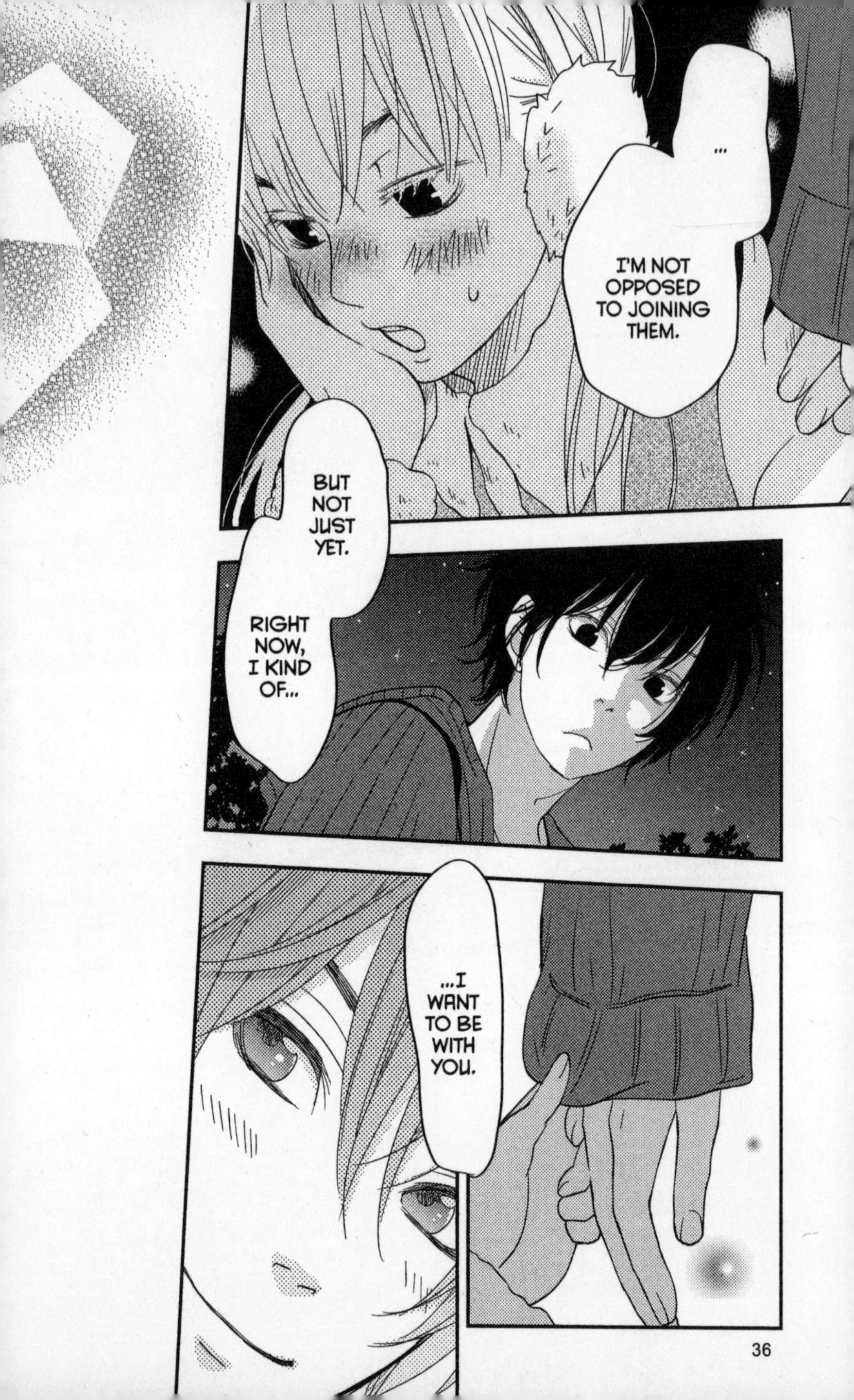
...
I'M NOT OPPOSED TO JOINING THEM.
BUT NOT JUST YET.
RIGHT NOW, I KIND OF...
...I WANT TO BE WITH YOU.

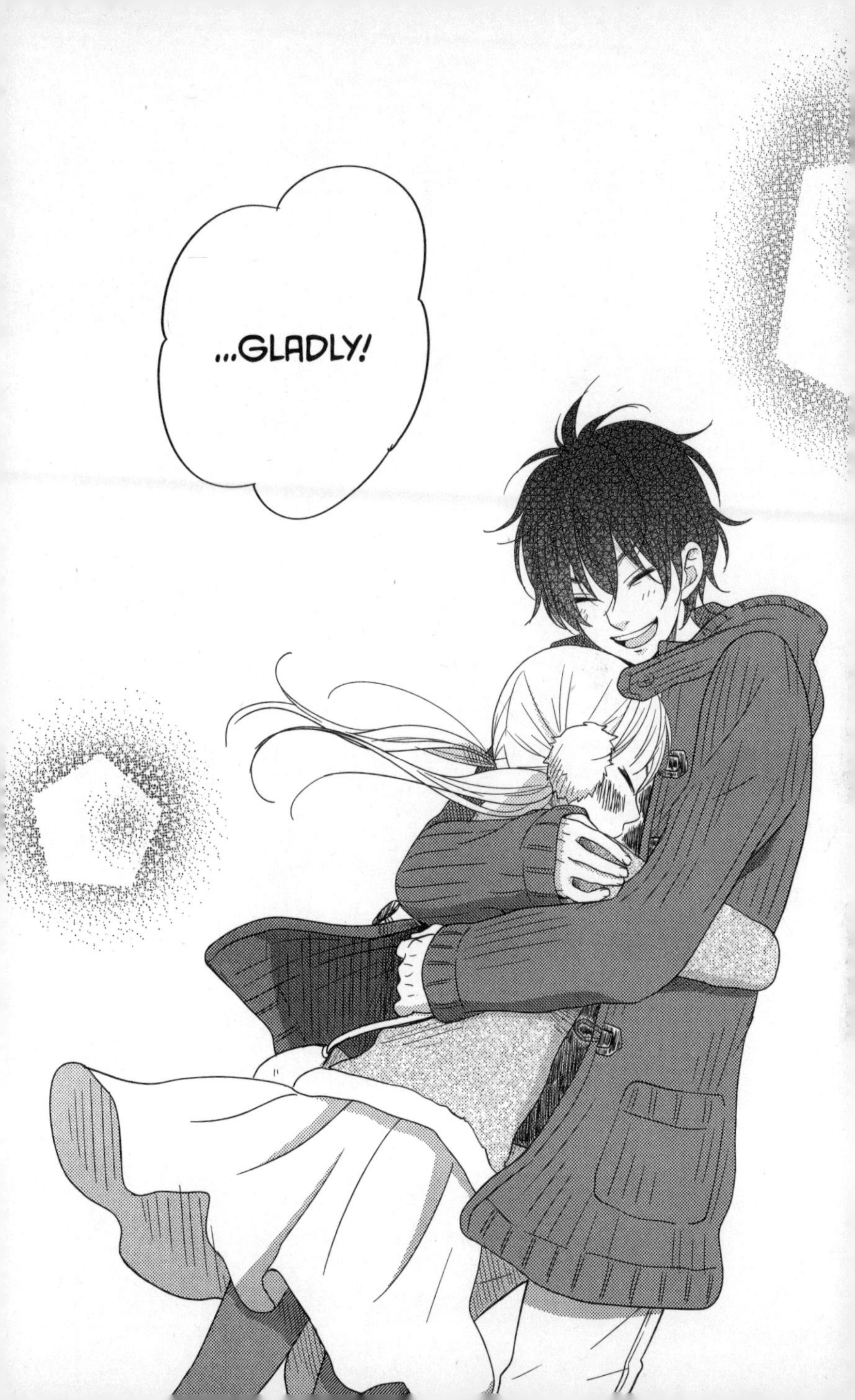
...GLADLY!

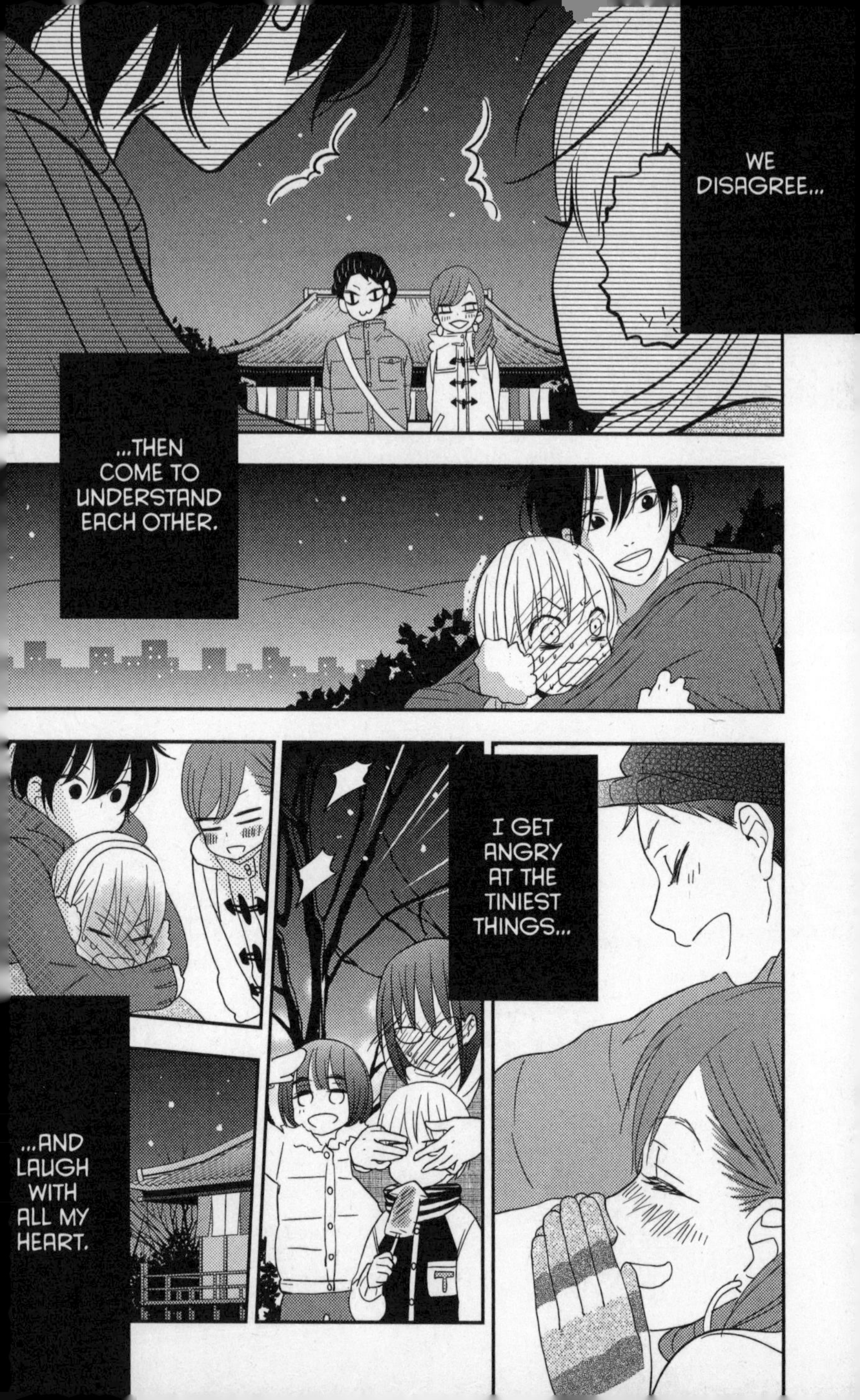
WE DISAGREE...
...THEN COME TO UNDERSTAND EACH OTHER.
I GET ANGRY AT THE TINIEST THINGS...
...AND LAUGH WITH ALL MY HEART.

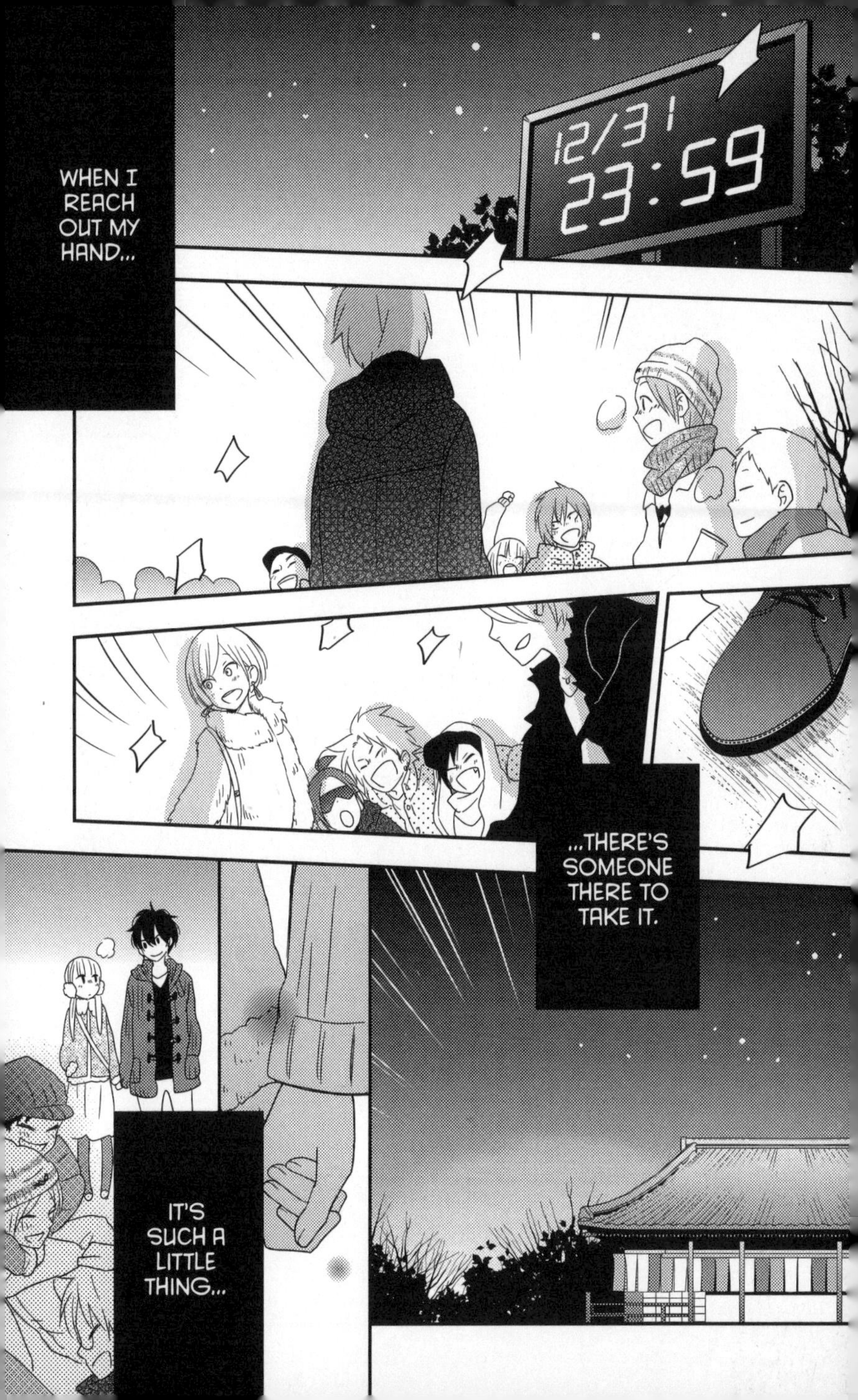
12/31
23:59
WHEN I REACH OUT MY HAND...
...THERE'S SOMEONE THERE TO TAKE IT.
IT'S SUCH A LITTLE THING...

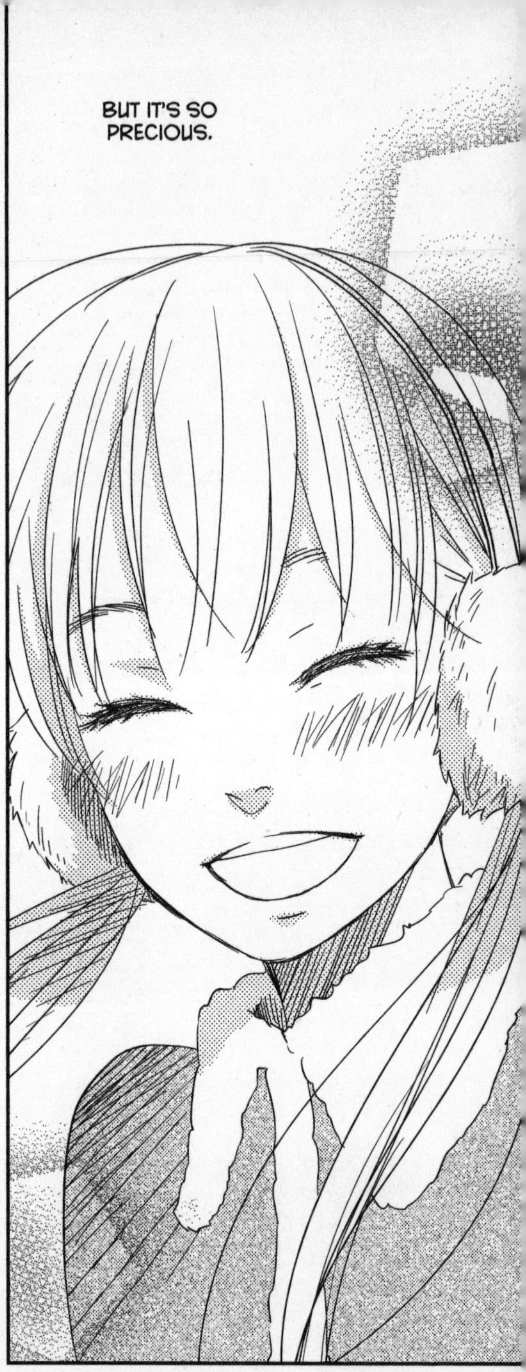
BUT IT'S SO PRECIOUS.
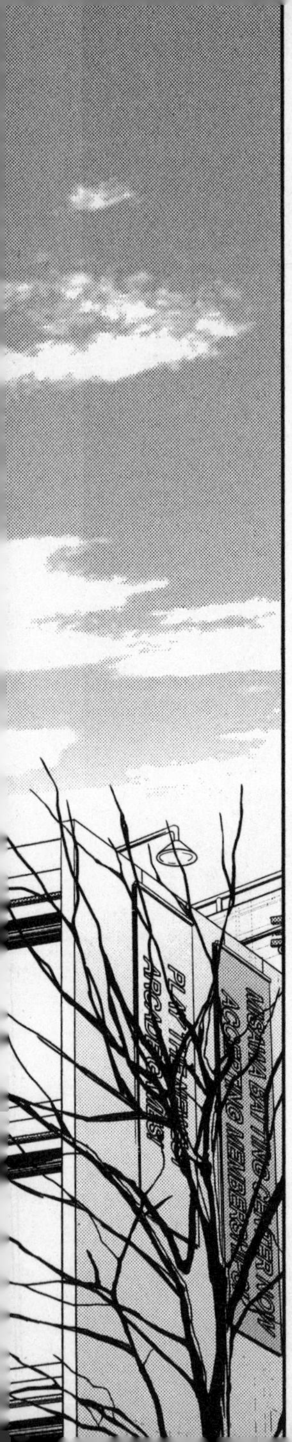

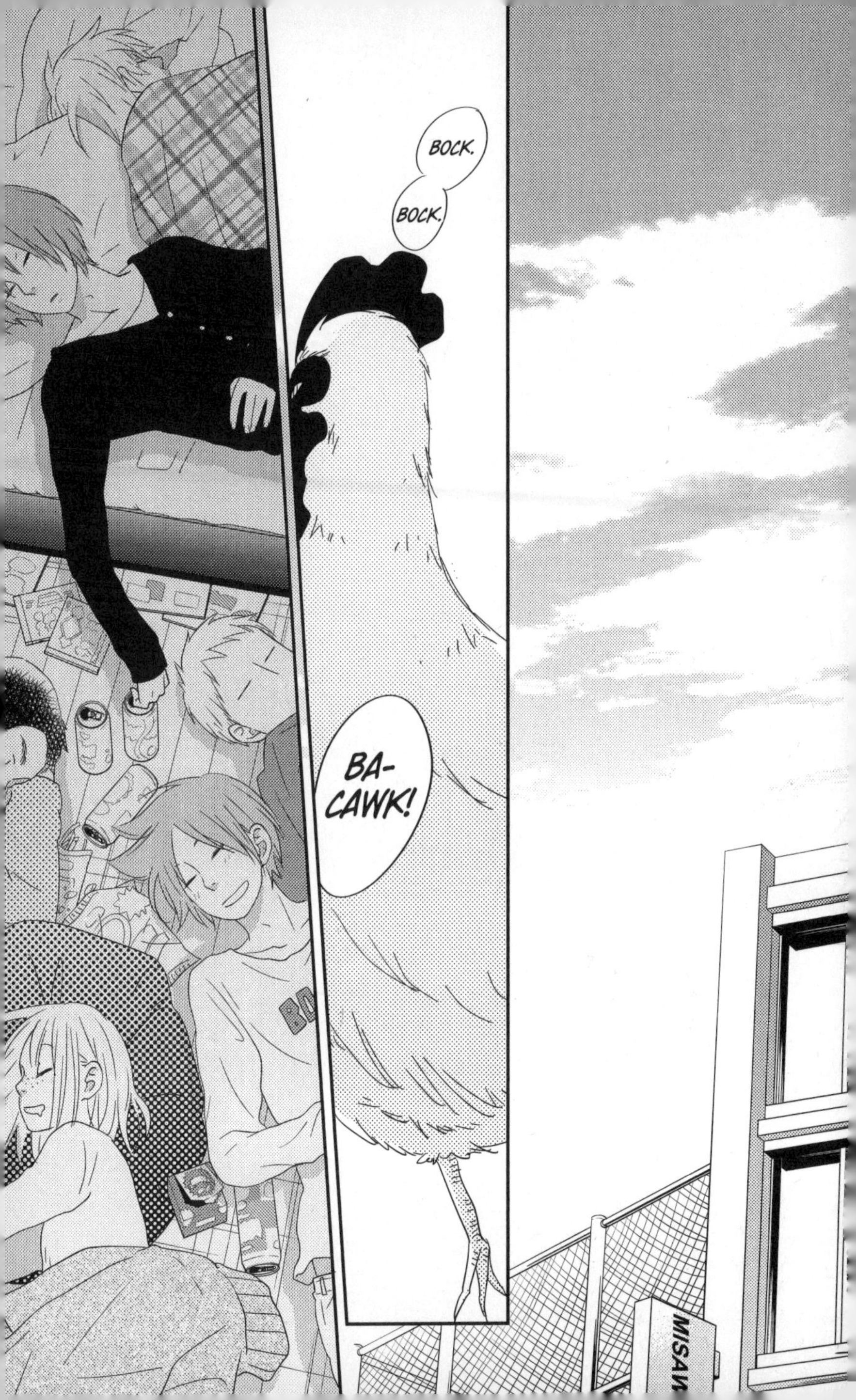
BOCK.
BOCK.
BA-CAWK!

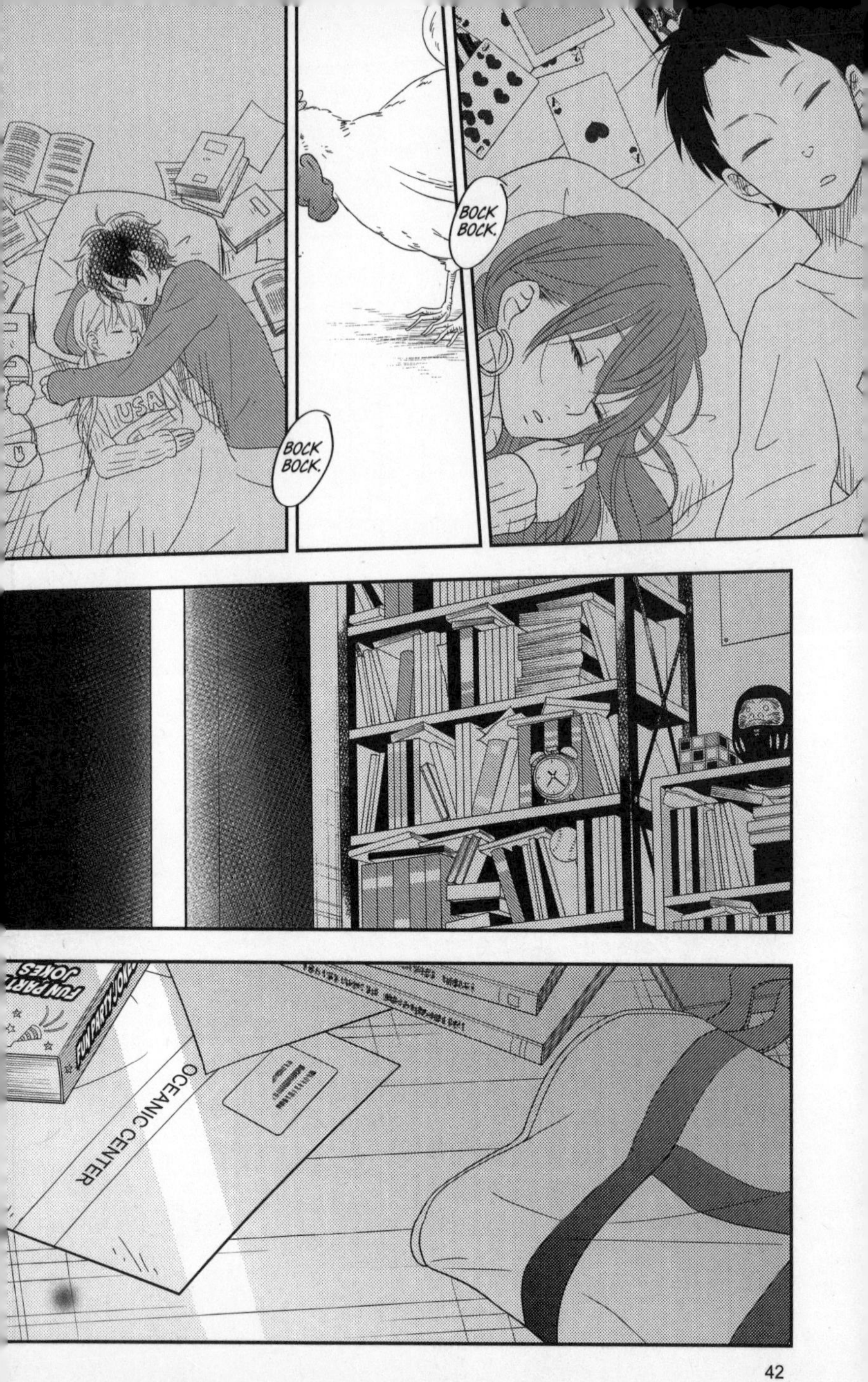
BOCK BOCK.
BOCK BOCK.
JOKES
OCEANIC CENTER

MOST PRIZED POSSESSION

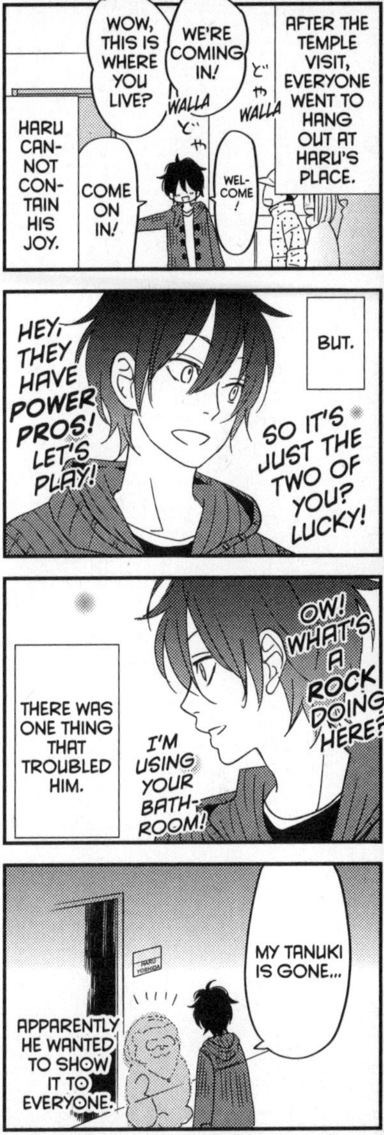
AFTER THE TEMPLE VISIT, EVERYONE WENT TO HANG OUT AT HARU'S PLACE.
WALLA
WE'RE COMING IN!
WELCOME!
WALLA
WOW, THIS IS WHERE YOU LIVE?
COME ON IN!
HARU CANNOT CONTAIN HIS JOY.
BUT.
SO IT'S JUST THE TWO OF YOU? LUCKY!
HEY, THEY HAVE POWER PROS! LET'S PLAY!
OW! WHAT'S A ROCK DOING HERE?
I'M USING YOUR BATHROOM!
THERE WAS ONE THING THAT TROUBLED HIM.
MY TANUKI IS GONE...
HARU YOSHIDA
APPARENTLY HE WANTED TO SHOW IT TO EVERYONE.

EARLY MORNING JOLT

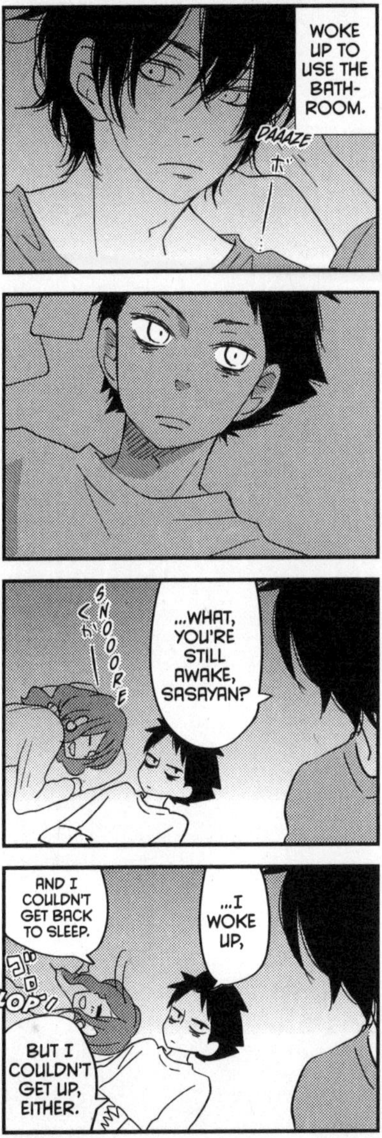
WOKE UP TO USE THE BATHROOM.
DAAAZE
...WHAT, YOU'RE STILL AWAKE, SASAYAN?
SNOOORE
...I WOKE UP,
AND I COULDN'T GET BACK TO SLEEP.
FLOP
BUT I COULDN'T GET UP, EITHER.

SLEEPTALK.

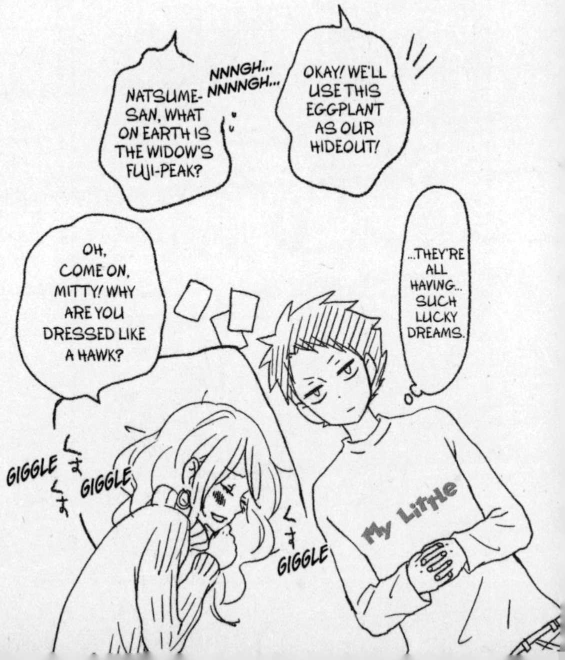
OKAY! WE'LL USE THIS EGGPLANT AS OUR HIDEOUT!
NNNGH... NNNNGH...
NATSUME-SAN, WHAT ON EARTH IS THE WIDOW'S FUJI-PEAK?
...THEY'RE ALL HAVING... SUCH LUCKY DREAMS.
OH, COME ON, MITTY! WHY ARE YOU DRESSED LIKE A HAWK?
くすくす
GIGGLE GIGGLE
くす
GIGGLE
My Little

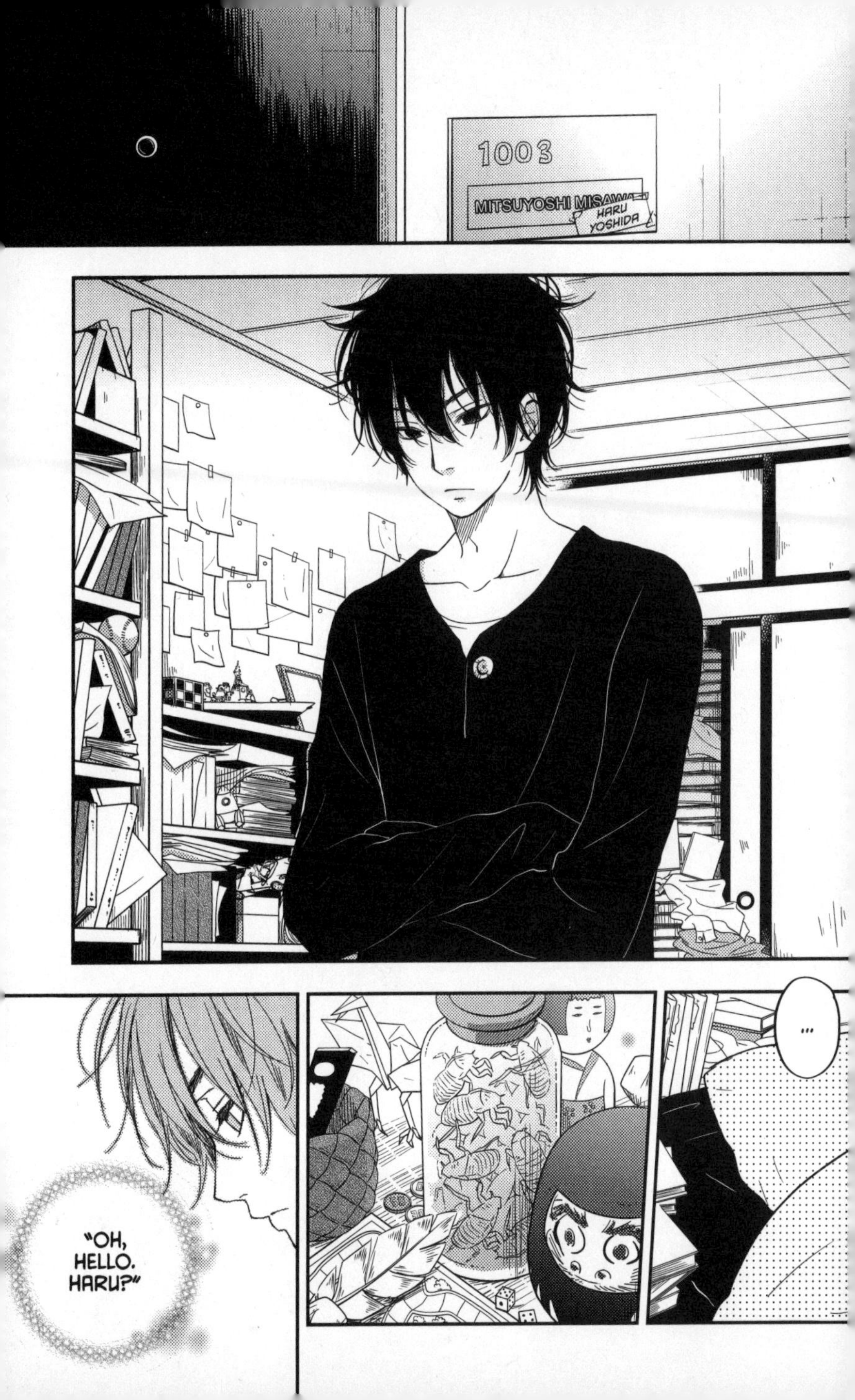
1003
MITSUYOSHI MISAWA
HARU YOSHIDA
...
“OH, HELLO. HARU?”

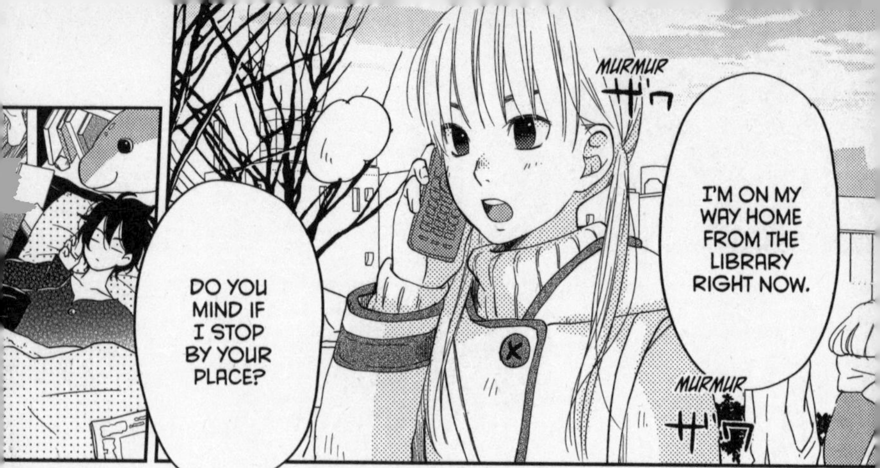
MURMUR
I'M ON MY WAY HOME FROM THE LIBRARY RIGHT NOW.
MURMUR
DO YOU MIND IF I STOP BY YOUR PLACE?

CHAPTER 46: HOME SWEET HOME

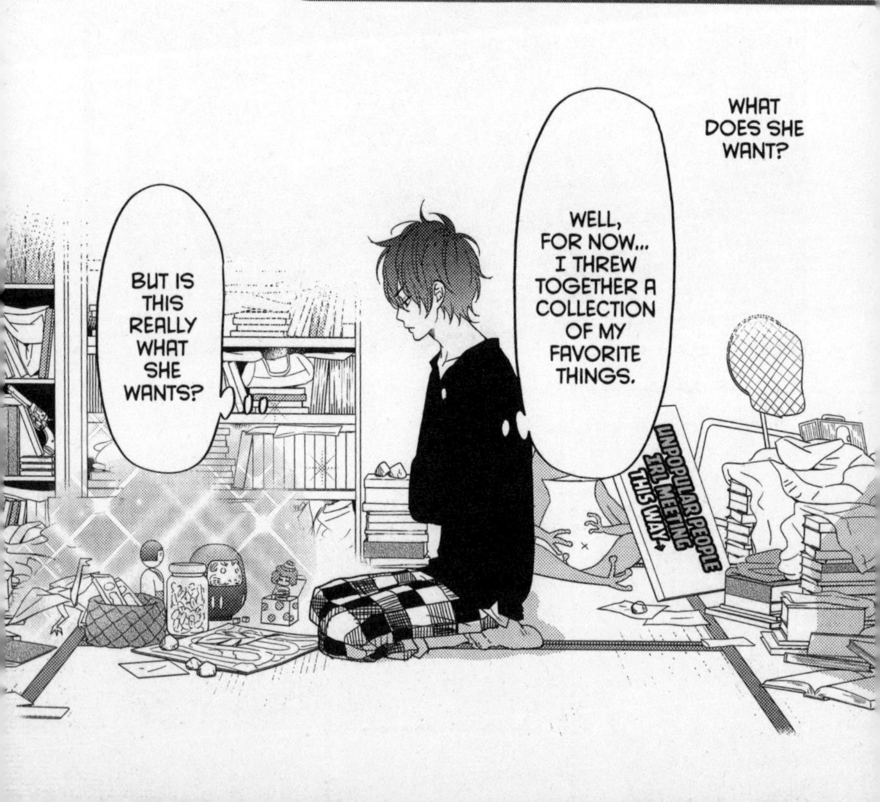
WHAT DOES SHE WANT?
WELL, FOR NOW... I THREW TOGETHER A COLLECTION OF MY FAVORITE THINGS.
UNPOPULAR PEOPLE IRL MEETING THIS WAY
BUT IS THIS REALLY WHAT SHE WANTS?

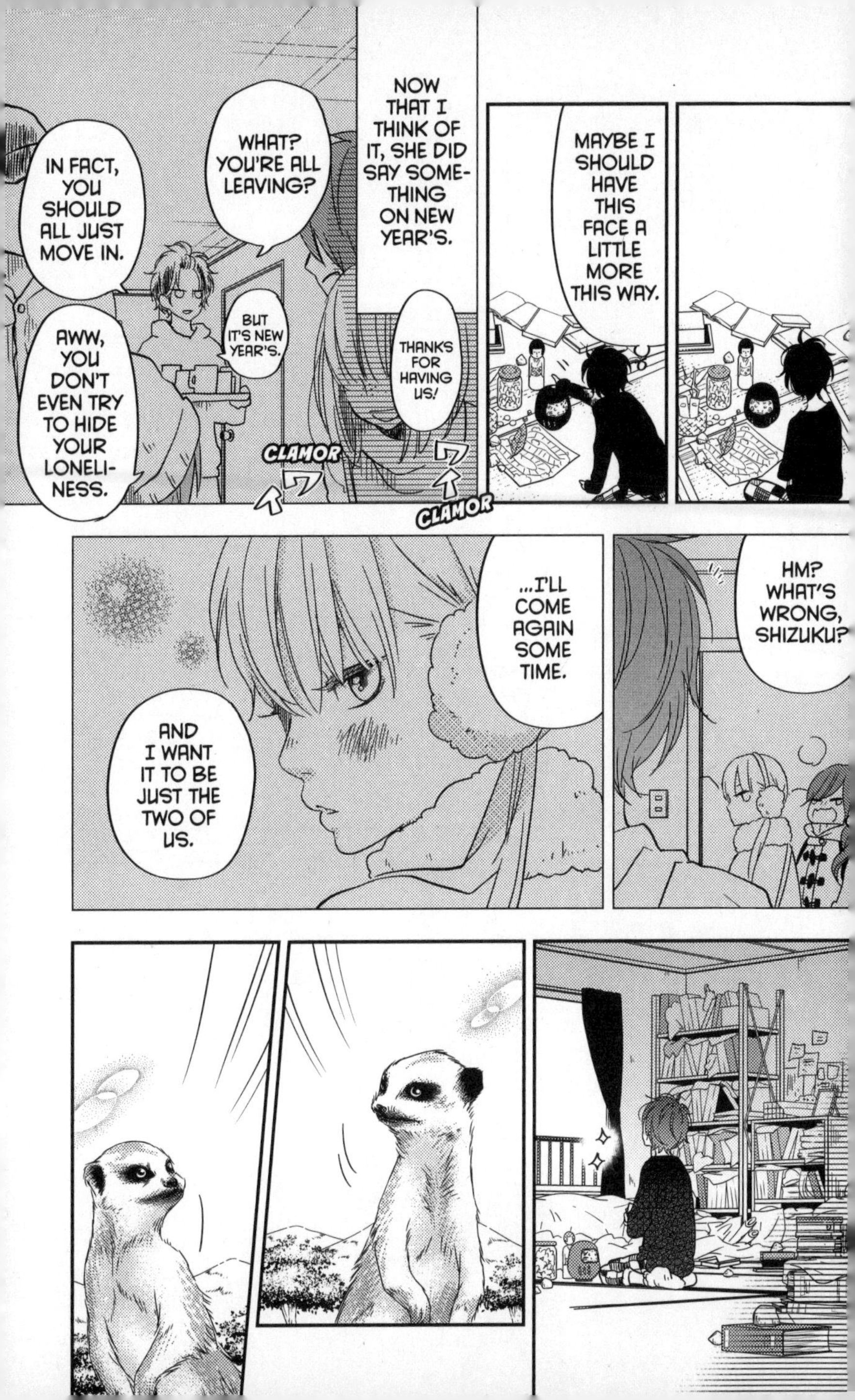
MAYBE I SHOULD HAVE THIS FACE A LITTLE MORE THIS WAY.
NOW THAT I THINK OF IT, SHE DID SAY SOME-THING ON NEW YEAR'S.
THANKS FOR HAVING US!
CLAMOR
WHAT? YOU'RE ALL LEAVING?
IN FACT, YOU SHOULD ALL JUST MOVE IN.
BUT IT'S NEW YEAR'S.
AWW, YOU DON'T EVEN TRY TO HIDE YOUR LONELI-NESS.
CLAMOR
HM? WHAT'S WRONG, SHIZUKU?
...I'LL COME AGAIN SOME TIME.
AND I WANT IT TO BE JUST THE TWO OF US.

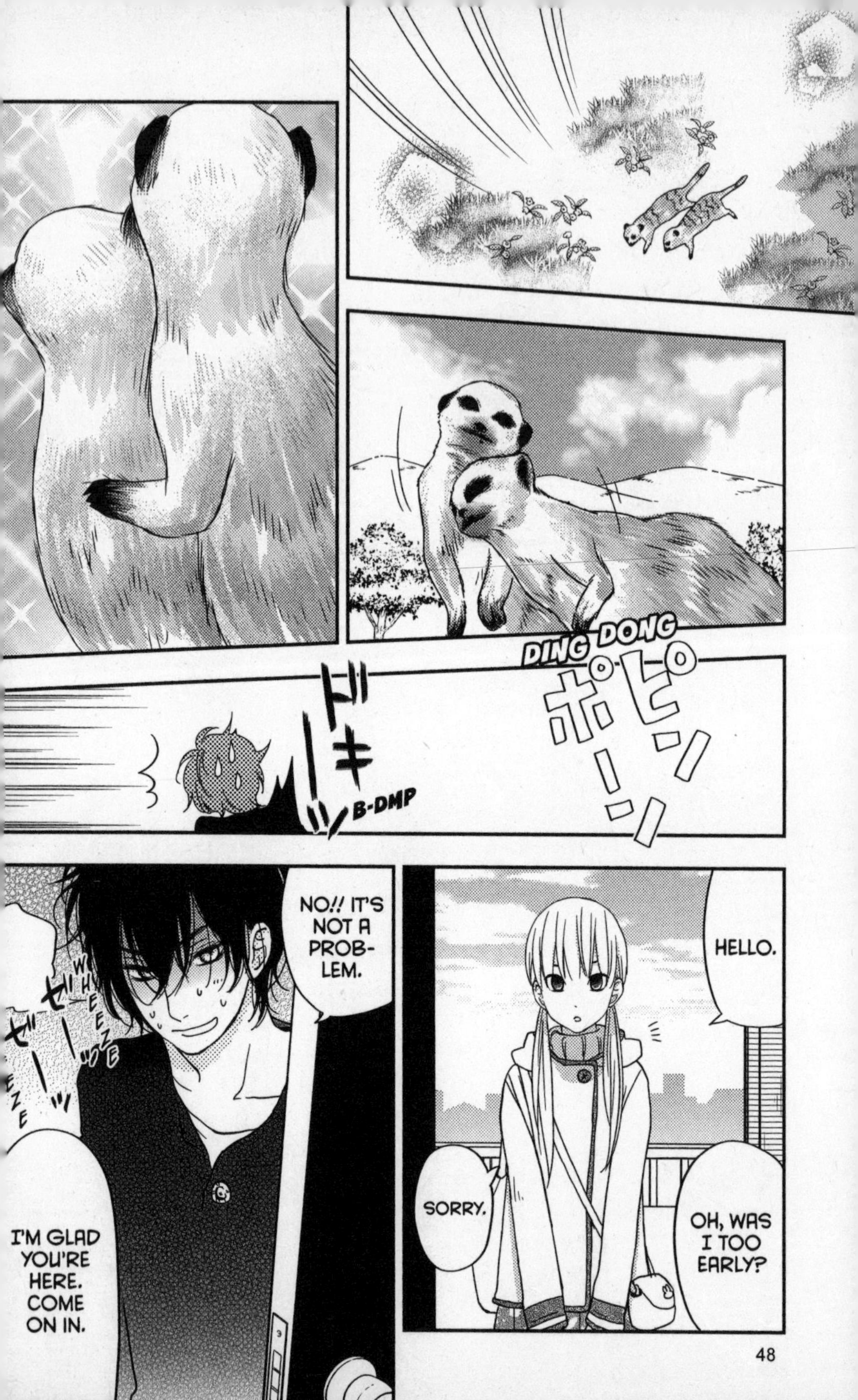
DING DONG
ポピーン
ドキッ
B-DMP
HELLO.
OH, WAS I TOO EARLY?
SORRY.
NO!! IT'S NOT A PROB-LEM.
WHEEZE
ゼーゼー
WHEEZE
I'M GLAD YOU'RE HERE. COME ON IN.

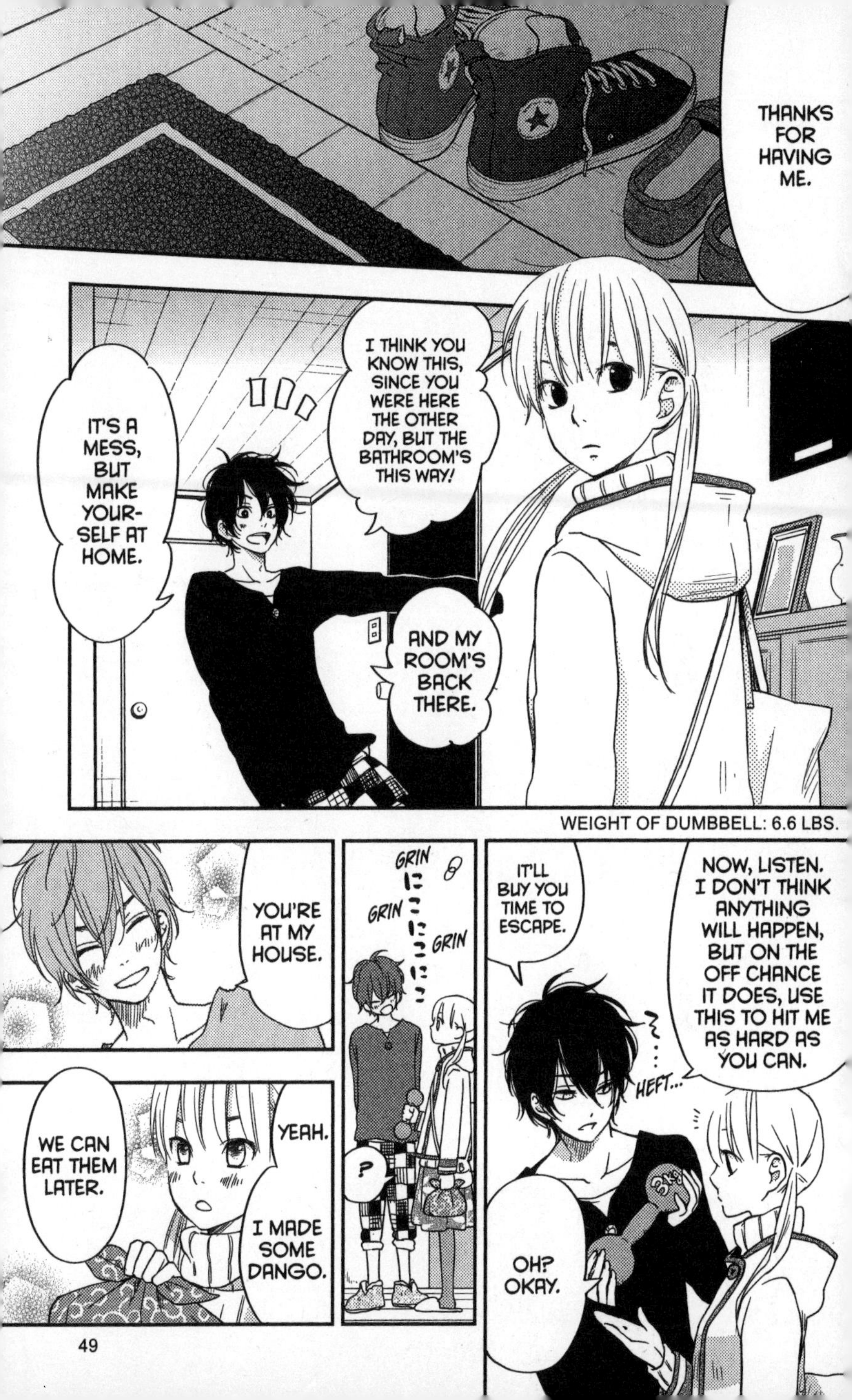
THANKS FOR HAVING ME.
I THINK YOU KNOW THIS, SINCE YOU WERE HERE THE OTHER DAY, BUT THE BATHROOM'S THIS WAY!
IT'S A MESS, BUT MAKE YOURSELF AT HOME.
AND MY ROOM'S BACK THERE.
WEIGHT OF DUMBBELL: 6.6 LBS.
NOW, LISTEN. I DON'T THINK ANYTHING WILL HAPPEN, BUT ON THE OFF CHANCE IT DOES, USE THIS TO HIT ME AS HARD AS YOU CAN.
IT'LL BUY YOU TIME TO ESCAPE.
HEFT...
OH? OKAY.
GRIN
にこにこにこ
GRIN GRIN
?
YOU'RE AT MY HOUSE.
YEAH.
I MADE SOME DANGO.
WE CAN EAT THEM LATER.

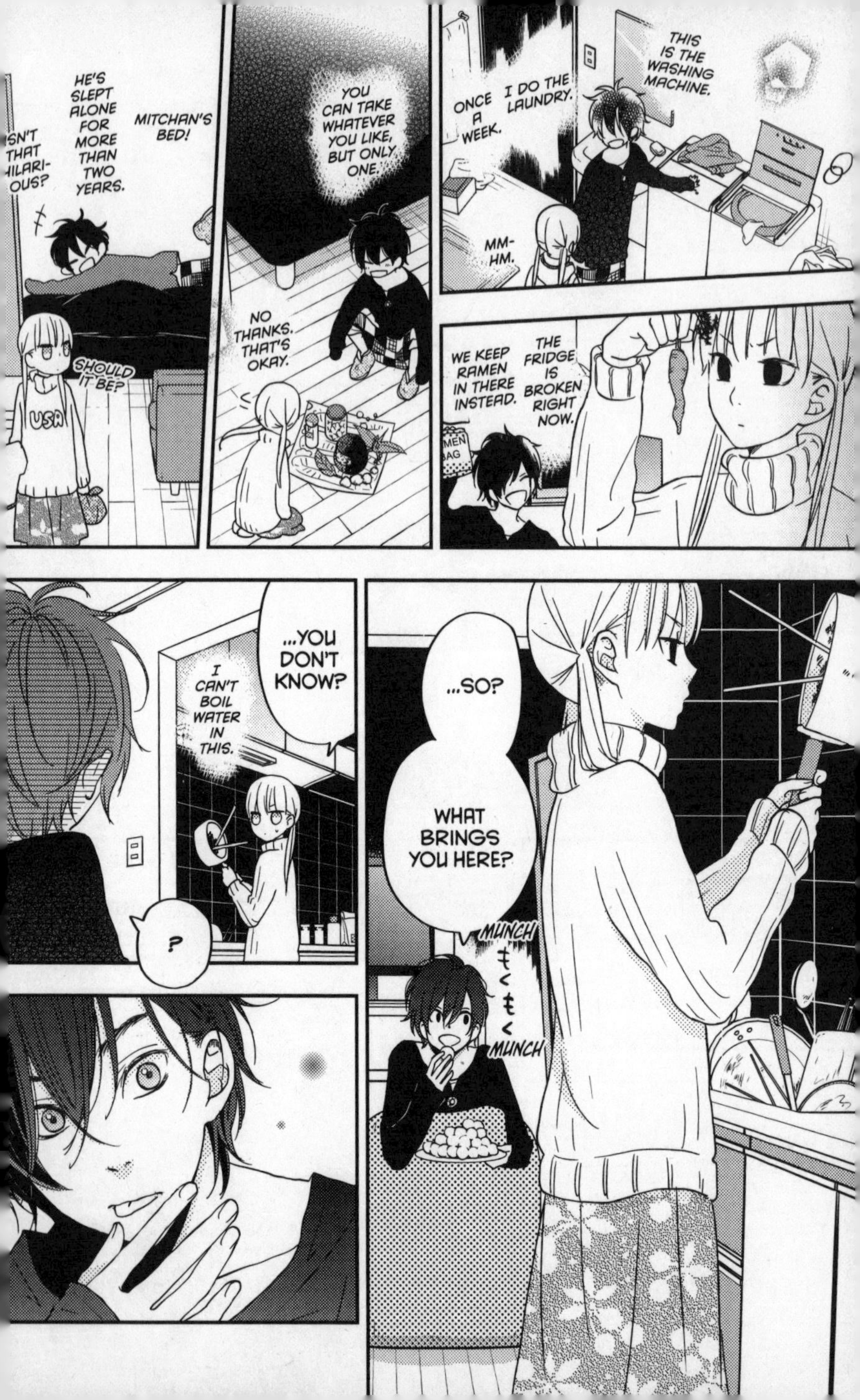
THIS IS THE WASHING MACHINE.
I DO THE LAUNDRY.
ONCE A WEEK.
MM-HM.
THE FRIDGE IS BROKEN RIGHT NOW.
WE KEEP RAMEN IN THERE INSTEAD.
YOU CAN TAKE WHATEVER YOU LIKE, BUT ONLY ONE.
NO THANKS. THAT'S OKAY.
MITCHAN'S BED!
HE'S SLEPT ALONE FOR MORE THAN TWO YEARS.
ISN'T THAT HILARIOUS?
SHOULD IT BE?
...SO?
WHAT BRINGS YOU HERE?
MUNCH もくもく MUNCH
...YOU DON'T KNOW?
I CAN'T BOIL WATER IN THIS.
?

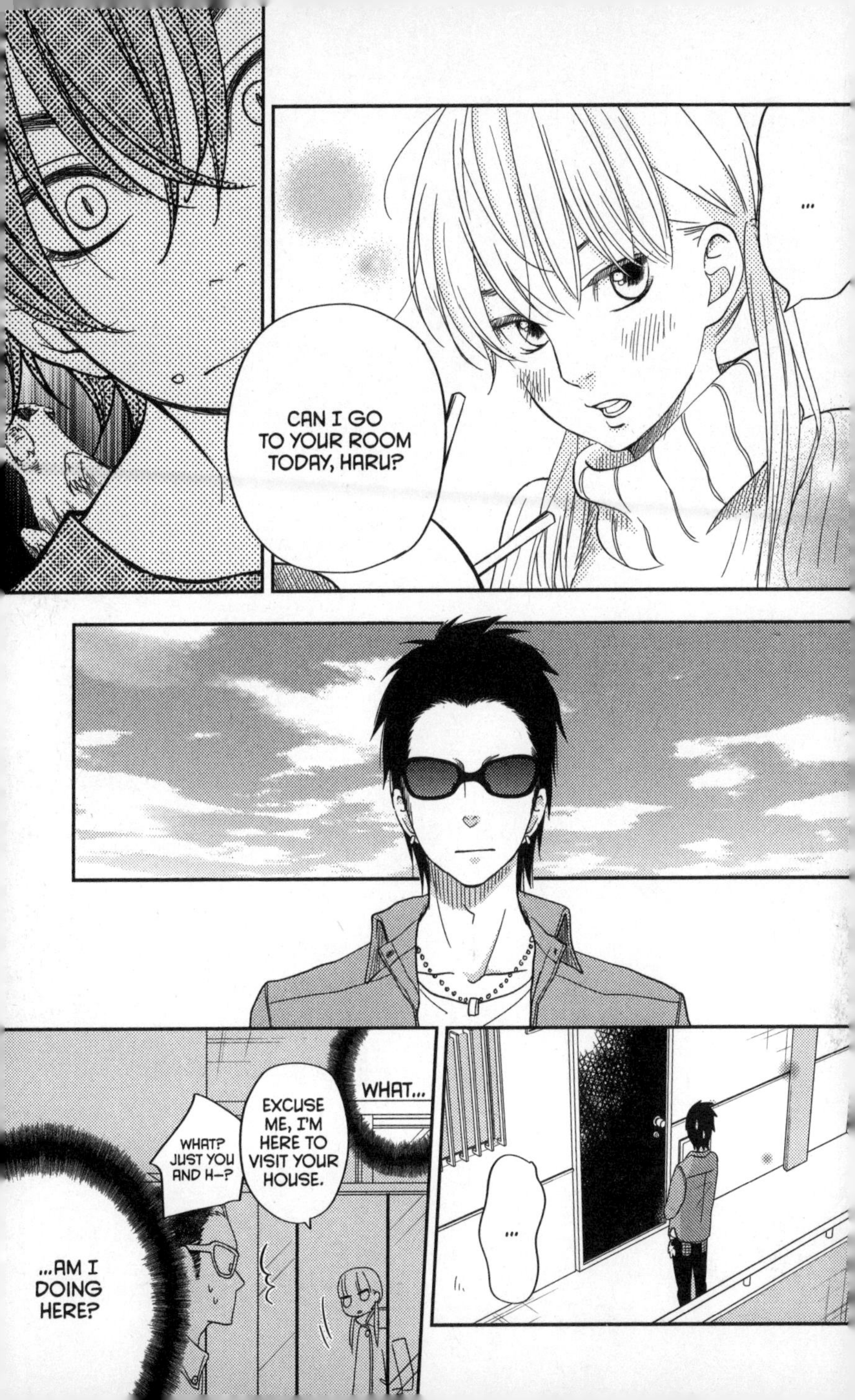
...
CAN I GO TO YOUR ROOM TODAY, HARU?
...
WHAT...
EXCUSE ME, I'M HERE TO VISIT YOUR HOUSE.
WHAT? JUST YOU AND H--?
...AM I DOING HERE?

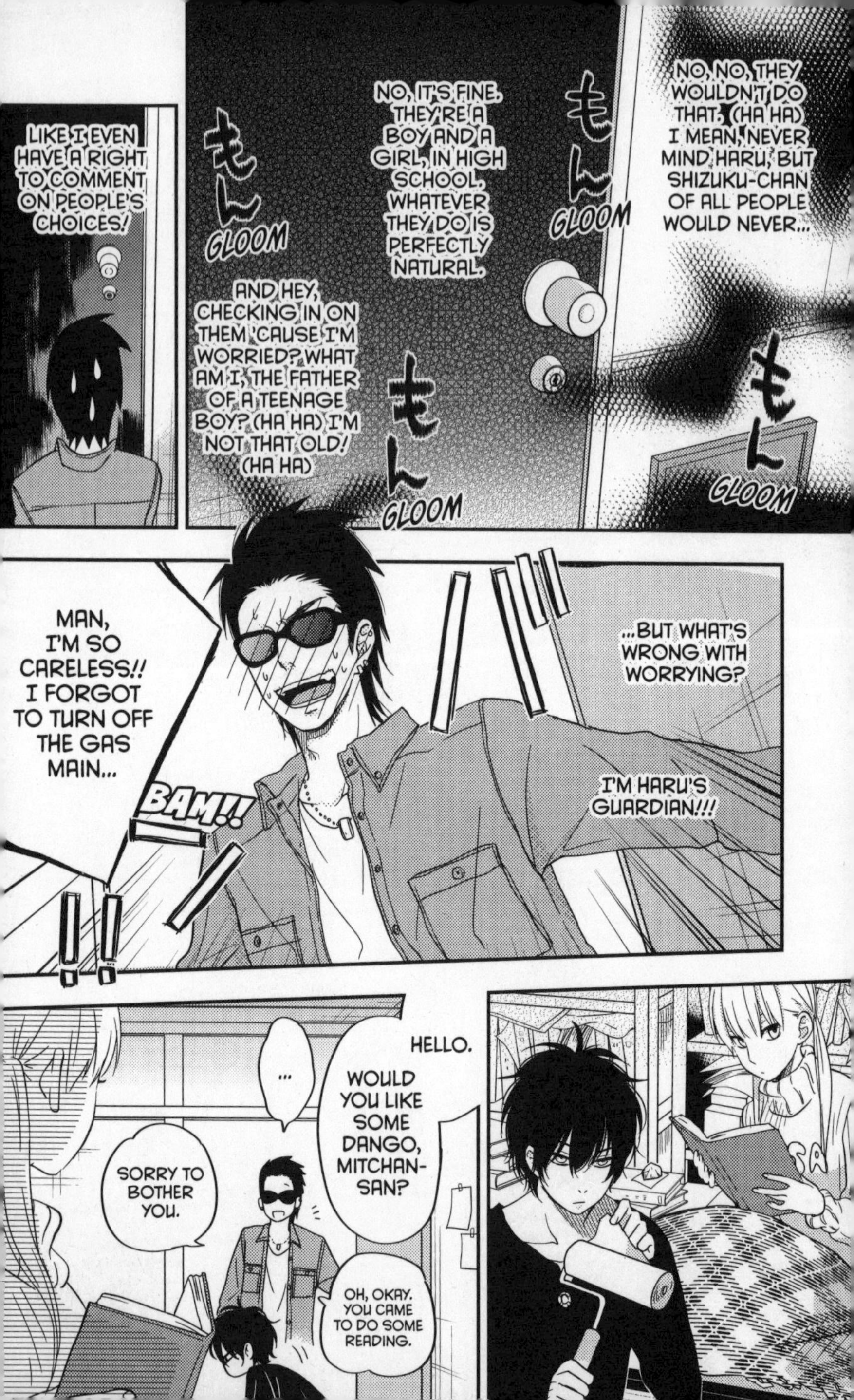
もん
GLOOM
NO, NO, THEY WOULDN'T DO THAT. (HA HA) I MEAN, NEVER MIND HARU, BUT SHIZUKU-CHAN OF ALL PEOPLE WOULD NEVER...
もん
GLOOM
NO, IT'S FINE. THEY'RE A BOY AND A GIRL, IN HIGH SCHOOL. WHATEVER THEY DO IS PERFECTLY NATURAL.
もん
GLOOM
AND HEY, CHECKING IN ON THEM 'CAUSE I'M WORRIED? WHAT AM I, THE FATHER OF A TEENAGE BOY? (HA HA) I'M NOT THAT OLD! (HA HA)
もん
GLOOM
LIKE I EVEN HAVE A RIGHT TO COMMENT ON PEOPLE'S CHOICES!
...BUT WHAT'S WRONG WITH WORRYING?
I'M HARU'S GUARDIAN!!!
BAM!!
MAN, I'M SO CARELESS!! I FORGOT TO TURN OFF THE GAS MAIN...
HELLO.
WOULD YOU LIKE SOME DANGO, MITCHAN-SAN?
...
SORRY TO BOTHER YOU.
OH, OKAY. YOU CAME TO DO SOME READING.

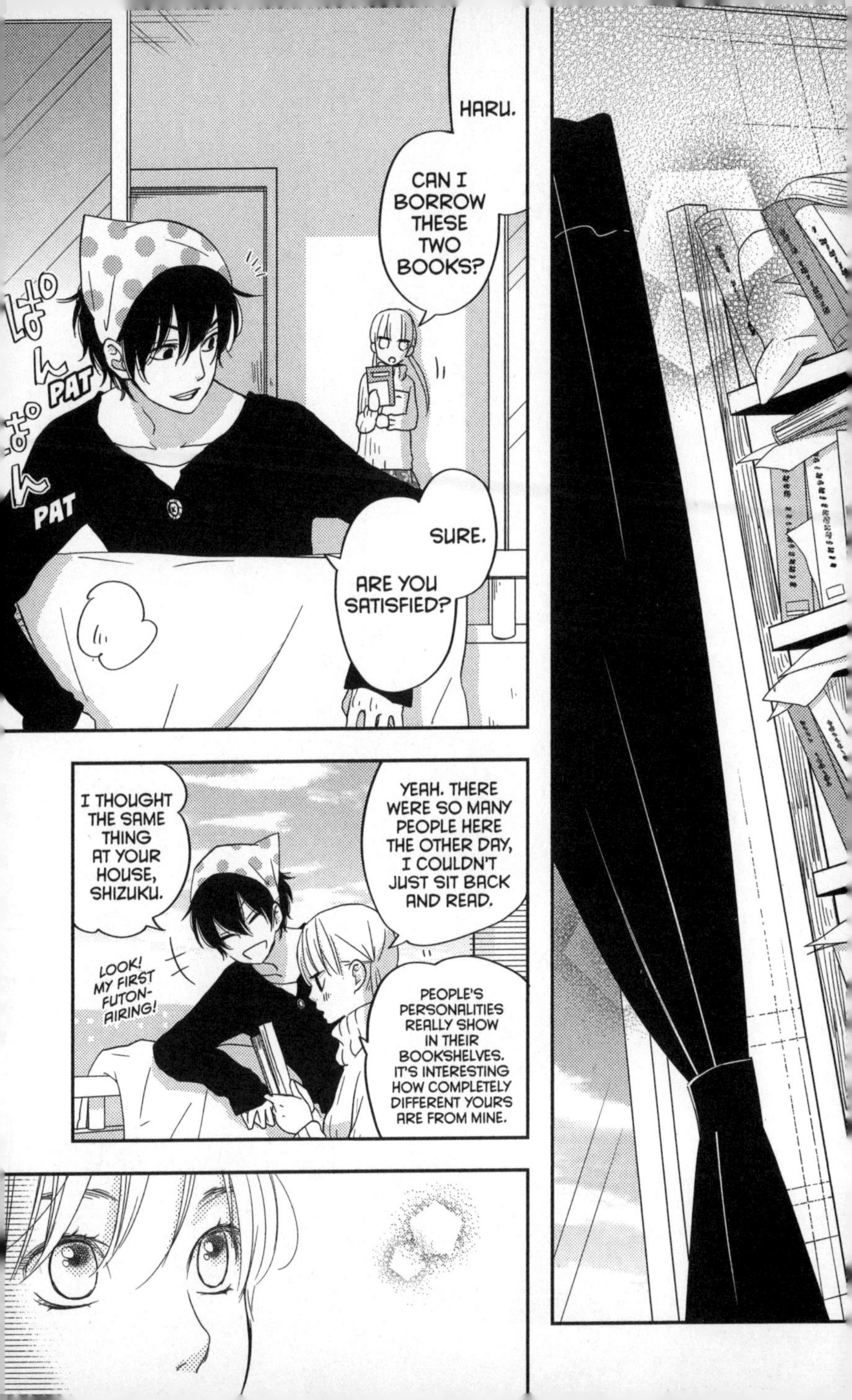
HARU.
CAN I BORROW THESE TWO BOOKS?
ぽん PAT
ぽん PAT
SURE.
ARE YOU SATISFIED?
YEAH. THERE WERE SO MANY PEOPLE HERE THE OTHER DAY, I COULDN'T JUST SIT BACK AND READ.
PEOPLE'S PERSONALITIES REALLY SHOW IN THEIR BOOKSHELVES. IT'S INTERESTING HOW COMPLETELY DIFFERENT YOURS ARE FROM MINE.
I THOUGHT THE SAME THING AT YOUR HOUSE, SHIZUKU.
LOOK! MY FIRST FUTON-AIRING!

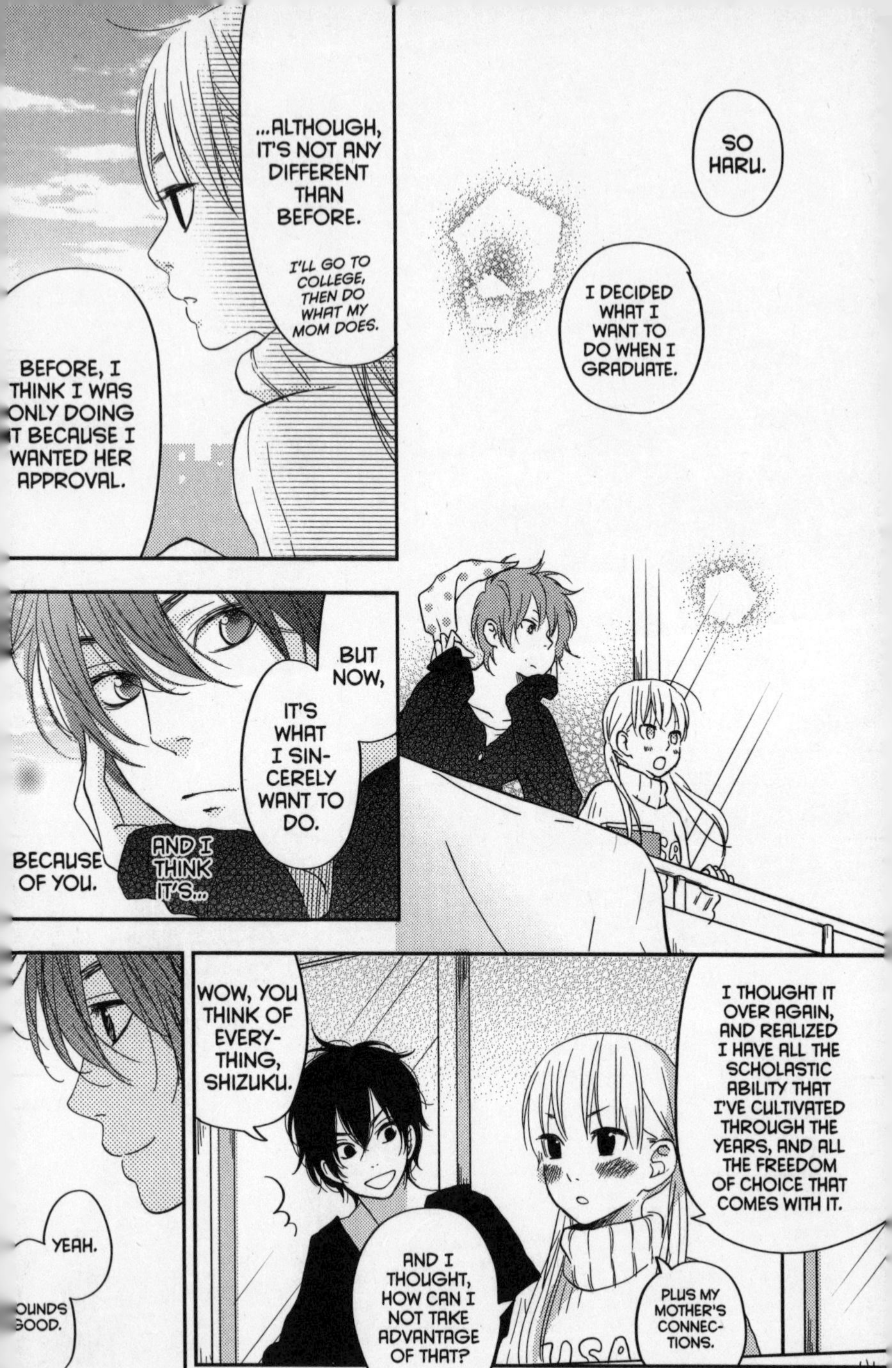
SO HARU.
I DECIDED WHAT I WANT TO DO WHEN I GRADUATE.
...ALTHOUGH, IT'S NOT ANY DIFFERENT THAN BEFORE.
I'LL GO TO COLLEGE, THEN DO WHAT MY MOM DOES.
BEFORE, I THINK I WAS ONLY DOING IT BECAUSE I WANTED HER APPROVAL.
BUT NOW,
IT'S WHAT I SIN-CERELY WANT TO DO.
AND I THINK IT'S...
BECAUSE OF YOU.
I THOUGHT IT OVER AGAIN, AND REALIZED I HAVE ALL THE SCHOLASTIC ABILITY THAT I'VE CULTIVATED THROUGH THE YEARS, AND ALL THE FREEDOM OF CHOICE THAT COMES WITH IT.
PLUS MY MOTHER'S CONNEC-TIONS.
AND I THOUGHT, HOW CAN I NOT TAKE ADVANTAGE OF THAT?
WOW, YOU THINK OF EVERY-THING, SHIZUKU.
YEAH.
OUNDS GOOD.

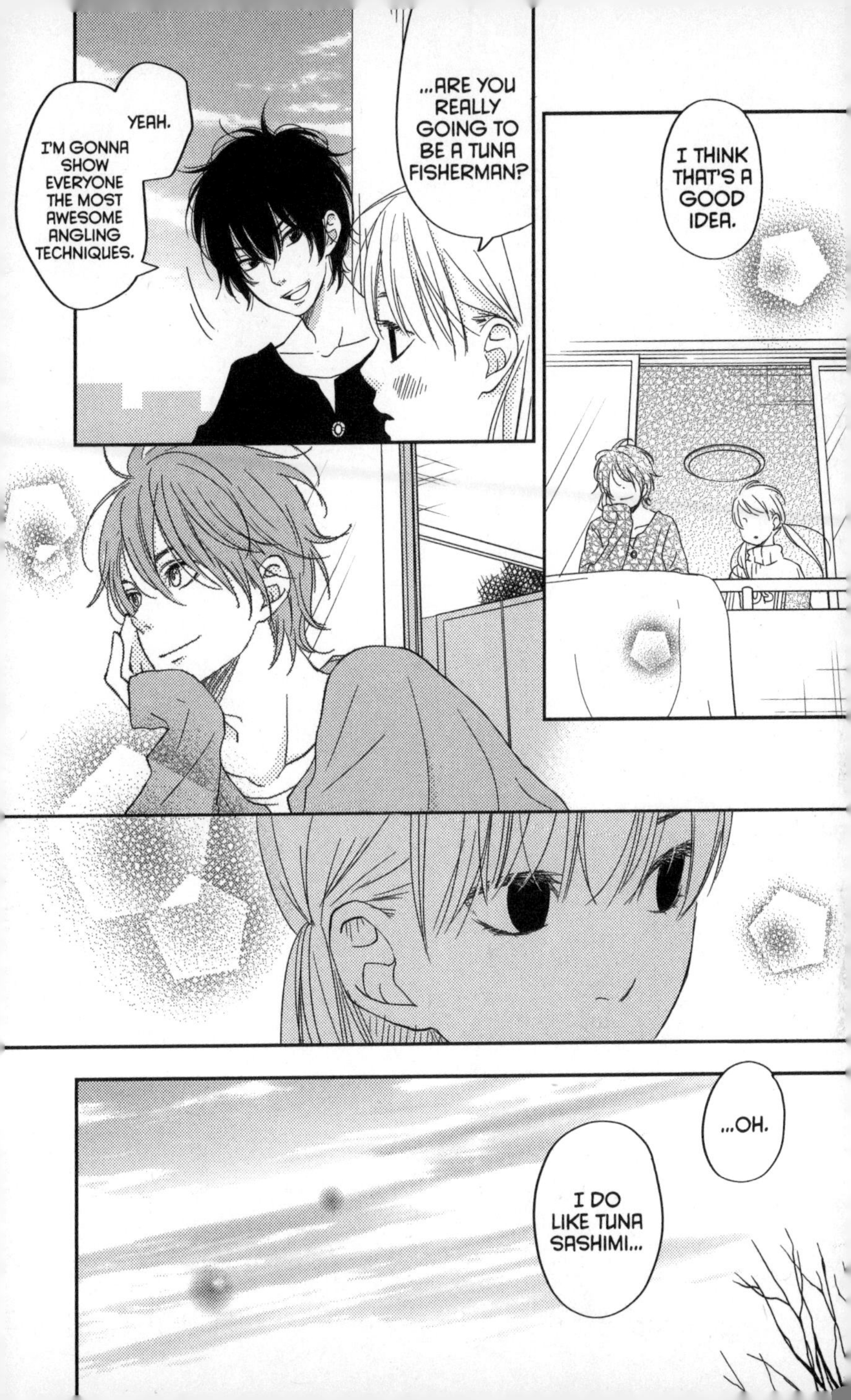
I THINK THAT'S A GOOD IDEA.
...ARE YOU REALLY GOING TO BE A TUNA FISHERMAN?
YEAH. I'M GONNA SHOW EVERYONE THE MOST AWESOME ANGLING TECHNIQUES.
...OH.
I DO LIKE TUNA SASHIMI...

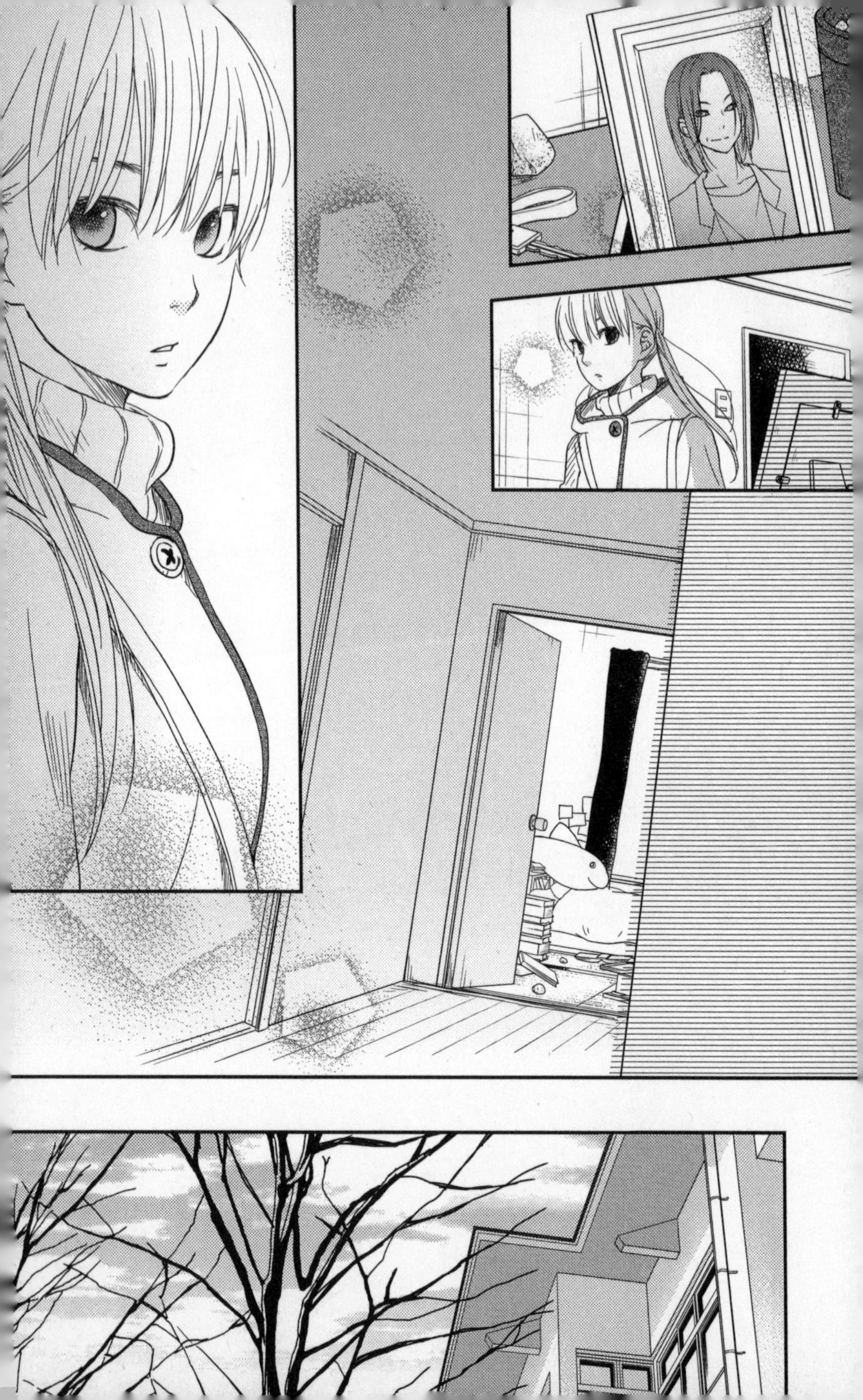

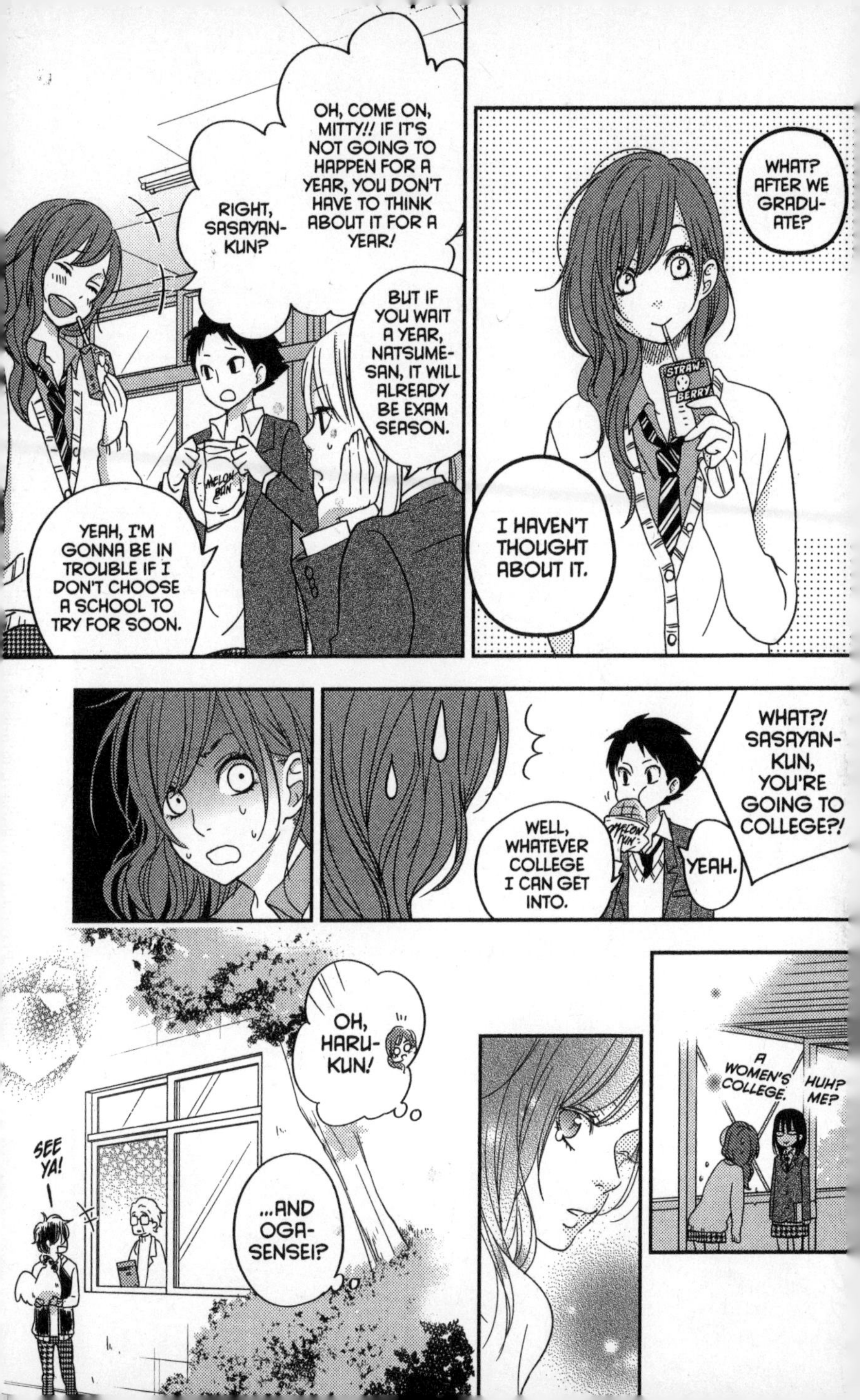
WHAT? AFTER WE GRADU-ATE?
STRAW-BERRY
I HAVEN'T THOUGHT ABOUT IT.
OH, COME ON, MITTY!! IF IT'S NOT GOING TO HAPPEN FOR A YEAR, YOU DON'T HAVE TO THINK ABOUT IT FOR A YEAR!
RIGHT, SASAYAN-KUN?
BUT IF YOU WAIT A YEAR, NATSUME-SAN, IT WILL ALREADY BE EXAM SEASON.
MELON BUN
YEAH, I'M GONNA BE IN TROUBLE IF I DON'T CHOOSE A SCHOOL TO TRY FOR SOON.
WHAT?! SASAYAN-KUN, YOU'RE GOING TO COLLEGE?!
YEAH.
WELL, WHATEVER COLLEGE I CAN GET INTO.
HUH? ME?
A WOMEN'S COLLEGE.
OH, HARU-KUN!
...AND OGA-SENSEI?
SEE YA!

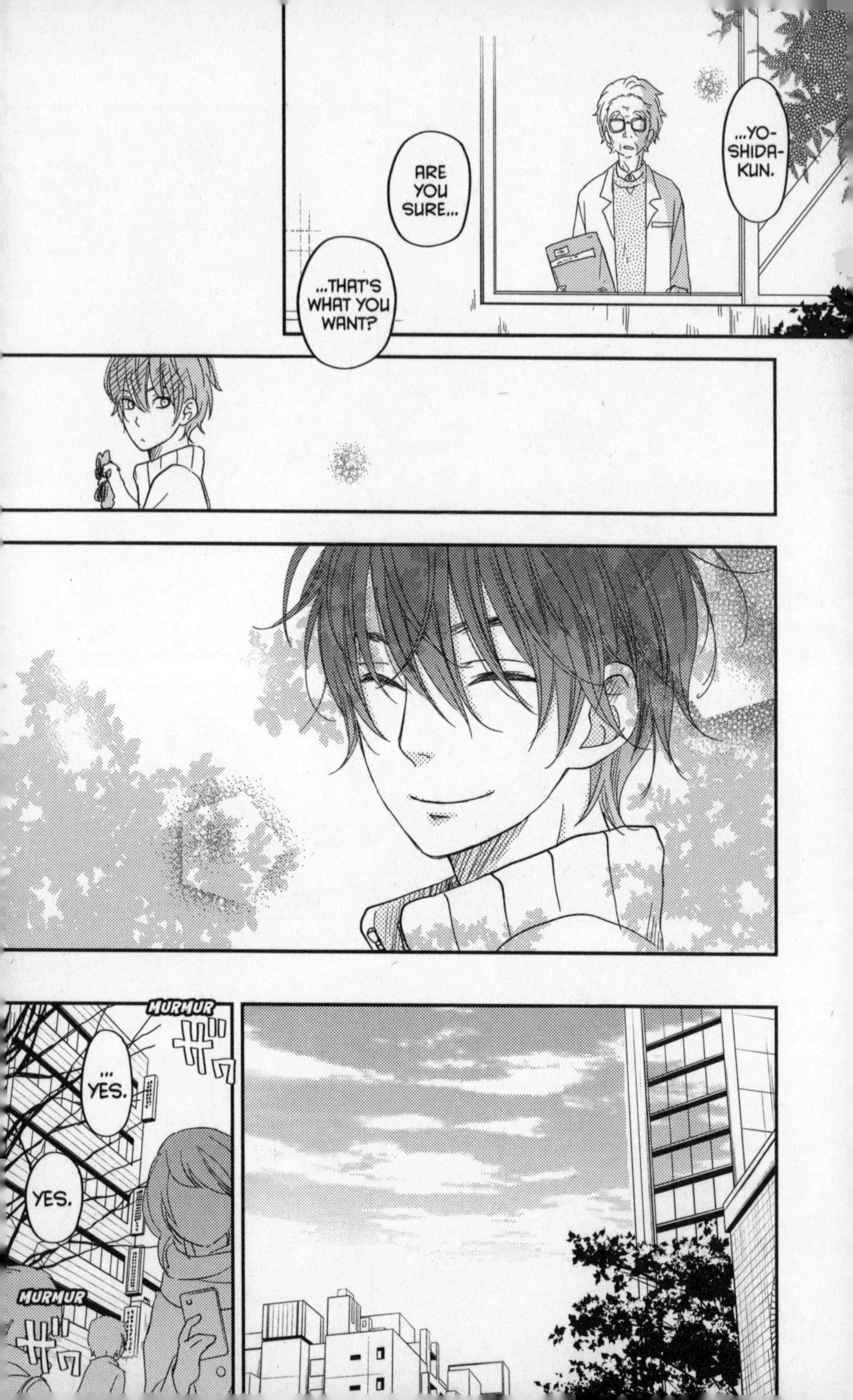
...YO-SHIDA-KUN.
ARE YOU SURE...
...THAT'S WHAT YOU WANT?
MURMUR
ザワ
... YES.
YES.
MURMUR
ザワ

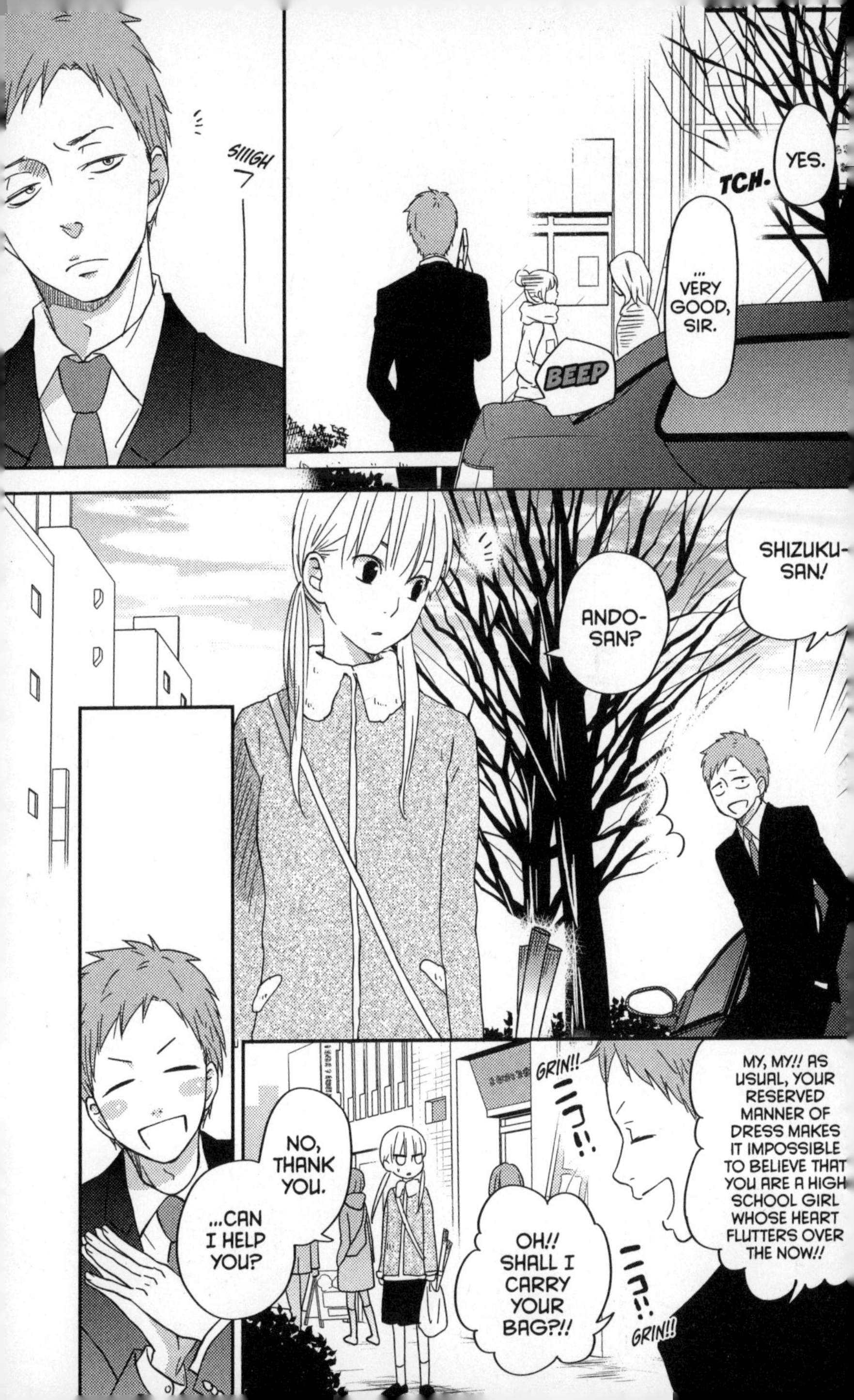
YES.
TCH.
...VERY GOOD, SIR.
BEEP
SIIGH
SHIZUKU-SAN!
ANDO-SAN?
MY, MY!! AS USUAL, YOUR RESERVED MANNER OF DRESS MAKES IT IMPOSSIBLE TO BELIEVE THAT YOU ARE A HIGH SCHOOL GIRL WHOSE HEART FLUTTERS OVER THE NOW!!
GRIN!!
OH!! SHALL I CARRY YOUR BAG?!!
GRIN!!
NO, THANK YOU.
...CAN I HELP YOU?

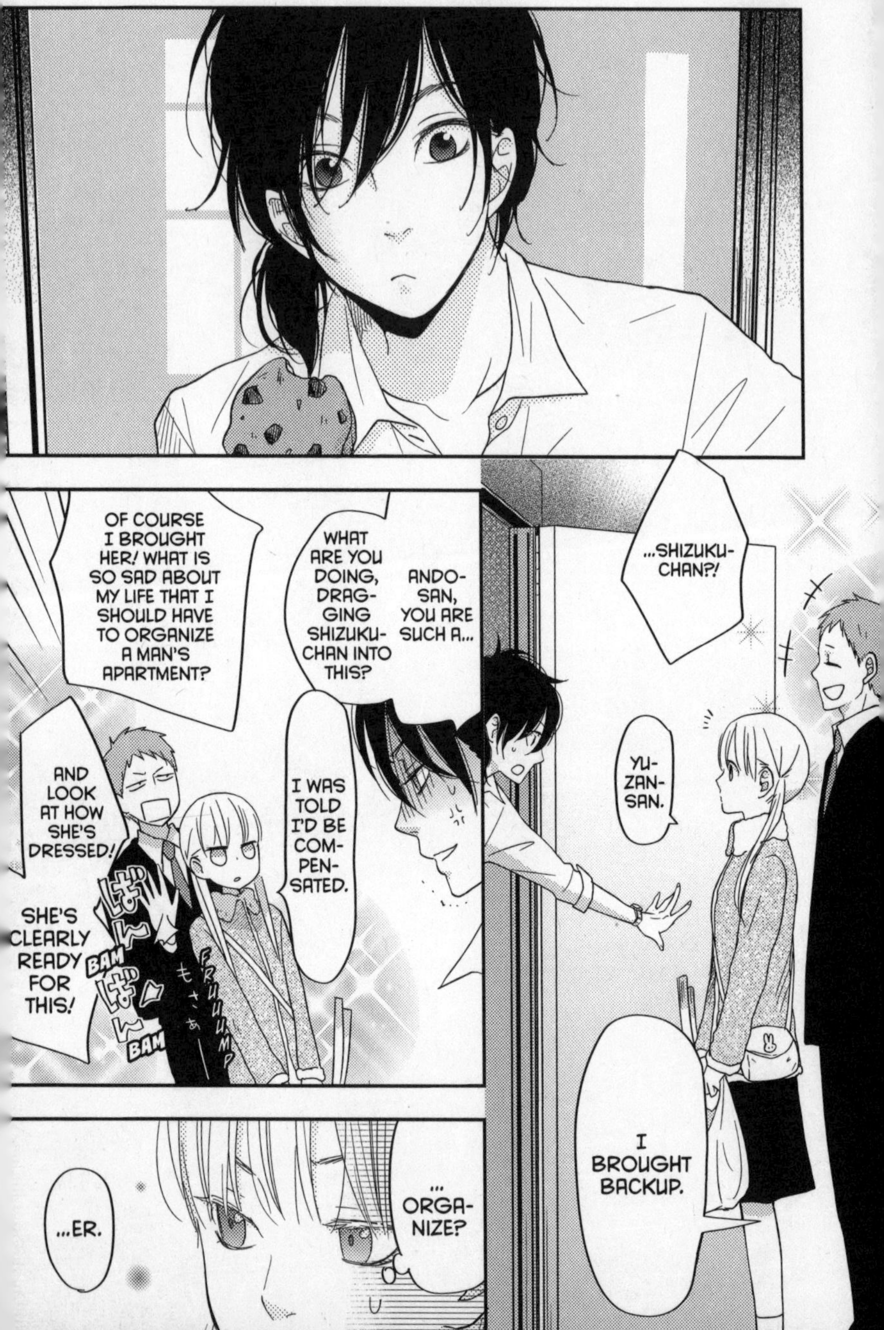
...SHIZUKU-CHAN?!
YU-ZAN-SAN.
I BROUGHT BACKUP.
ANDO-SAN, YOU ARE SUCH A...
WHAT ARE YOU DOING, DRAGGING SHIZUKU-CHAN INTO THIS?
OF COURSE I BROUGHT HER! WHAT IS SO SAD ABOUT MY LIFE THAT I SHOULD HAVE TO ORGANIZE A MAN'S APARTMENT?
I WAS TOLD I'D BE COMPENSATED.
AND LOOK AT HOW SHE'S DRESSED!
FRUUUMP
BAM
BAM
SHE'S CLEARLY READY FOR THIS!
...ORGANIZE?
...ER.

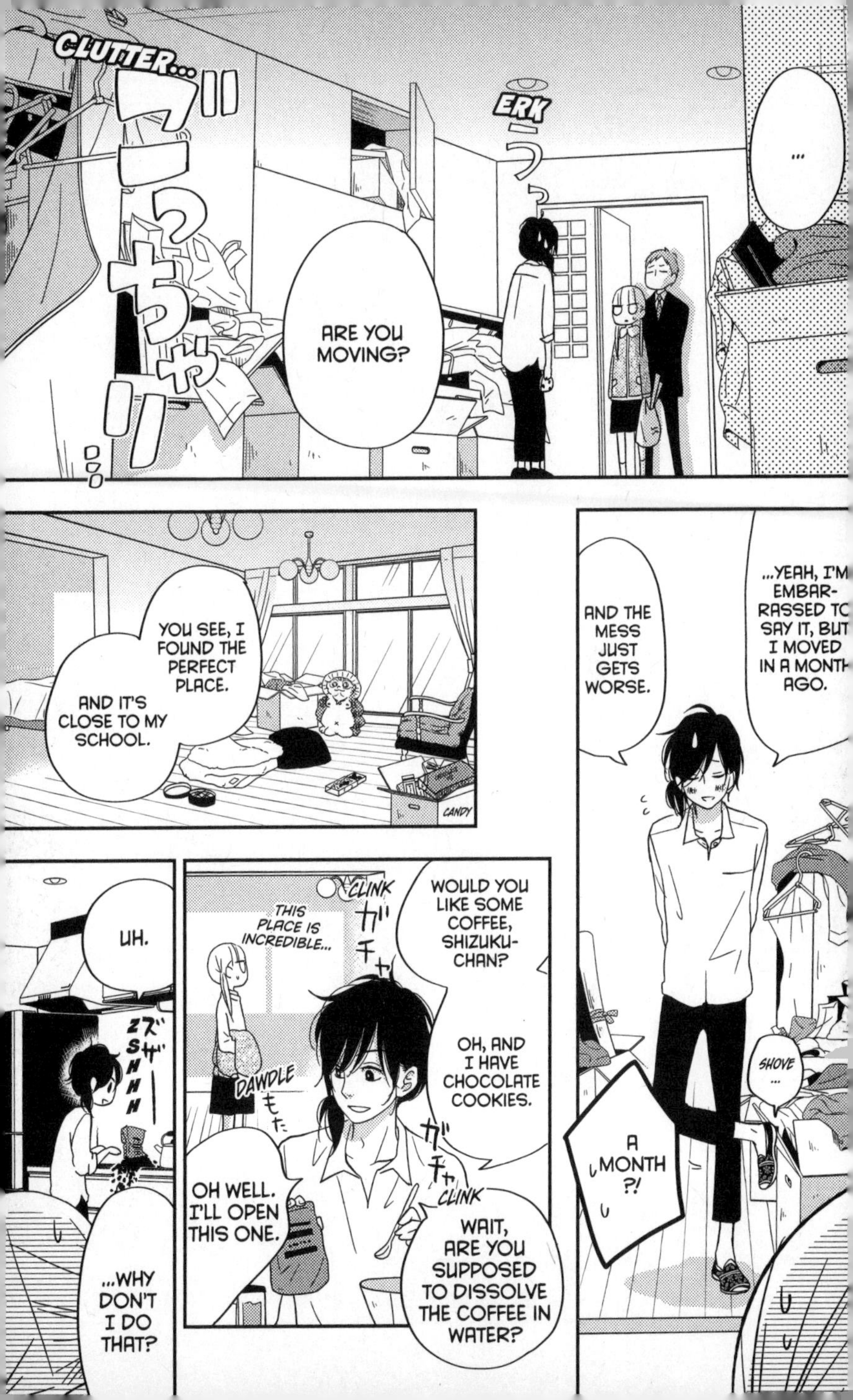
...
ERK
うっ
ARE YOU MOVING?
CLUTTER...
ごっちゃり
...YEAH, I'M EMBARRASSED TO SAY IT, BUT I MOVED IN A MONTH AGO.
AND THE MESS JUST GETS WORSE.
SHOVE...
A MONTH?!
YOU SEE, I FOUND THE PERFECT PLACE.
AND IT'S CLOSE TO MY SCHOOL.
CANDY
WOULD YOU LIKE SOME COFFEE, SHIZUKU-CHAN?
CLINK
ガチャ
THIS PLACE IS INCREDIBLE...
OH, AND I HAVE CHOCOLATE COOKIES.
DAWDLE
もた
CLINK
ガチャ
OH WELL. I'LL OPEN THIS ONE.
WAIT, ARE YOU SUPPOSED TO DISSOLVE THE COFFEE IN WATER?
UH.
ZSHHH
ズザー
...WHY DON'T I DO THAT?

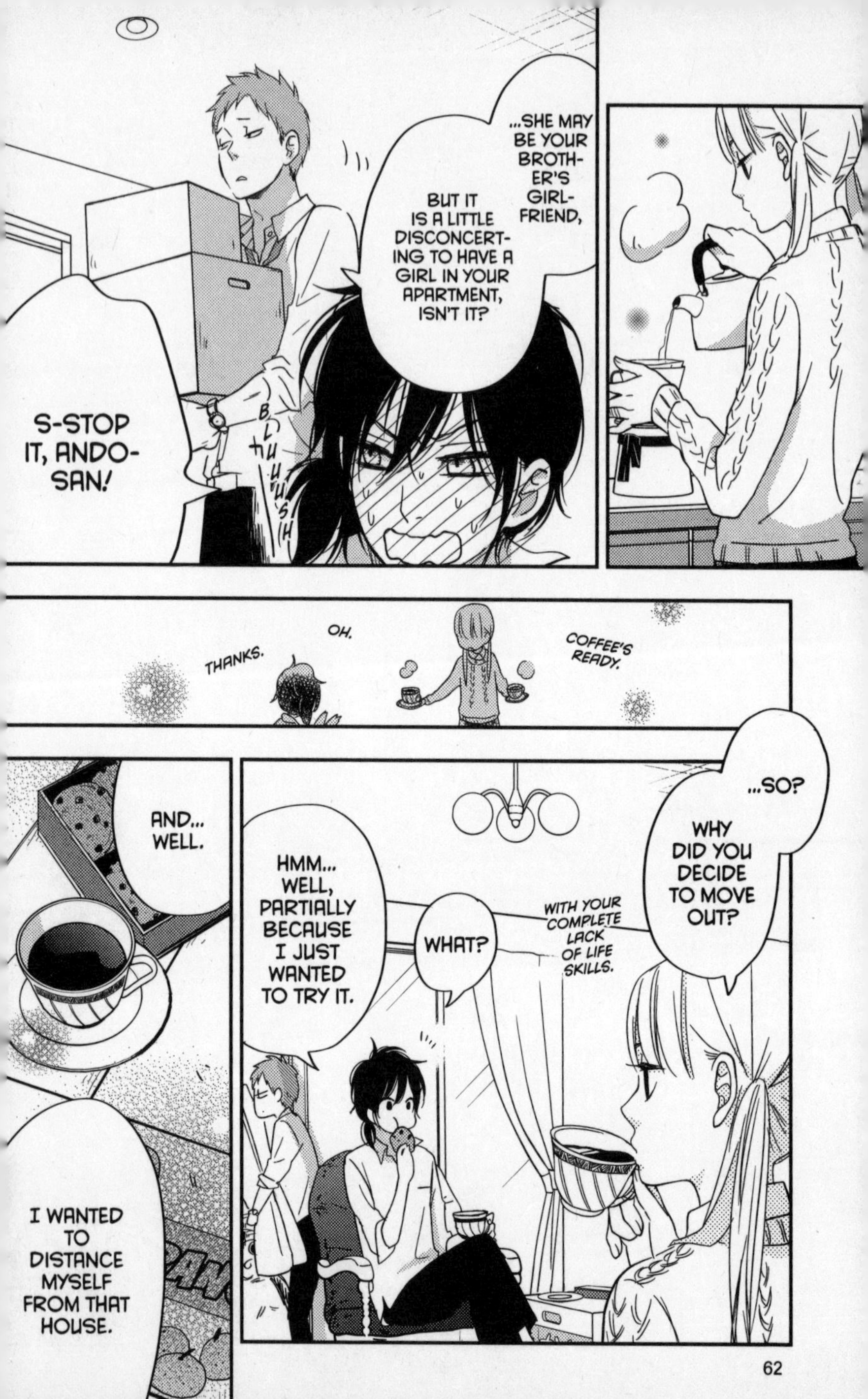
...SHE MAY BE YOUR BROTHER'S GIRL-FRIEND,
BUT IT IS A LITTLE DISCONCERTING TO HAVE A GIRL IN YOUR APARTMENT, ISN'T IT?
S-STOP IT, ANDO-SAN!
BLUUUUSH
COFFEE'S READY.
OH.
THANKS.
...SO?
WHY DID YOU DECIDE TO MOVE OUT?
WITH YOUR COMPLETE LACK OF LIFE SKILLS.
WHAT?
HMM... WELL, PARTIALLY BECAUSE I JUST WANTED TO TRY IT.
AND... WELL.
I WANTED TO DISTANCE MYSELF FROM THAT HOUSE.

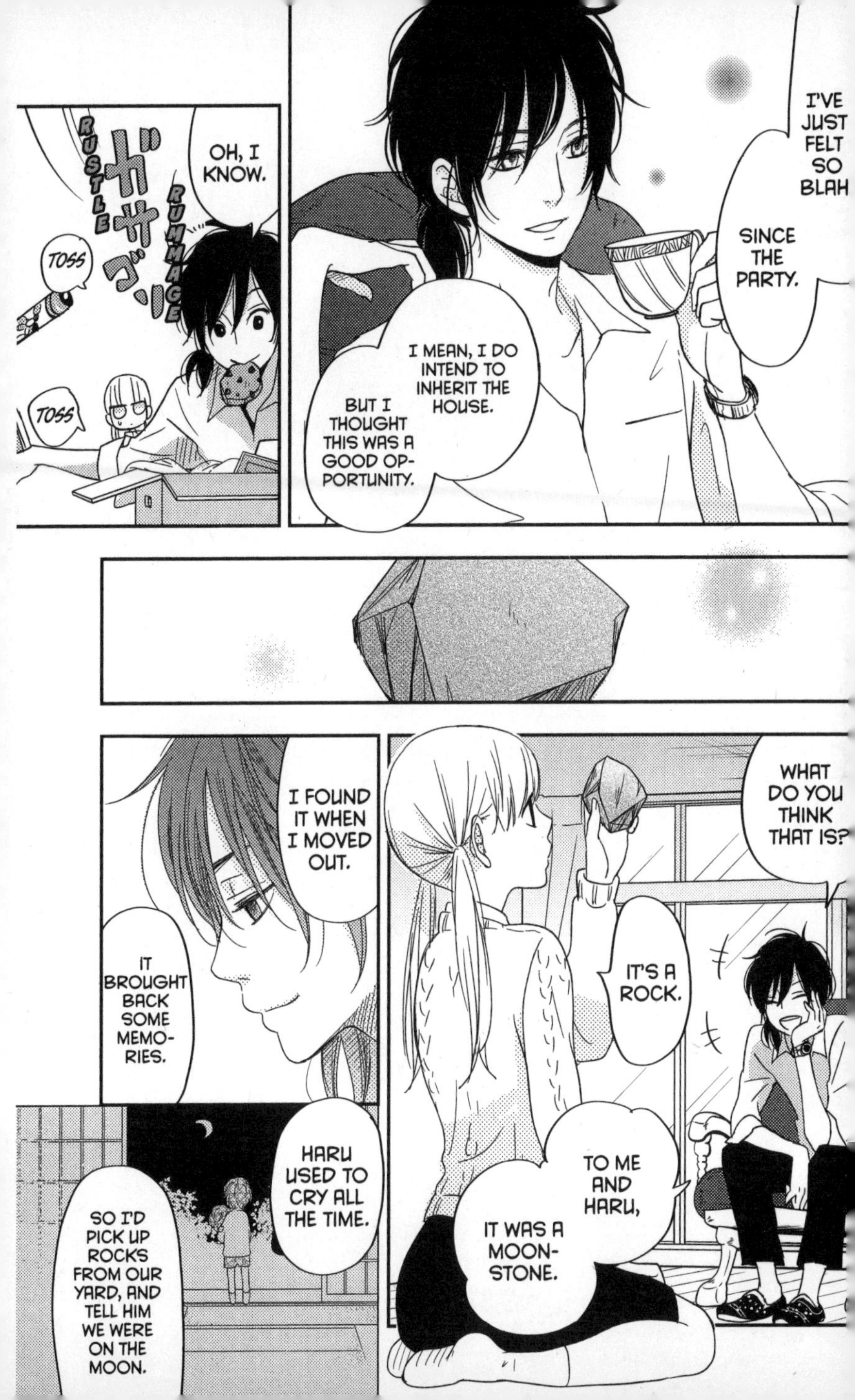

I'VE JUST FELT SO BLAH
SINCE THE PARTY.
I MEAN, I DO INTEND TO INHERIT THE HOUSE.
BUT I THOUGHT THIS WAS A GOOD OP-PORTUNITY.
OH, I KNOW.
ガサゴソ
RUSTLE
RUMMAGE
TOSS
TOSS
WHAT DO YOU THINK THAT IS?
IT'S A ROCK.
TO ME AND HARU,
IT WAS A MOON-STONE.
I FOUND IT WHEN I MOVED OUT.
IT BROUGHT BACK SOME MEMO-RIES.
HARU USED TO CRY ALL THE TIME.
SO I'D PICK UP ROCKS FROM OUR YARD, AND TELL HIM WE WERE ON THE MOON.

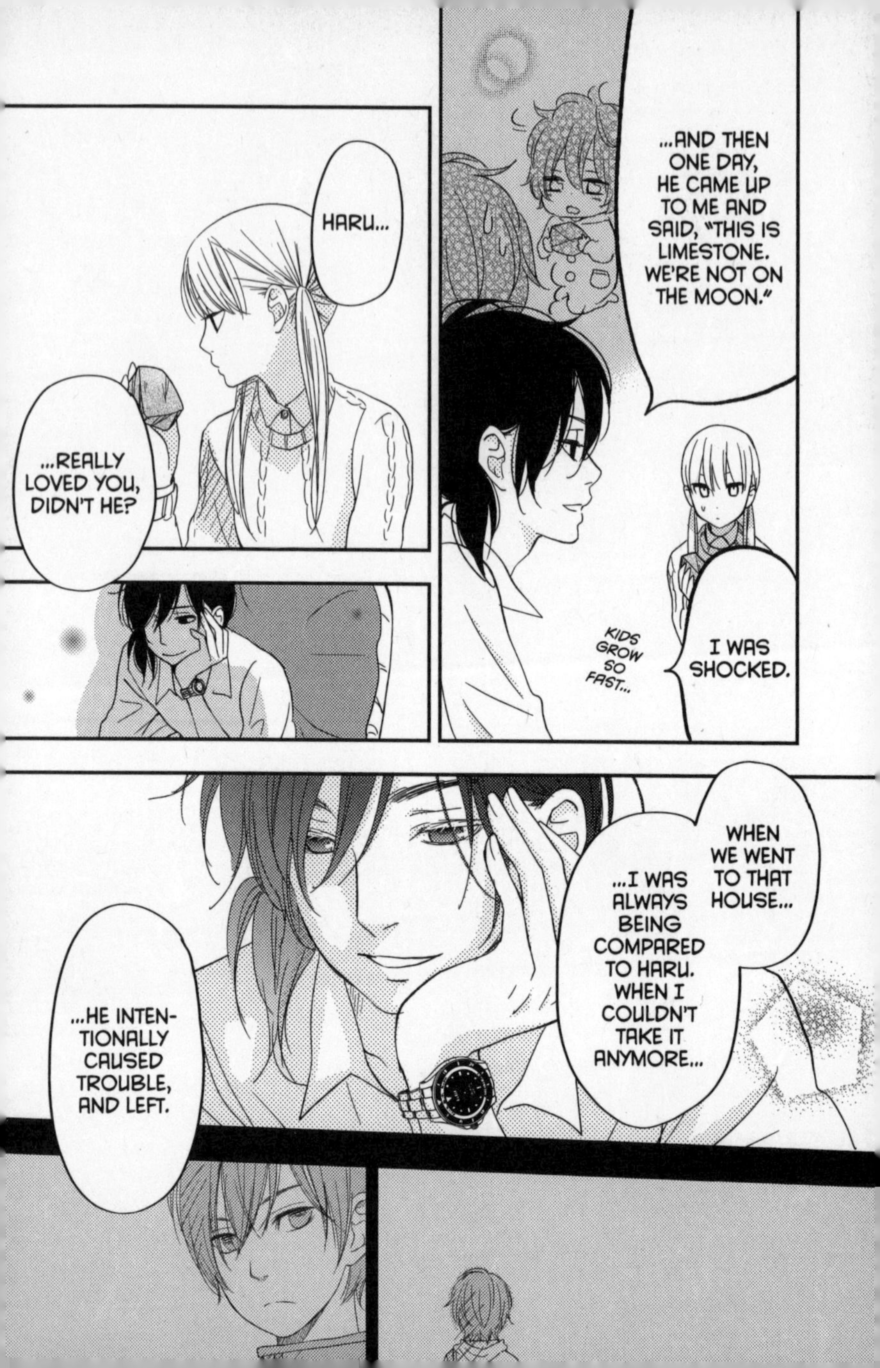
...AND THEN ONE DAY, HE CAME UP TO ME AND SAID, "THIS IS LIMESTONE. WE'RE NOT ON THE MOON."
I WAS SHOCKED.
KIDS GROW SO FAST...
HARU...
...REALLY LOVED YOU, DIDN'T HE?
WHEN WE WENT TO THAT HOUSE...
...I WAS ALWAYS BEING COMPARED TO HARU. WHEN I COULDN'T TAKE IT ANYMORE...
...HE INTENTIONALLY CAUSED TROUBLE, AND LEFT.

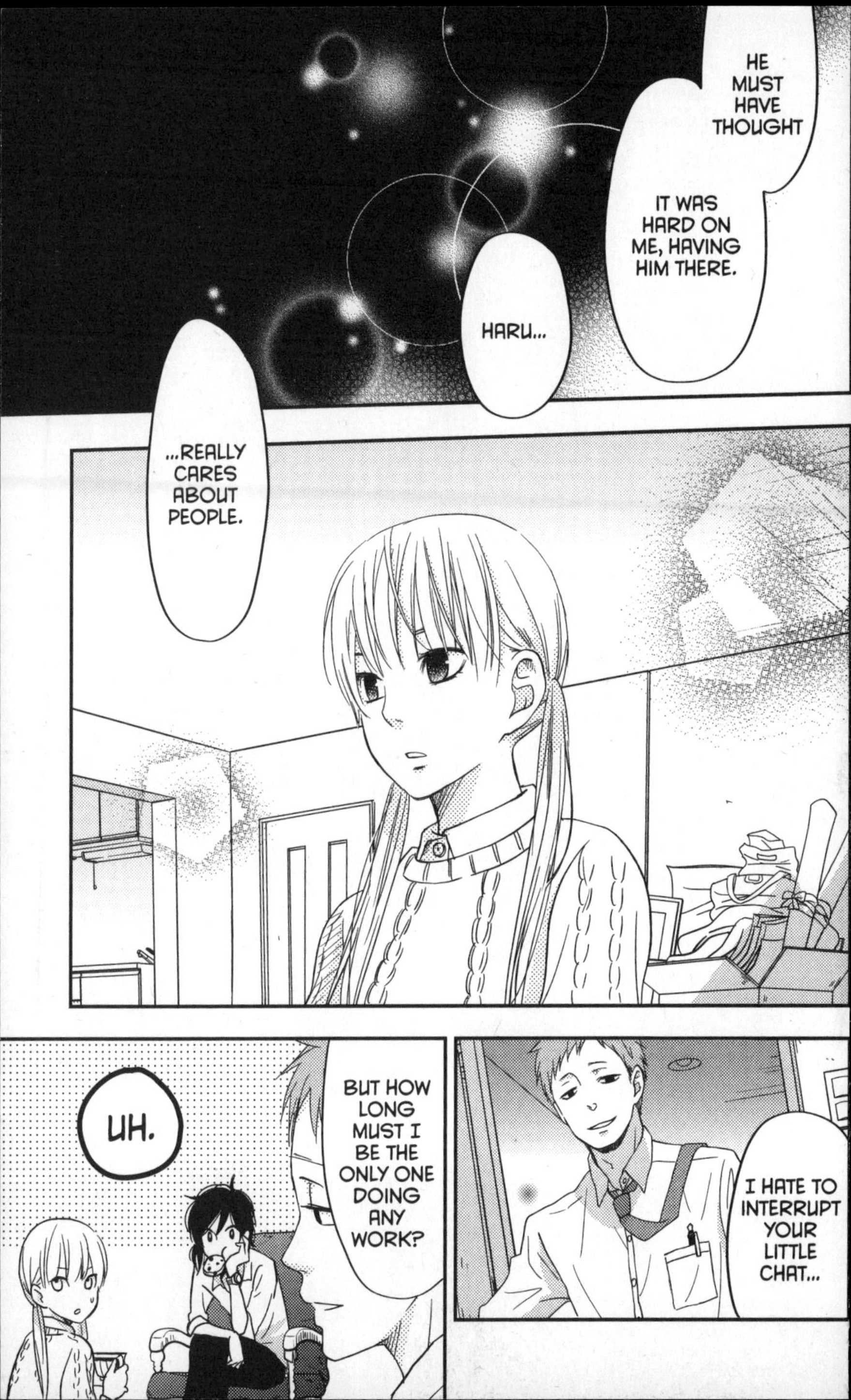
HE MUST HAVE THOUGHT
IT WAS HARD ON ME, HAVING HIM THERE.
HARU...
...REALLY CARES ABOUT PEOPLE.
I HATE TO INTERRUPT YOUR LITTLE CHAT...
BUT HOW LONG MUST I BE THE ONLY ONE DOING ANY WORK?
UH.

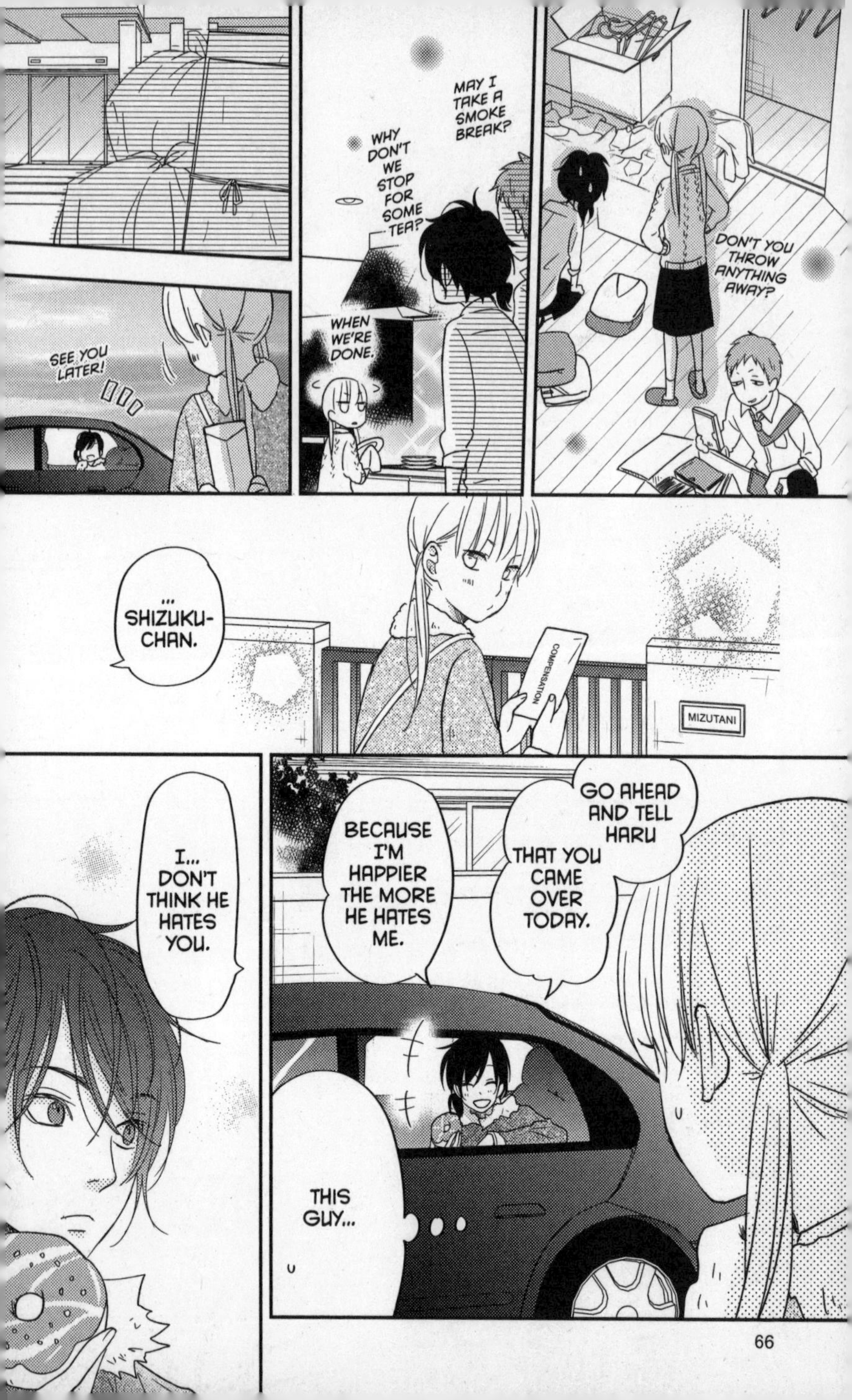
DON'T YOU THROW ANYTHING AWAY?
MAY I TAKE A SMOKE BREAK?
WHY DON'T WE STOP FOR SOME TEA?
WHEN WE'RE DONE.
SEE YOU LATER!
...SHIZUKU-CHAN.
COMPENSATION
MIZUTANI
GO AHEAD AND TELL HARU THAT YOU CAME OVER TODAY.
BECAUSE I'M HAPPIER THE MORE HE HATES ME.
THIS GUY...
I... DON'T THINK HE HATES YOU.

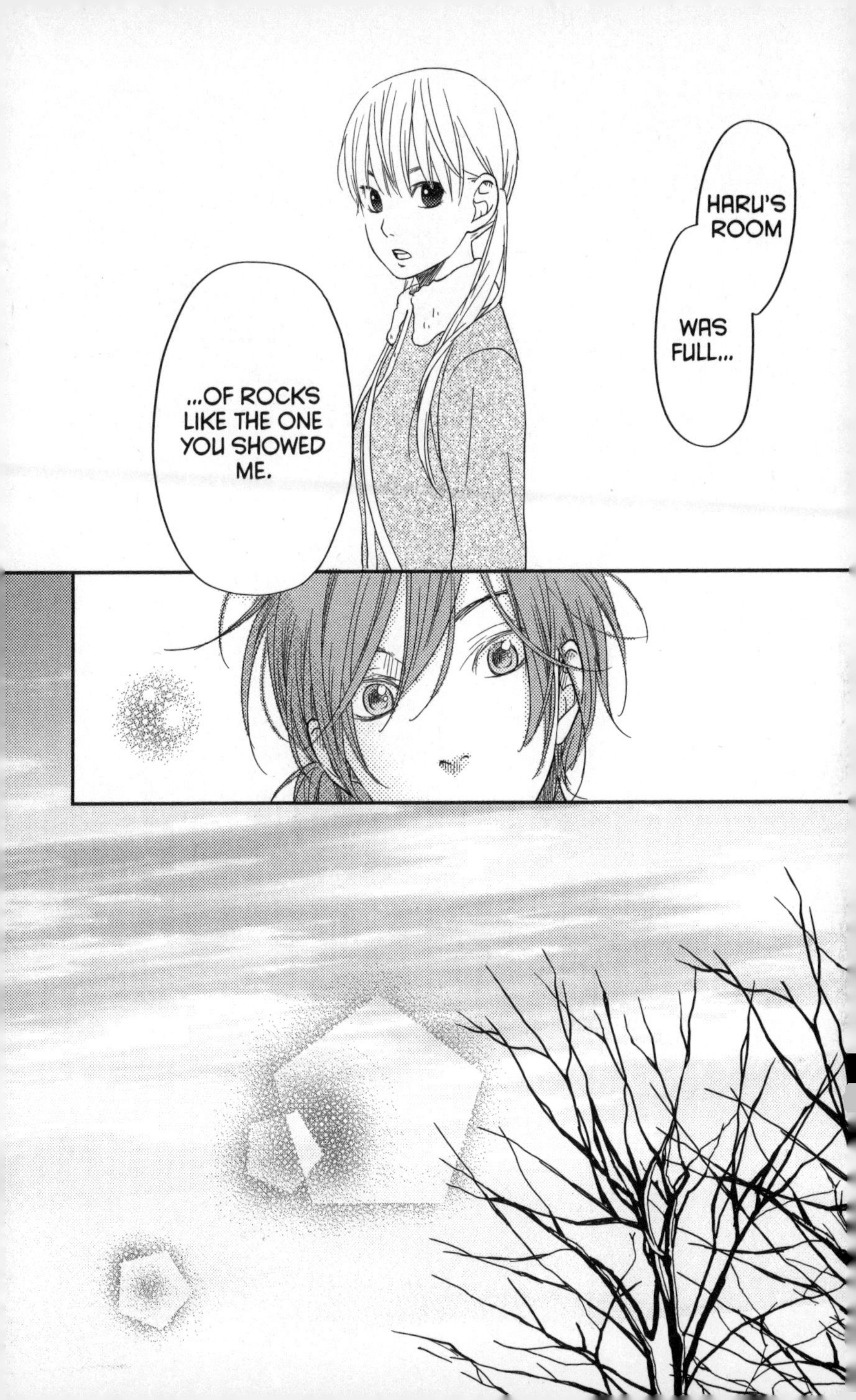
HARU'S ROOM
WAS FULL...
...OF ROCKS LIKE THE ONE YOU SHOWED ME.

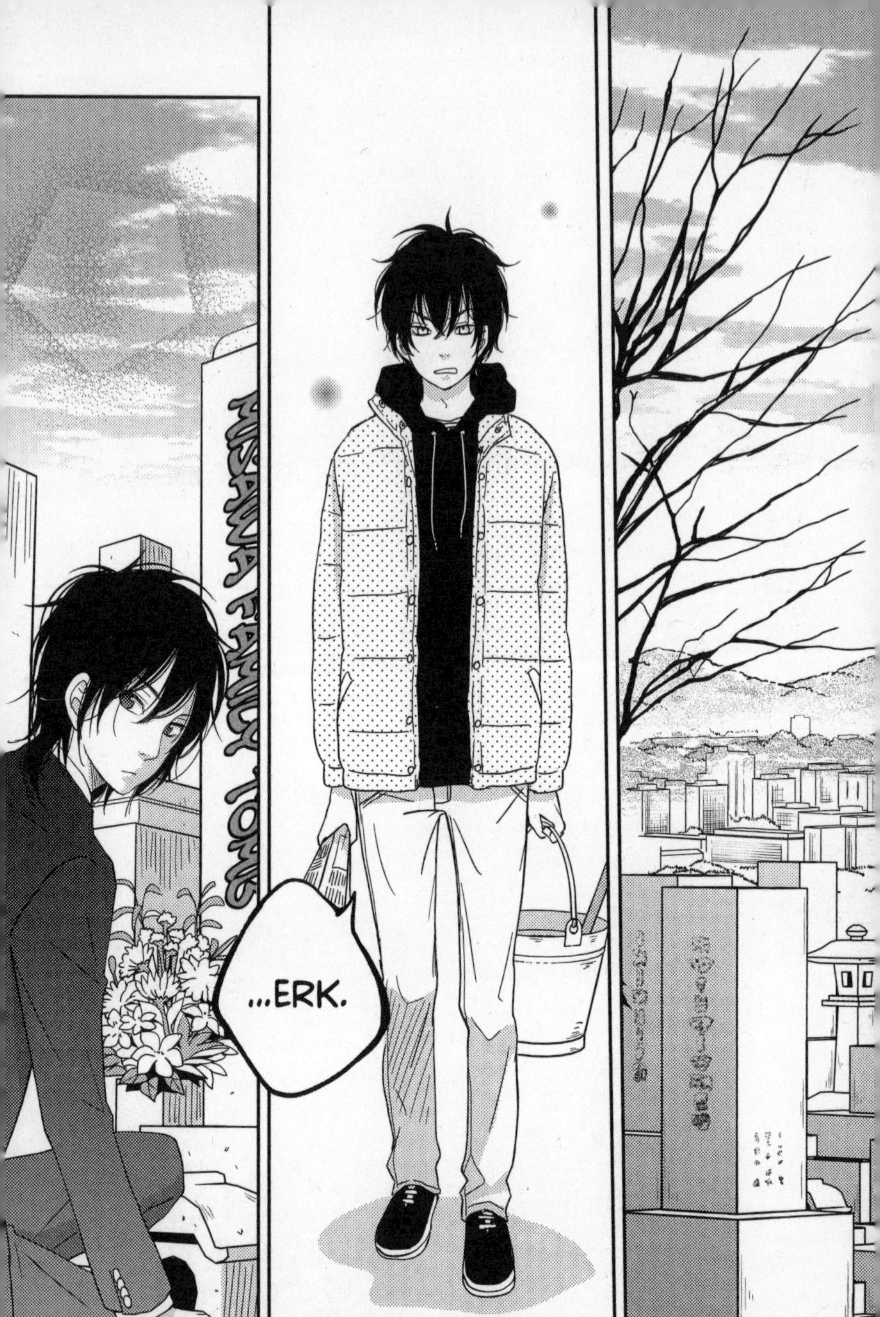
...ERK.
MISAWA FAMILY TOMB

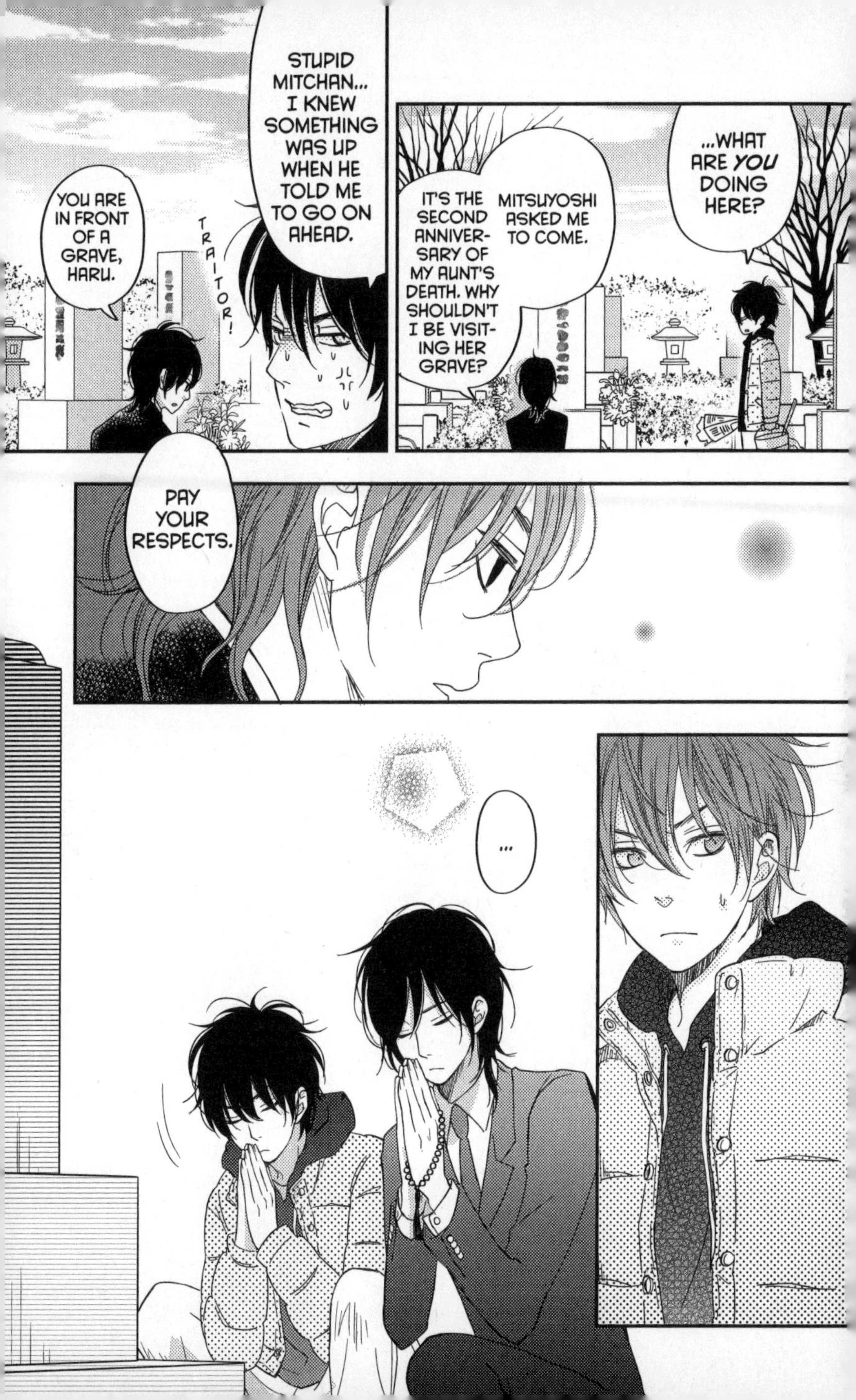
...WHAT ARE *YOU* DOING HERE?
MITSUYOSHI ASKED ME TO COME.
IT'S THE SECOND ANNIVERSARY OF MY AUNT'S DEATH. WHY SHOULDN'T I BE VISITING HER GRAVE?
STUPID MITCHAN... I KNEW SOMETHING WAS UP WHEN HE TOLD ME TO GO ON AHEAD.
TRAITOR!
YOU ARE IN FRONT OF A GRAVE, HARU.
PAY YOUR RESPECTS.
...

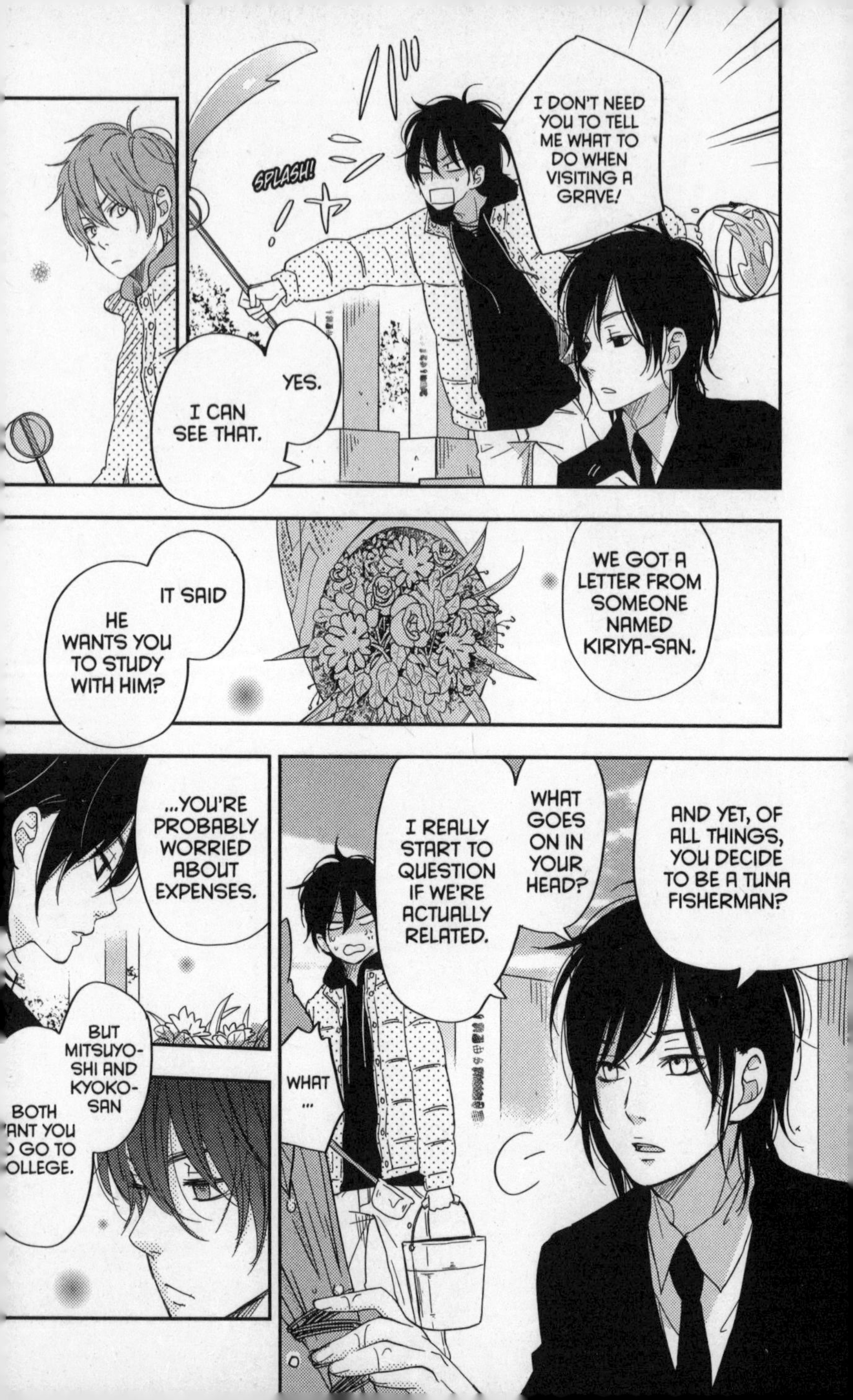

I DON'T NEED YOU TO TELL ME WHAT TO DO WHEN VISITING A GRAVE!
SPLASH!
YES.
I CAN SEE THAT.
WE GOT A LETTER FROM SOMEONE NAMED KIRIYA-SAN.
IT SAID
HE WANTS YOU TO STUDY WITH HIM?
AND YET, OF ALL THINGS, YOU DECIDE TO BE A TUNA FISHERMAN?
WHAT GOES ON IN YOUR HEAD?
I REALLY START TO QUESTION IF WE'RE ACTUALLY RELATED.
WHAT ...
...YOU'RE PROBABLY WORRIED ABOUT EXPENSES.
BUT MITSUYOSHI AND KYOKO-SAN
BOTH ANT YOU O GO TO OLLEGE.

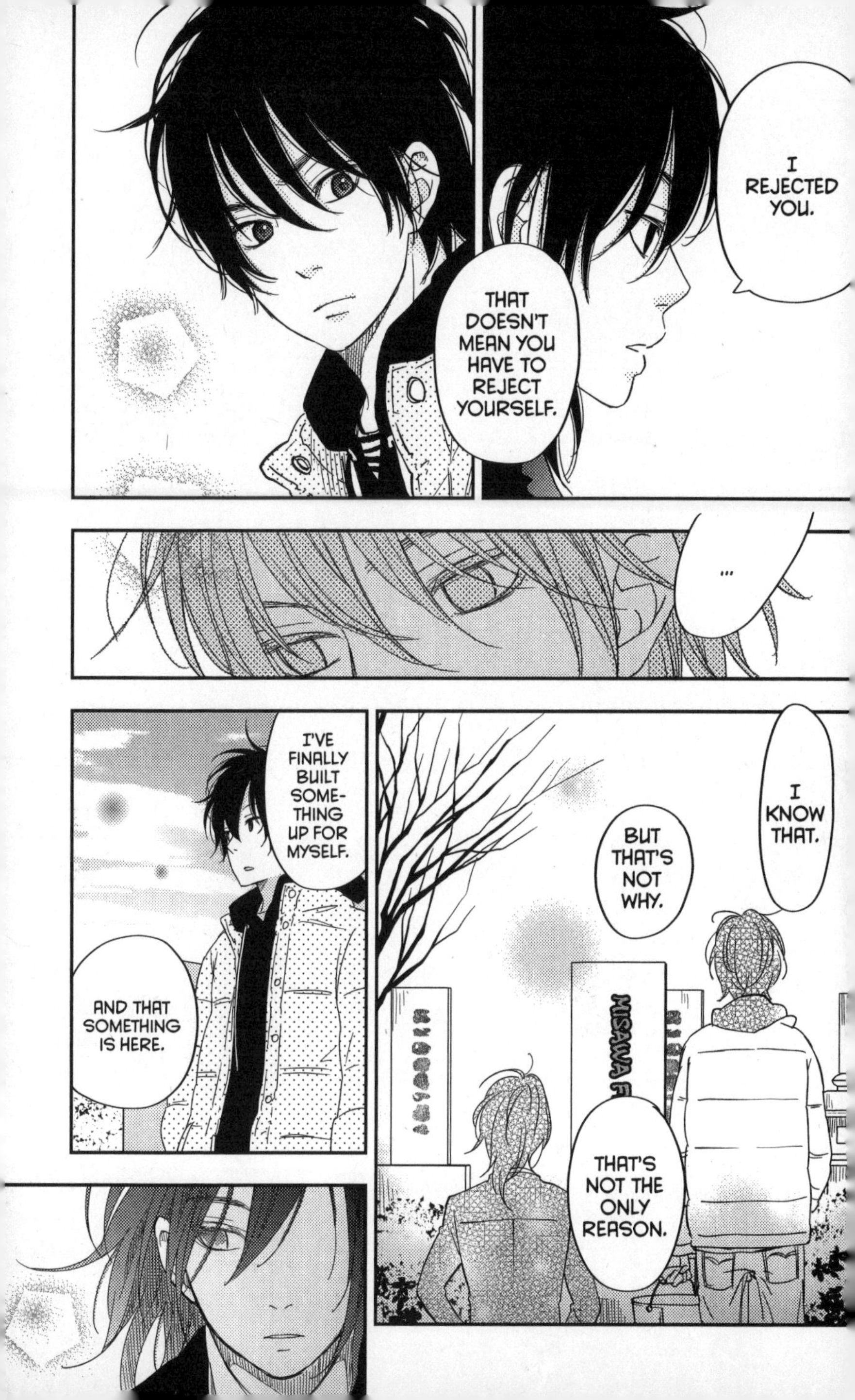
I REJECTED YOU.
THAT DOESN'T MEAN YOU HAVE TO REJECT YOURSELF.
...
I KNOW THAT.
BUT THAT'S NOT WHY.
MISAWA F
THAT'S NOT THE ONLY REASON.
I'VE FINALLY BUILT SOME-THING UP FOR MYSELF.
AND THAT SOMETHING IS HERE.

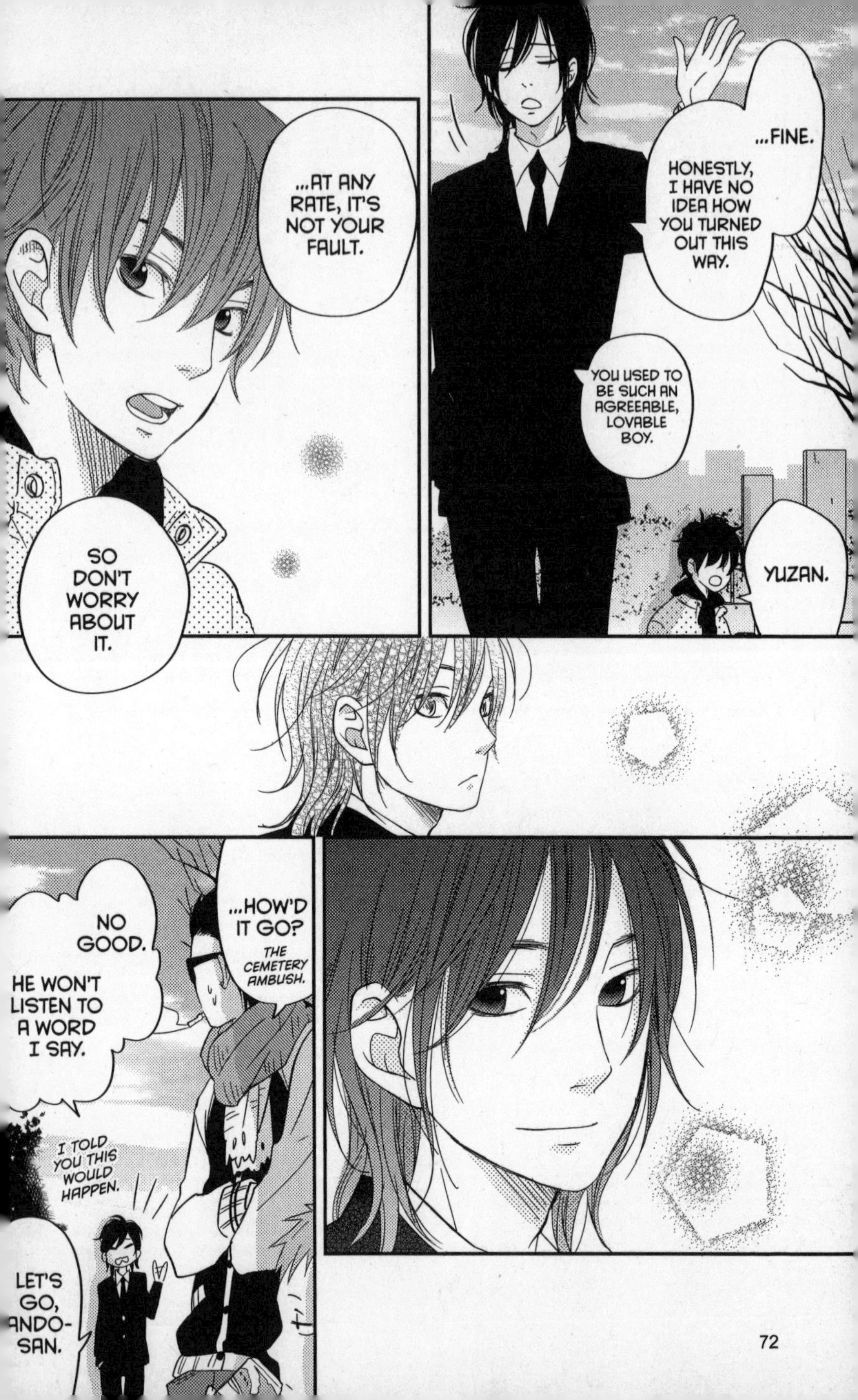
...FINE.
HONESTLY, I HAVE NO IDEA HOW YOU TURNED OUT THIS WAY.
YOU USED TO BE SUCH AN AGREEABLE, LOVABLE BOY.
YUZAN.
...AT ANY RATE, IT'S NOT YOUR FAULT.
SO DON'T WORRY ABOUT IT.
...HOW'D IT GO?
THE CEMETERY AMBUSH.
NO GOOD.
HE WON'T LISTEN TO A WORD I SAY.
I TOLD YOU THIS WOULD HAPPEN.
LET'S GO, ANDO-SAN.

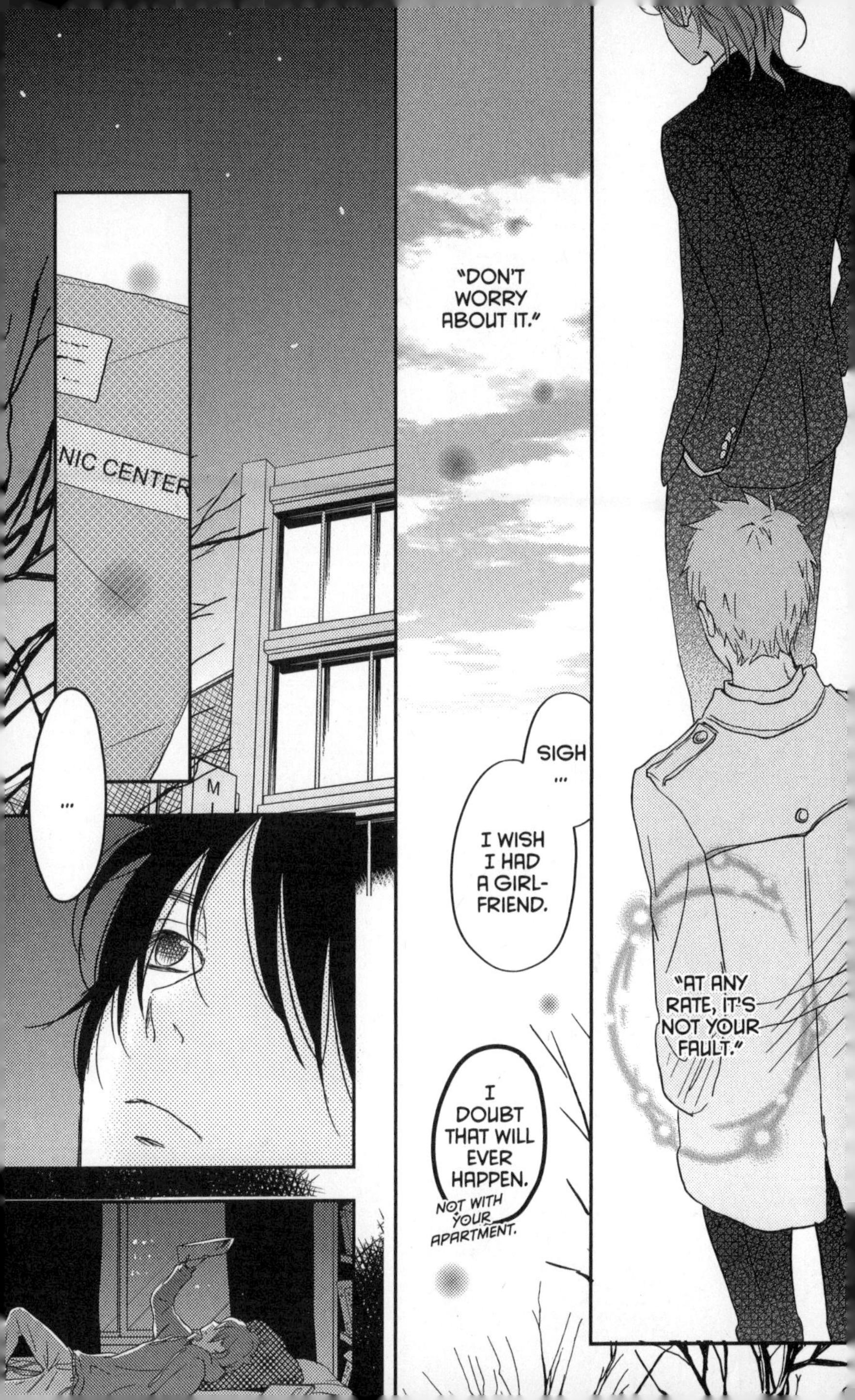
"AT ANY RATE, IT'S NOT YOUR FAULT."
"DON'T WORRY ABOUT IT."
SIGH ...
I WISH I HAD A GIRL-FRIEND.
I DOUBT THAT WILL EVER HAPPEN.
NOT WITH YOUR APARTMENT.
NIC CENTER
M
...

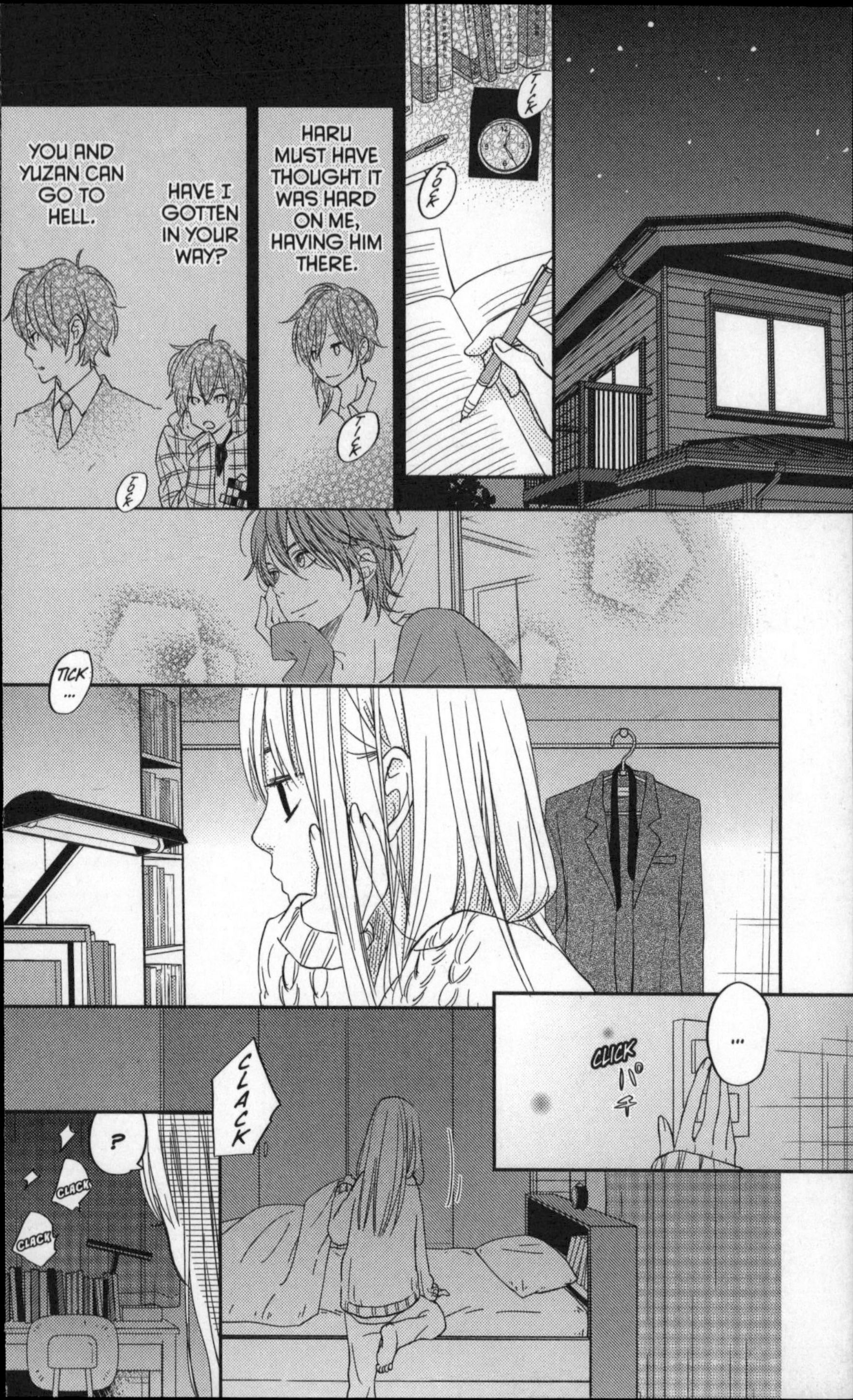

TICK
TOCK
HARU MUST HAVE THOUGHT IT WAS HARD ON ME, HAVING HIM THERE.
TICK
HAVE I GOTTEN IN YOUR WAY?
YOU AND YUZAN CAN GO TO HELL.
TOCK
TICK ...
...
CLICK
パチ
CLACK
?
CLACK
CLACK

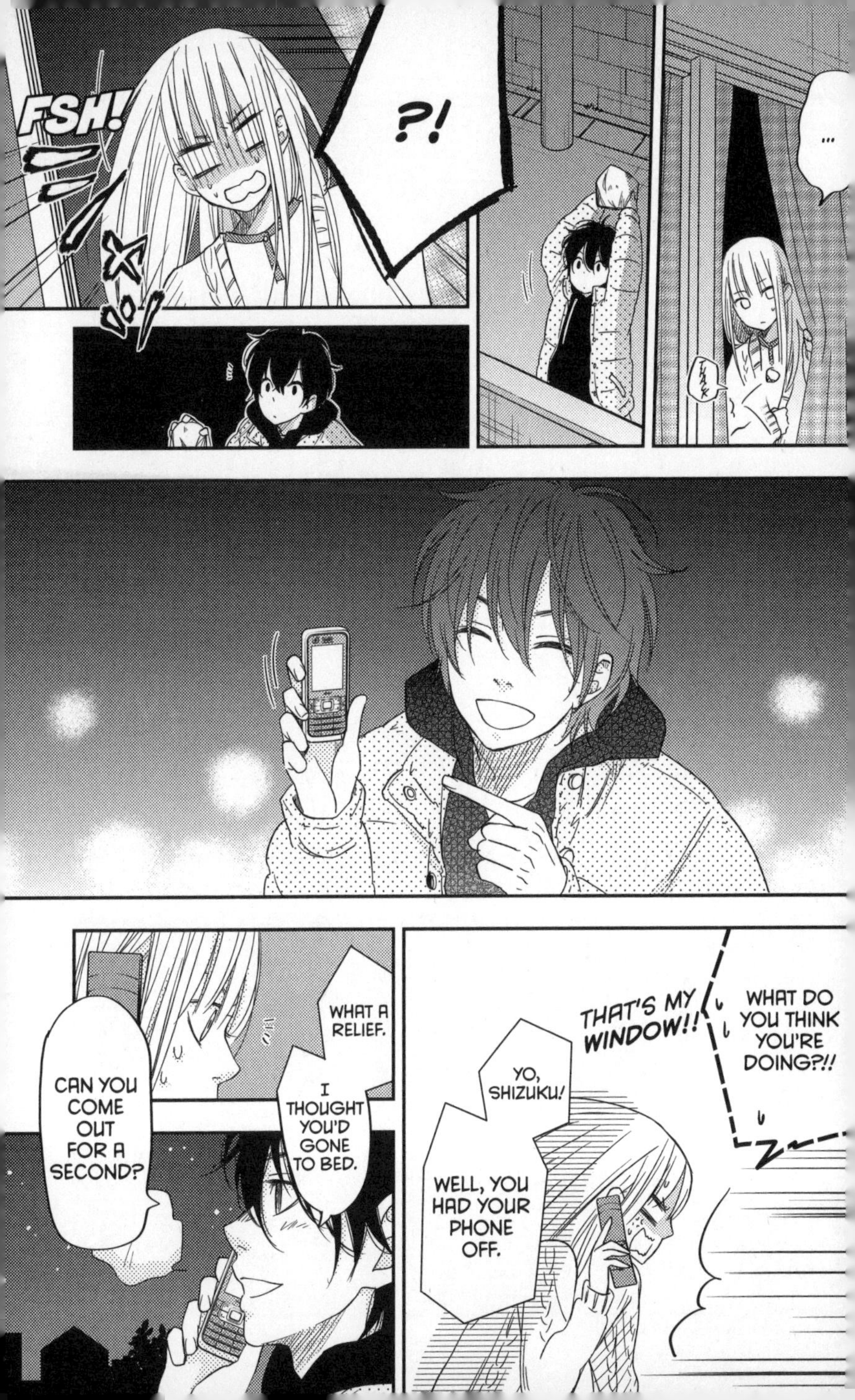
...
THACK
?!
FSH!
WHAT DO YOU THINK YOU'RE DOING?!!
THAT'S MY WINDOW!!
YO, SHIZUKU!
WELL, YOU HAD YOUR PHONE OFF.
WHAT A RELIEF.
I THOUGHT YOU'D GONE TO BED.
CAN YOU COME OUT FOR A SECOND?

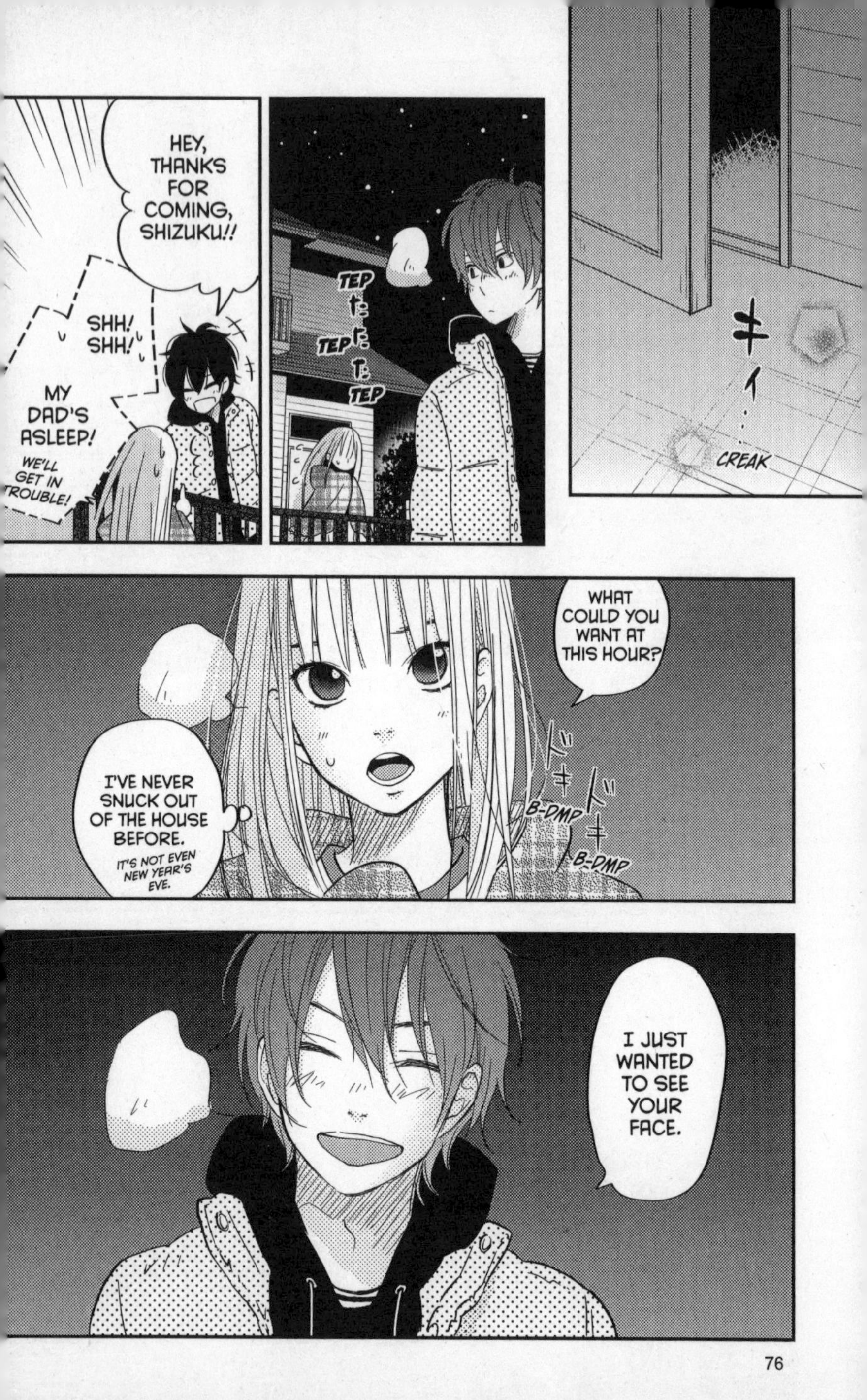
キィ…
CREAK
TEP たたた TEP TEP
HEY, THANKS FOR COMING, SHIZUKU!!
SHH! SHH!
MY DAD'S ASLEEP!
WE'LL GET IN TROUBLE!
WHAT COULD YOU WANT AT THIS HOUR?
ドキドキ B-DMP B-DMP
I'VE NEVER SNUCK OUT OF THE HOUSE BEFORE.
IT'S NOT EVEN NEW YEAR'S EVE.
I JUST WANTED TO SEE YOUR FACE.

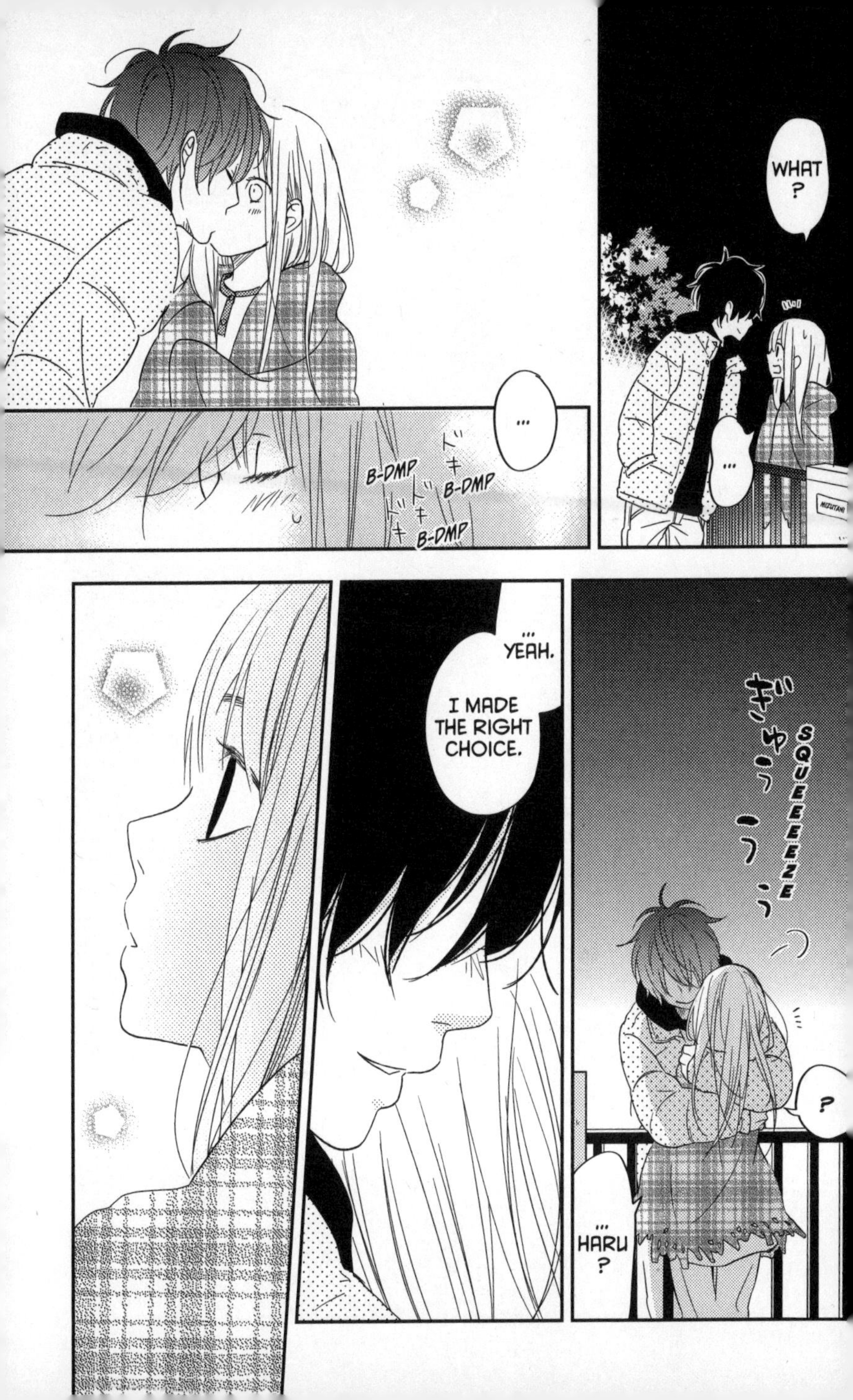
WHAT?
...
MIZUTANI
...
ドキ
B-DMP
ドキ
B-DMP
ドキ
B-DMP
ぎゅううう
SQUEEEEZE
?
...HARU?
...YEAH.
I MADE THE RIGHT CHOICE.

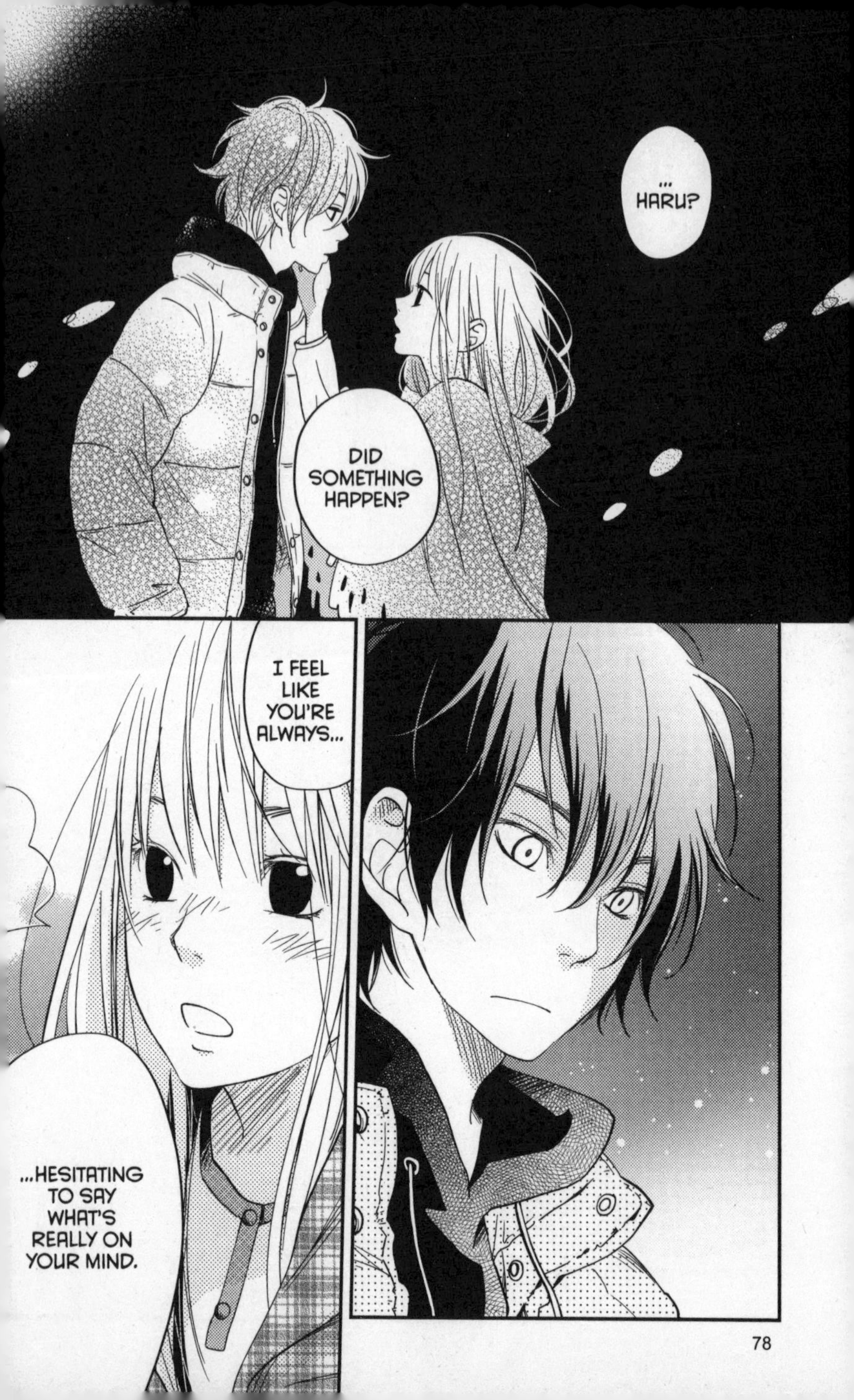
...HARU?
DID SOMETHING HAPPEN?
I FEEL LIKE YOU'RE ALWAYS...
...HESITATING TO SAY WHAT'S REALLY ON YOUR MIND.

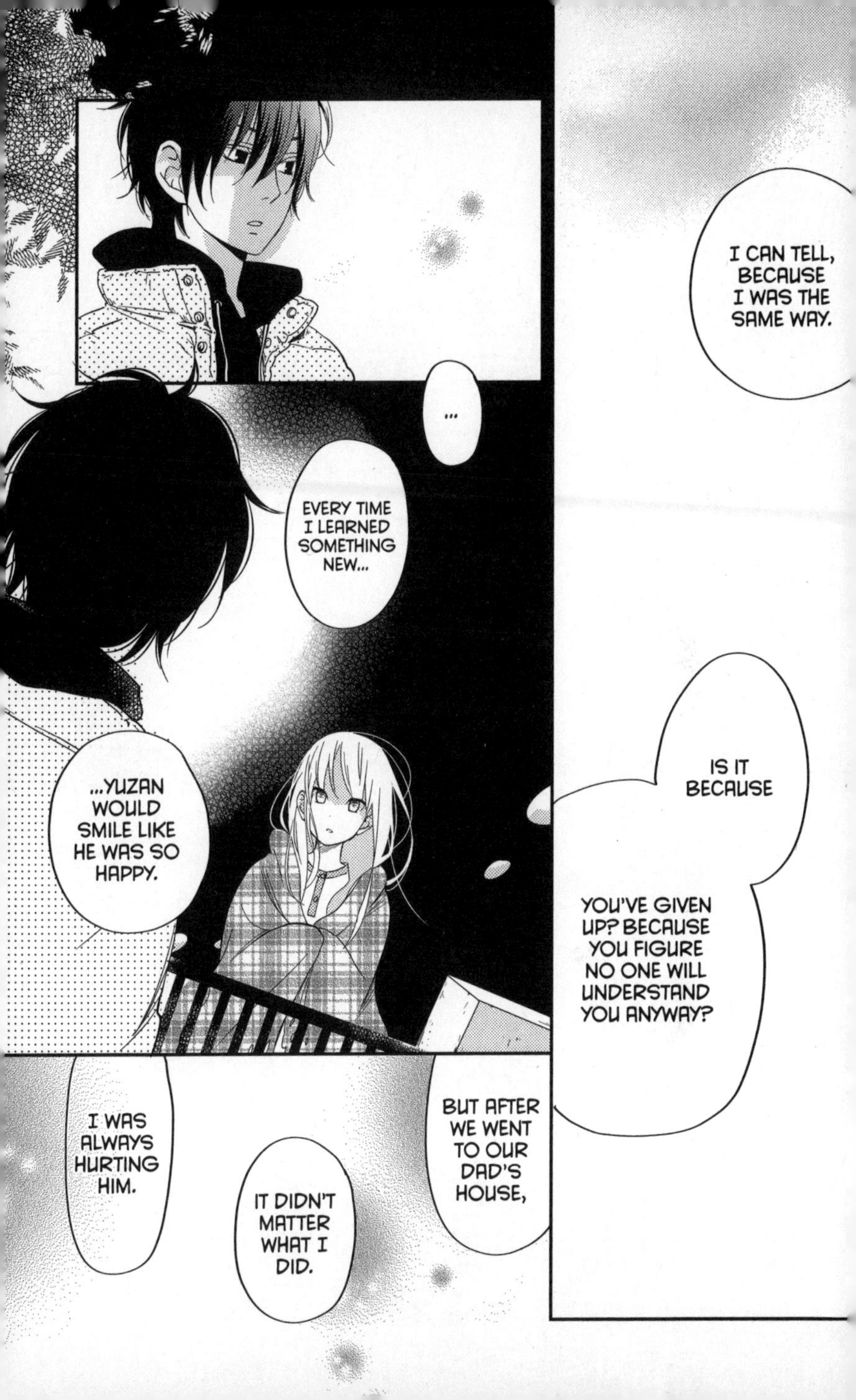
I CAN TELL, BECAUSE I WAS THE SAME WAY.
IS IT BECAUSE
YOU'VE GIVEN UP? BECAUSE YOU FIGURE NO ONE WILL UNDERSTAND YOU ANYWAY?
...
EVERY TIME I LEARNED SOMETHING NEW...
...YUZAN WOULD SMILE LIKE HE WAS SO HAPPY.
BUT AFTER WE WENT TO OUR DAD'S HOUSE,
IT DIDN'T MATTER WHAT I DID.
I WAS ALWAYS HURTING HIM.

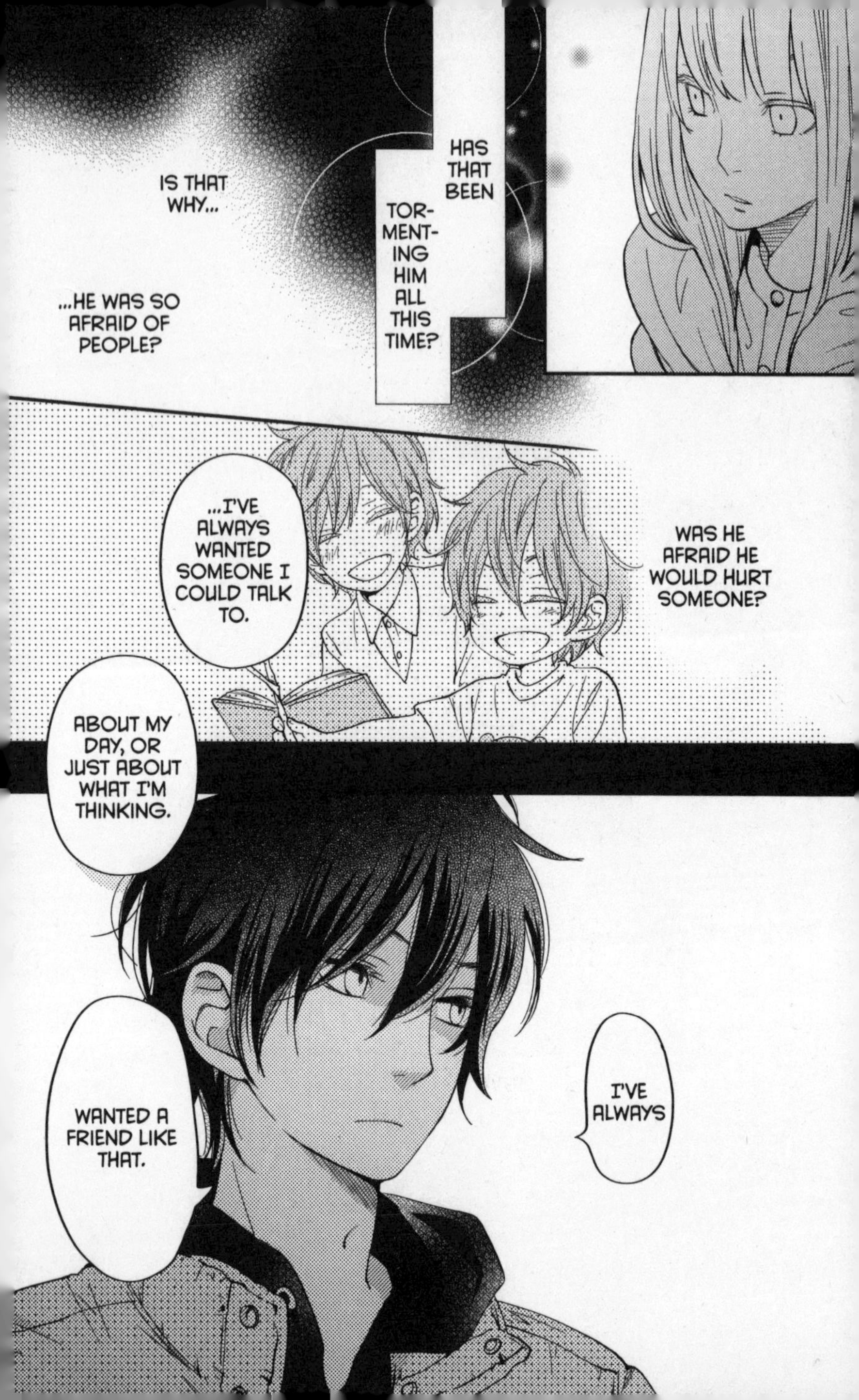
HAS THAT BEEN TORMENTING HIM ALL THIS TIME?
IS THAT WHY...
...HE WAS SO AFRAID OF PEOPLE?
WAS HE AFRAID HE WOULD HURT SOMEONE?
...I'VE ALWAYS WANTED SOMEONE I COULD TALK TO.
ABOUT MY DAY, OR JUST ABOUT WHAT I'M THINKING.
I'VE ALWAYS
WANTED A FRIEND LIKE THAT.

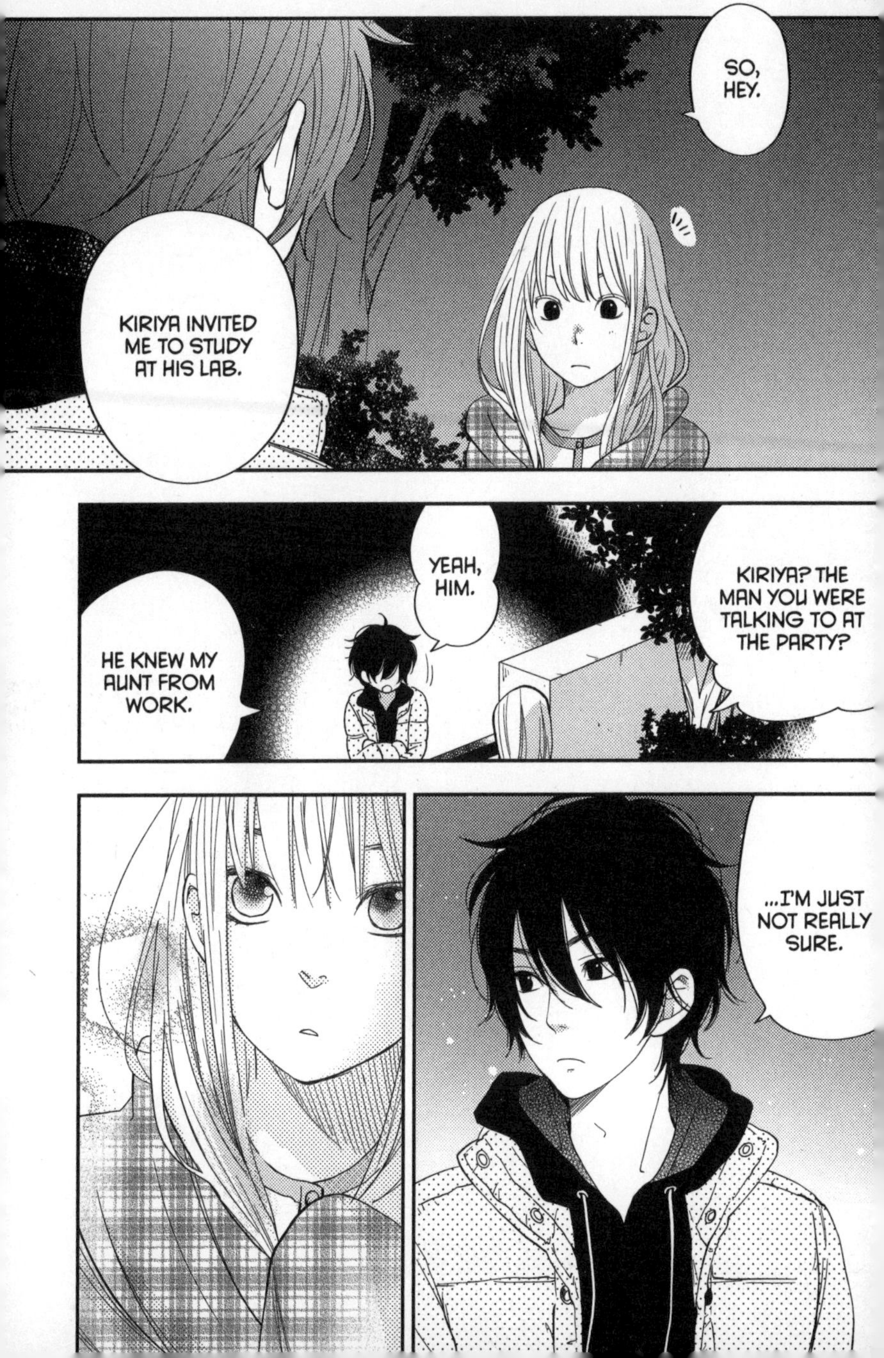
SO, HEY.
KIRIYA INVITED ME TO STUDY AT HIS LAB.
KIRIYA? THE MAN YOU WERE TALKING TO AT THE PARTY?
YEAH, HIM.
HE KNEW MY AUNT FROM WORK.
...I'M JUST NOT REALLY SURE.

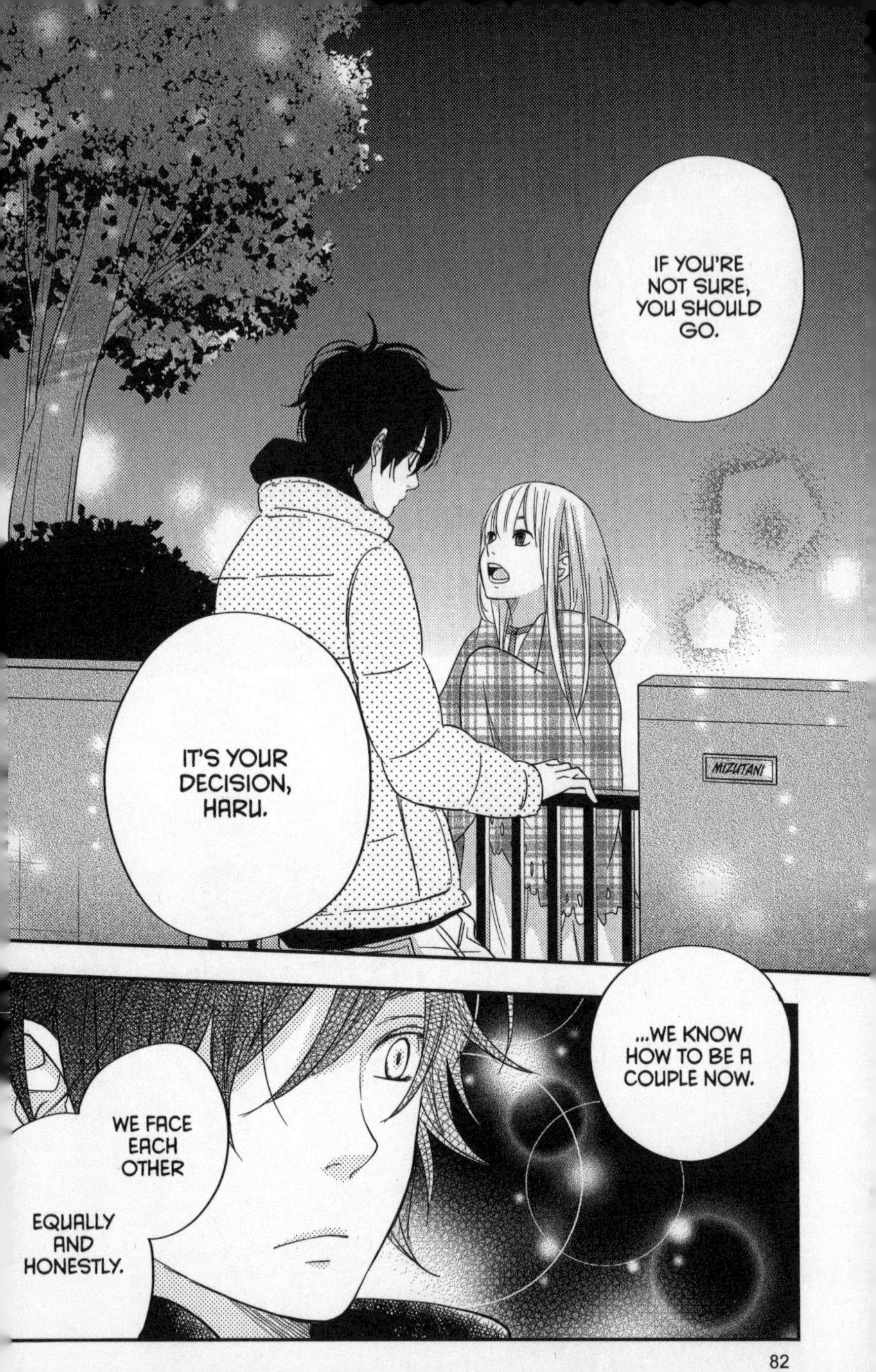
IF YOU'RE NOT SURE, YOU SHOULD GO.
MIZUTANI
IT'S YOUR DECISION, HARU.
...WE KNOW HOW TO BE A COUPLE NOW.
WE FACE EACH OTHER
EQUALLY AND HONESTLY.

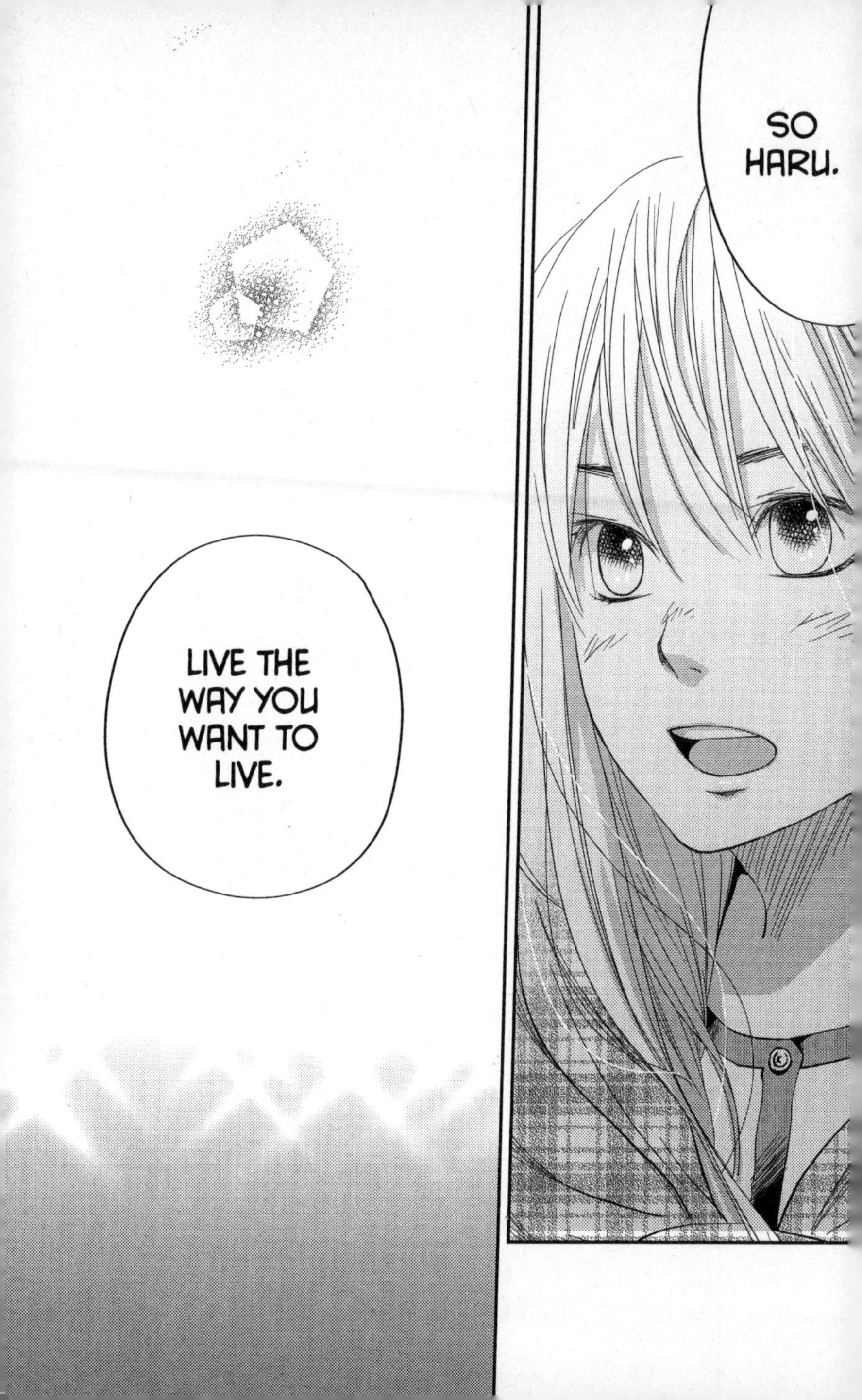
SO HARU.
LIVE THE WAY YOU WANT TO LIVE.

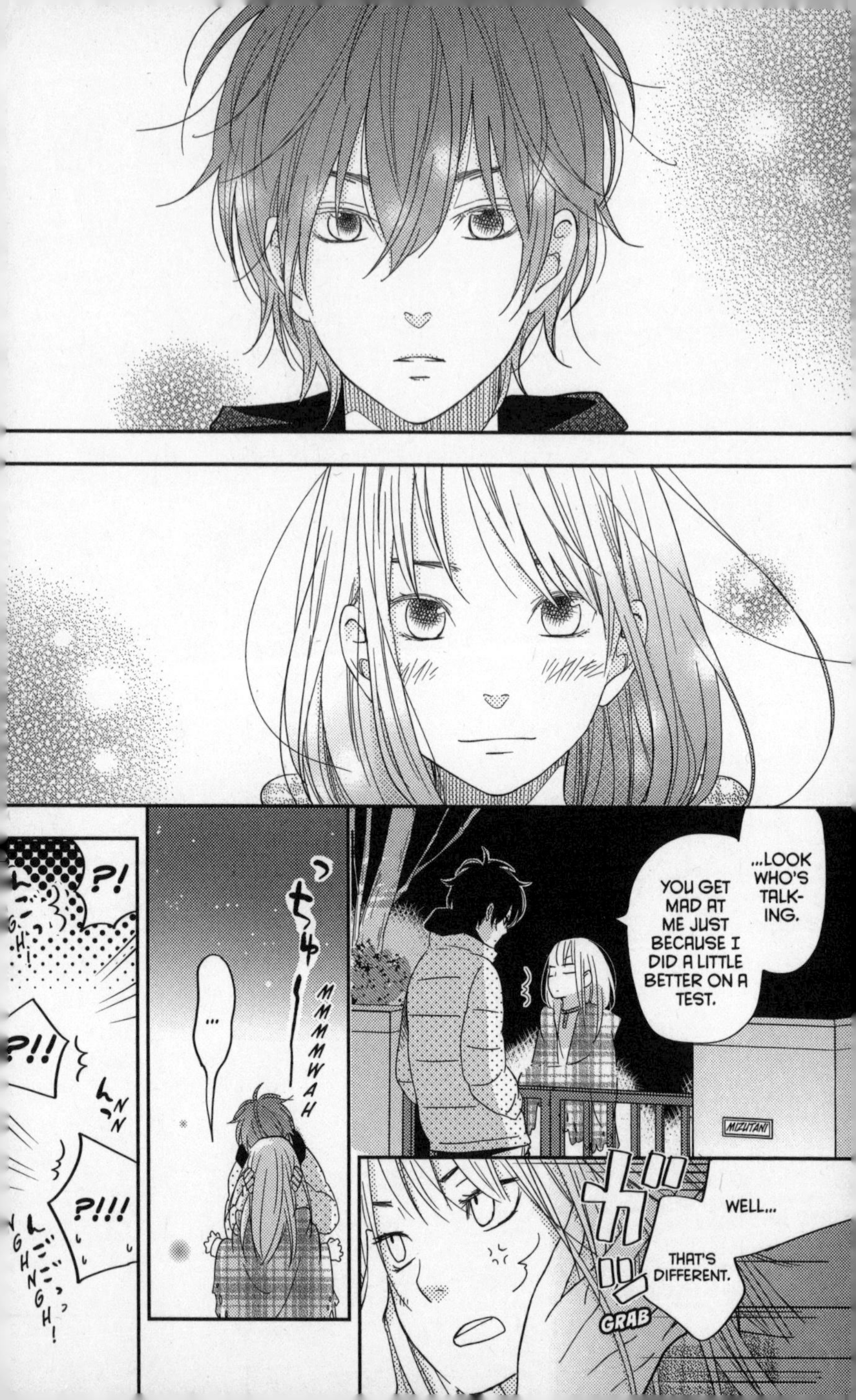

...LOOK WHO'S TALK-ING.
YOU GET MAD AT ME JUST BECAUSE I DID A LITTLE BETTER ON A TEST.
MIZUTANI
WELL...
THAT'S DIFFERENT.
GRAB
MMMMWAH
...
?!
?!!
NN
?!!!
NGHNGHNGH!

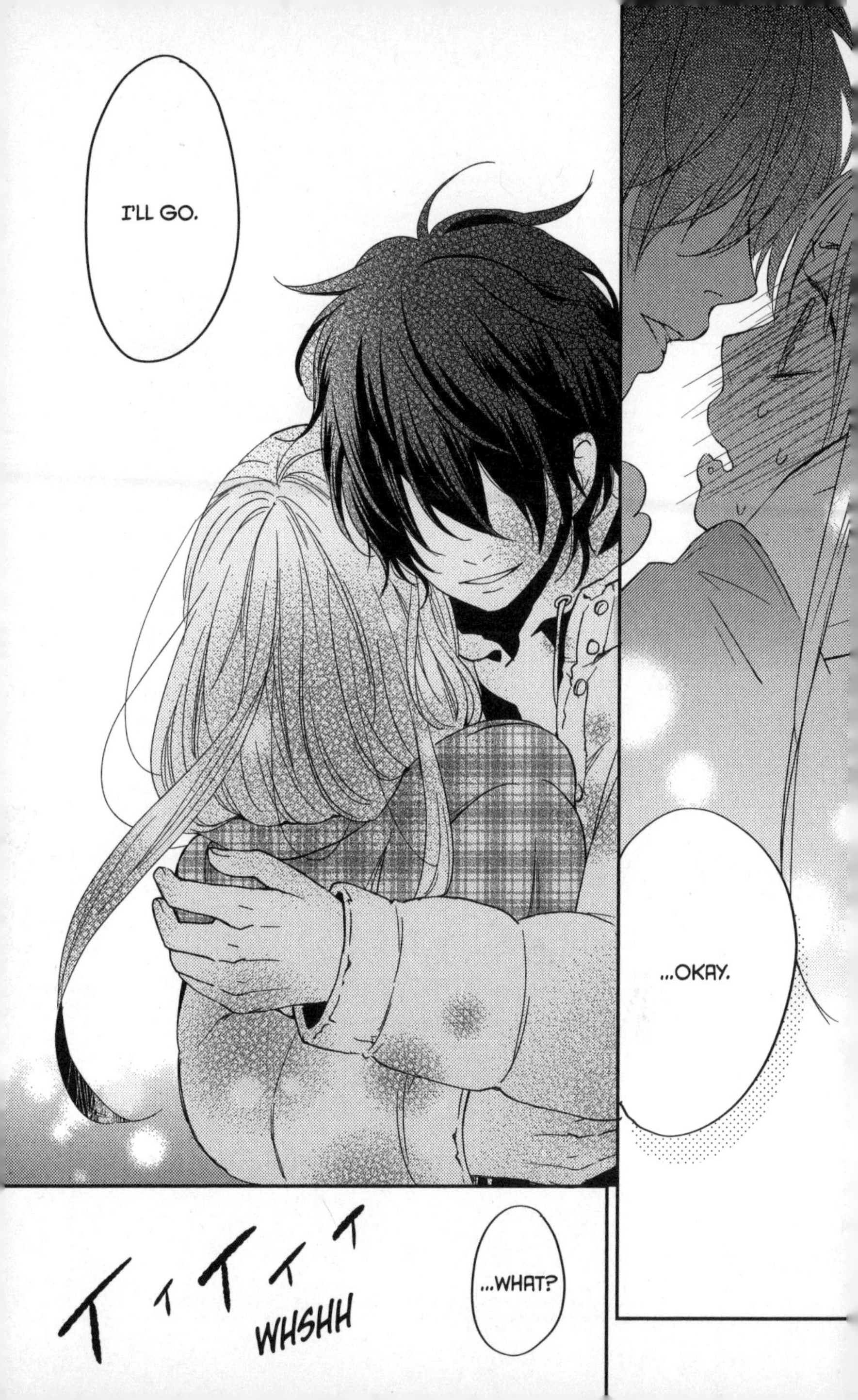
...OKAY.
I'LL GO.
...WHAT?
WHSHH

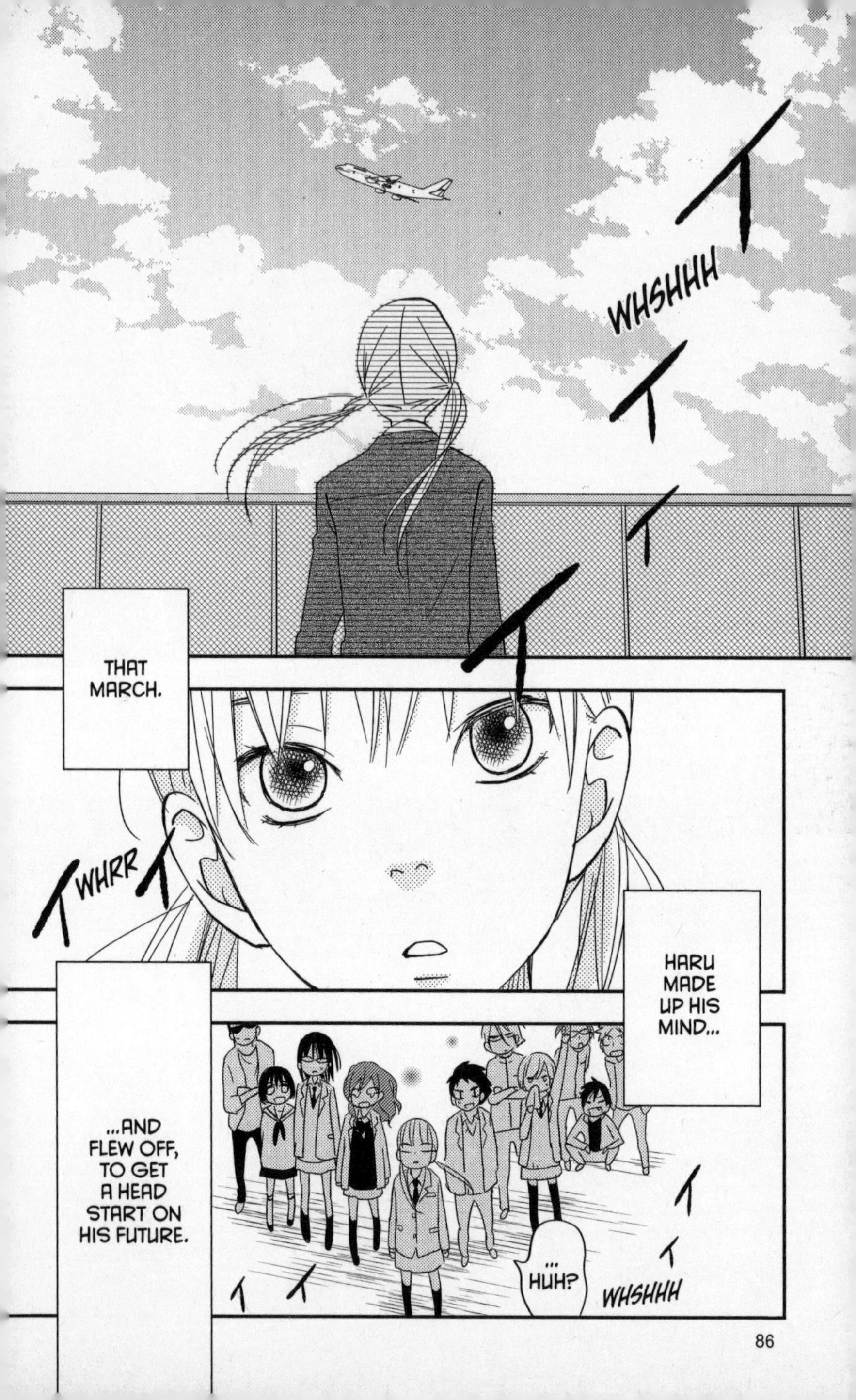
WHSHHH
THAT MARCH.
TWHRR
HARU MADE UP HIS MIND...
...AND FLEW OFF, TO GET A HEAD START ON HIS FUTURE.
WHSHHH
...HUH?

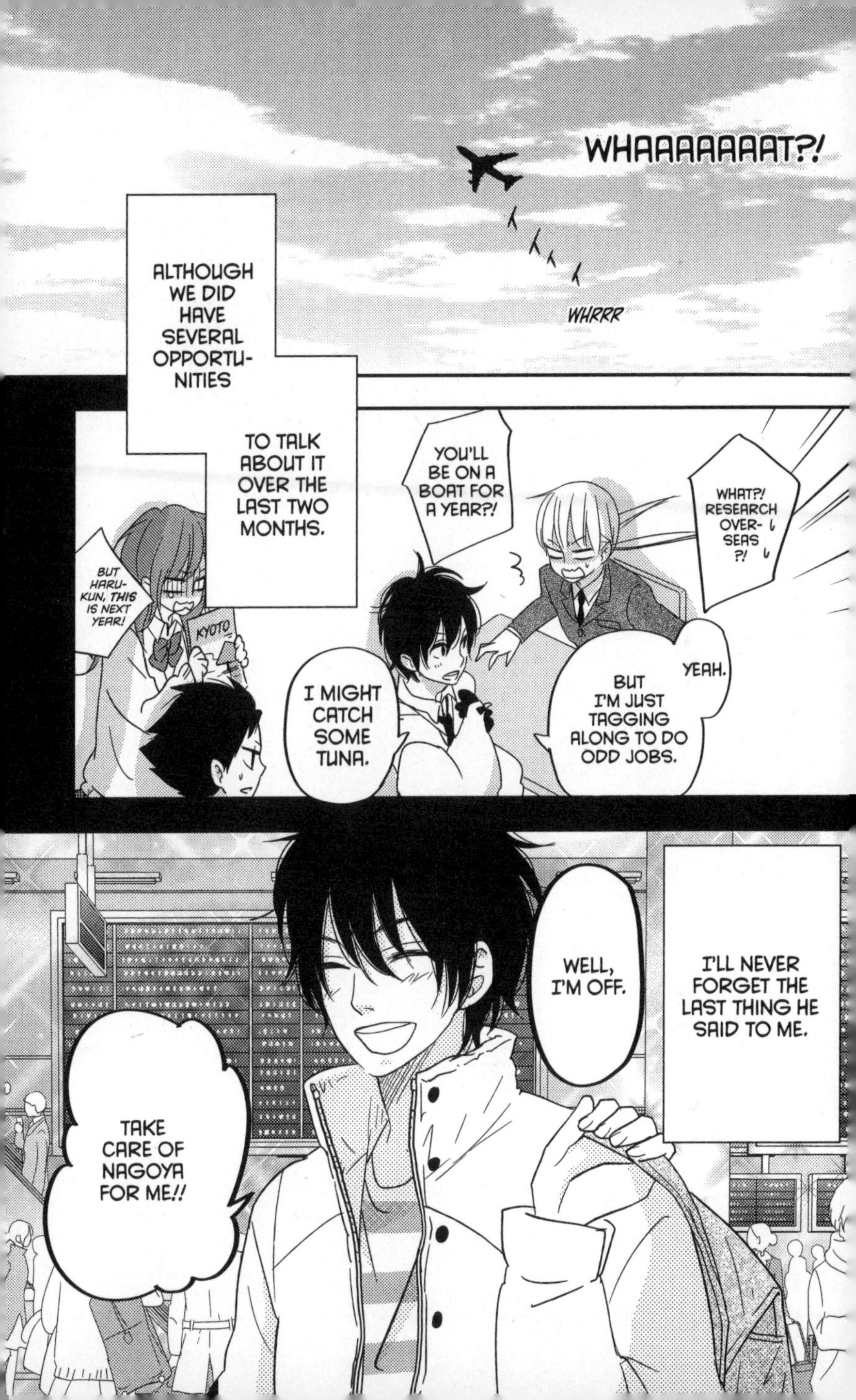
WHAAAAAAAT?!
WHRRR
ALTHOUGH WE DID HAVE SEVERAL OPPORTUNITIES
WHAT?! RESEARCH OVERSEAS?!
YOU'LL BE ON A BOAT FOR A YEAR?!
YEAH.
BUT I'M JUST TAGGING ALONG TO DO ODD JOBS.
I MIGHT CATCH SOME TUNA.
TO TALK ABOUT IT OVER THE LAST TWO MONTHS.
BUT HARU-KUN, THIS IS NEXT YEAR!
KYOTO
I'LL NEVER FORGET THE LAST THING HE SAID TO ME.
WELL, I'M OFF.
TAKE CARE OF NAGOYA FOR ME!!

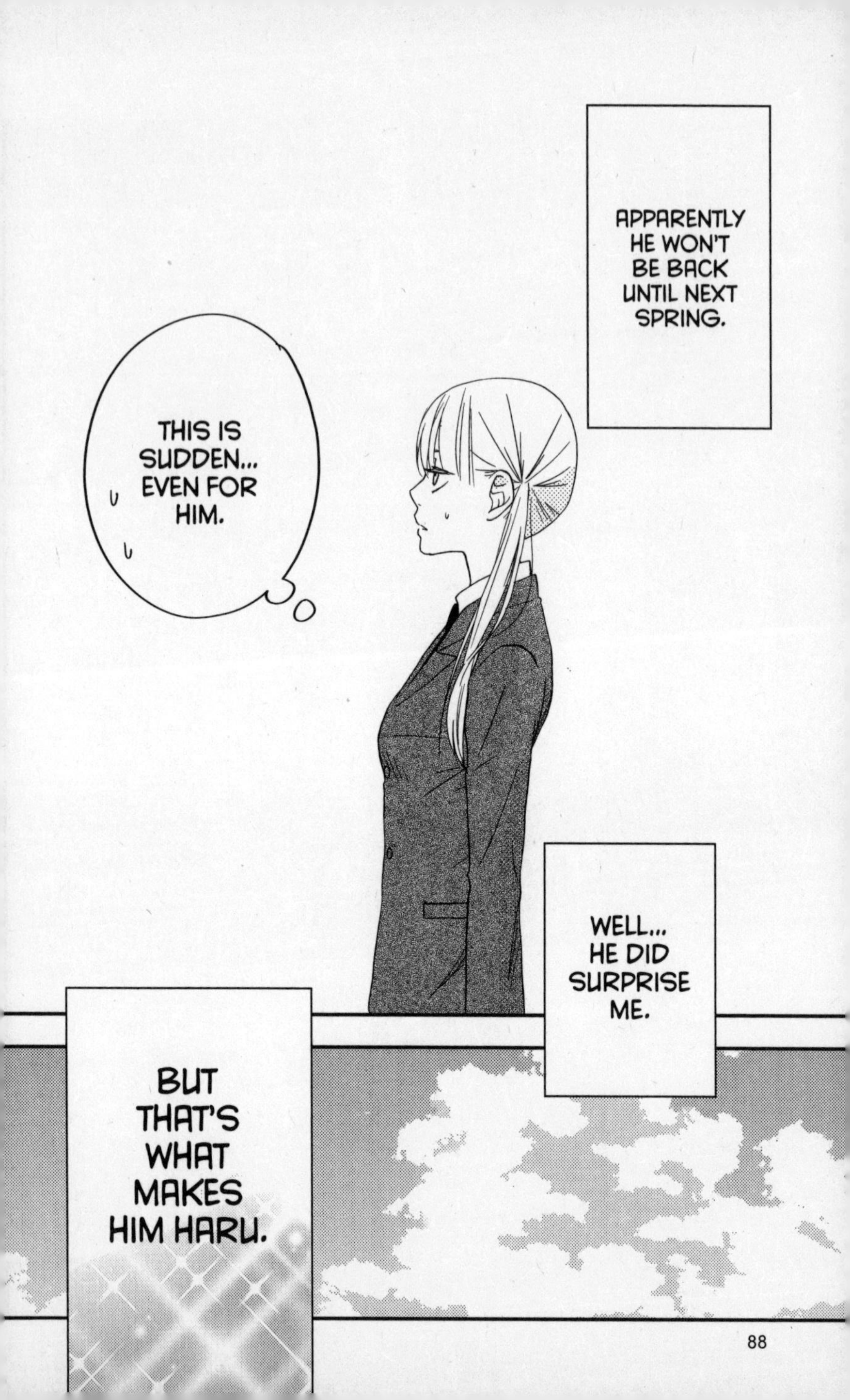
APPARENTLY HE WON'T BE BACK UNTIL NEXT SPRING.
THIS IS SUDDEN... EVEN FOR HIM.
WELL... HE DID SURPRISE ME.
BUT THAT'S WHAT MAKES HIM HARU.

AT YUZAN-SAN'S HOUSE

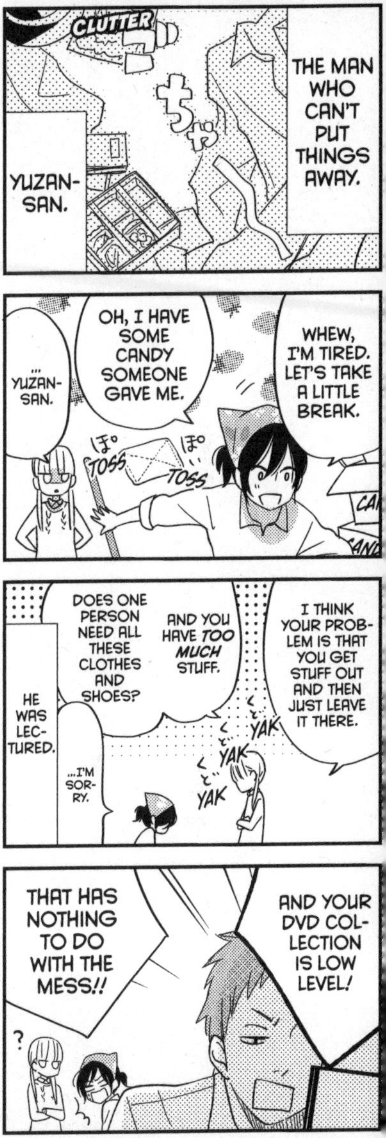
THE MAN WHO CAN'T PUT THINGS AWAY.
CLUTTER
ちゃ
YUZAN-SAN.
WHEW, I'M TIRED. LET'S TAKE A LITTLE BREAK.
OH, I HAVE SOME CANDY SOMEONE GAVE ME.
...YUZAN-SAN.
ぽい TOSS
ぽ TOSS
I THINK YOUR PROBLEM IS THAT YOU GET STUFF OUT AND THEN JUST LEAVE IT THERE.
AND YOU HAVE *TOO MUCH* STUFF.
DOES ONE PERSON NEED ALL THESE CLOTHES AND SHOES?
くど YAK
くど YAK
くど YAK
HE WAS LECTURED.
...I'M SORRY.
AND YOUR DVD COLLECTION IS LOW LEVEL!
THAT HAS NOTHING TO DO WITH THE MESS!!
?

BIG BROTHER

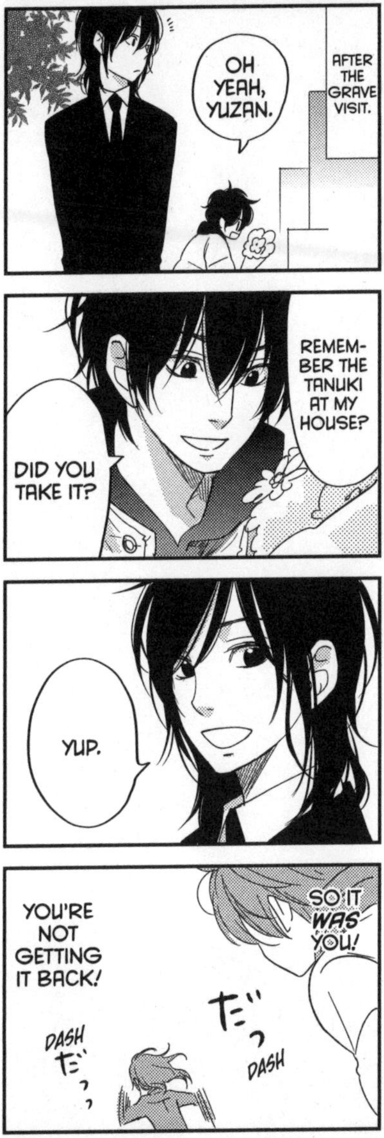
AFTER THE GRAVE VISIT.
OH YEAH, YUZAN.
REMEMBER THE TANUKI AT MY HOUSE?
DID YOU TAKE IT?
YUP.
SO IT *WAS* YOU!
YOU'RE NOT GETTING IT BACK!
だっ DASH
DASH だっ

CHAPTER 47: THIRD-YEAR STUDENTS

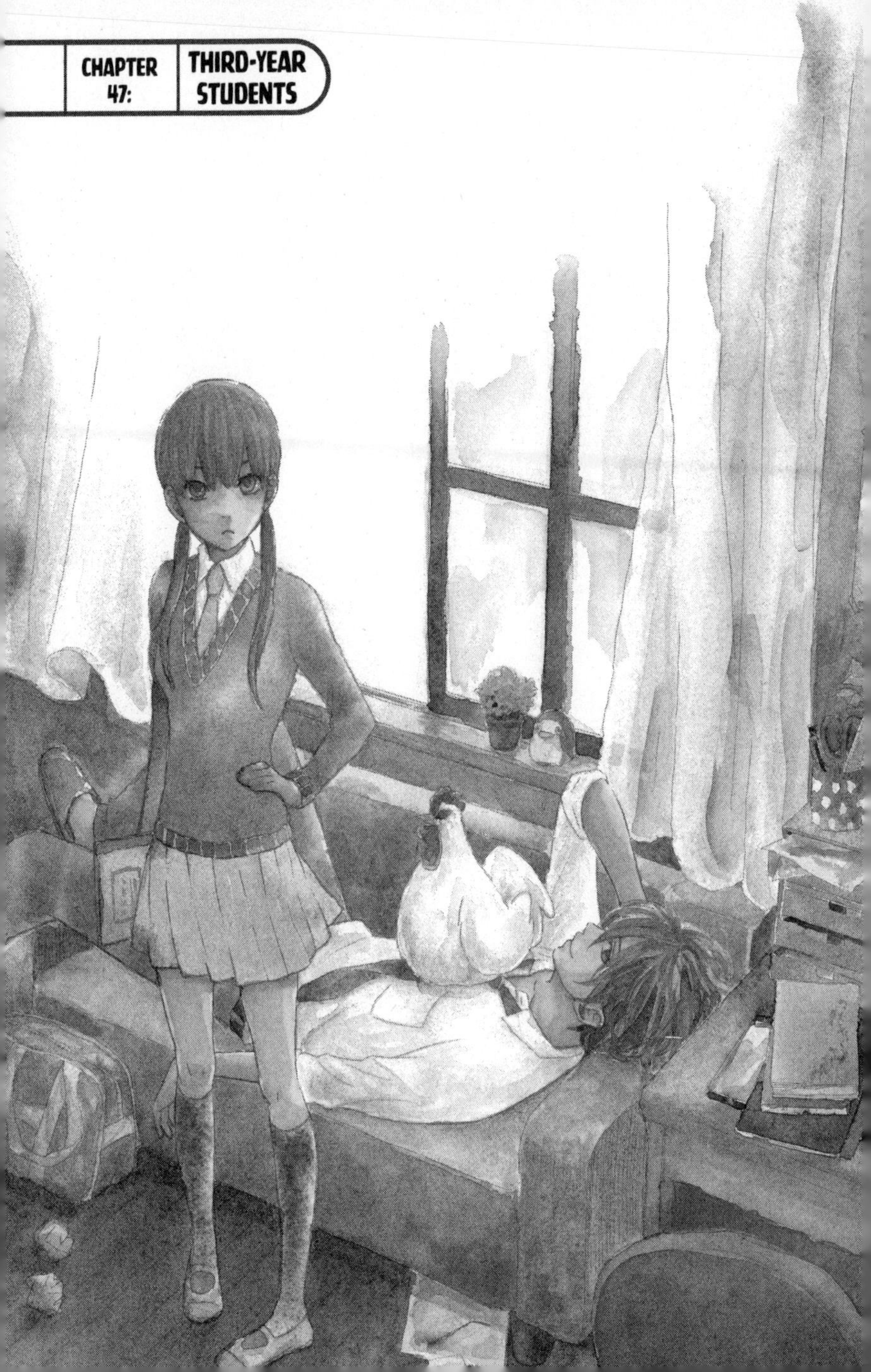

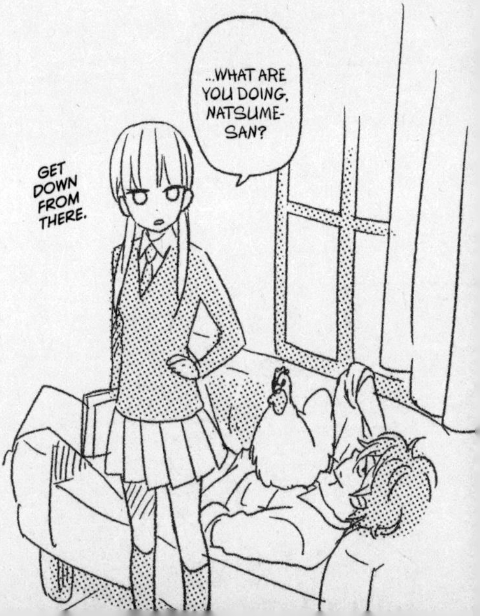
...WHAT ARE YOU DOING, NATSUME-SAN?
GET DOWN FROM THERE.

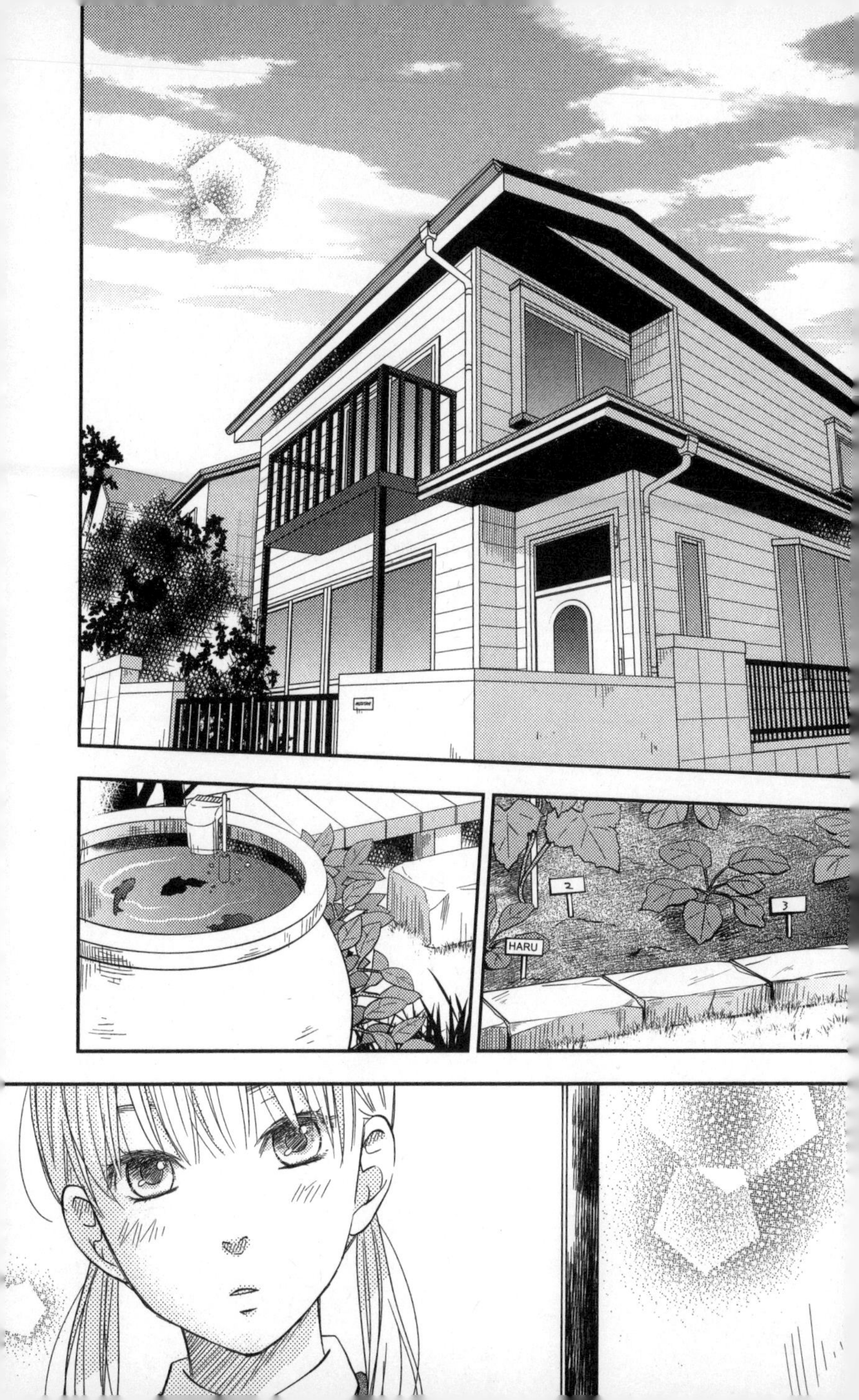
2
3
HARU

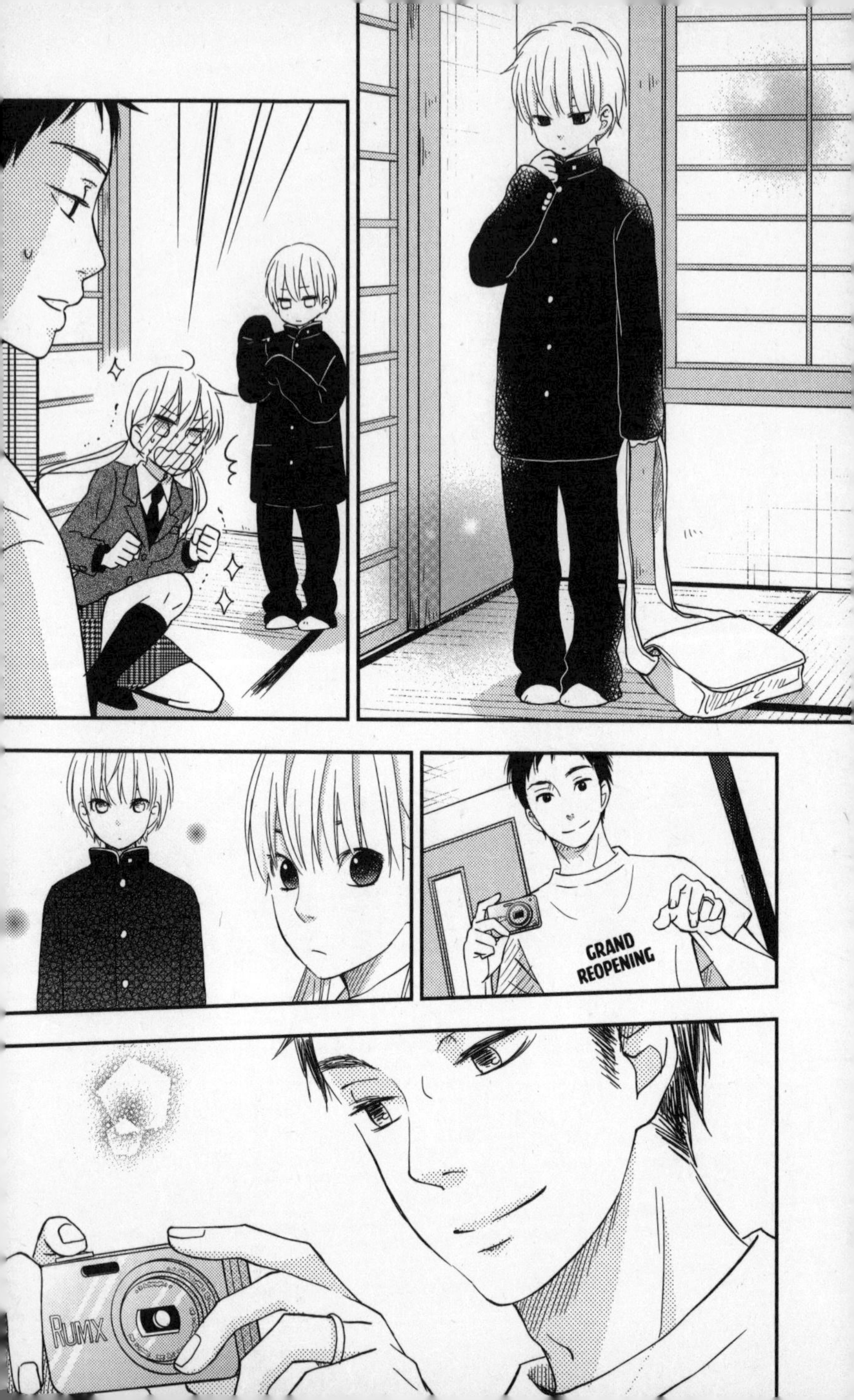
GRAND
REOPENING
RUMX

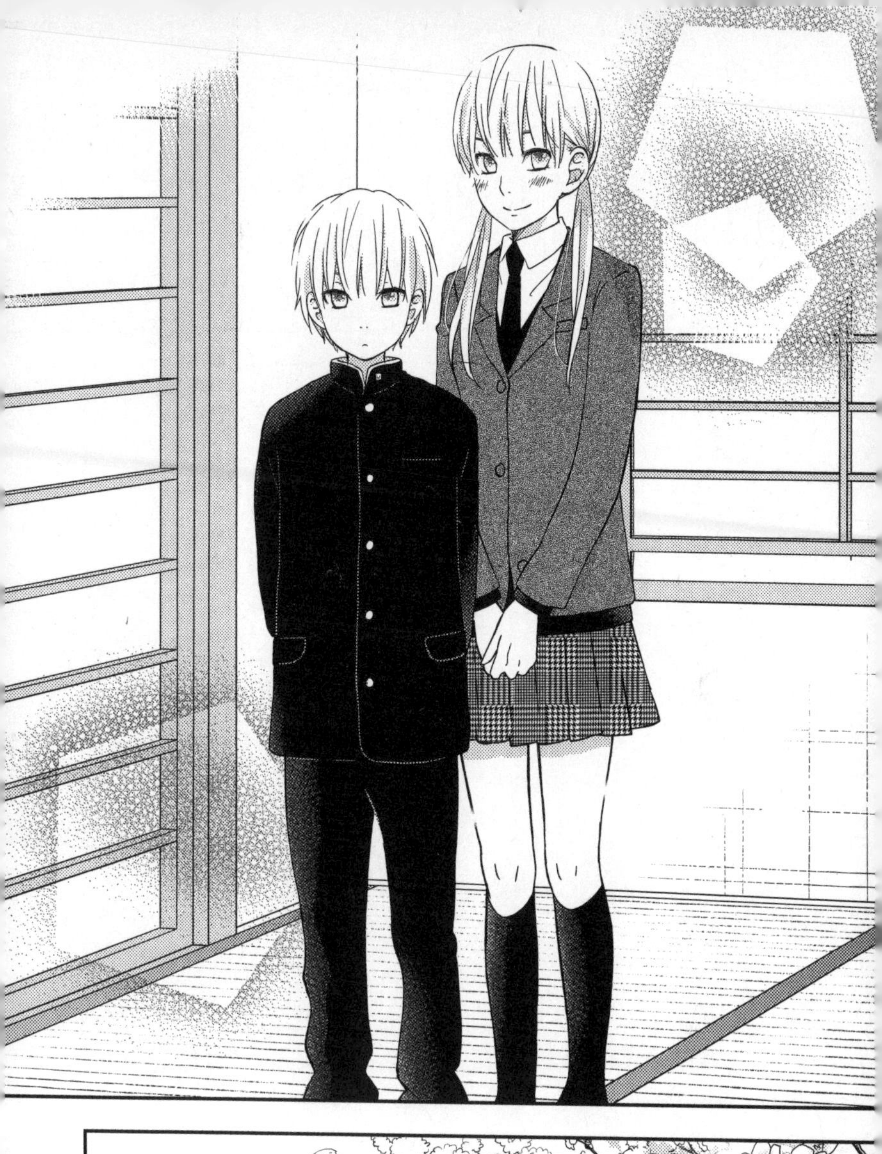
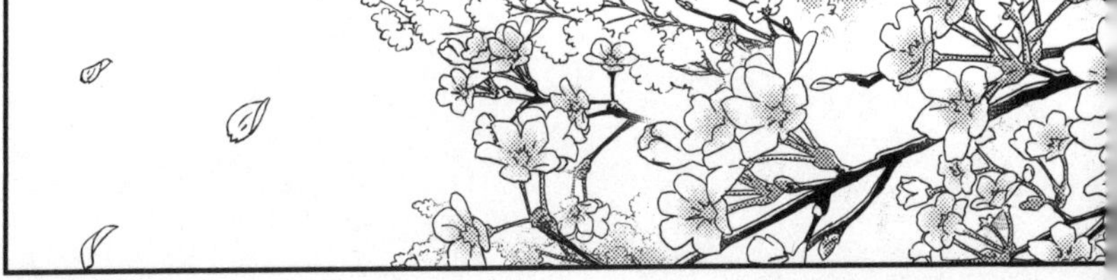

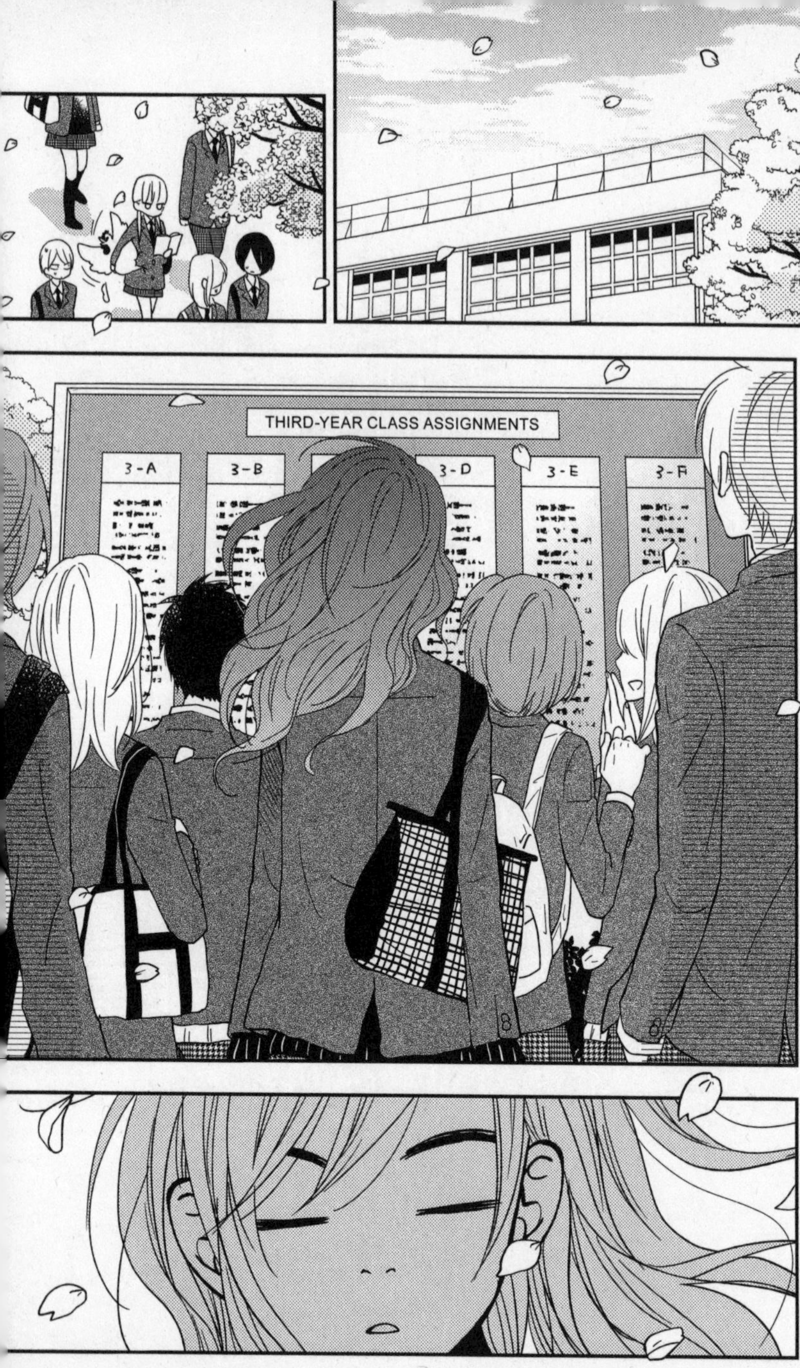
THIRD-YEAR CLASS ASSIGNMENTS
3-A
3-B
3-D
3-E
3-F

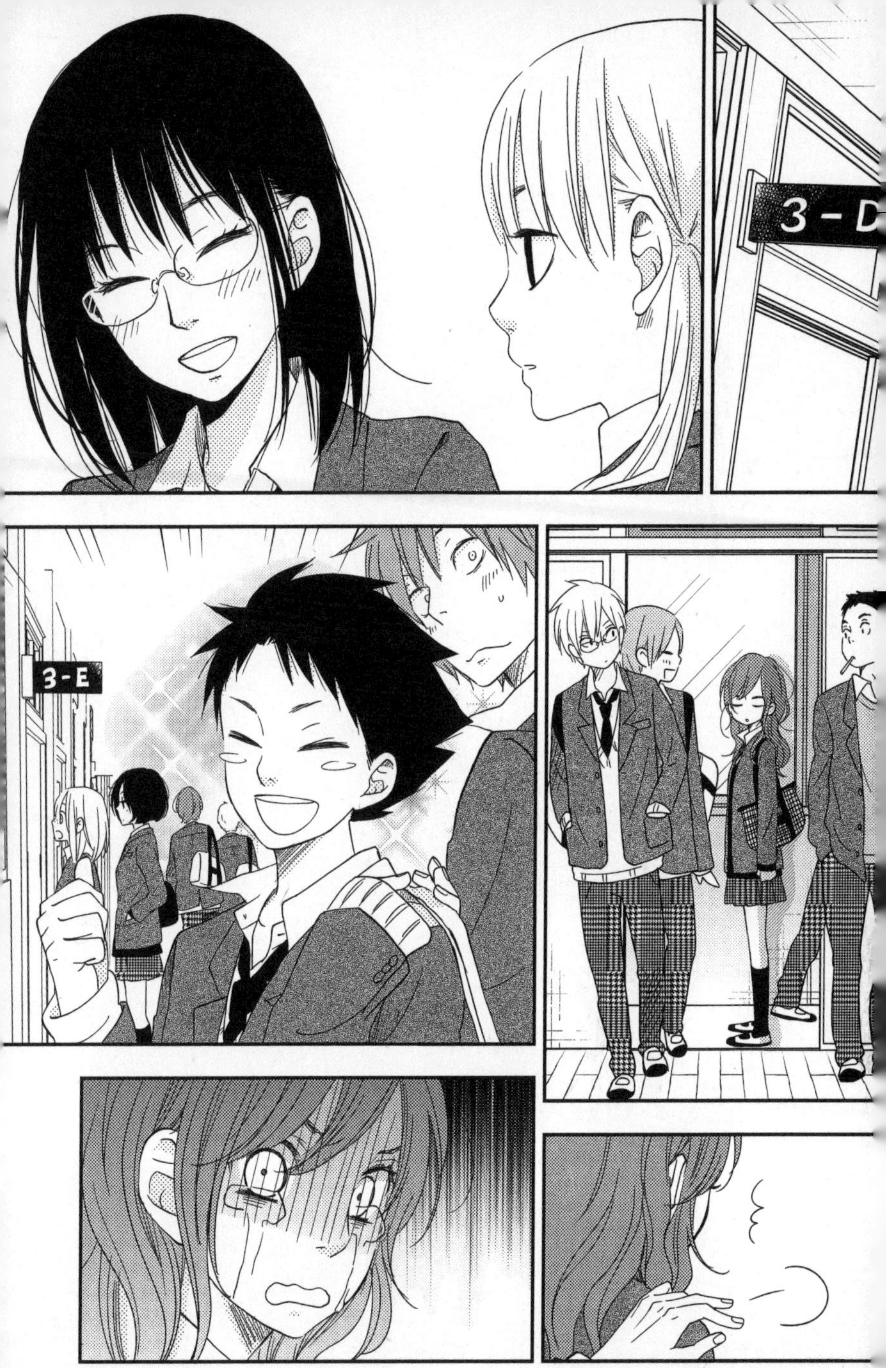
3-D
3-E

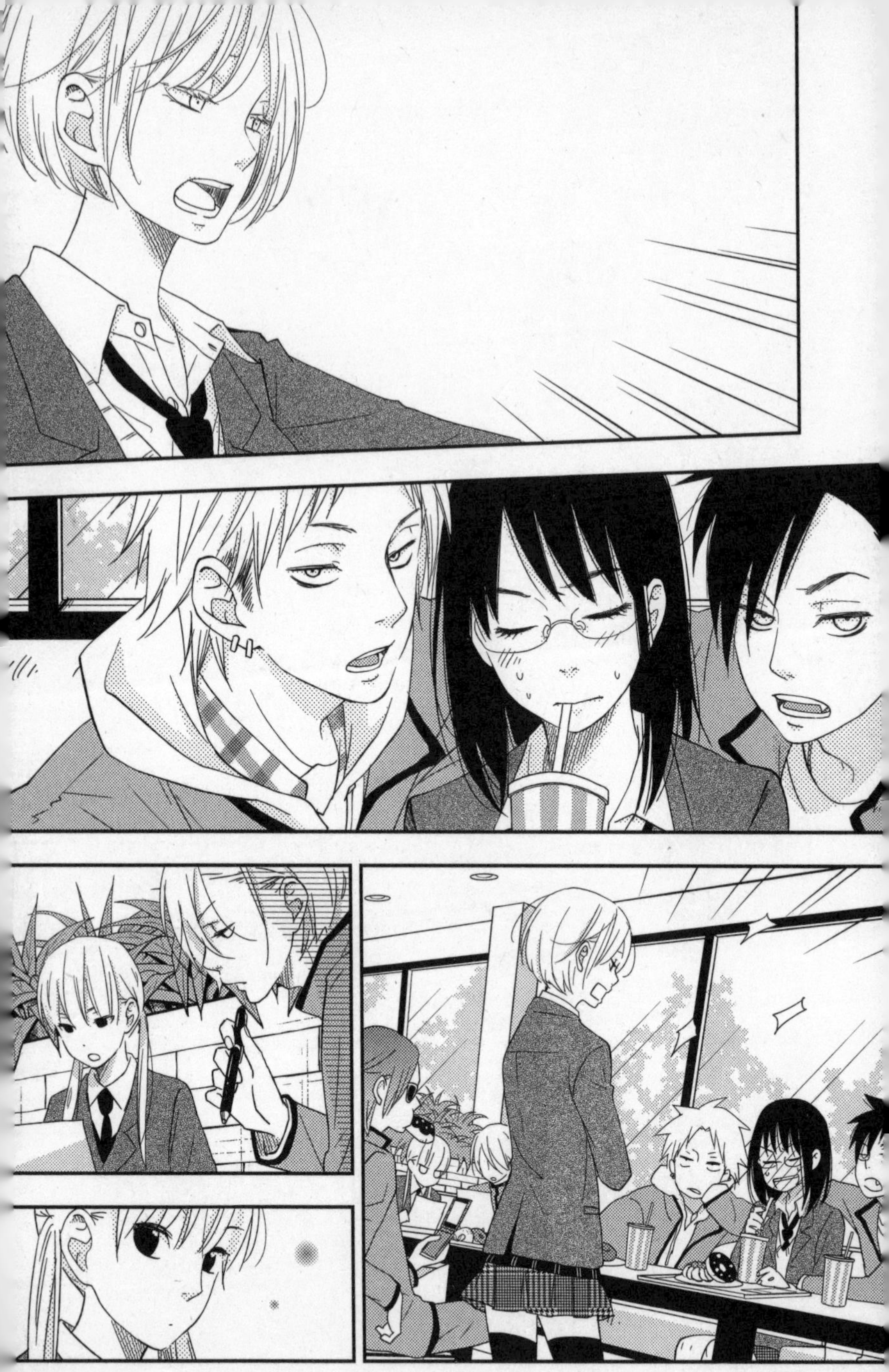

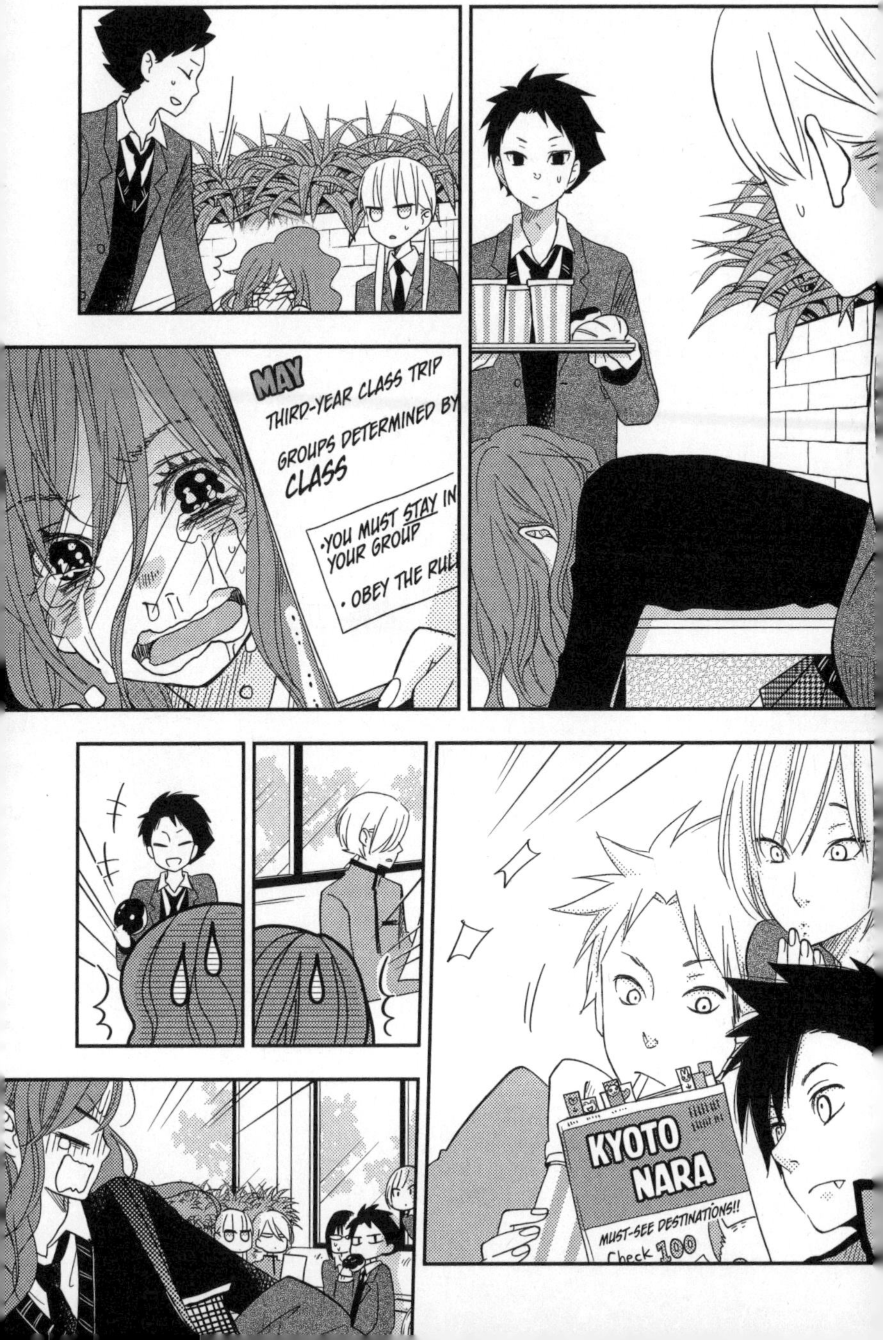
MAY
THIRD-YEAR CLASS TRIP
GROUPS DETERMINED BY CLASS
•YOU MUST STAY IN YOUR GROUP
• OBEY THE RUL
KYOTO NARA
MUST-SEE DESTINATIONS!!
Check 100

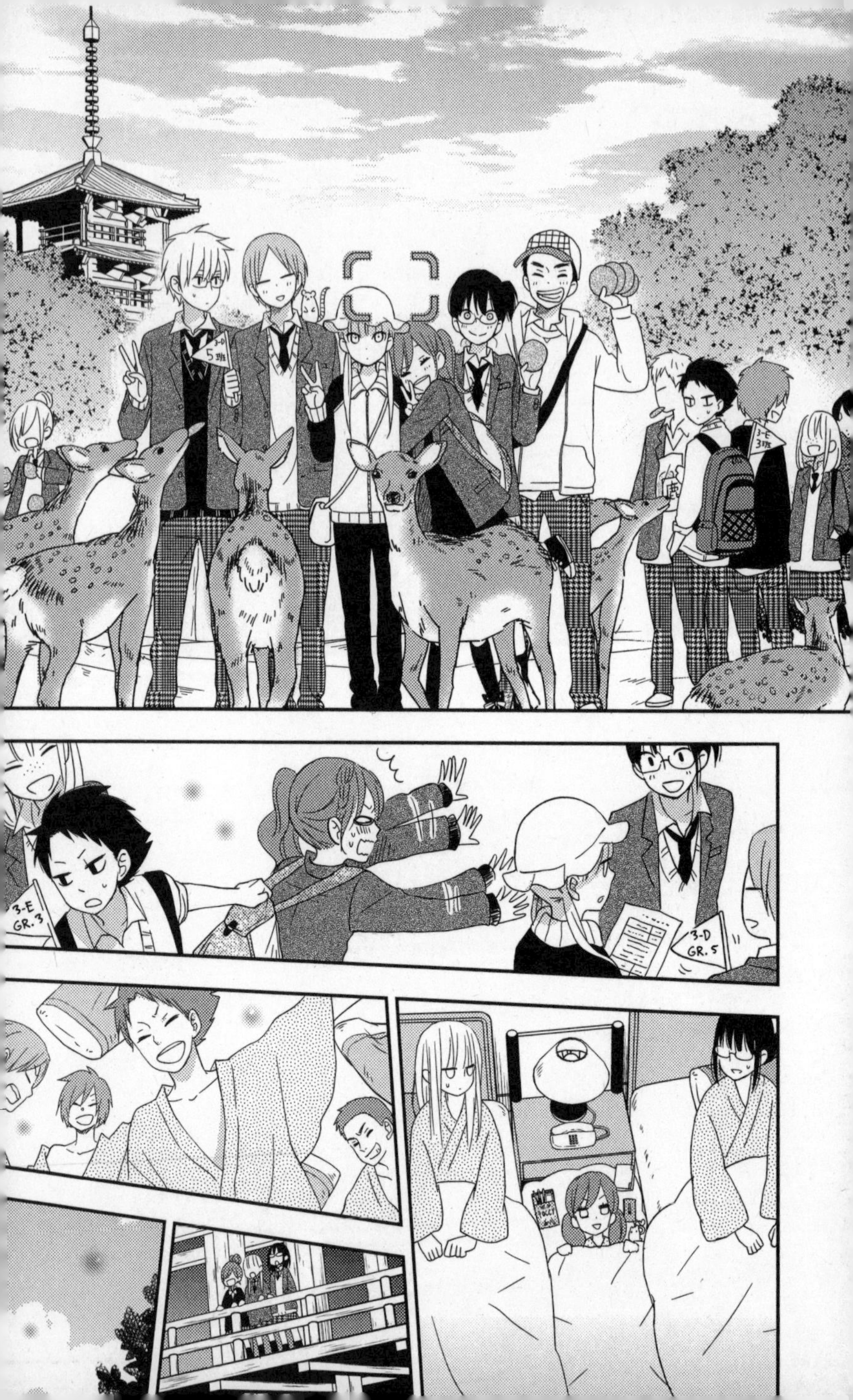
3-E 3班
3-D 5班
3-D GR. 5
3-E GR. 3

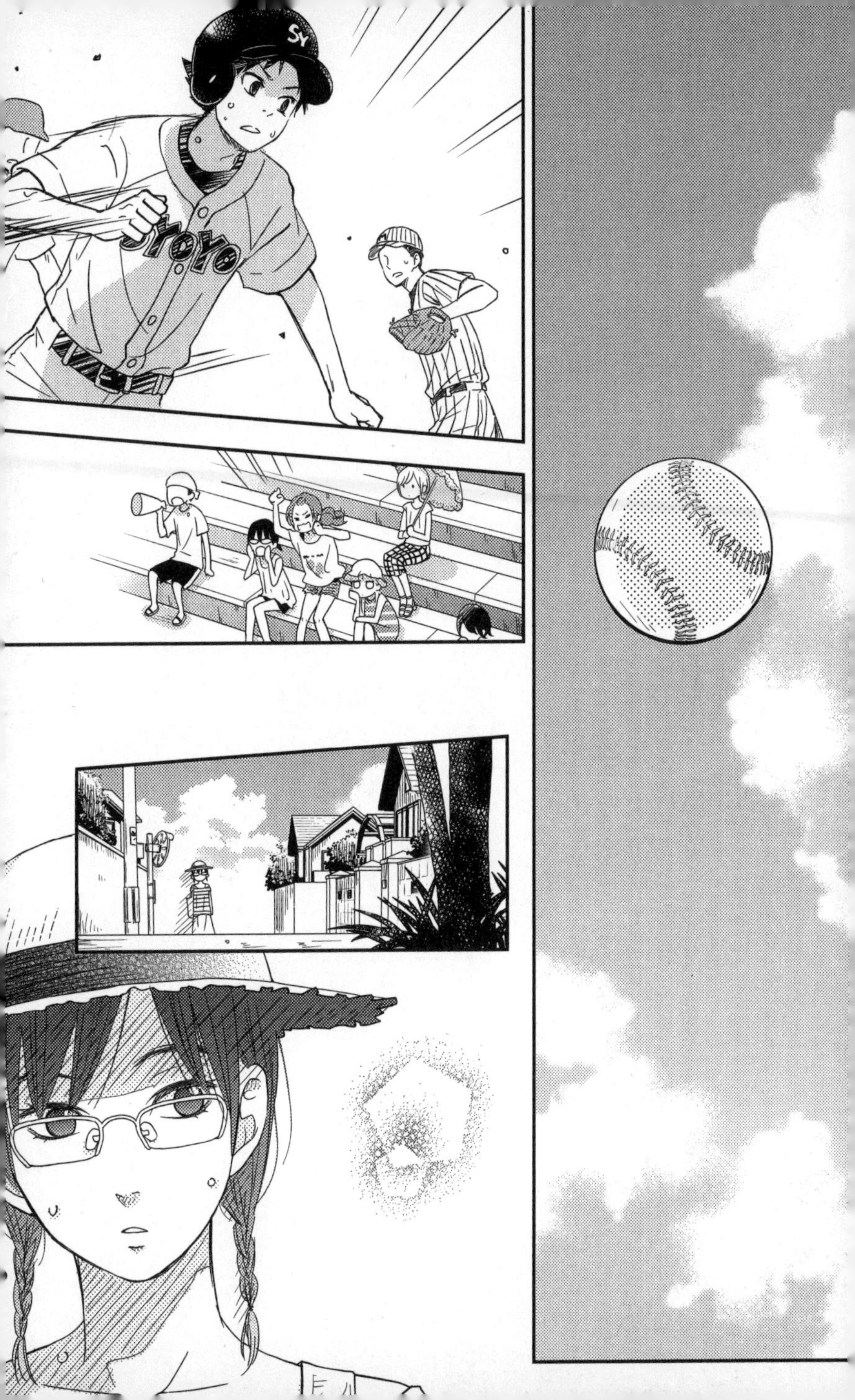

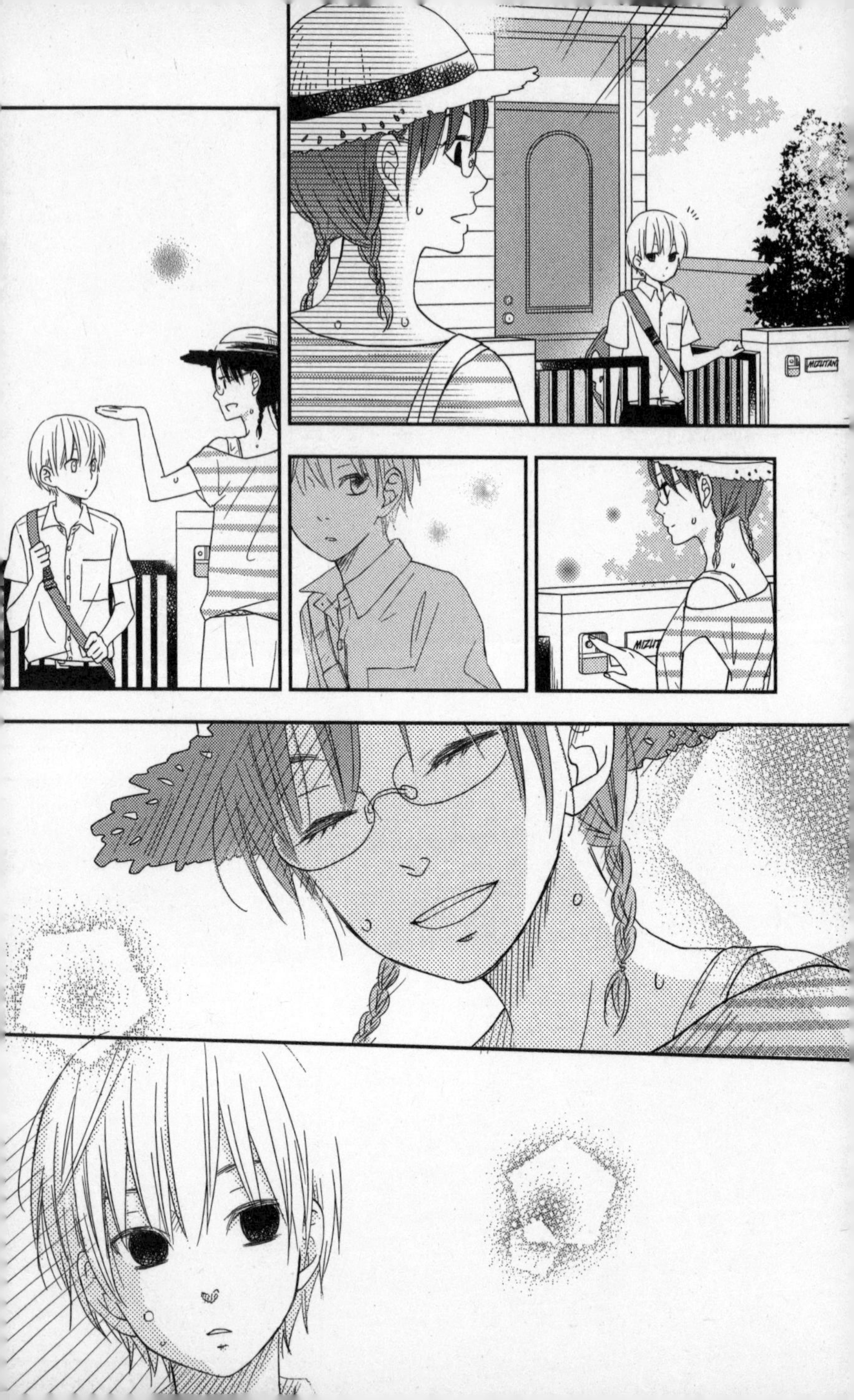
MIZUTAN

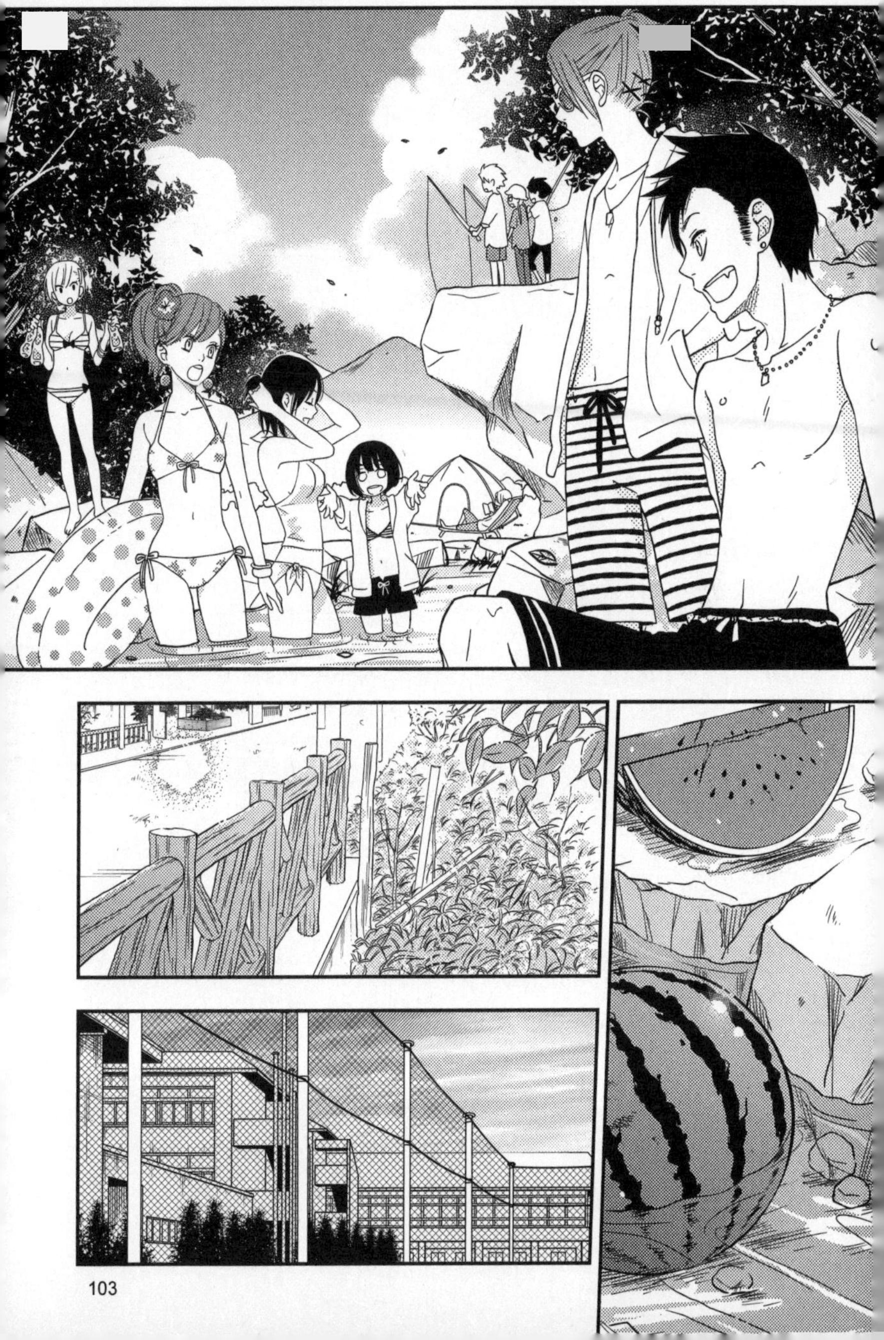

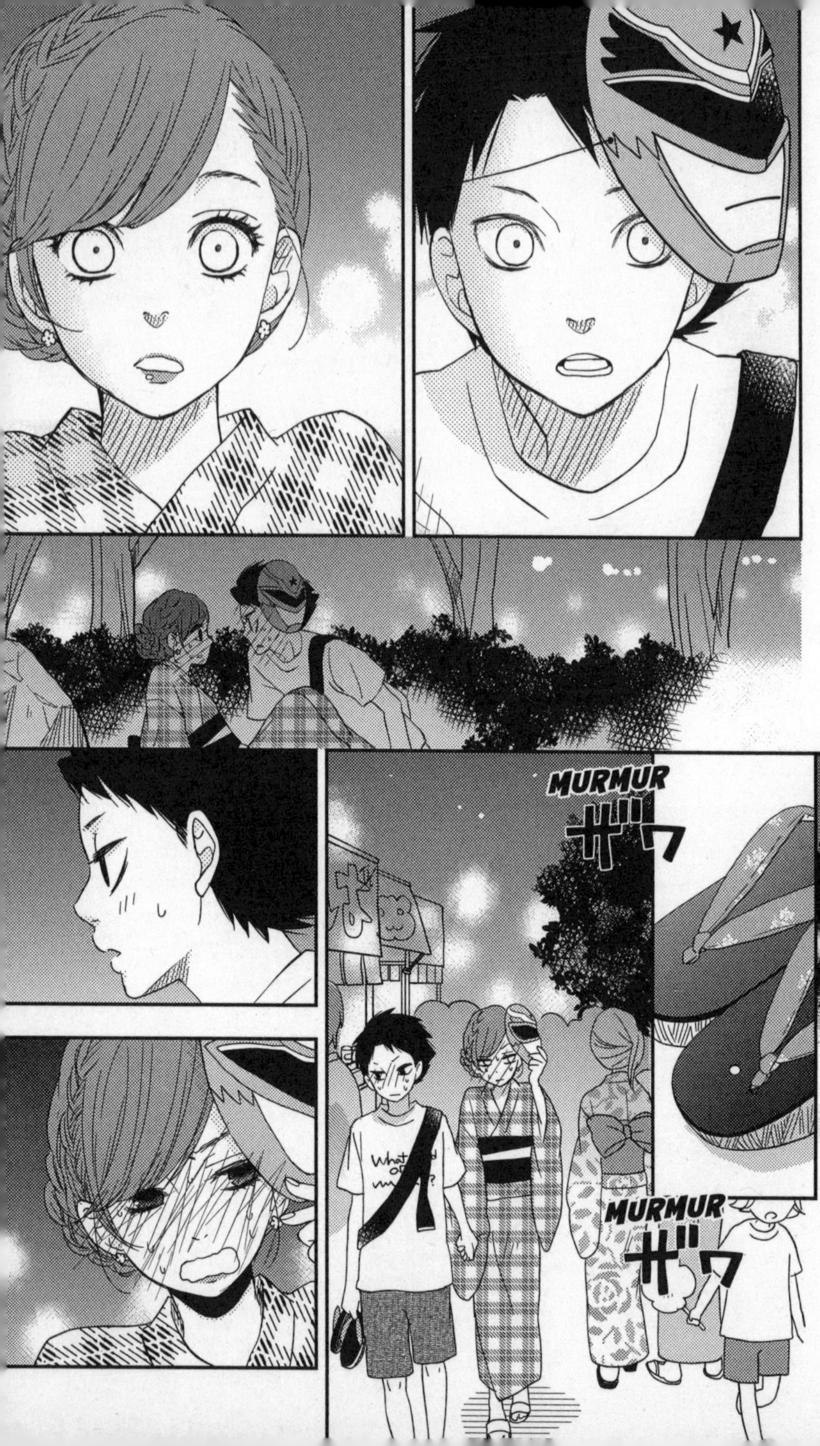
MURMUR
ザワ
MURMUR
ザワ

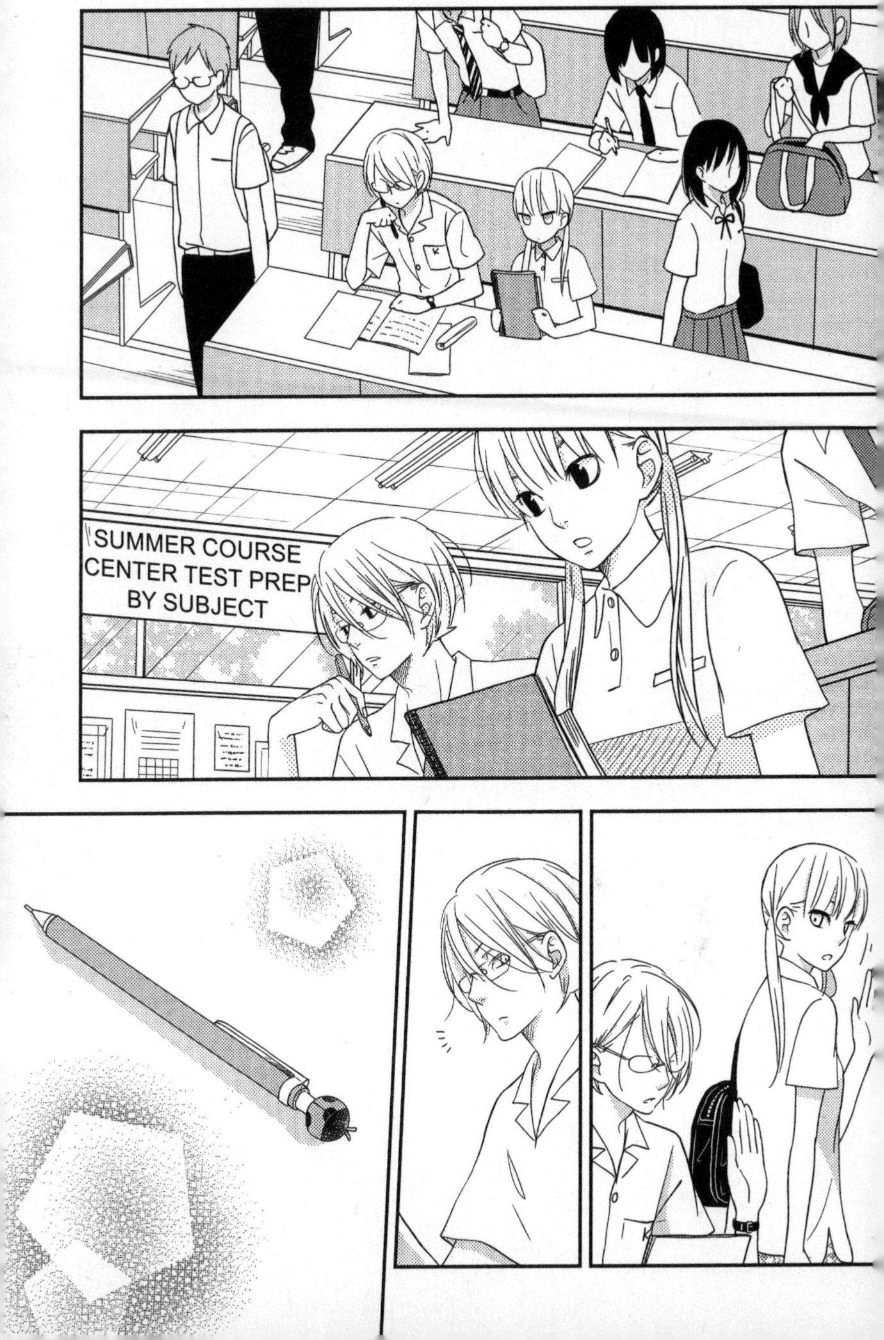
SUMMER COURSE
CENTER TEST PREP
BY SUBJECT

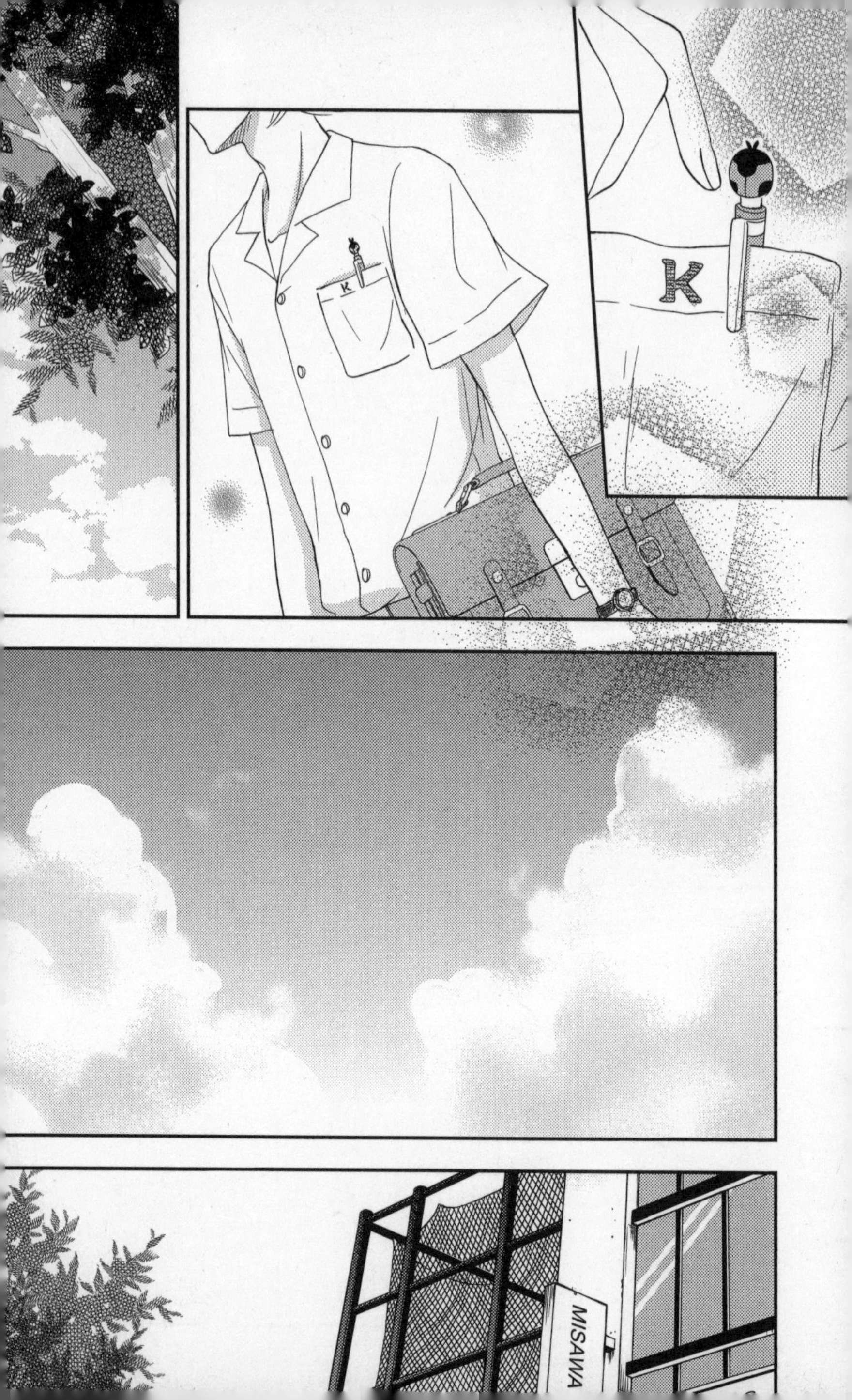
K
MISAWA

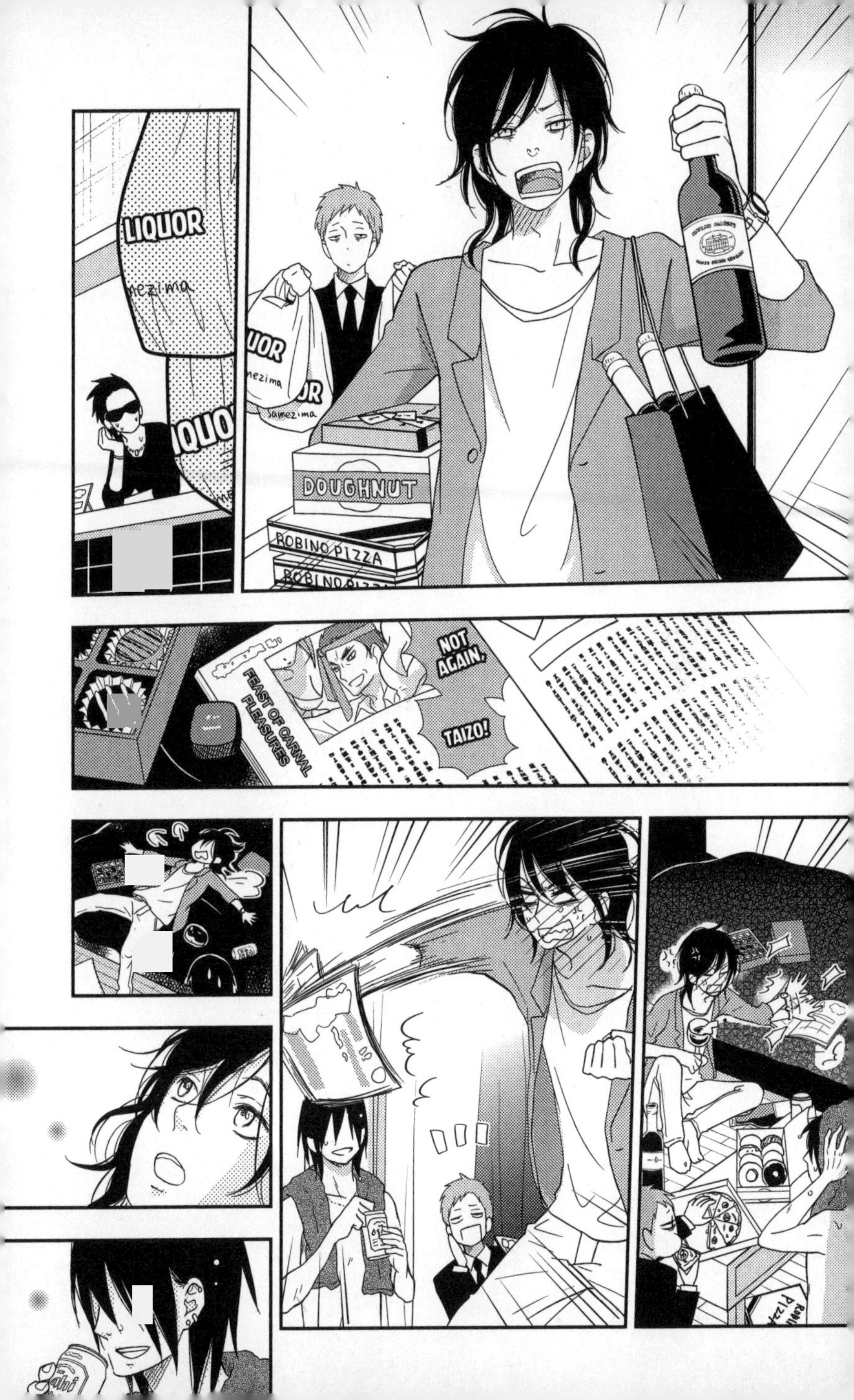

LIQUOR
mezima
LIQUOR
DOUGHNUT
ROBINO PIZZA
LIQUOR
mezima
LIQUOR
FEAST OF CARNAL PLEASURES
NOT AGAIN, TAIZO!
Pizza

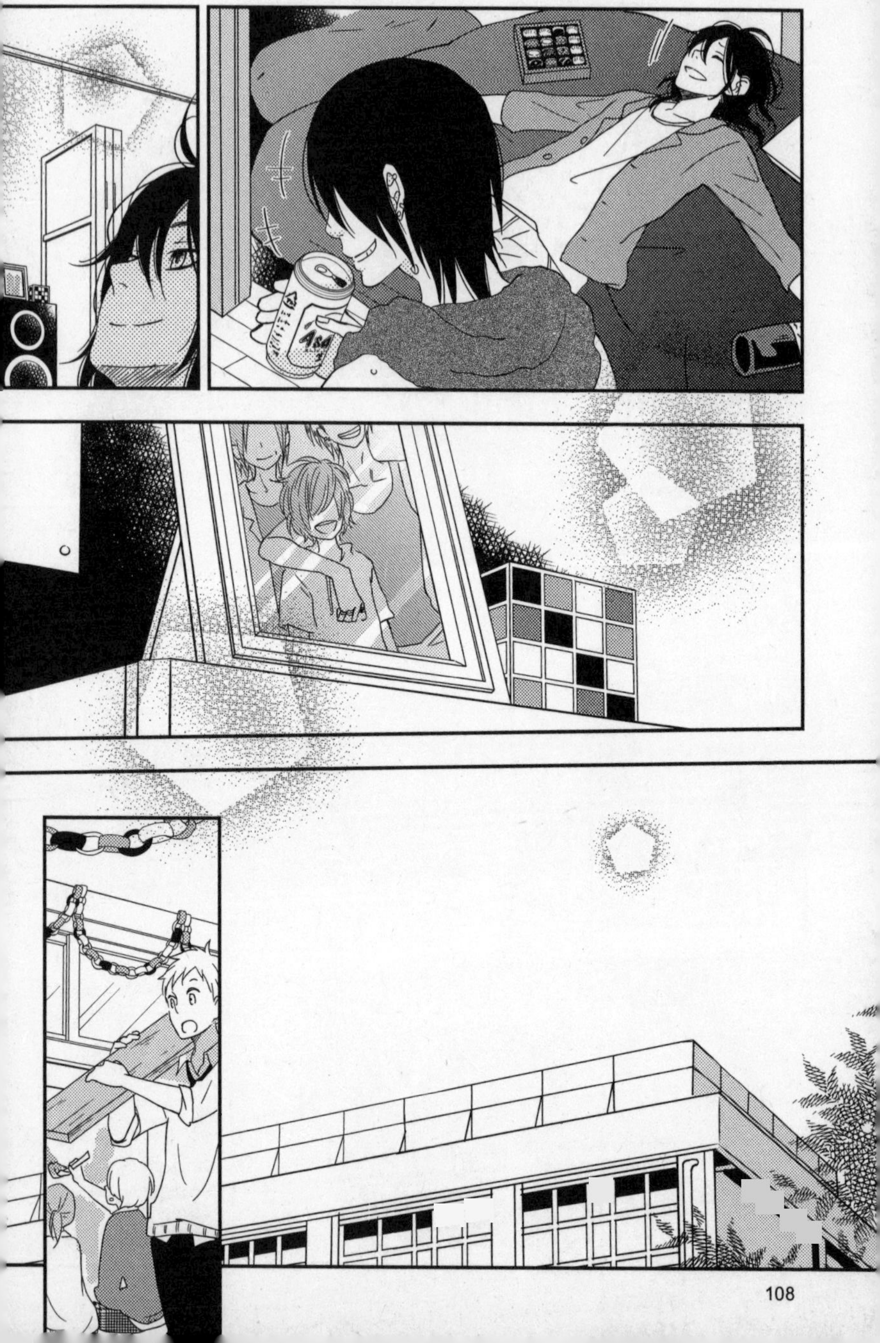

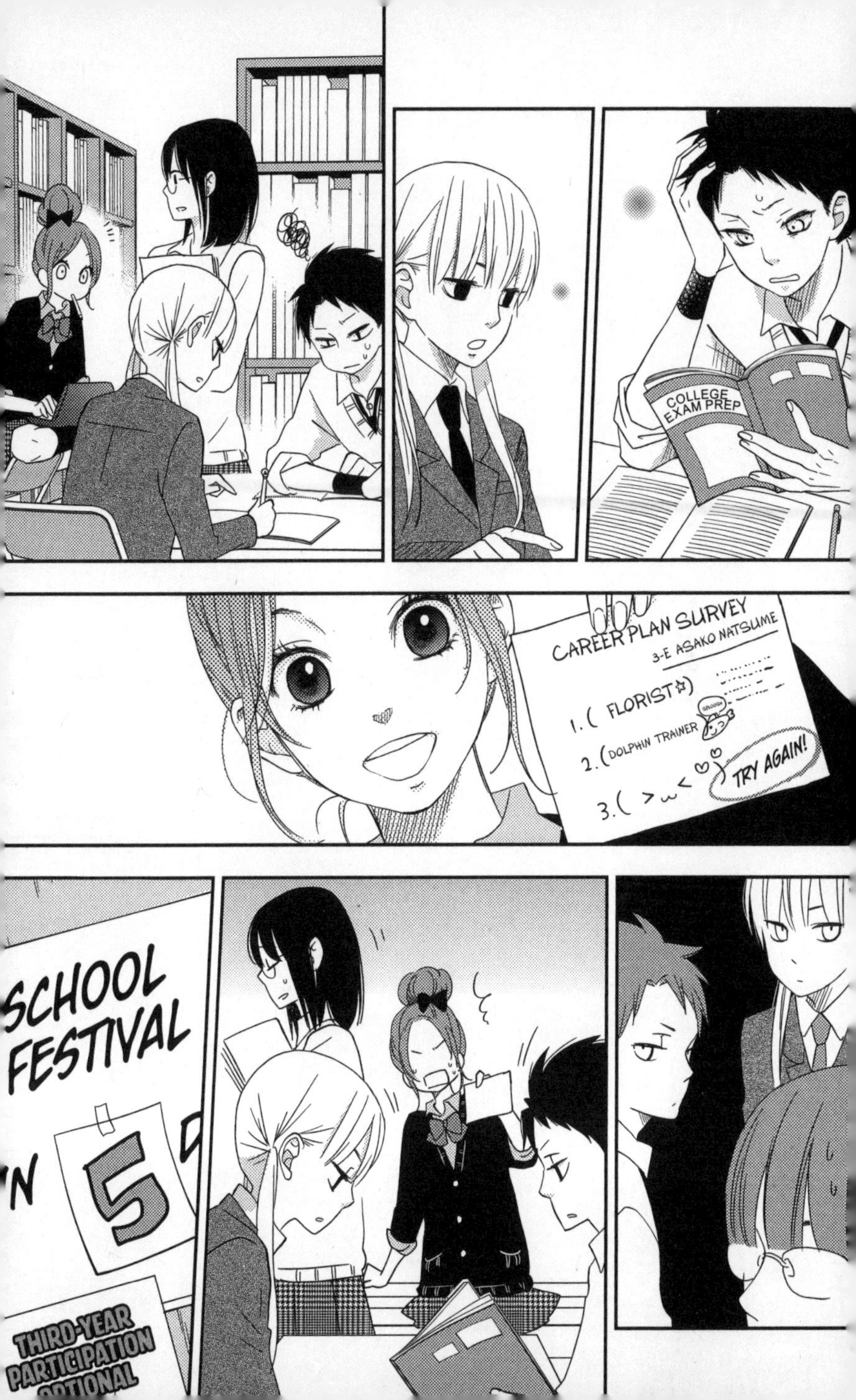
COLLEGE EXAM PREP
CAREER PLAN SURVEY
3-E ASAKO NATSUME
1. (FLORIST☆)
2. (DOLPHIN TRAINER
3. (>ω< ♡)
TRY AGAIN!
SCHOOL FESTIVAL
5
THIRD-YEAR PARTICIPATION OPTIONAL

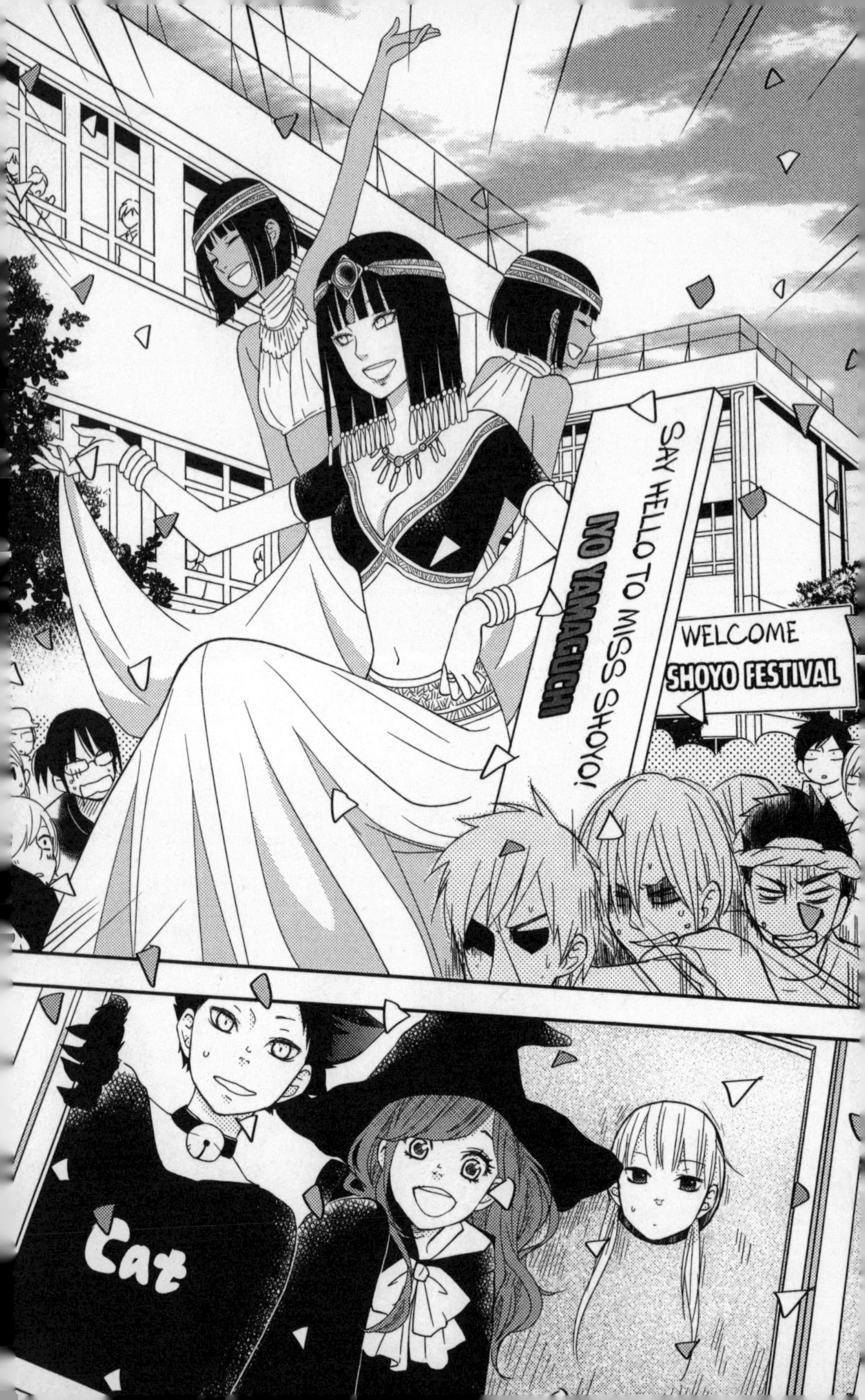
SAY HELLO TO MISS SHOYO!
IYO YAMAGUCHI
WELCOME
SHOYO FESTIVAL
Cat

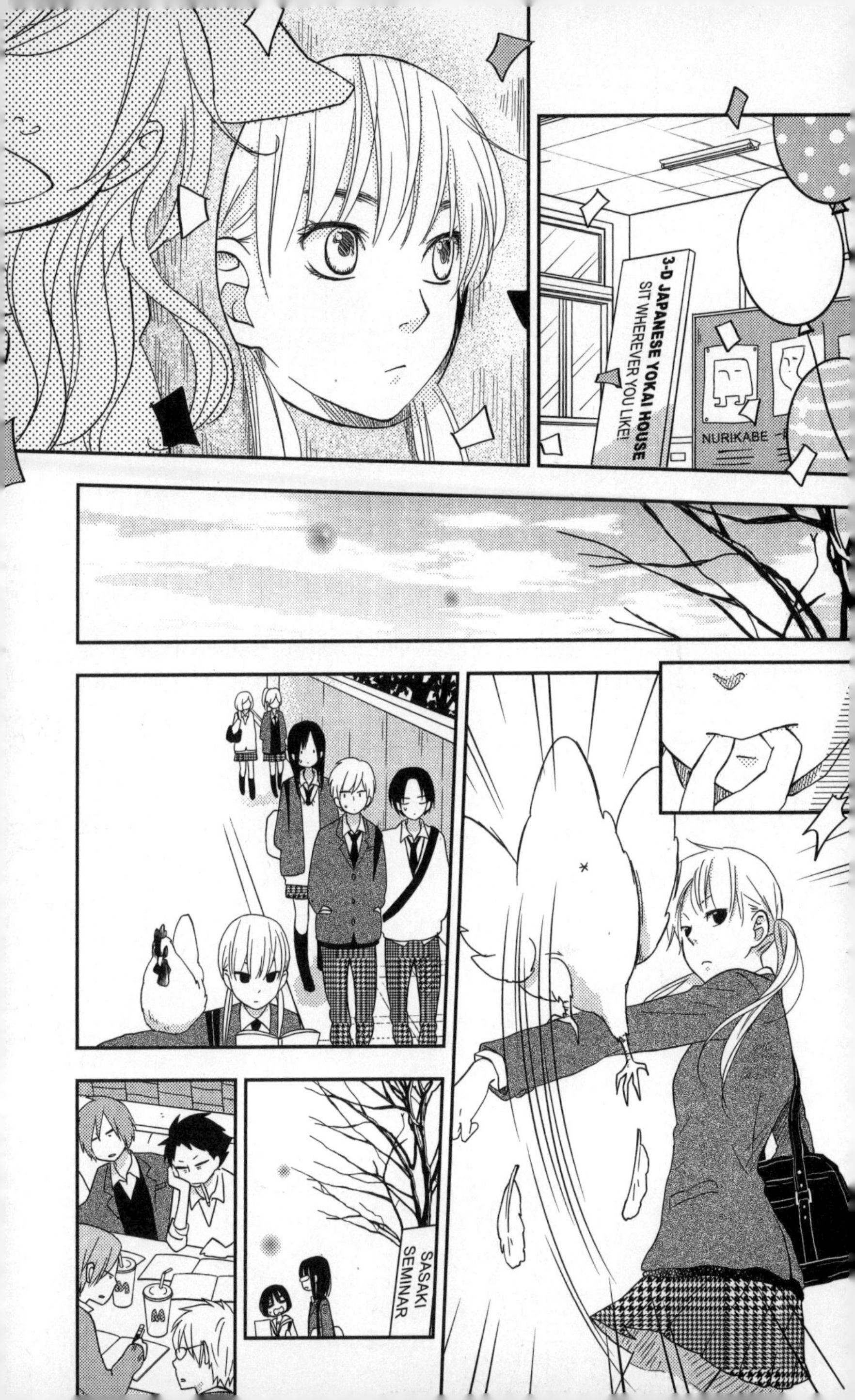
3-D JAPANESE YOKAI HOUSE
SIT WHEREVER YOU LIKE!
NURIKABE
SASAKI SEMINAR

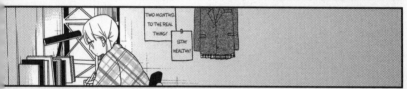

TWO MONTHS
TO THE REAL
THING!

STAY
HEALTHY!

NEW YEAR'S BELL 23:30

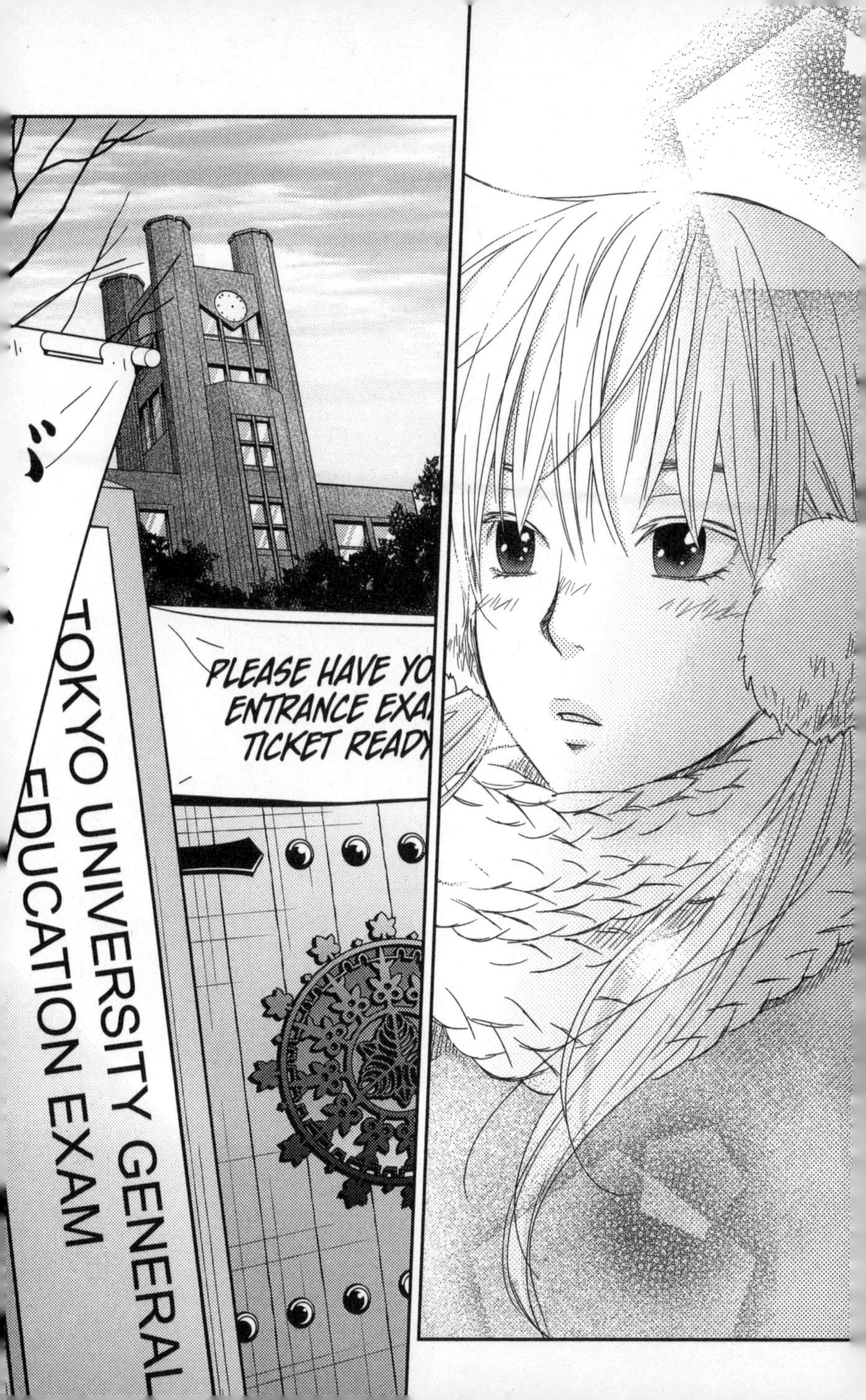
PLEASE HAVE YO
ENTRANCE EXA
TICKET READY
TOKYO UNIVERSITY GENERAL
EDUCATION EXAM

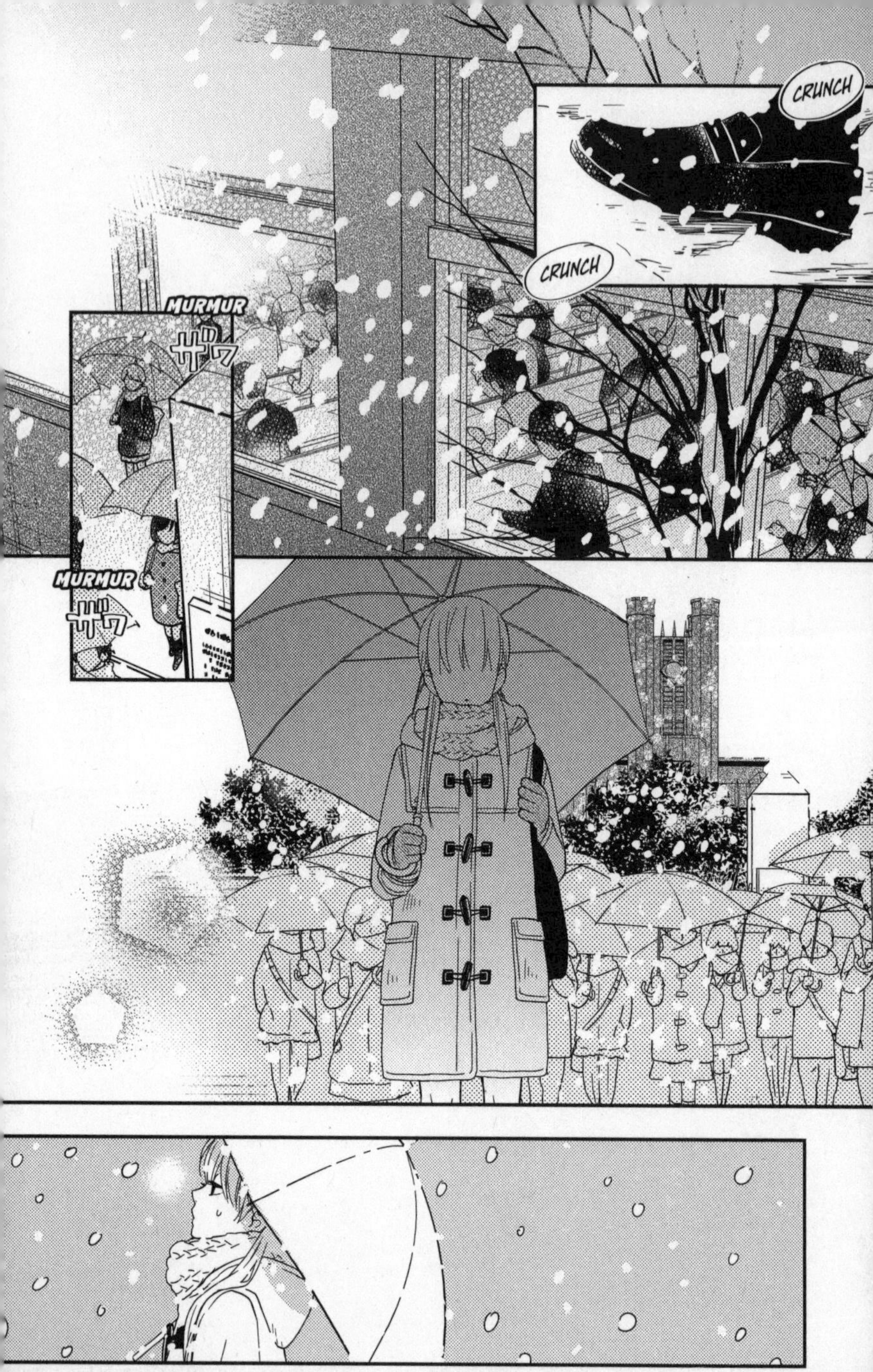
CRUNCH
CRUNCH
MURMUR
ザワ
MURMUR
ザワ

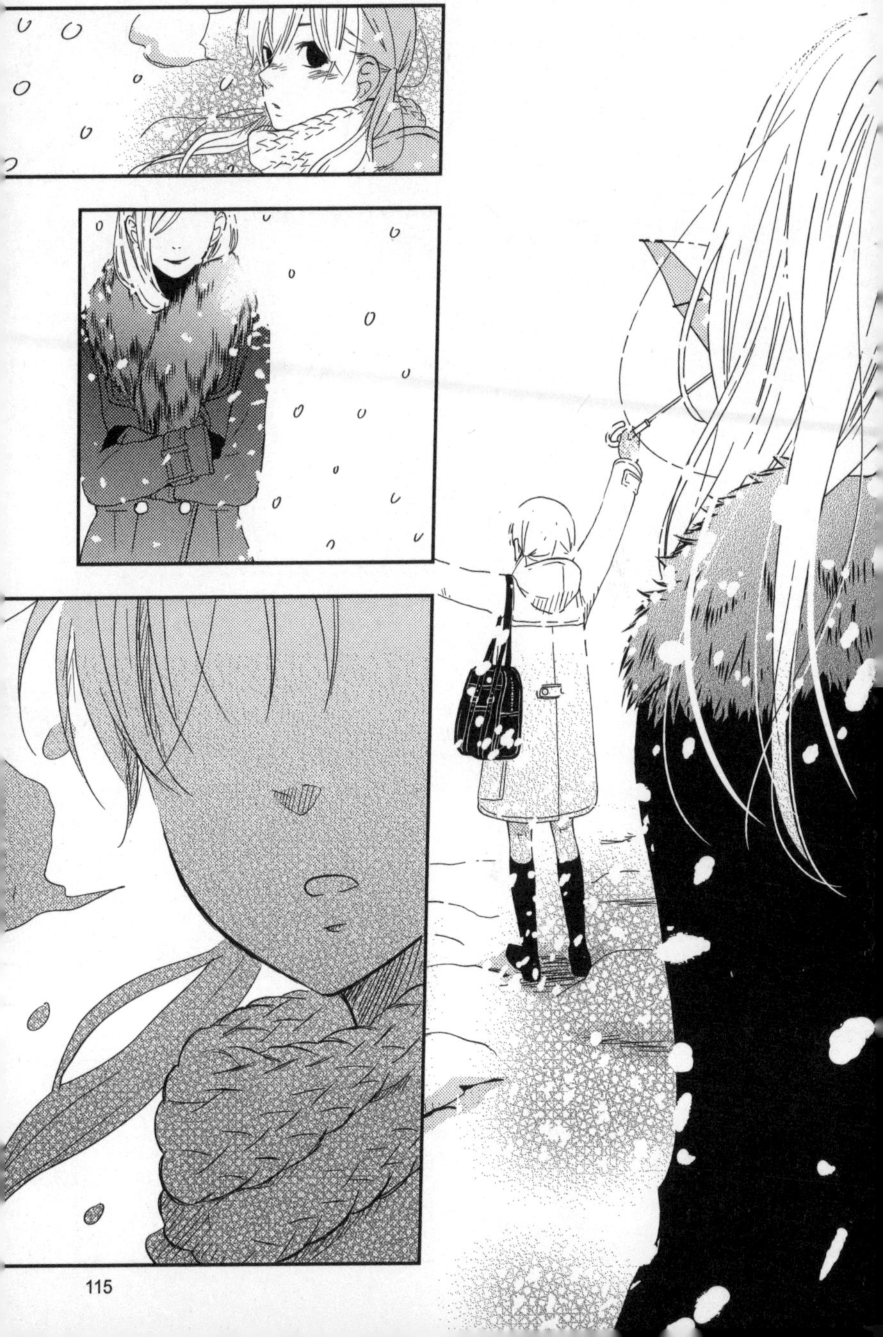

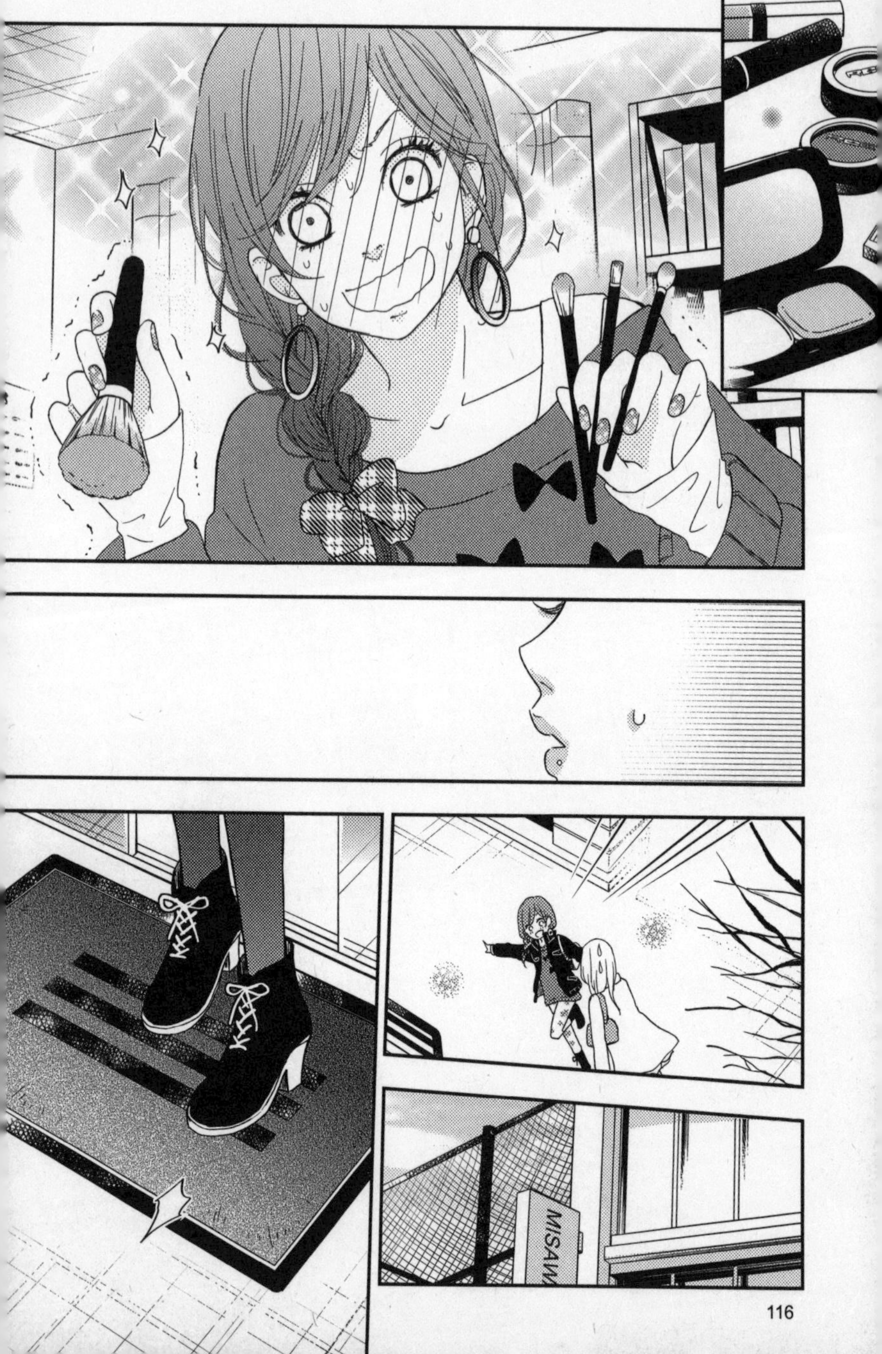
MISAW

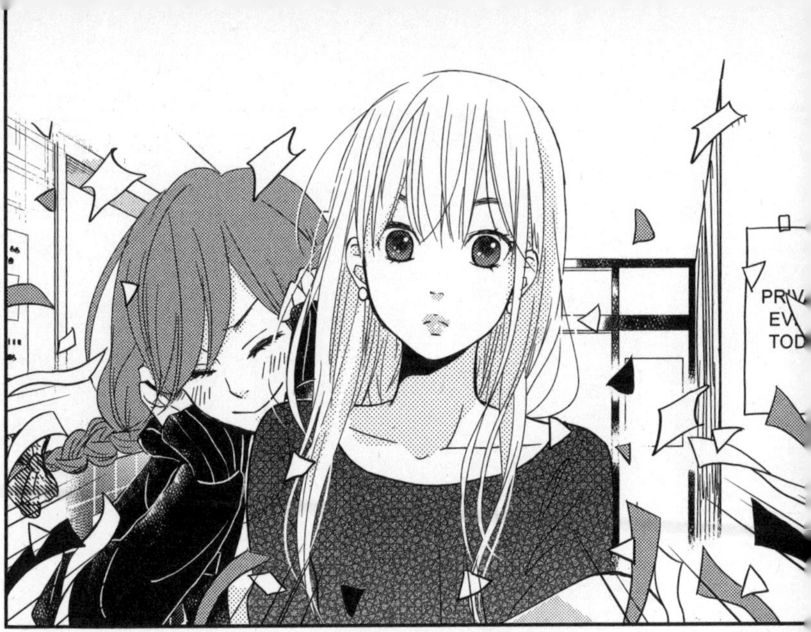
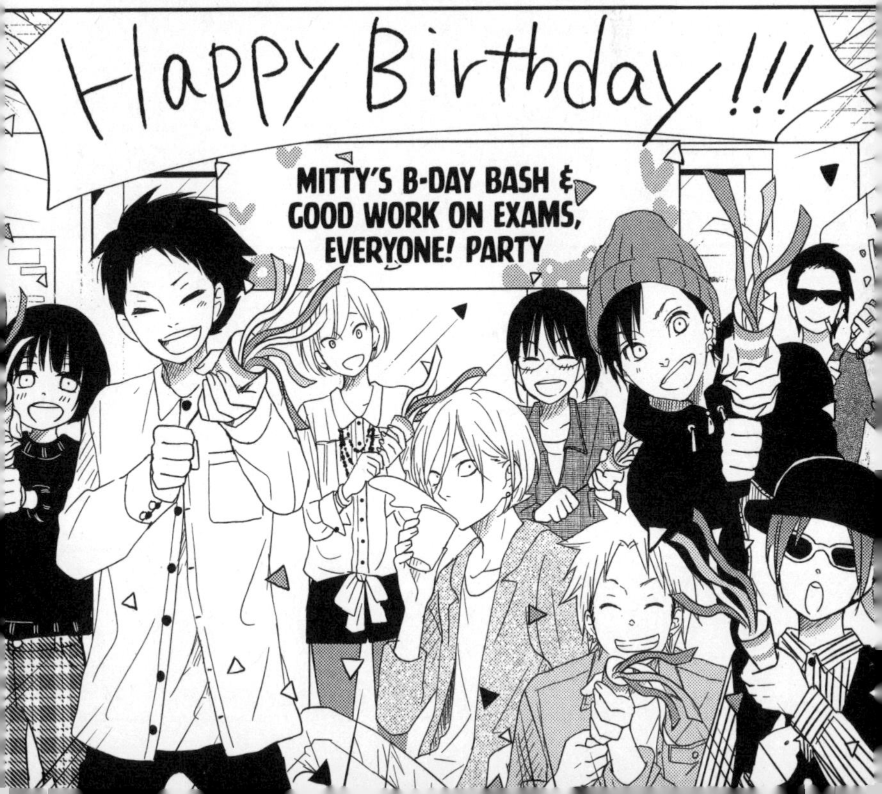
Happy Birthday!!!
MITTY'S B-DAY BASH & GOOD WORK ON EXAMS, EVERYONE! PARTY

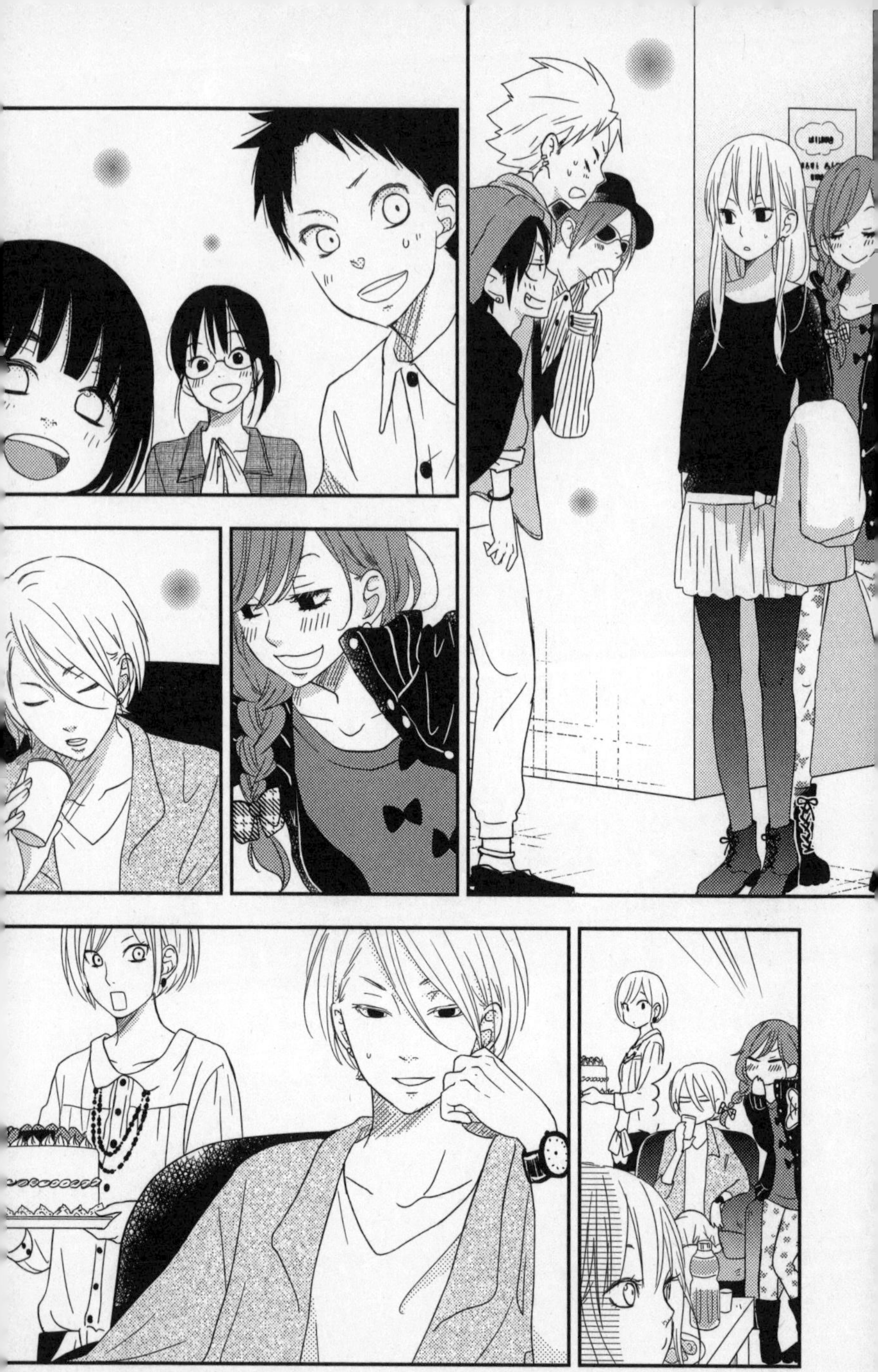

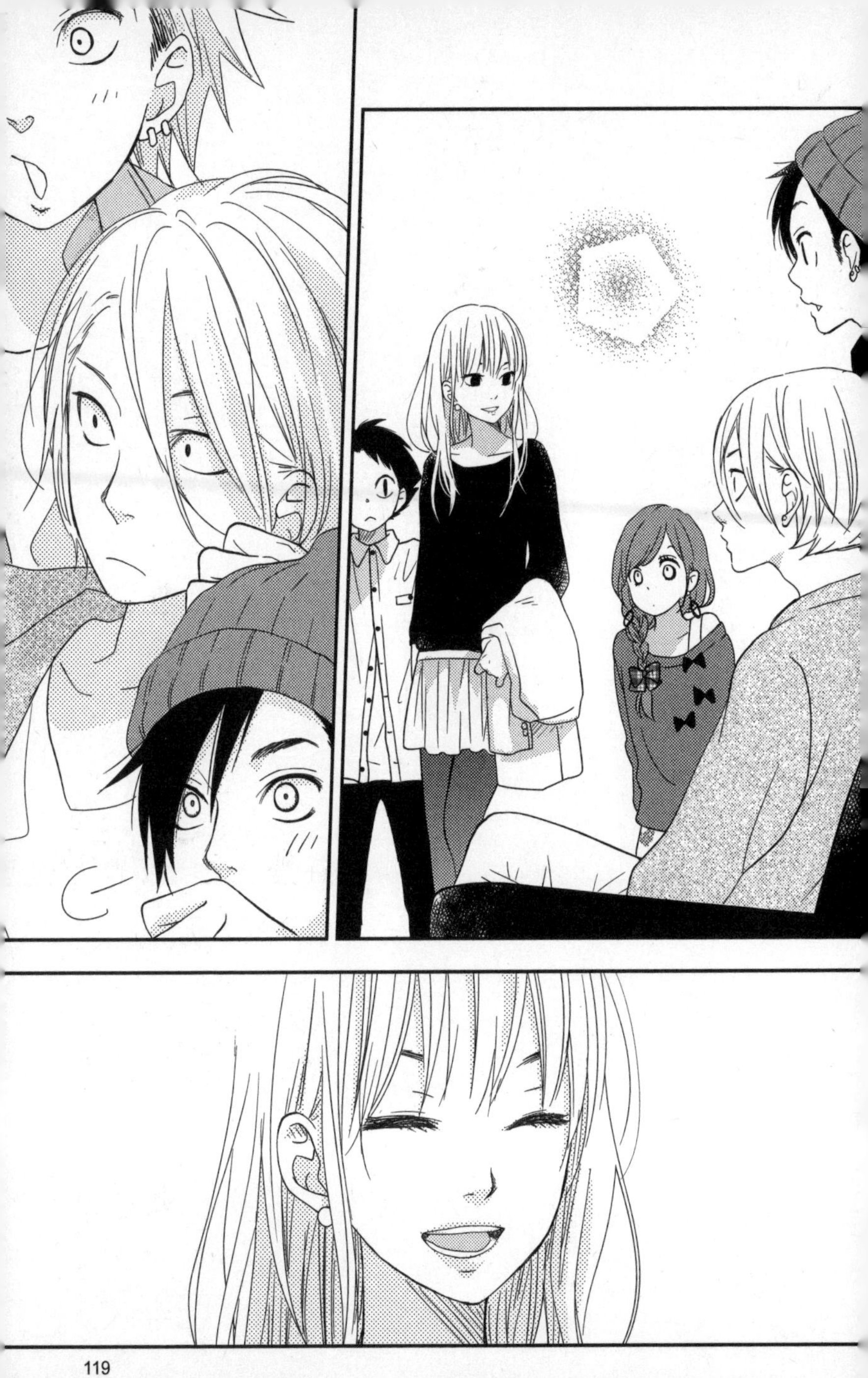

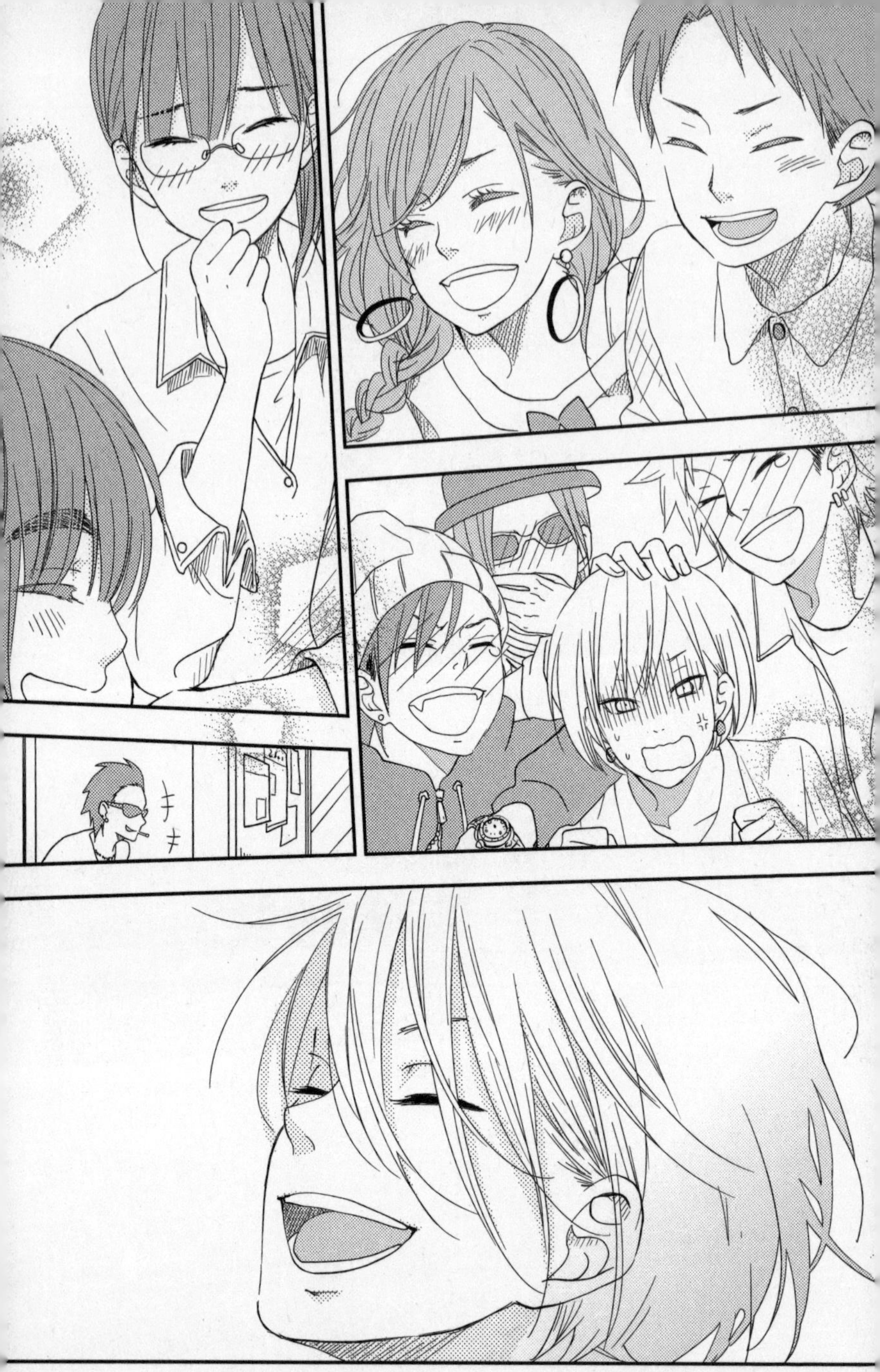
キ キ

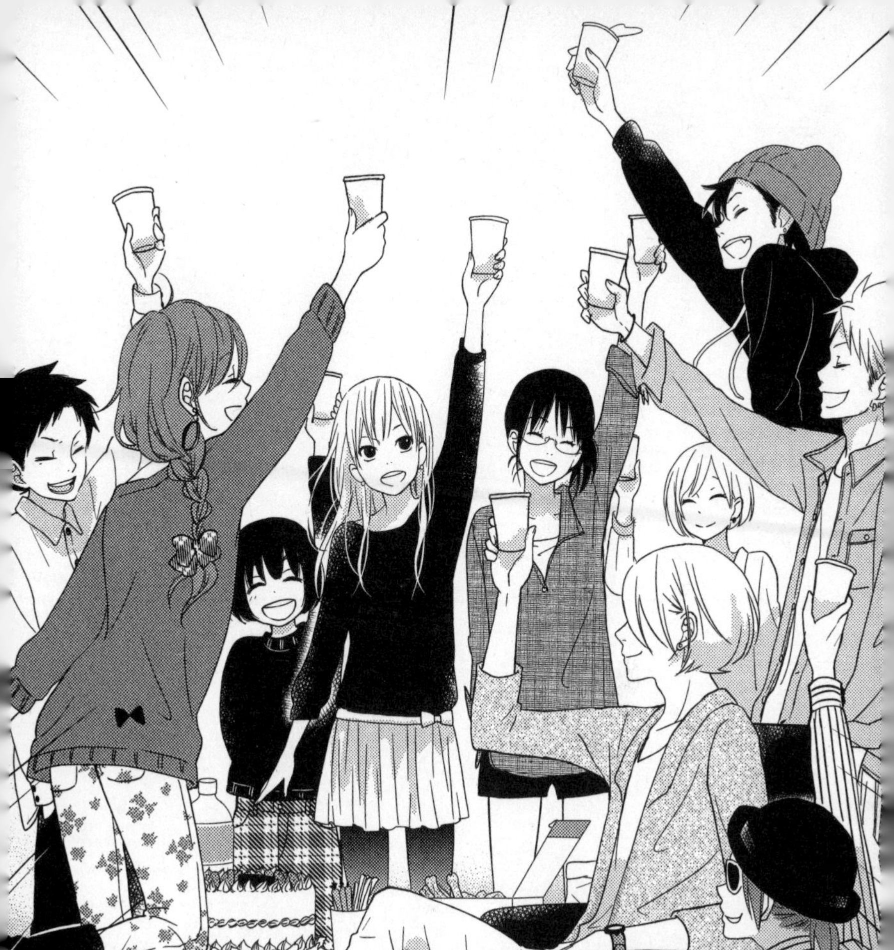
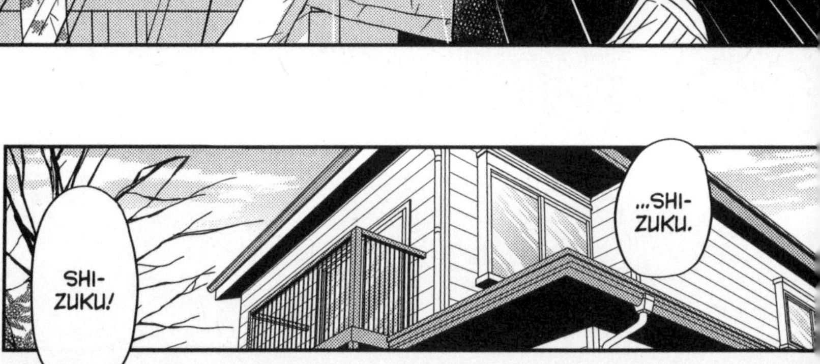
...SHI-ZUKU.
SHI-ZUKU!

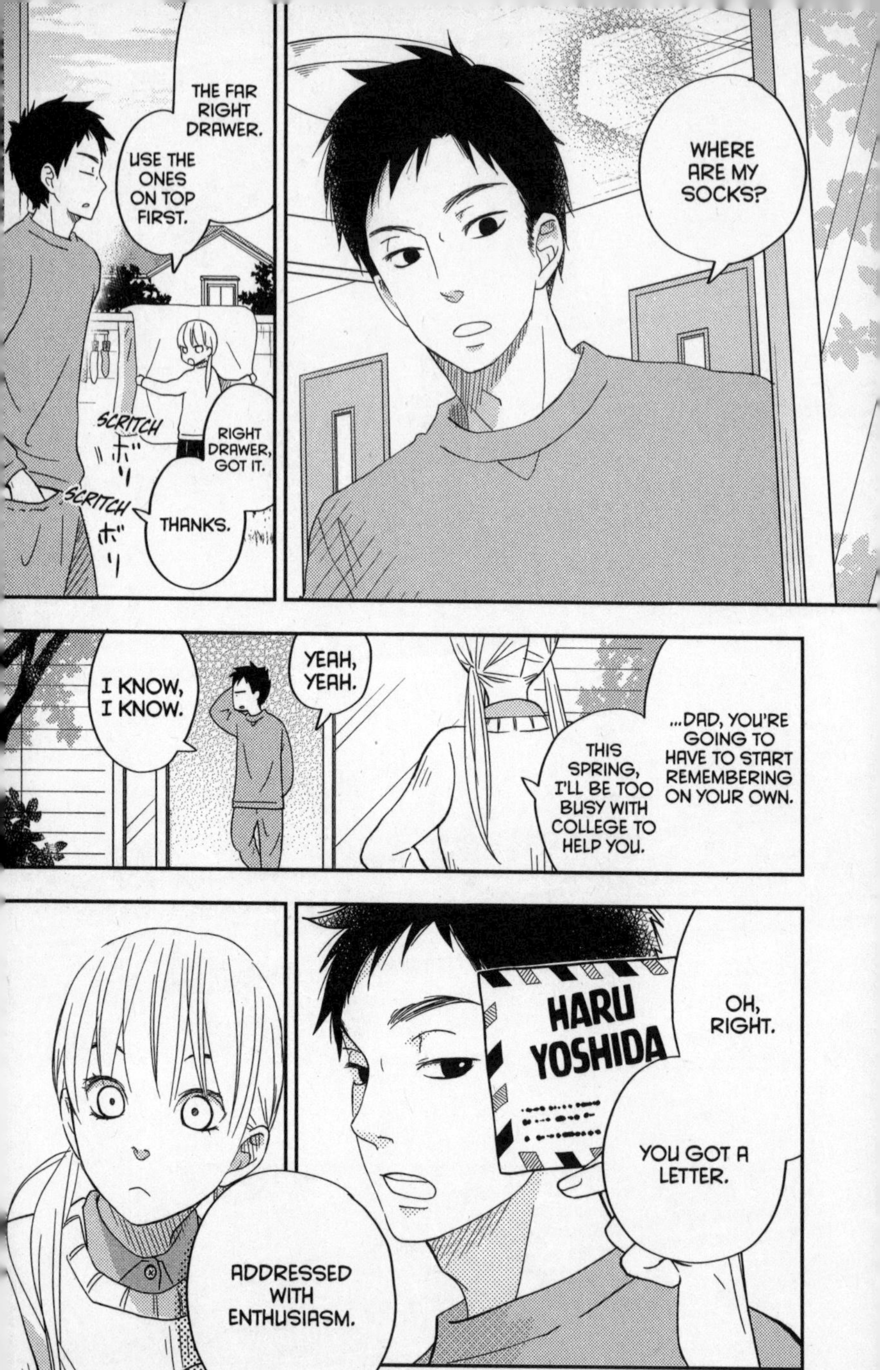

WHERE ARE MY SOCKS?
THE FAR RIGHT DRAWER.
USE THE ONES ON TOP FIRST.
RIGHT DRAWER, GOT IT.
SCRITCH
THANKS.
SCRITCH
...DAD, YOU'RE GOING TO HAVE TO START REMEMBERING ON YOUR OWN.
THIS SPRING, I'LL BE TOO BUSY WITH COLLEGE TO HELP YOU.
YEAH, YEAH.
I KNOW, I KNOW.
OH, RIGHT.
HARU YOSHIDA
YOU GOT A LETTER.
ADDRESSED WITH ENTHUSIASM.

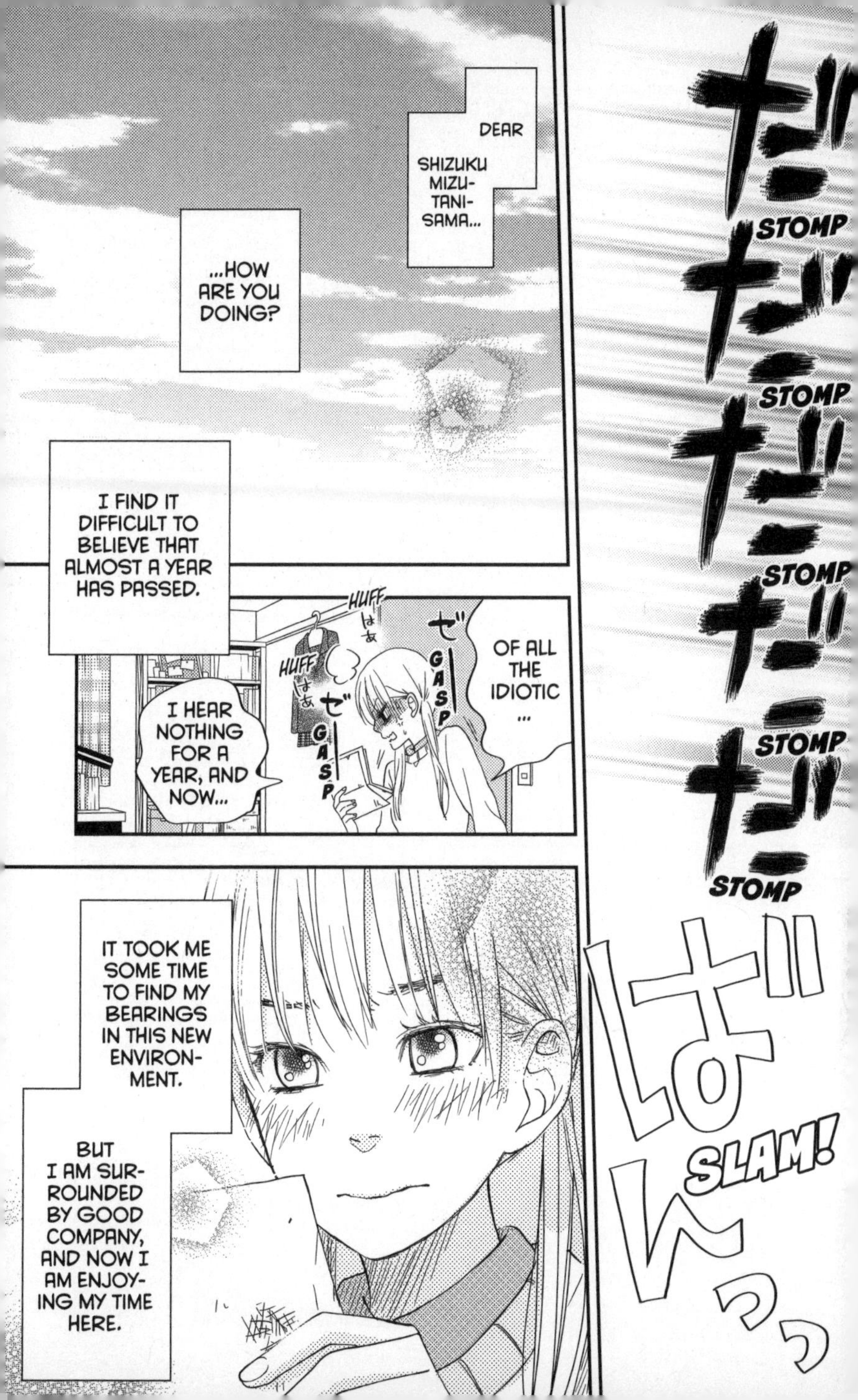

STOMP
STOMP
STOMP
STOMP
STOMP
ばんっっ
SLAM!
DEAR SHIZUKU MIZUTANI-SAMA...
...HOW ARE YOU DOING?
I FIND IT DIFFICULT TO BELIEVE THAT ALMOST A YEAR HAS PASSED.
OF ALL THE IDIOTIC ...
ぜ GASP
HUFF はぁ
ぜ GASP
HUFF はぁ
I HEAR NOTHING FOR A YEAR, AND NOW...
IT TOOK ME SOME TIME TO FIND MY BEARINGS IN THIS NEW ENVIRONMENT.
BUT I AM SURROUNDED BY GOOD COMPANY, AND NOW I AM ENJOYING MY TIME HERE.

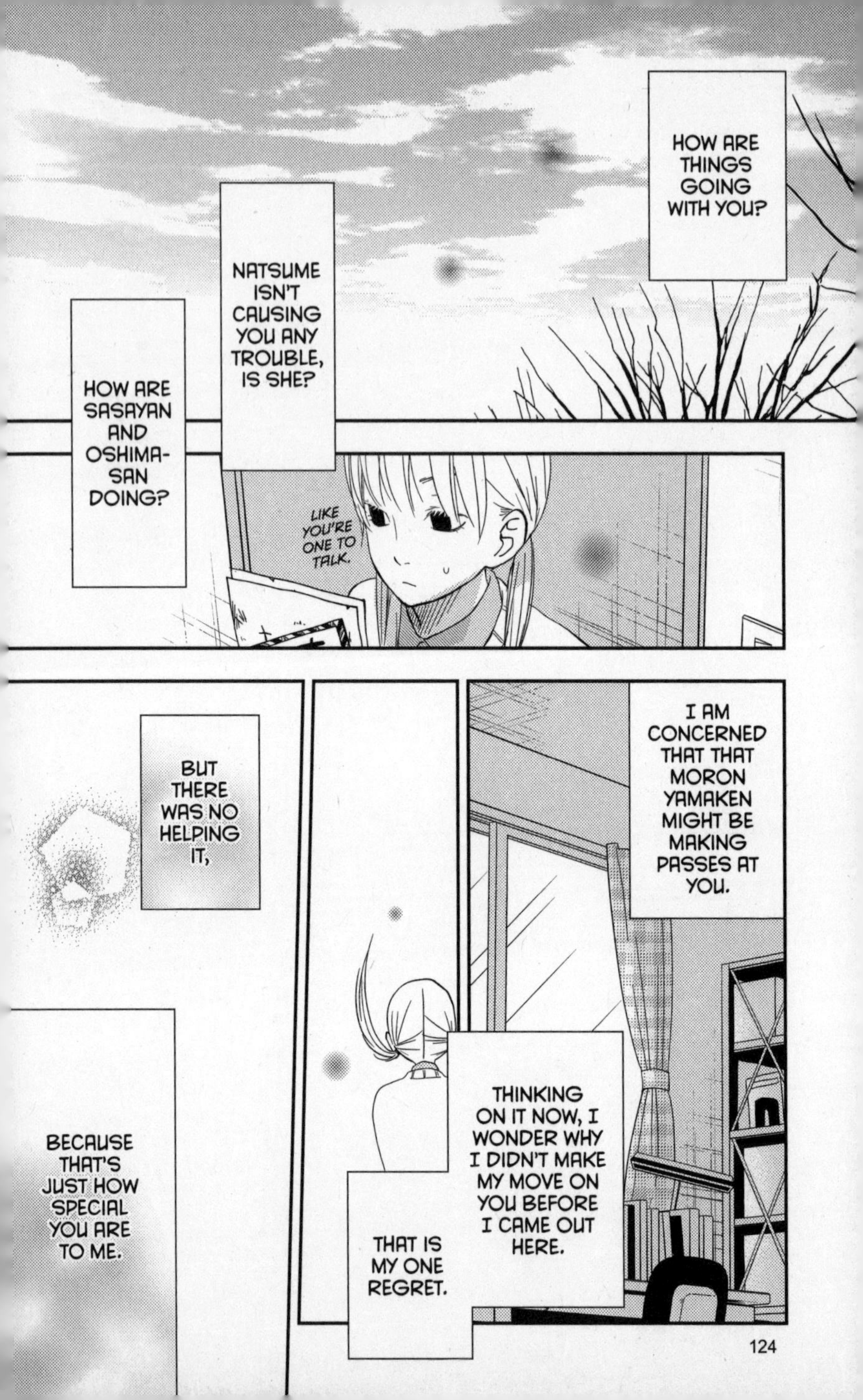
HOW ARE THINGS GOING WITH YOU?
NATSUME ISN'T CAUSING YOU ANY TROUBLE, IS SHE?
HOW ARE SASAYAN AND OSHIMA-SAN DOING?
LIKE YOU'RE ONE TO TALK.
I AM CONCERNED THAT THAT MORON YAMAKEN MIGHT BE MAKING PASSES AT YOU.
THINKING ON IT NOW, I WONDER WHY I DIDN'T MAKE MY MOVE ON YOU BEFORE I CAME OUT HERE.
THAT IS MY ONE REGRET.
BUT THERE WAS NO HELPING IT,
BECAUSE THAT'S JUST HOW SPECIAL YOU ARE TO ME.

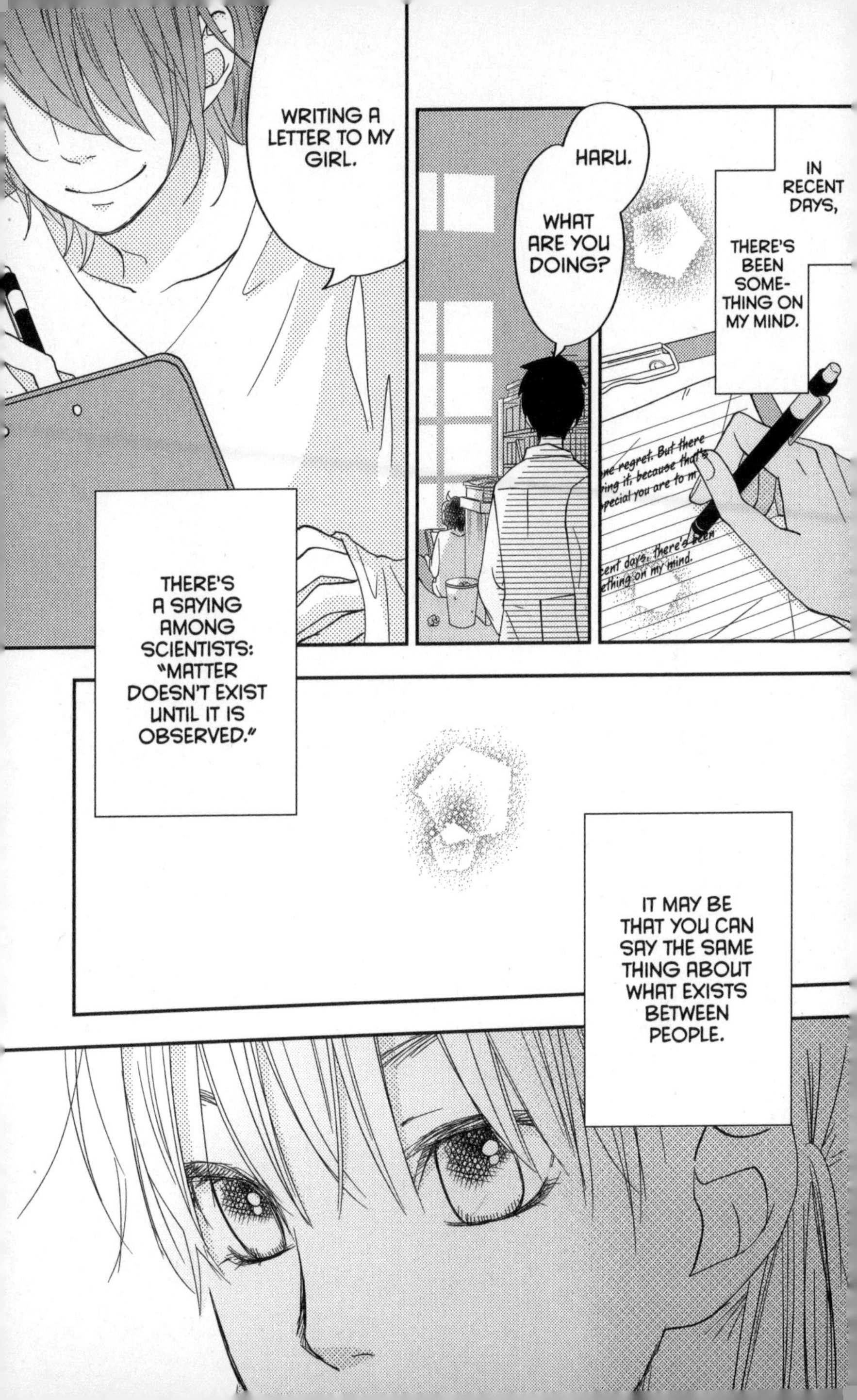
IN RECENT DAYS,
THERE'S BEEN SOME-THING ON MY MIND.
HARU.
WHAT ARE YOU DOING?
WRITING A LETTER TO MY GIRL.
THERE'S A SAYING AMONG SCIENTISTS: "MATTER DOESN'T EXIST UNTIL IT IS OBSERVED."
IT MAY BE THAT YOU CAN SAY THE SAME THING ABOUT WHAT EXISTS BETWEEN PEOPLE.

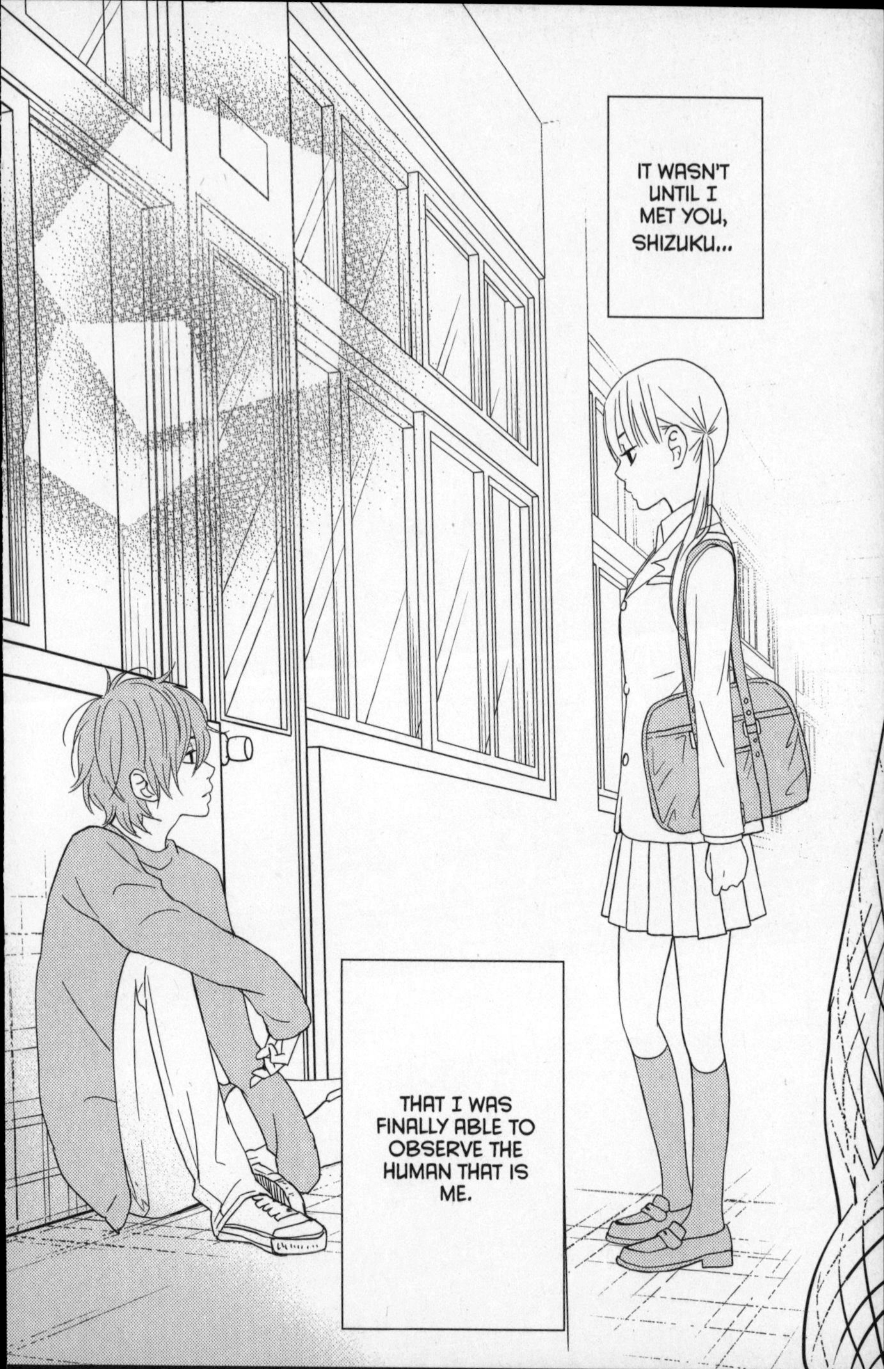
IT WASN'T UNTIL I MET YOU, SHIZUKU...
THAT I WAS FINALLY ABLE TO OBSERVE THE HUMAN THAT IS ME.

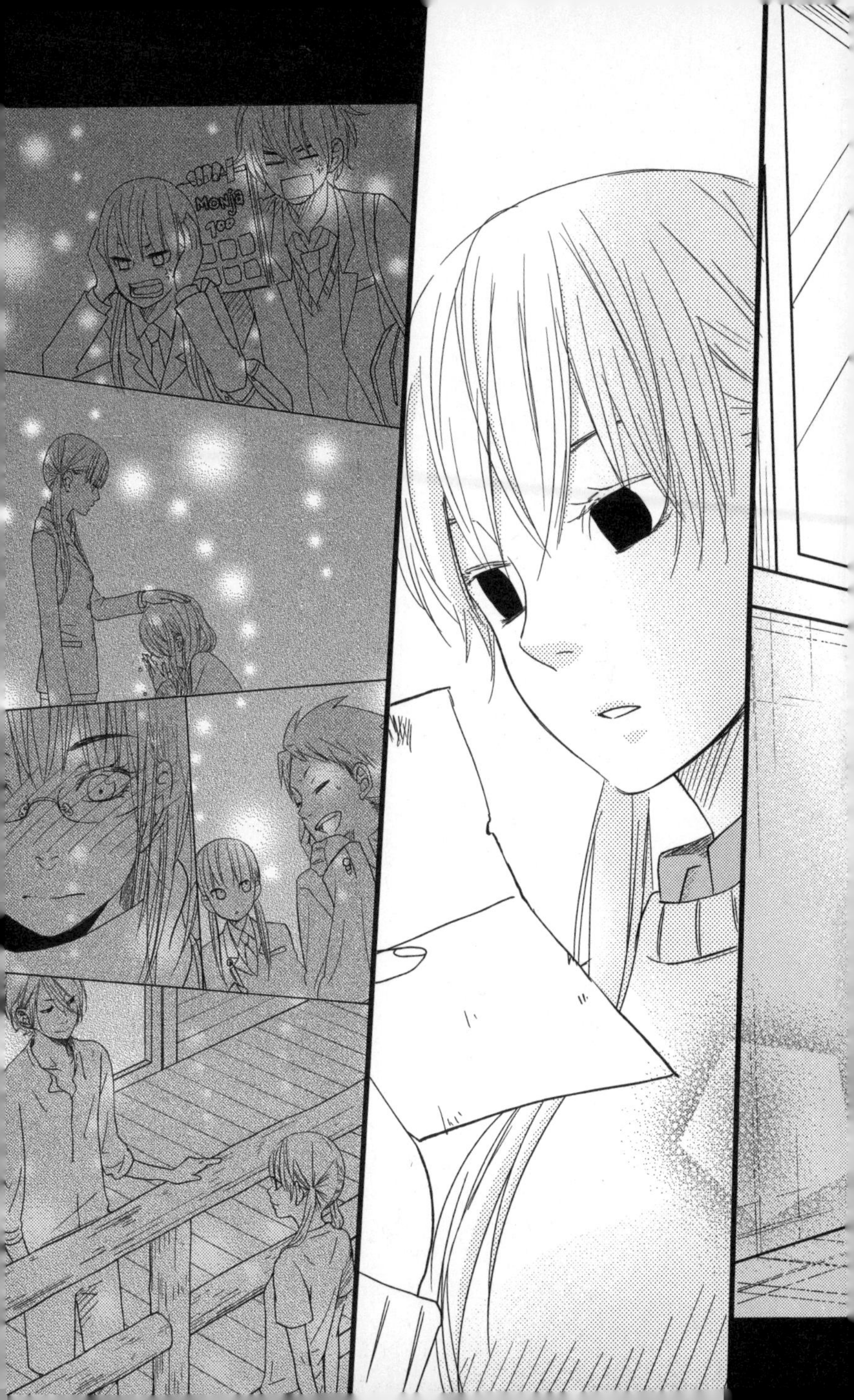
Monja
100

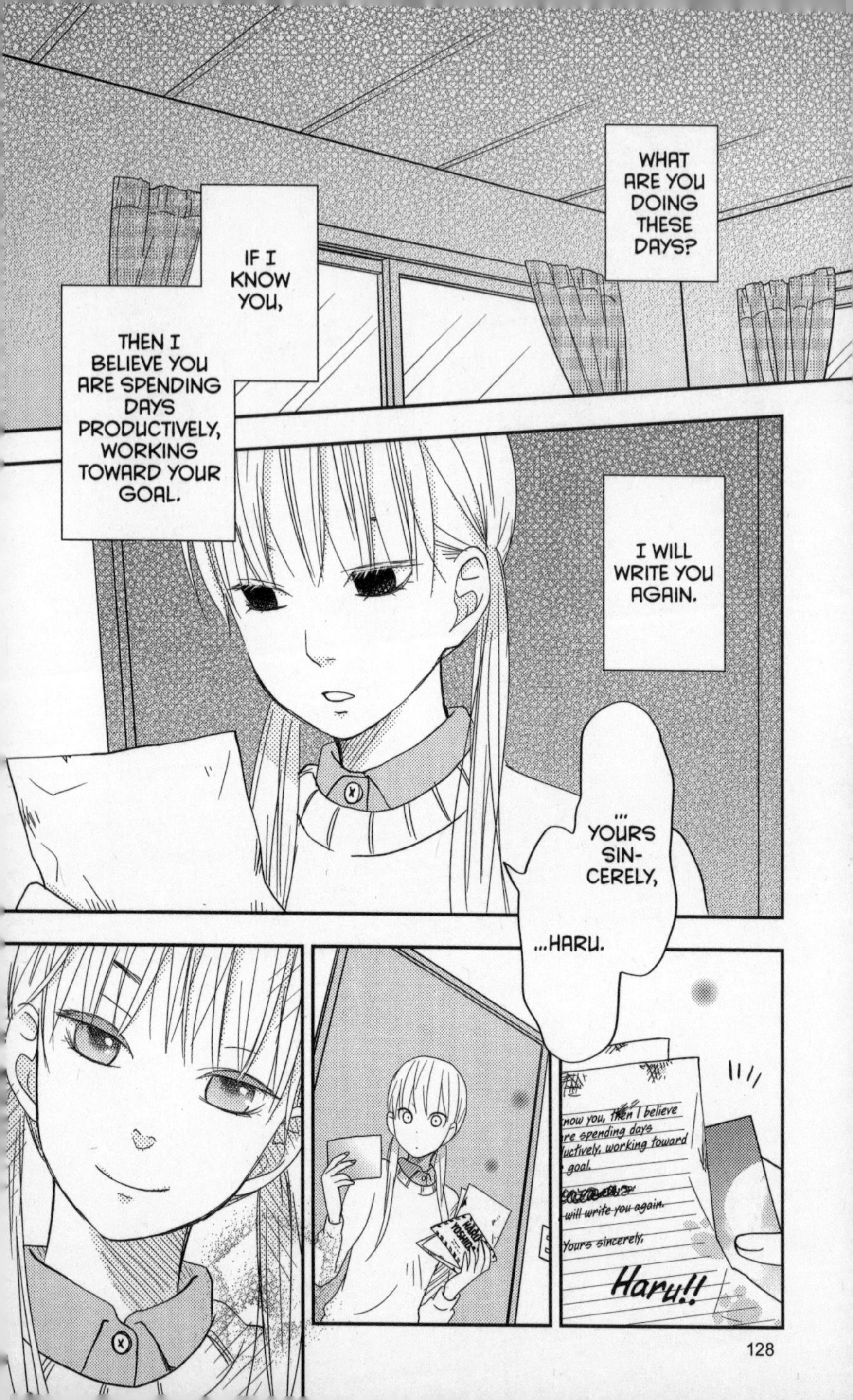
WHAT ARE YOU DOING THESE DAYS?
IF I KNOW YOU,
THEN I BELIEVE YOU ARE SPENDING DAYS PRODUCTIVELY, WORKING TOWARD YOUR GOAL.
I WILL WRITE YOU AGAIN.
... YOURS SIN-CERELY,
...HARU.
know you, then I believe
re spending days
ductively, working toward
goal.
will write you again.
Yours sincerely,
Haru!!

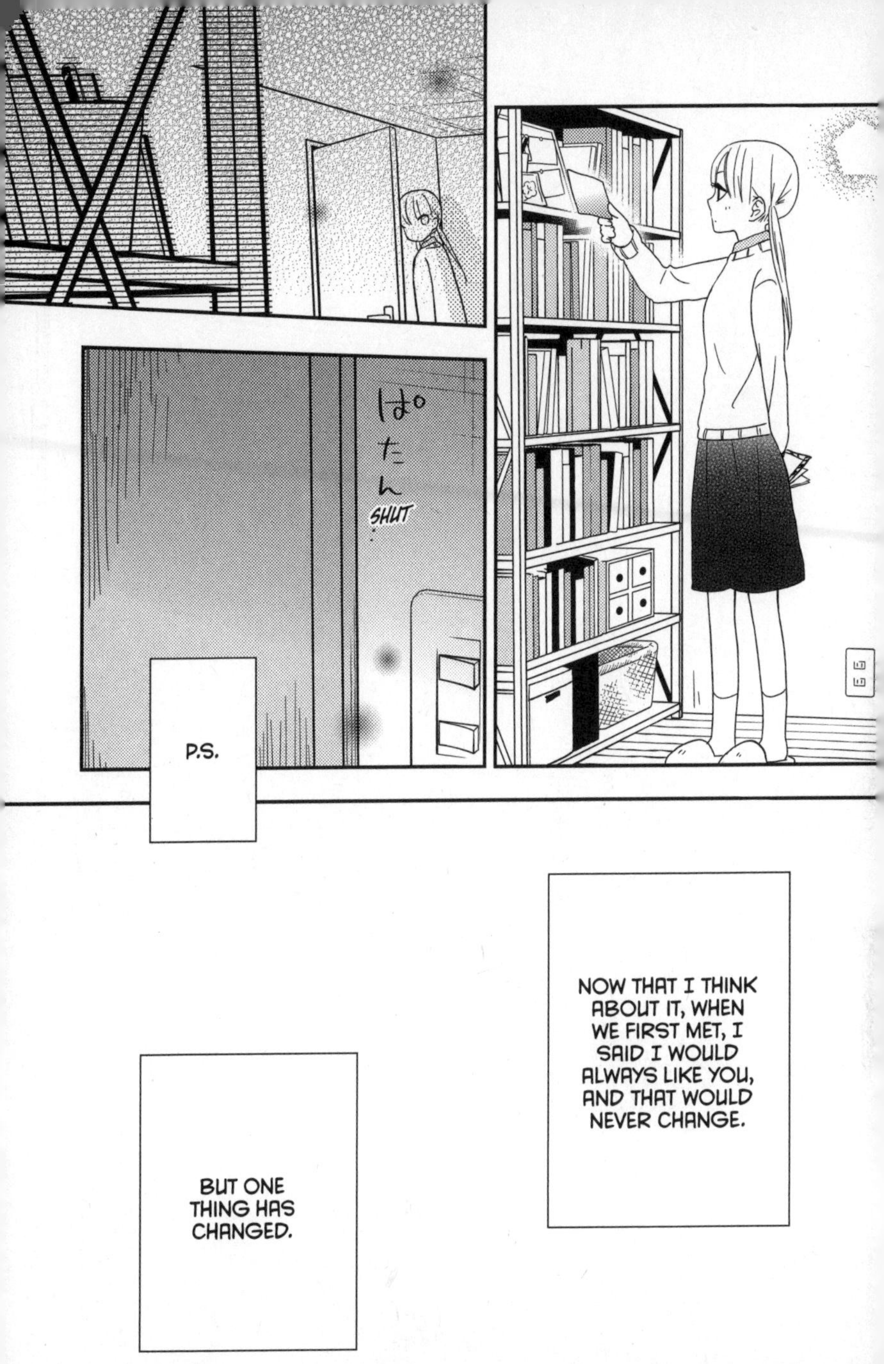
ぱたん
SHUT
P.S.
NOW THAT I THINK ABOUT IT, WHEN WE FIRST MET, I SAID I WOULD ALWAYS LIKE YOU, AND THAT WOULD NEVER CHANGE.
BUT ONE THING HAS CHANGED.

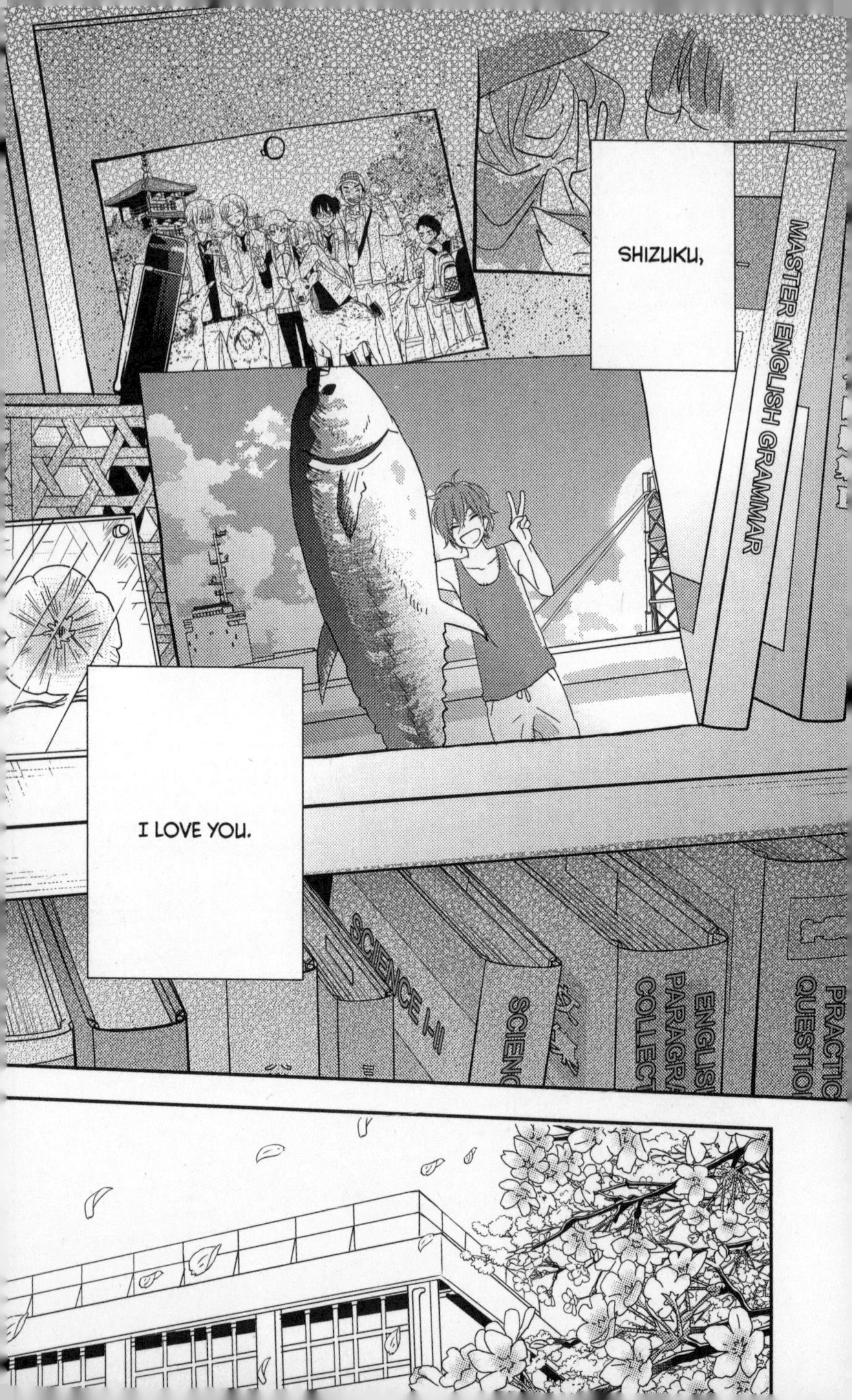
SHIZUKU,
MASTER ENGLISH GRAMMAR
I LOVE YOU.
SCIENCE I-II

THIRD-YEAR STUDENTS, PART 1

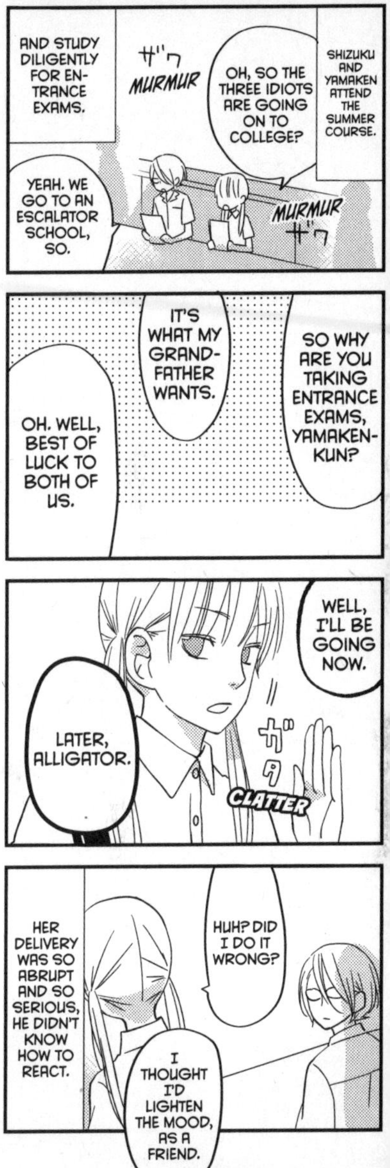
SHIZUKU AND YAMAKEN ATTEND THE SUMMER COURSE.
OH, SO THE THREE IDIOTS ARE GOING ON TO COLLEGE?
ザワ MURMUR
AND STUDY DILIGENTLY FOR ENTRANCE EXAMS.
YEAH. WE GO TO AN ESCALATOR SCHOOL, SO.
MURMUR ザワ
SO WHY ARE YOU TAKING ENTRANCE EXAMS, YAMAKEN-KUN?
IT'S WHAT MY GRANDFATHER WANTS.
OH. WELL, BEST OF LUCK TO BOTH OF US.
WELL, I'LL BE GOING NOW.
ガタ CLATTER
LATER, ALLIGATOR.
HUH? DID I DO IT WRONG?
I THOUGHT I'D LIGHTEN THE MOOD, AS A FRIEND.
HER DELIVERY WAS SO ABRUPT AND SO SERIOUS, HE DIDN'T KNOW HOW TO REACT.

THIRD-YEAR STUDENTS, PART 2

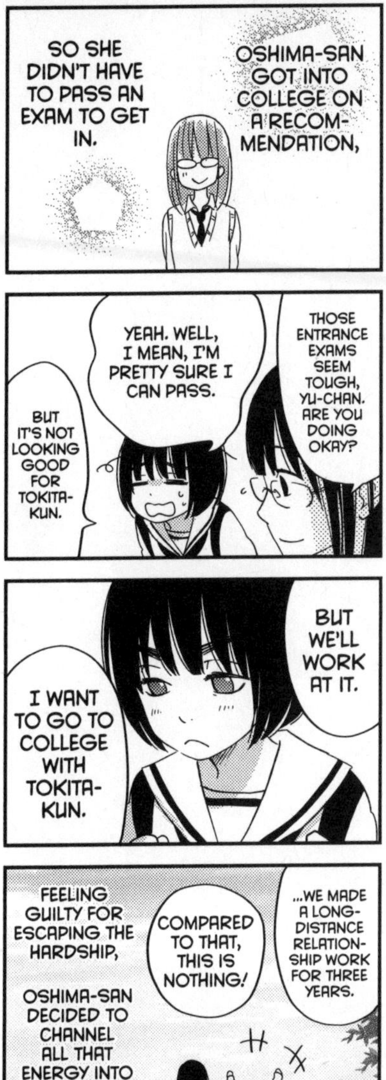
OSHIMA-SAN GOT INTO COLLEGE ON A RECOMMENDATION,
SO SHE DIDN'T HAVE TO PASS AN EXAM TO GET IN.
THOSE ENTRANCE EXAMS SEEM TOUGH, YU-CHAN. ARE YOU DOING OKAY?
YEAH. WELL, I MEAN, I'M PRETTY SURE I CAN PASS.
BUT IT'S NOT LOOKING GOOD FOR TOKITA-KUN.
BUT WE'LL WORK AT IT.
I WANT TO GO TO COLLEGE WITH TOKITA-KUN.
...WE MADE A LONG-DISTANCE RELATIONSHIP WORK FOR THREE YEARS.
COMPARED TO THAT, THIS IS NOTHING!
FEELING GUILTY FOR ESCAPING THE HARDSHIP,
OSHIMA-SAN DECIDED TO CHANNEL ALL THAT ENERGY INTO SUPPORTING HER FRIEND.

THIRD-YEAR STUDENTS, PART 3

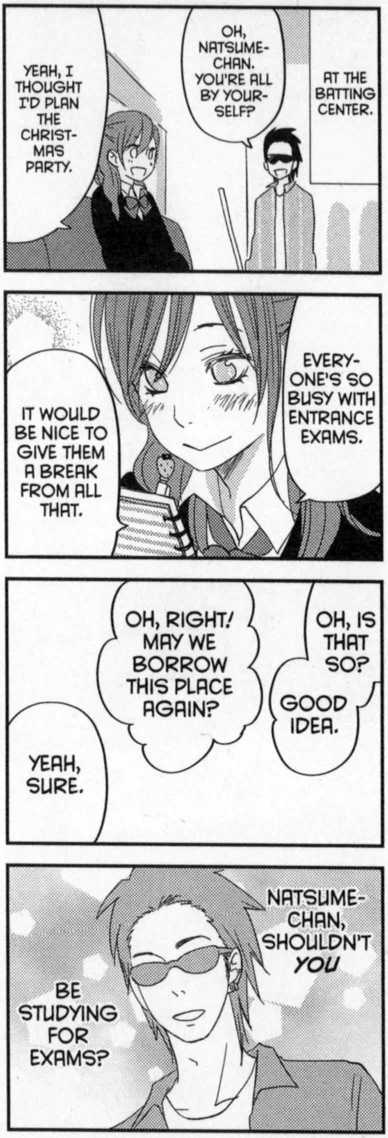
AT THE BATTING CENTER.
OH, NATSUME-CHAN. YOU'RE ALL BY YOURSELF?
YEAH, I THOUGHT I'D PLAN THE CHRISTMAS PARTY.
EVERYONE'S SO BUSY WITH ENTRANCE EXAMS.
IT WOULD BE NICE TO GIVE THEM A BREAK FROM ALL THAT.
OH, IS THAT SO?
GOOD IDEA.
OH, RIGHT! MAY WE BORROW THIS PLACE AGAIN?
YEAH, SURE.
NATSUME-CHAN, SHOULDN'T *YOU*
BE STUDYING FOR EXAMS?

THIRD-YEAR STUDENTS, PART 4

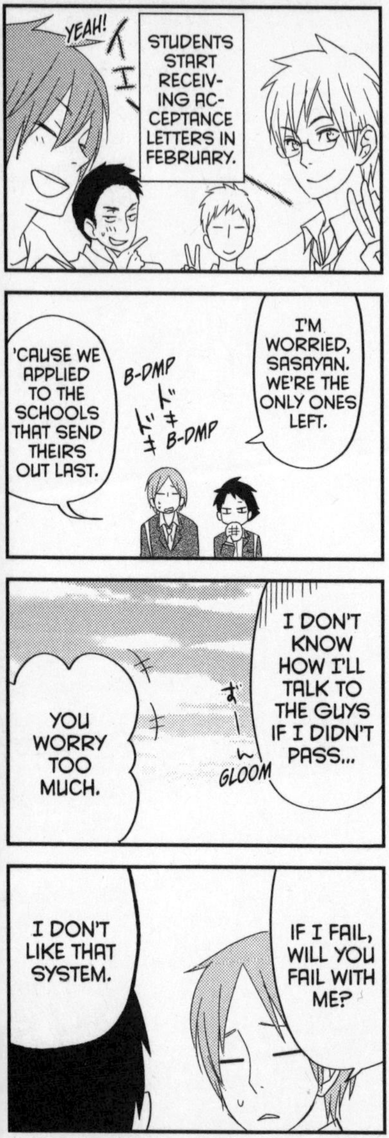
STUDENTS START RECEIVING ACCEPTANCE LETTERS IN FEBRUARY.
イエー
YEAH!
I'M WORRIED, SASAYAN. WE'RE THE ONLY ONES LEFT.
ドキ ドキ
B-DMP
B-DMP
'CAUSE WE APPLIED TO THE SCHOOLS THAT SEND THEIRS OUT LAST.
I DON'T KNOW HOW I'LL TALK TO THE GUYS IF I DIDN'T PASS...
ずーん
GLOOM
YOU WORRY TOO MUCH.
IF I FAIL, WILL YOU FAIL WITH ME?
I DON'T LIKE THAT SYSTEM.

THIRD-YEAR STUDENTS, PART 5

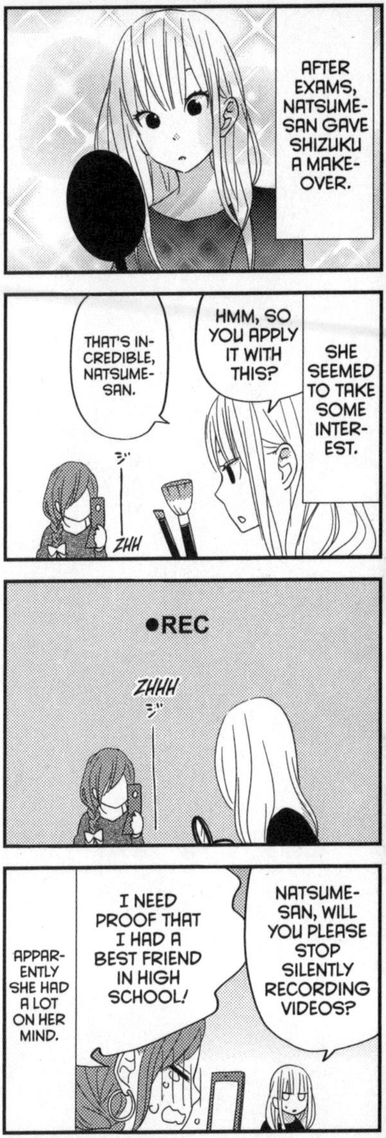
AFTER EXAMS, NATSUME-SAN GAVE SHIZUKU A MAKE-OVER.
SHE SEEMED TO TAKE SOME INTER-EST.
HMM, SO YOU APPLY IT WITH THIS?
THAT'S IN-CREDIBLE, NATSUME-SAN.
ジ
ZHH
●REC
ZHHH
ジ
NATSUME-SAN, WILL YOU PLEASE STOP SILENTLY RECORDING VIDEOS?
I NEED PROOF THAT I HAD A BEST FRIEND IN HIGH SCHOOL!
APPAR-ENTLY SHE HAD A LOT ON HER MIND.

SECOND-YEAR STUDENT

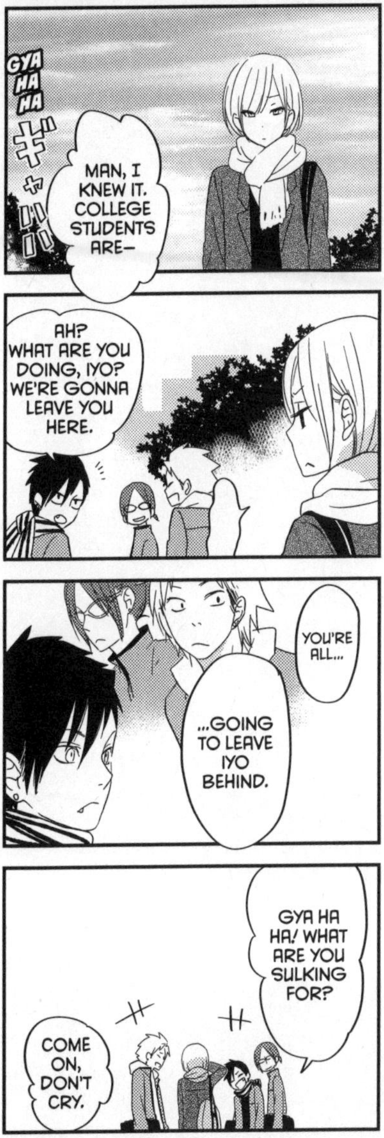
GYA HA HA
MAN, I KNEW IT. COLLEGE STUDENTS ARE—
AH? WHAT ARE YOU DOING, IYO? WE'RE GONNA LEAVE YOU HERE.
YOU'RE ALL...
...GOING TO LEAVE IYO BEHIND.
GYA HA HA! WHAT ARE YOU SULKING FOR?
COME ON, DON'T CRY.

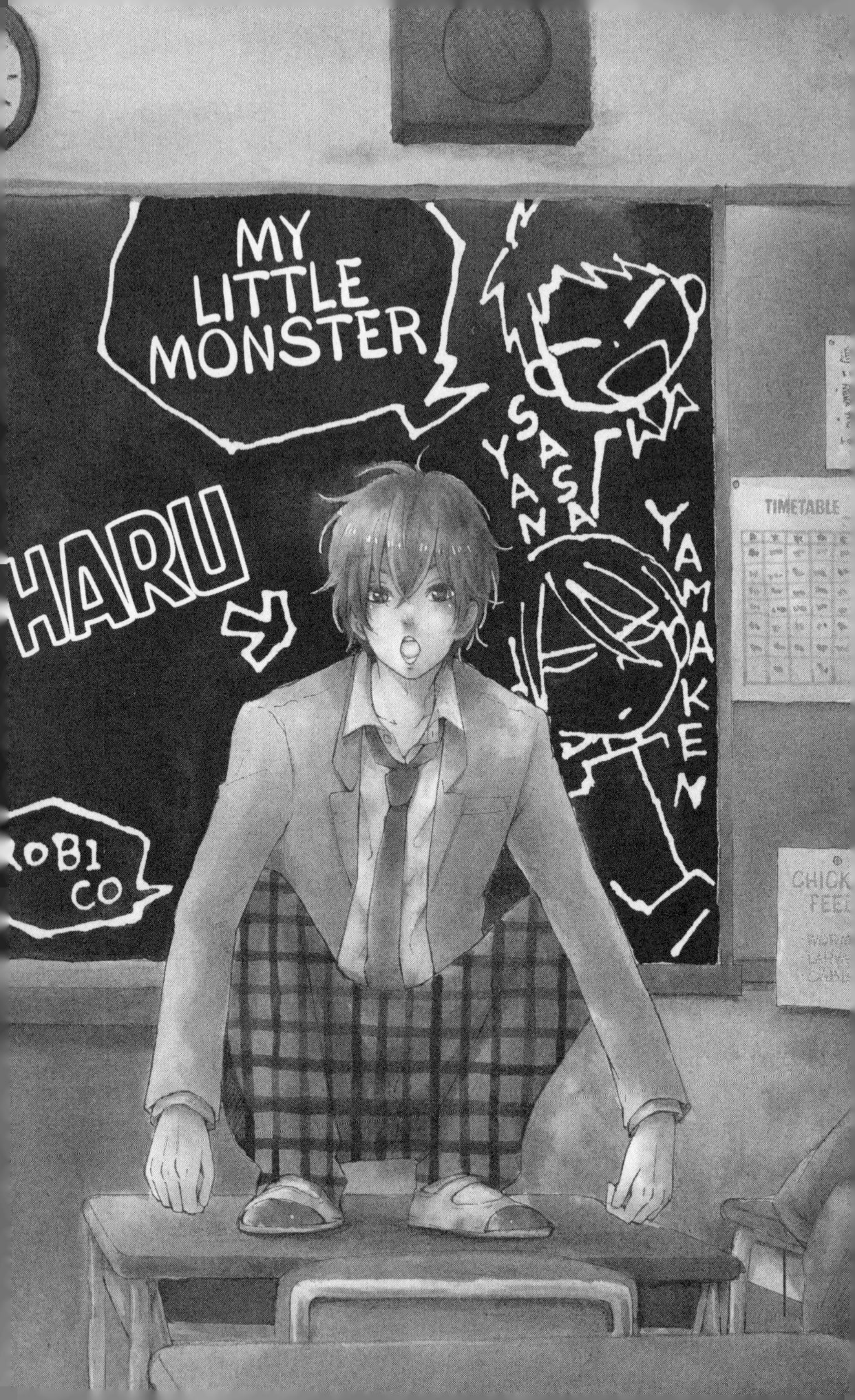

MY LITTLE MONSTER
HARU
ROBICO
SASAYAN
YAMAKEN
TIMETABLE

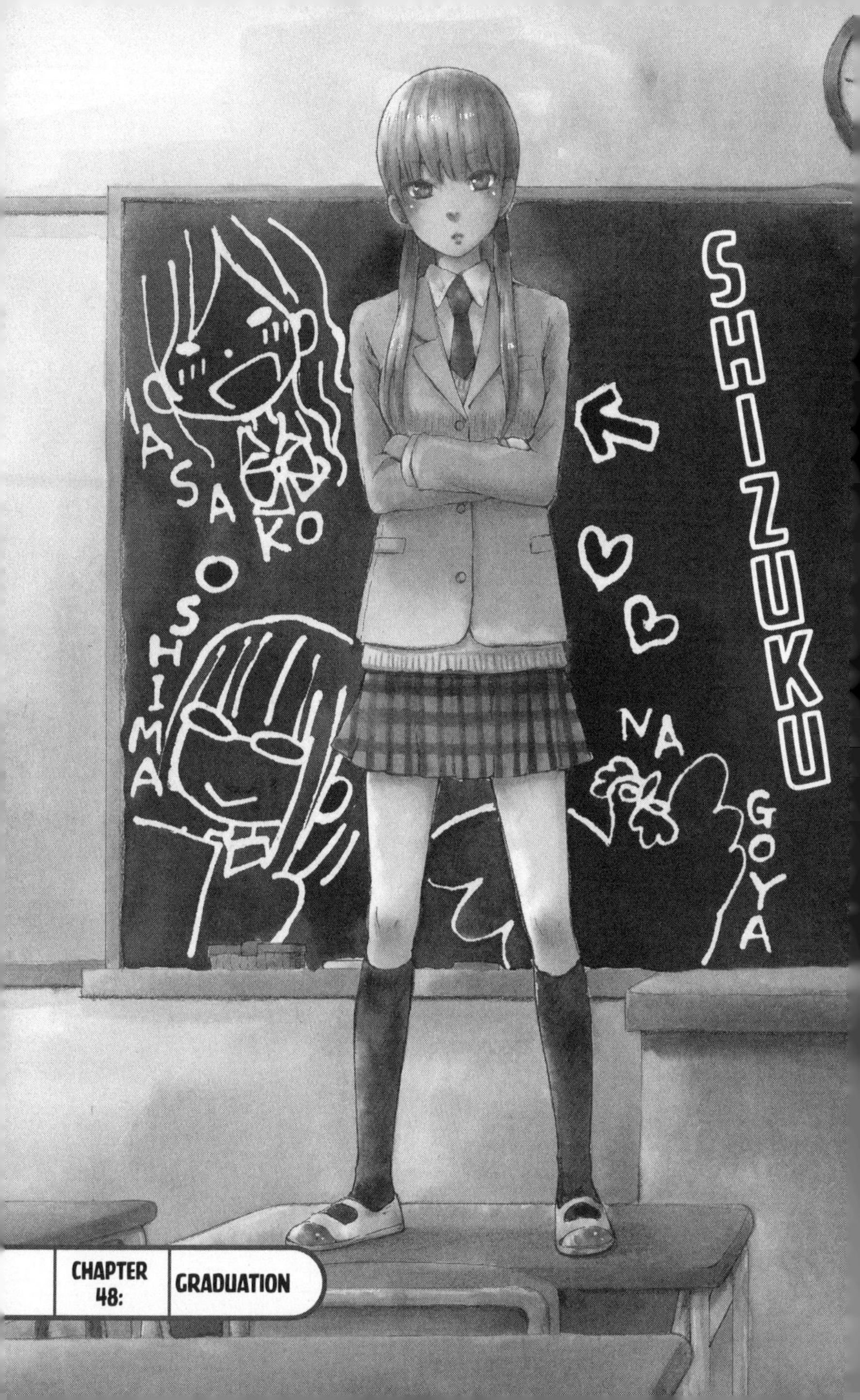
SHIZUKU
ASAKO
OSHIMA
NAGOYA

CHAPTER 48: GRADUATION

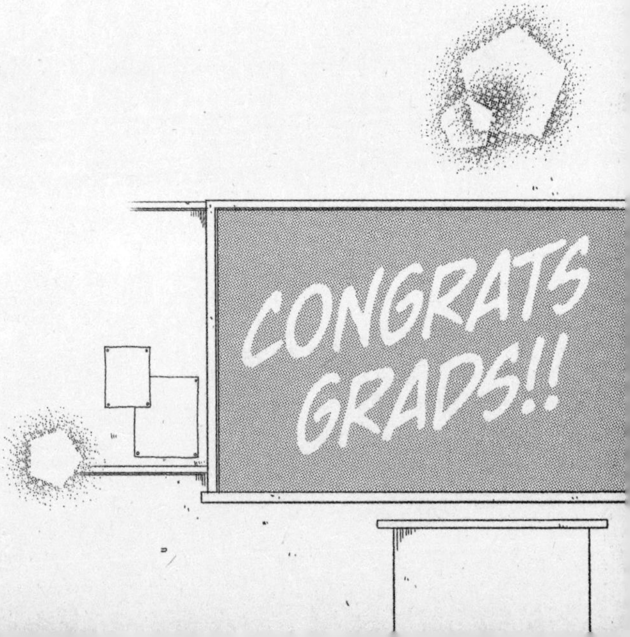
CONGRATS
GRADS!!

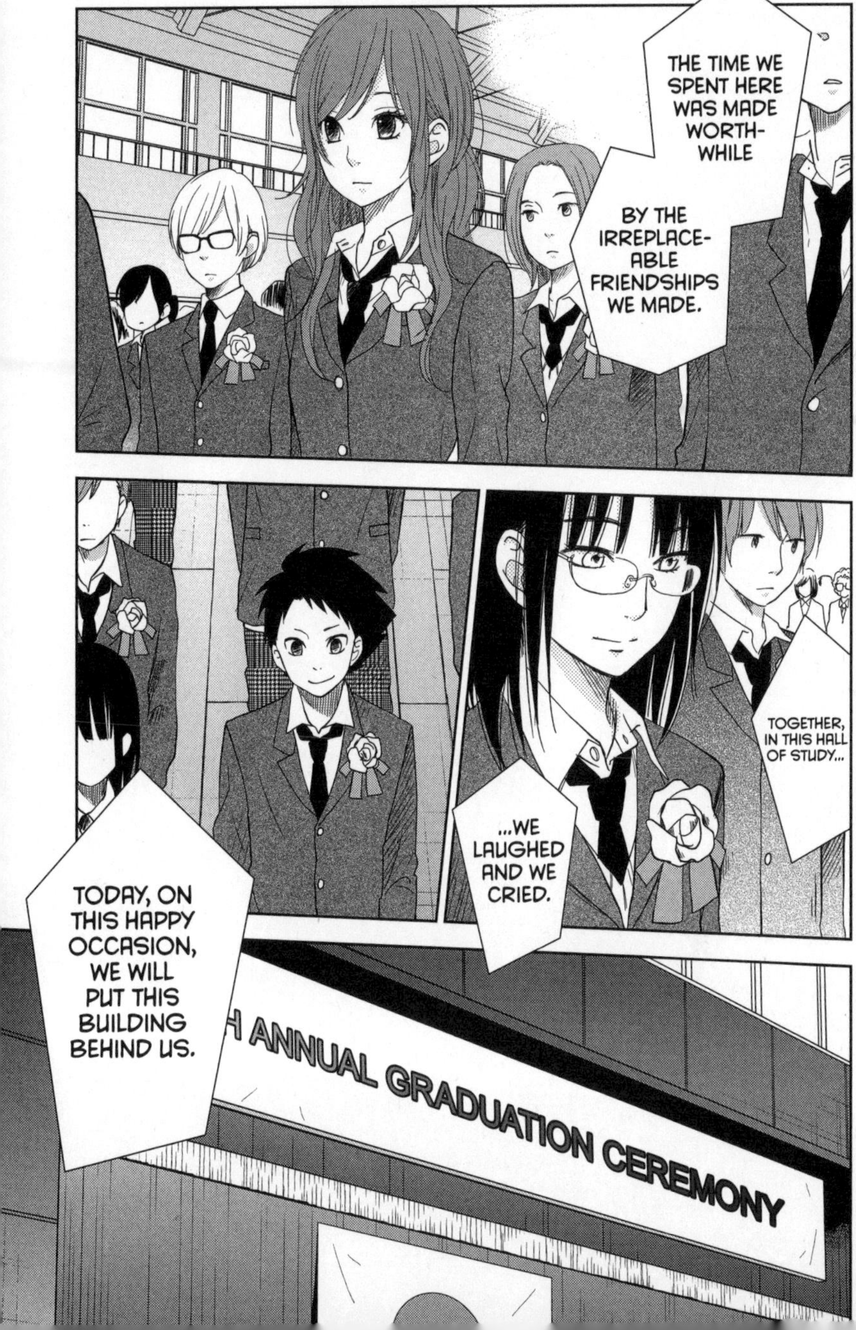

THE TIME WE SPENT HERE WAS MADE WORTHWHILE
BY THE IRREPLACEABLE FRIENDSHIPS WE MADE.
TOGETHER, IN THIS HALL OF STUDY...
...WE LAUGHED AND WE CRIED.
TODAY, ON THIS HAPPY OCCASION, WE WILL PUT THIS BUILDING BEHIND US.
H ANNUAL GRADUATION CEREMONY

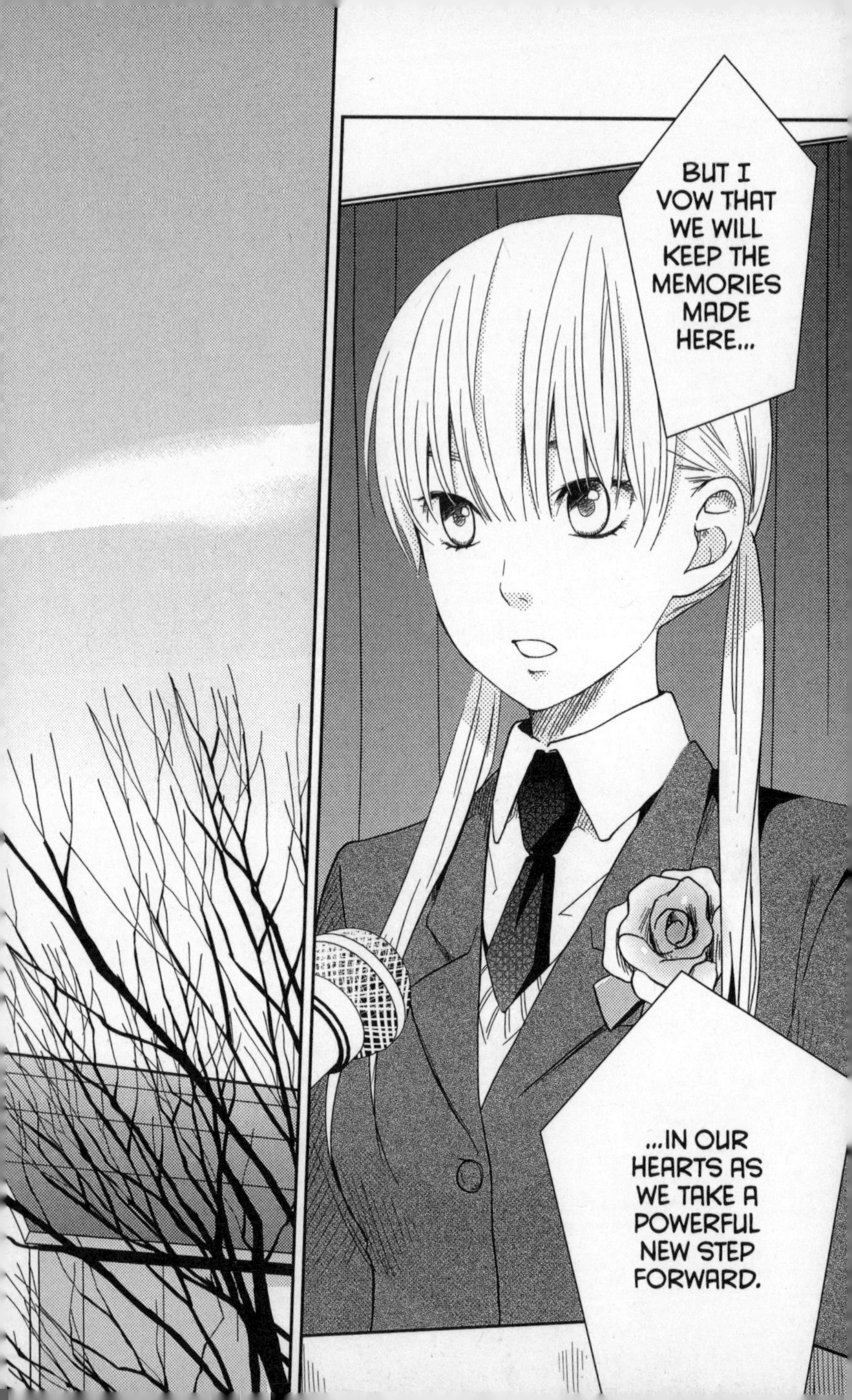
BUT I VOW THAT WE WILL KEEP THE MEMORIES MADE HERE...
...IN OUR HEARTS AS WE TAKE A POWERFUL NEW STEP FORWARD.

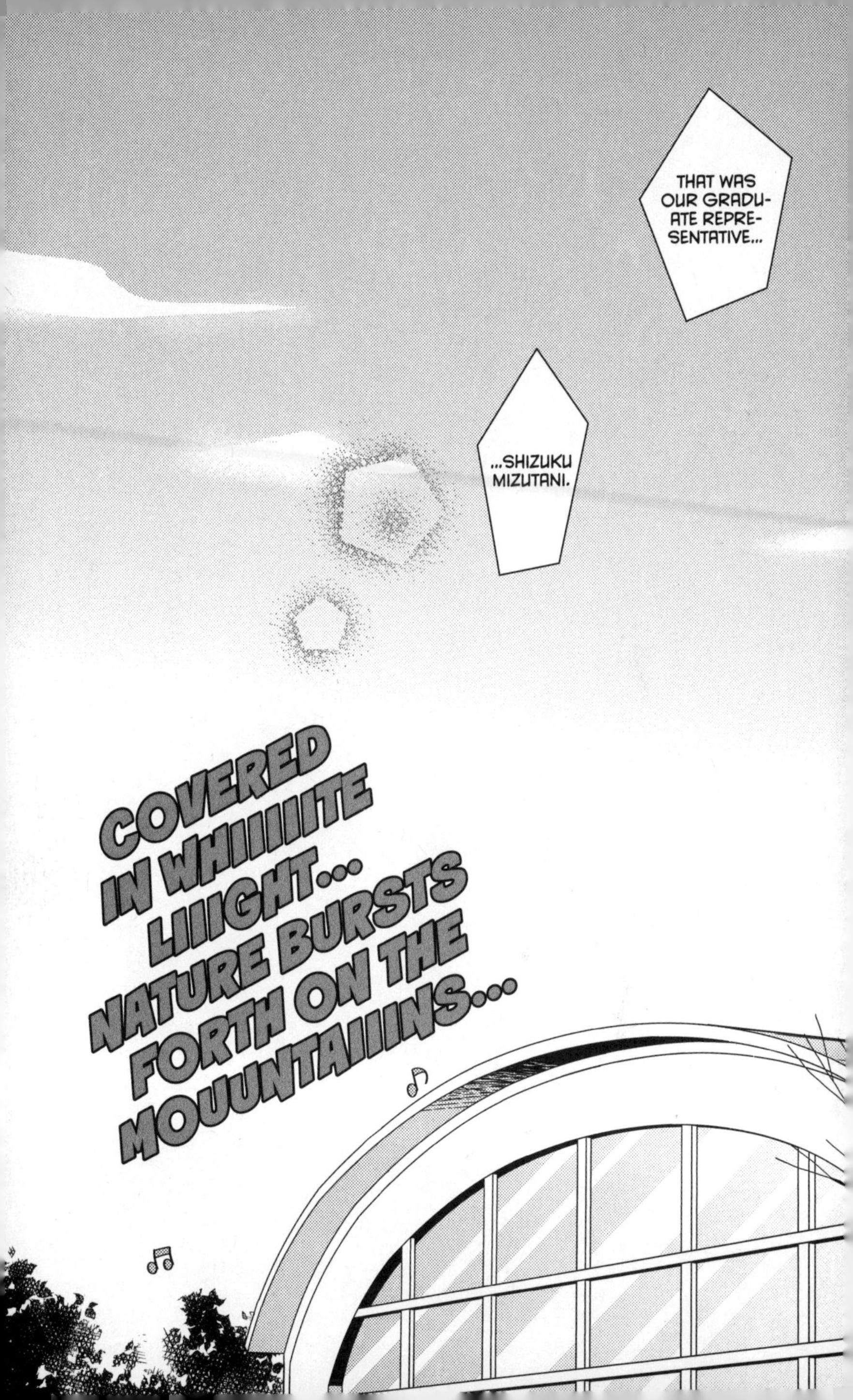
THAT WAS OUR GRADUATE REPRESENTATIVE...
...SHIZUKU MIZUTANI.
COVERED IN WHIIIIIITE LIIIGHT... NATURE BURSTS FORTH ON THE MOUUNTAIIINS...

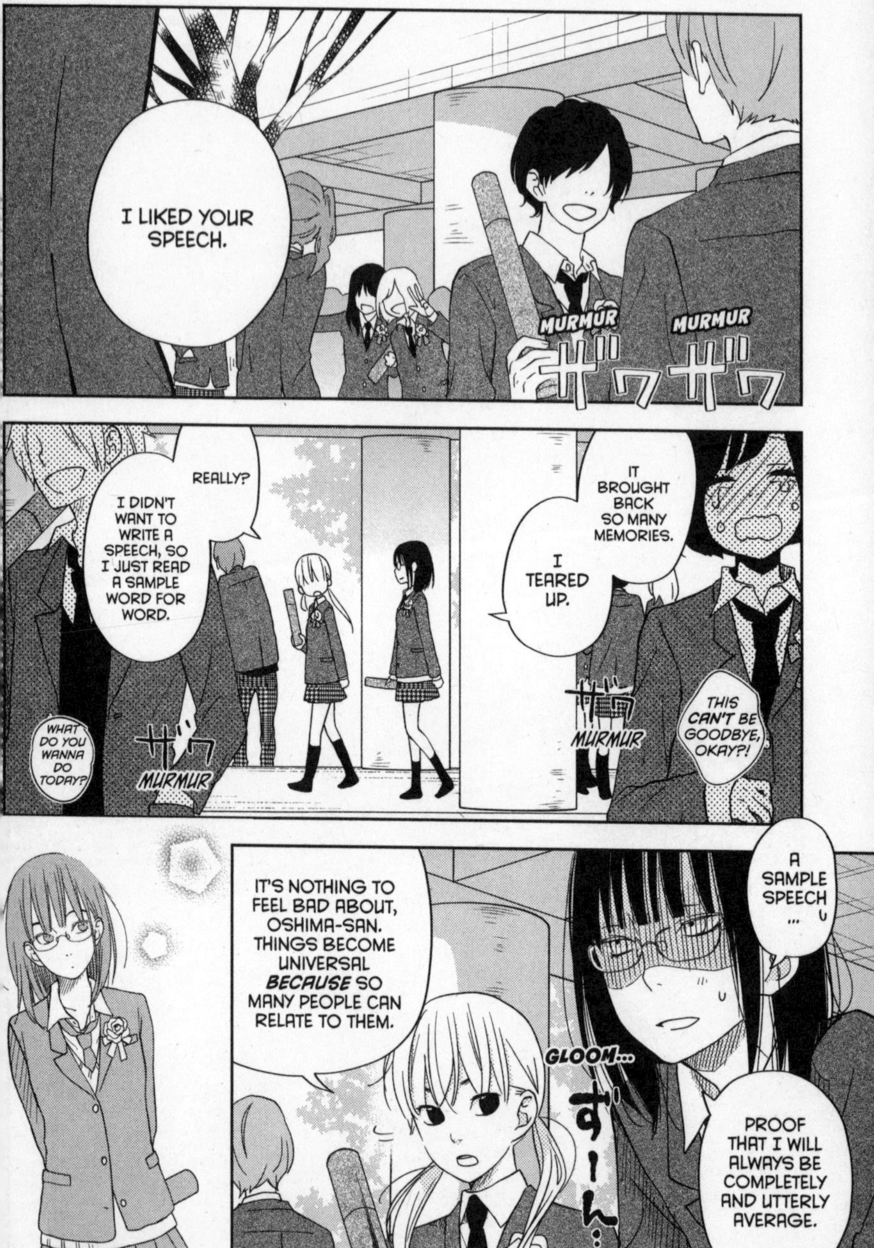
I LIKED YOUR SPEECH.
MURMUR
ザワ
MURMUR
ザワ
IT BROUGHT BACK SO MANY MEMORIES.
I TEARED UP.
THIS CAN'T BE GOODBYE, OKAY?!
ザワ
MURMUR
REALLY?
I DIDN'T WANT TO WRITE A SPEECH, SO I JUST READ A SAMPLE WORD FOR WORD.
ザワ
MURMUR
WHAT DO YOU WANNA DO TODAY?
A SAMPLE SPEECH...
PROOF THAT I WILL ALWAYS BE COMPLETELY AND UTTERLY AVERAGE.
GLOOM...
ずーん...
IT'S NOTHING TO FEEL BAD ABOUT, OSHIMA-SAN. THINGS BECOME UNIVERSAL BECAUSE SO MANY PEOPLE CAN RELATE TO THEM.

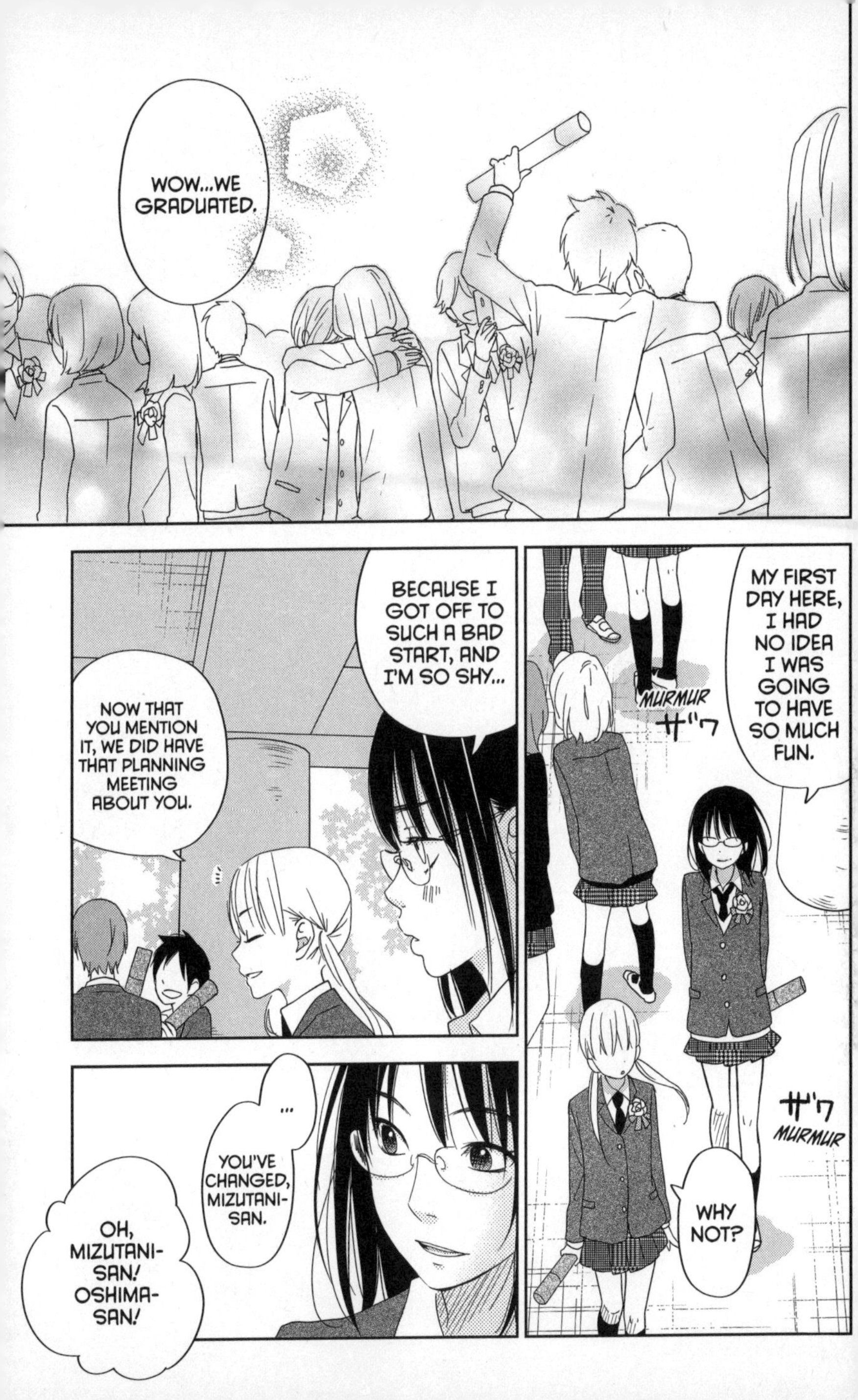
WOW...WE GRADUATED.
MY FIRST DAY HERE, I HAD NO IDEA I WAS GOING TO HAVE SO MUCH FUN.
MURMUR ザワ
ザワ MURMUR
WHY NOT?
BECAUSE I GOT OFF TO SUCH A BAD START, AND I'M SO SHY...
NOW THAT YOU MENTION IT, WE DID HAVE THAT PLANNING MEETING ABOUT YOU.
...
...
YOU'VE CHANGED, MIZUTANI-SAN.
OH, MIZUTANI-SAN! OSHIMA-SAN!

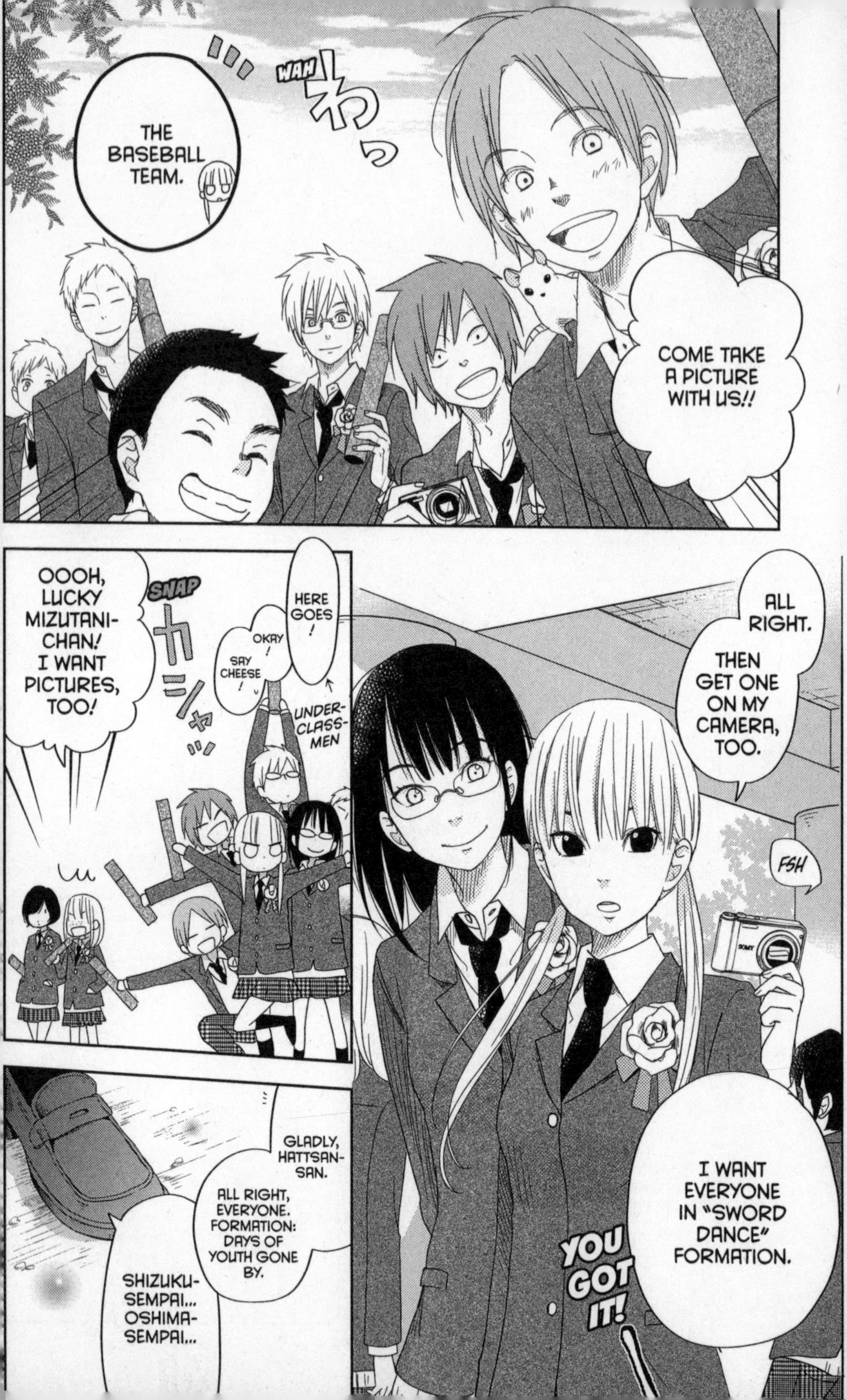
WAH
わっ
COME TAKE A PICTURE WITH US!!
THE BASEBALL TEAM.
ALL RIGHT.
THEN GET ONE ON MY CAMERA, TOO.
FSH
I WANT EVERYONE IN "SWORD DANCE" FORMATION.
YOU GOT IT!
HERE GOES!
OKAY!
SAY CHEESE!
UNDER-CLASS-MEN
SNAP
カシャッ
OOOH, LUCKY MIZUTANI-CHAN! I WANT PICTURES, TOO!
GLADLY, HATTSAN-SAN.
ALL RIGHT, EVERYONE. FORMATION: DAYS OF YOUTH GONE BY.
SHIZUKU-SEMPAI... OSHIMA-SEMPAI...

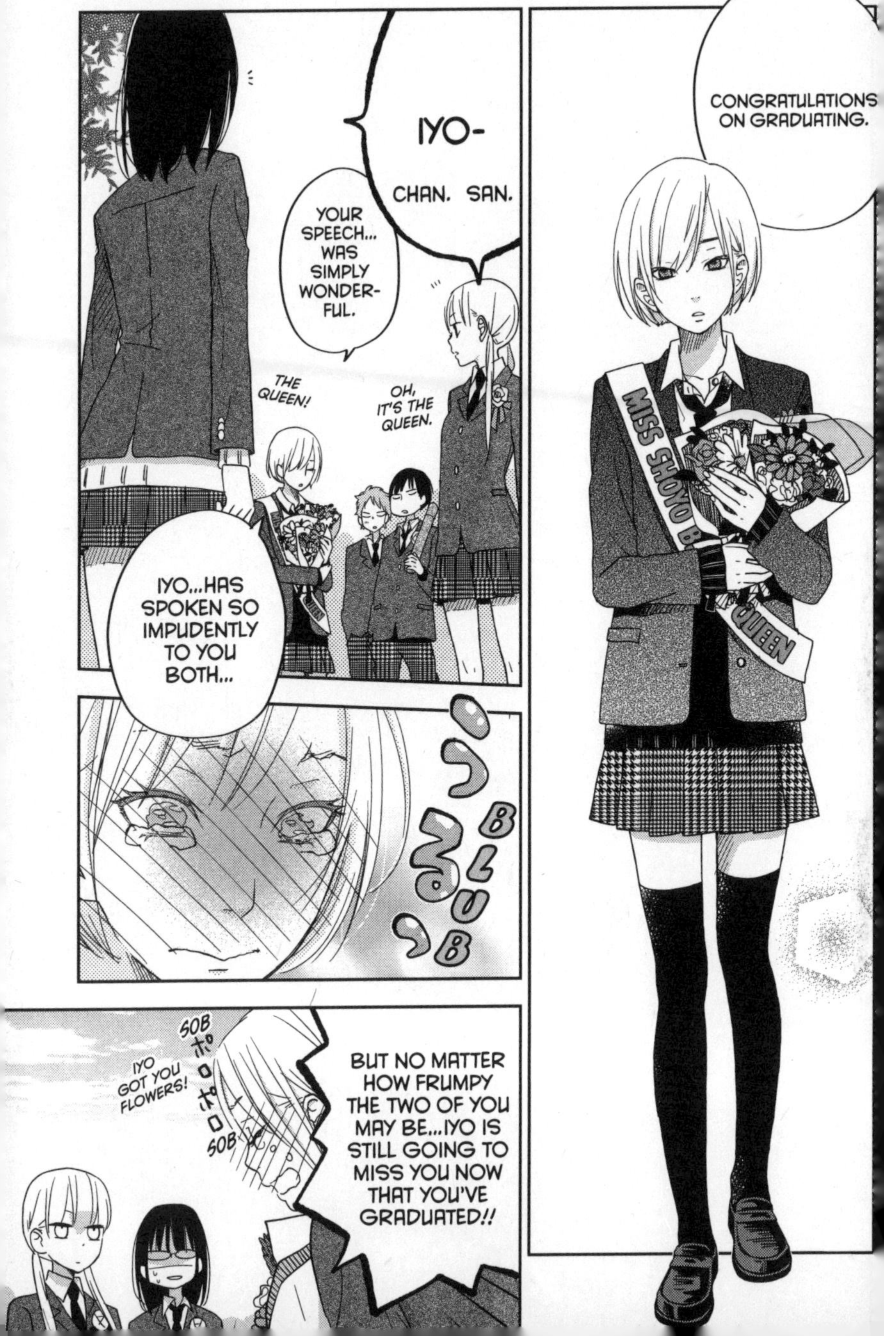
CONGRATULATIONS ON GRADUATING.
MISS SHOYO B
QUEEN
IYO-
CHAN. SAN.
YOUR SPEECH... WAS SIMPLY WONDERFUL.
OH, IT'S THE QUEEN.
THE QUEEN!
IYO...HAS SPOKEN SO IMPUDENTLY TO YOU BOTH...
BLUB
BUT NO MATTER HOW FRUMPY THE TWO OF YOU MAY BE...IYO IS STILL GOING TO MISS YOU NOW THAT YOU'VE GRADUATED!!
SOB
ポロポロ
SOB
IYO GOT YOU FLOWERS!

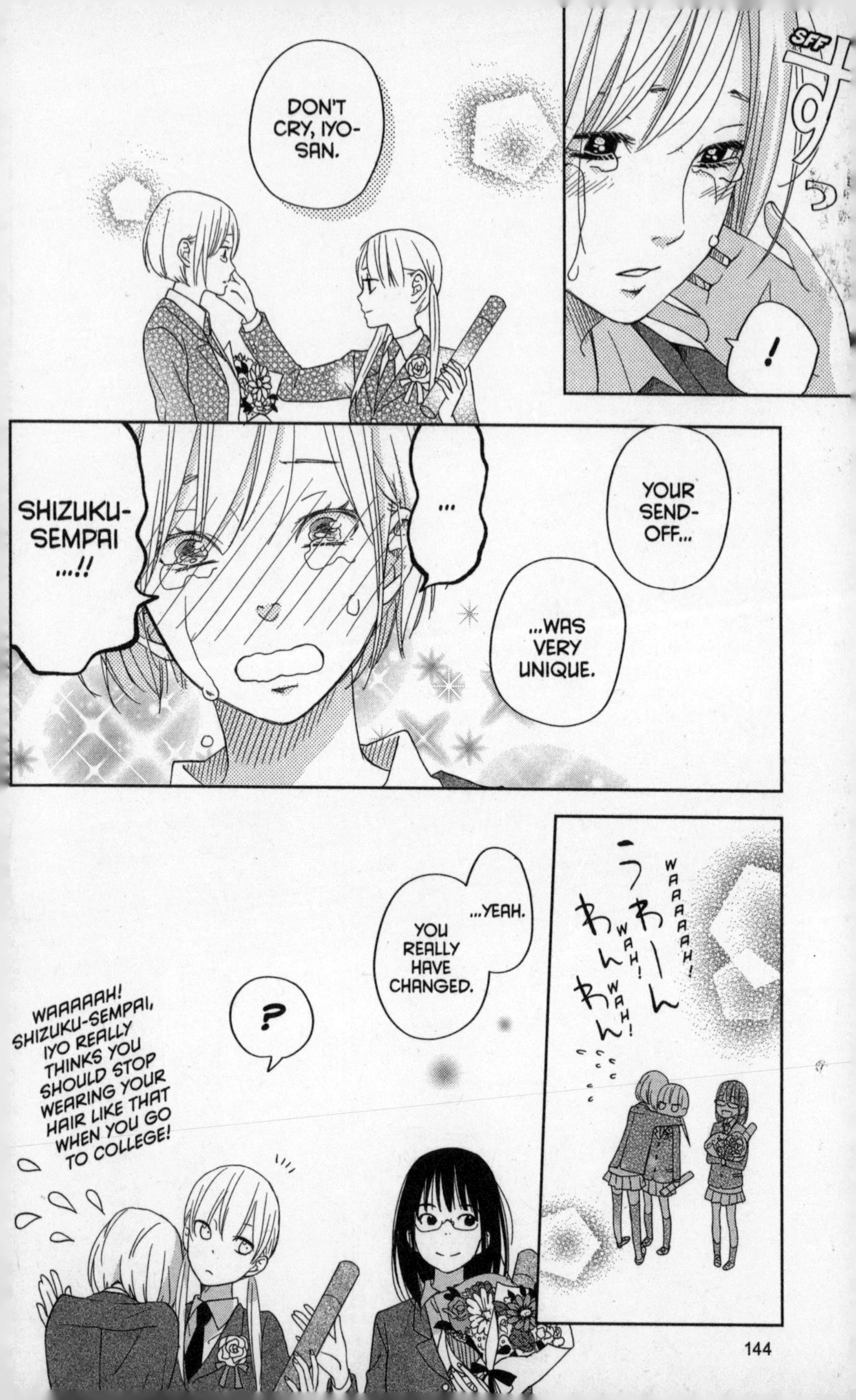
SFF
す
つ
!
DON'T CRY, IYO-SAN.
YOUR SEND-OFF...
...WAS VERY UNIQUE.
...
SHIZUKU-SEMPAI ...!!
うわーん
WAAAAAH!
わんわん
WAH! WAH!
...YEAH. YOU REALLY HAVE CHANGED.
?
WAAAAAH! SHIZUKU-SEMPAI, IYO REALLY THINKS YOU SHOULD STOP WEARING YOUR HAIR LIKE THAT WHEN YOU GO TO COLLEGE!

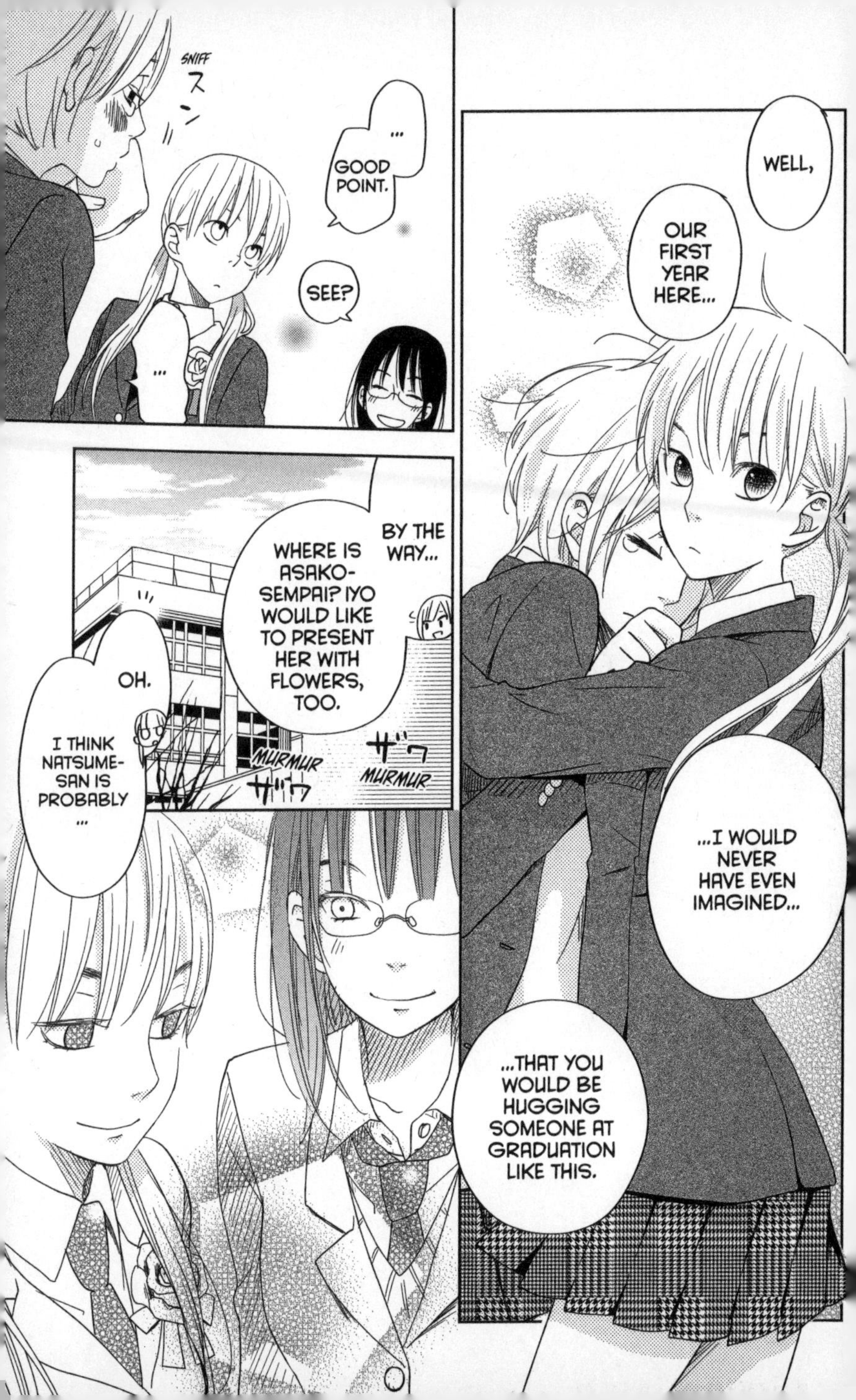
... GOOD POINT.
SEE?
SNIFF スン
...
BY THE WAY...
WHERE IS ASAKO-SEMPAI? IYO WOULD LIKE TO PRESENT HER WITH FLOWERS, TOO.
OH.
ザワ MURMUR
MURMUR ザワ
I THINK NATSUME-SAN IS PROBABLY ...
WELL,
OUR FIRST YEAR HERE...
...I WOULD NEVER HAVE EVEN IMAGINED...
...THAT YOU WOULD BE HUGGING SOMEONE AT GRADUATION LIKE THIS.

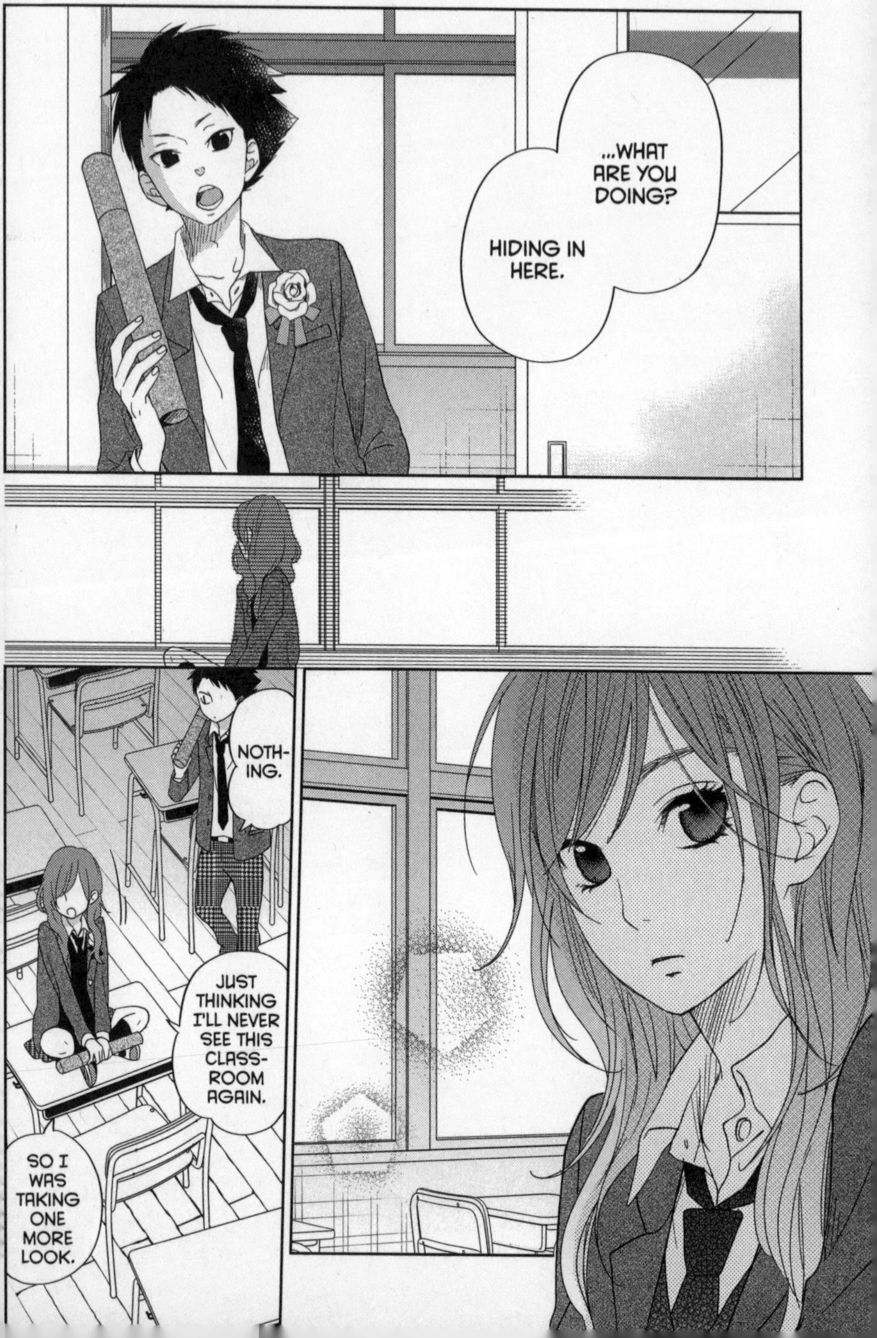
...WHAT ARE YOU DOING?
HIDING IN HERE.
NOTH-ING.
JUST THINKING I'LL NEVER SEE THIS CLASS-ROOM AGAIN.
SO I WAS TAKING ONE MORE LOOK.

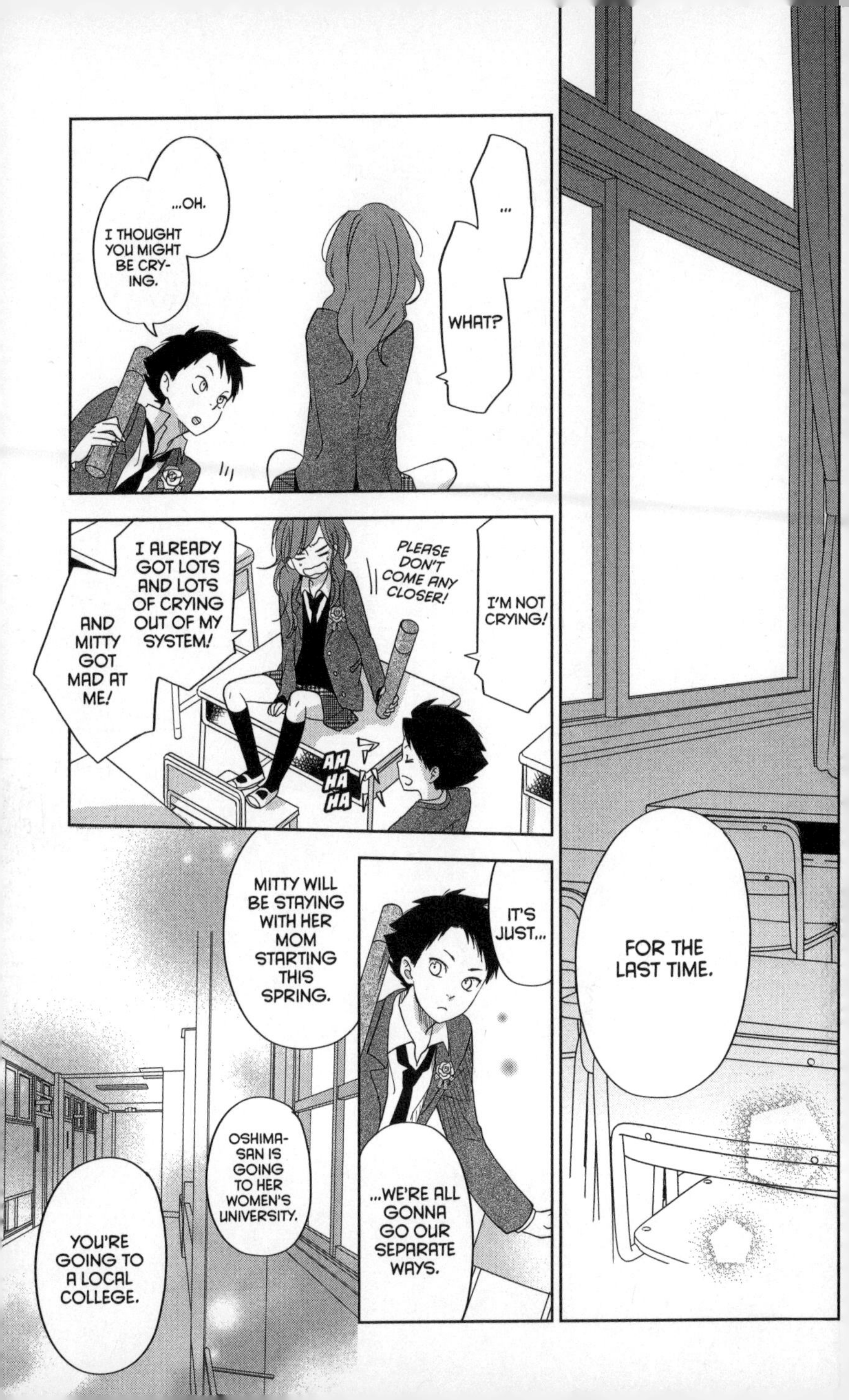
FOR THE LAST TIME.
...
WHAT?
...OH.
I THOUGHT YOU MIGHT BE CRY-ING.
I'M NOT CRYING!
PLEASE DON'T COME ANY CLOSER!
I ALREADY GOT LOTS AND LOTS OF CRYING OUT OF MY SYSTEM!
AND MITTY GOT MAD AT ME!
AH HA HA
IT'S JUST...
MITTY WILL BE STAYING WITH HER MOM STARTING THIS SPRING.
OSHIMA-SAN IS GOING TO HER WOMEN'S UNIVERSITY.
YOU'RE GOING TO A LOCAL COLLEGE.
...WE'RE ALL GONNA GO OUR SEPARATE WAYS.

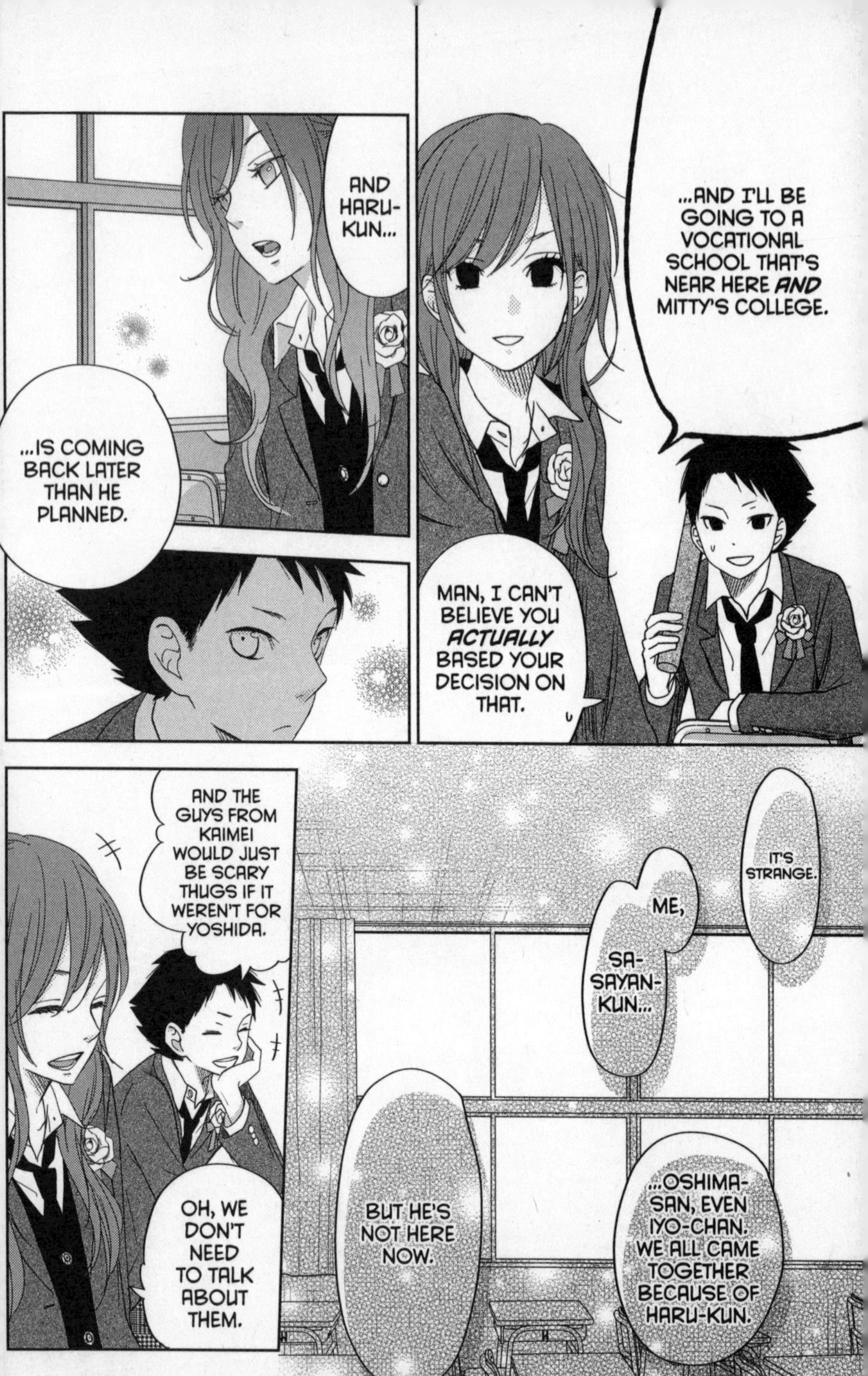
...AND I'LL BE GOING TO A VOCATIONAL SCHOOL THAT'S NEAR HERE *AND* MITTY'S COLLEGE.
MAN, I CAN'T BELIEVE YOU *ACTUALLY* BASED YOUR DECISION ON THAT.
AND HARU-KUN...
...IS COMING BACK LATER THAN HE PLANNED.
IT'S STRANGE.
ME,
SA-SAYAN-KUN...
...OSHIMA-SAN, EVEN IYO-CHAN. WE ALL CAME TOGETHER BECAUSE OF HARU-KUN.
BUT HE'S NOT HERE NOW.
AND THE GUYS FROM KAIMEI WOULD JUST BE SCARY THUGS IF IT WEREN'T FOR YOSHIDA.
OH, WE DON'T NEED TO TALK ABOUT THEM.

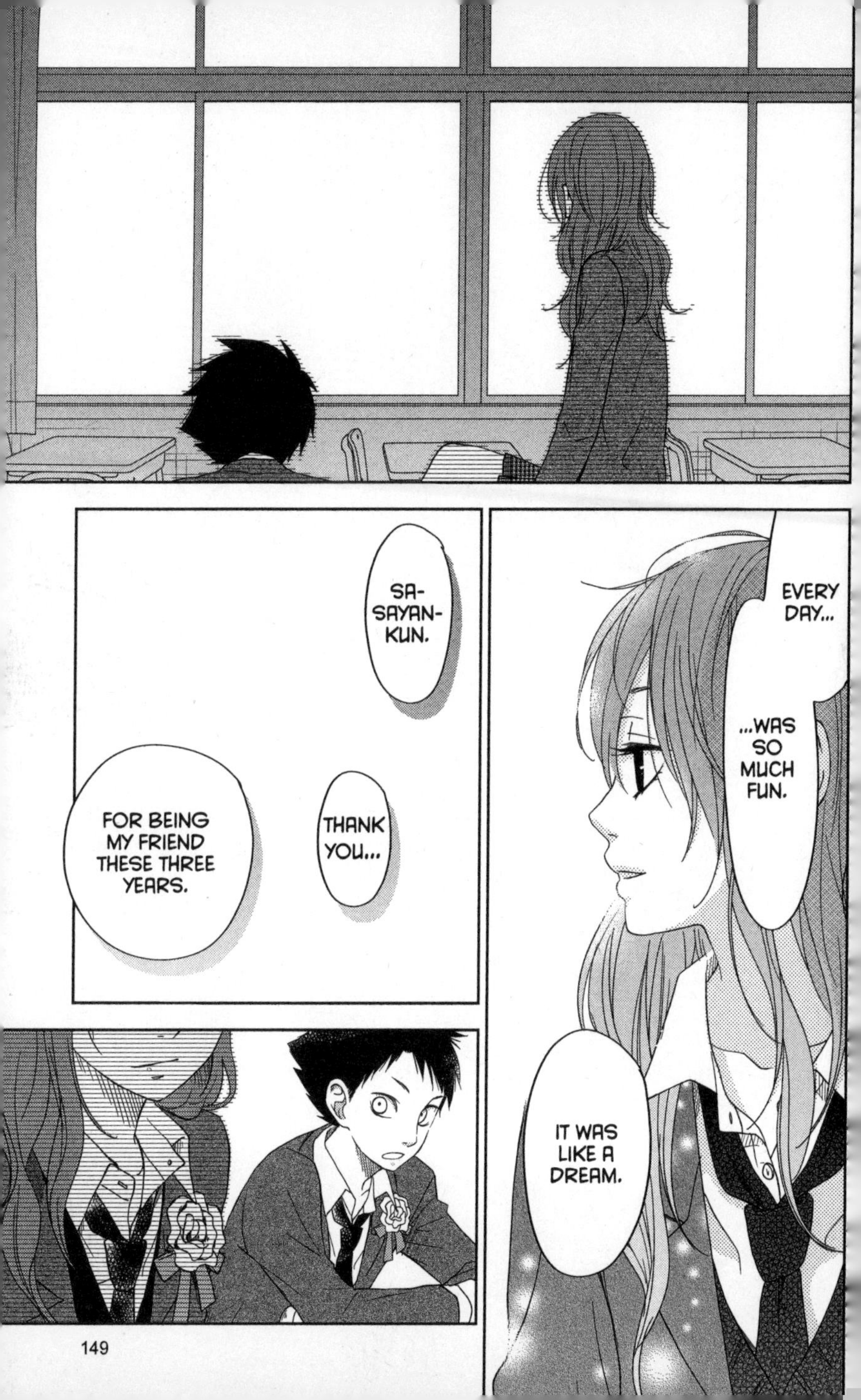
EVERY DAY...
...WAS SO MUCH FUN.
IT WAS LIKE A DREAM.
SA-SAYAN-KUN.
THANK YOU...
FOR BEING MY FRIEND THESE THREE YEARS.

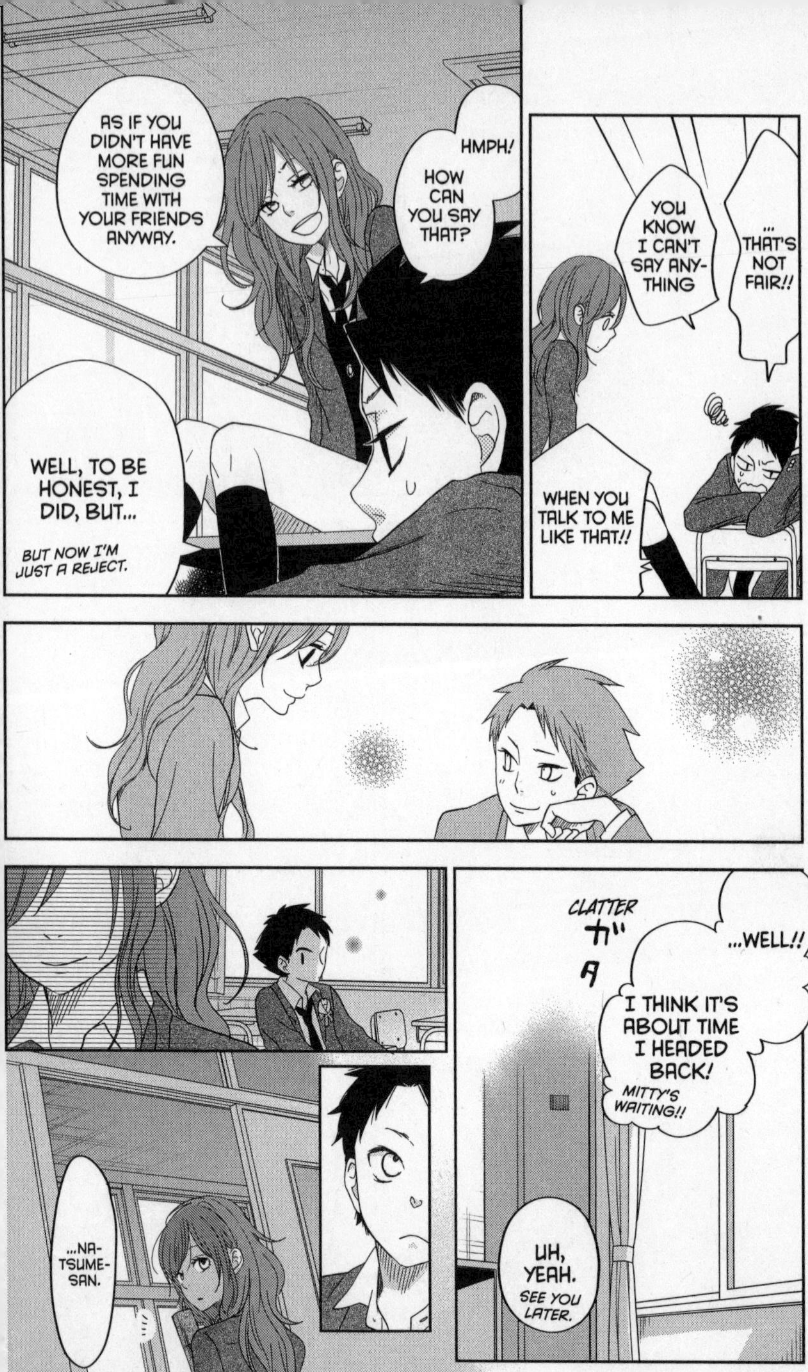
...THAT'S NOT FAIR!!
YOU KNOW I CAN'T SAY ANYTHING
WHEN YOU TALK TO ME LIKE THAT!!
HMPH! HOW CAN YOU SAY THAT?
AS IF YOU DIDN'T HAVE MORE FUN SPENDING TIME WITH YOUR FRIENDS ANYWAY.
WELL, TO BE HONEST, I DID, BUT...
BUT NOW I'M JUST A REJECT.
CLATTER
ガタ
...WELL!!
I THINK IT'S ABOUT TIME I HEADED BACK!
MITTY'S WAITING!!
UH, YEAH.
SEE YOU LATER.
...NA-TSUME-SAN.
...!

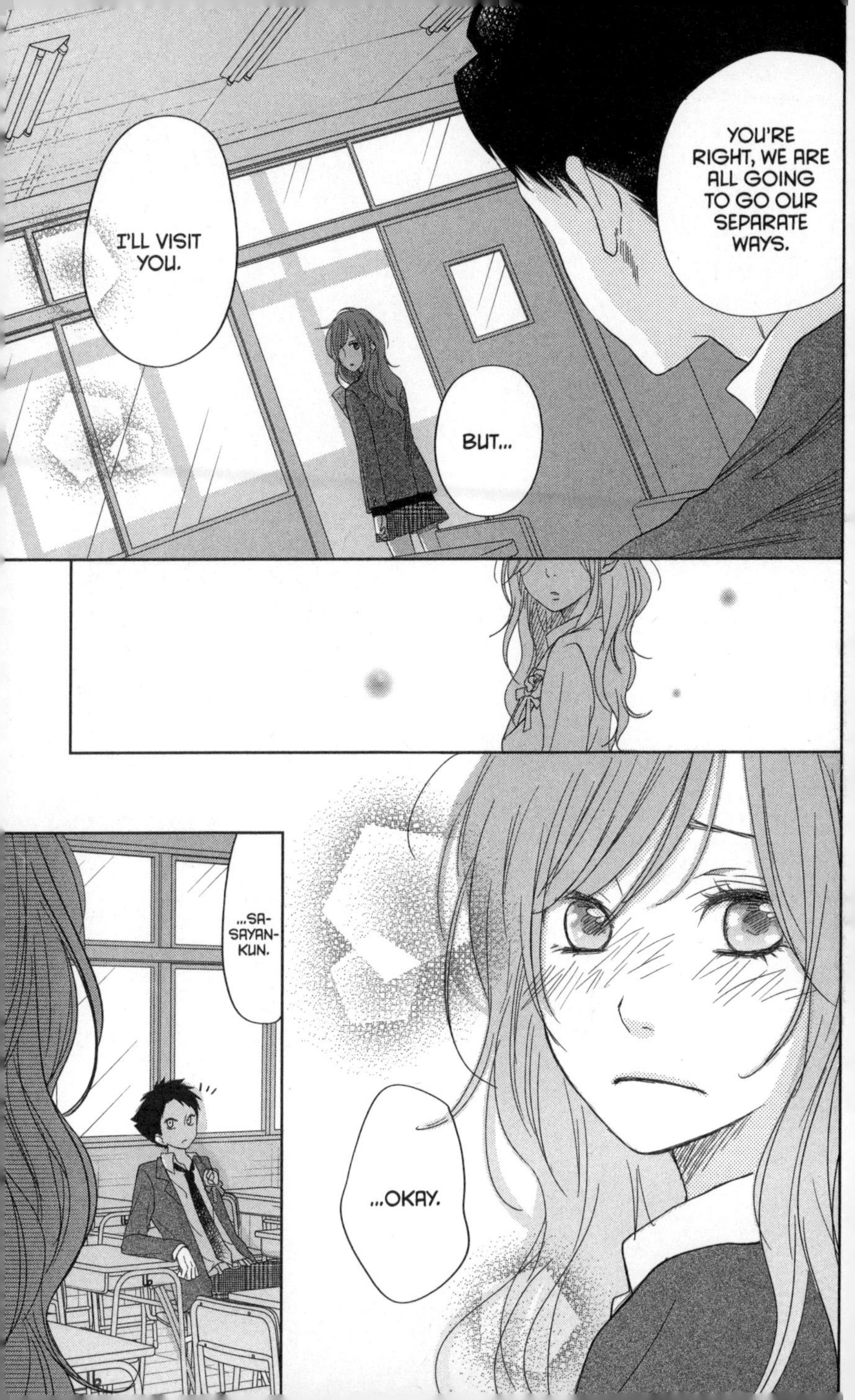
YOU'RE RIGHT, WE ARE ALL GOING TO GO OUR SEPARATE WAYS.
I'LL VISIT YOU.
BUT...
...OKAY.
...SA-SAYAN-KUN.

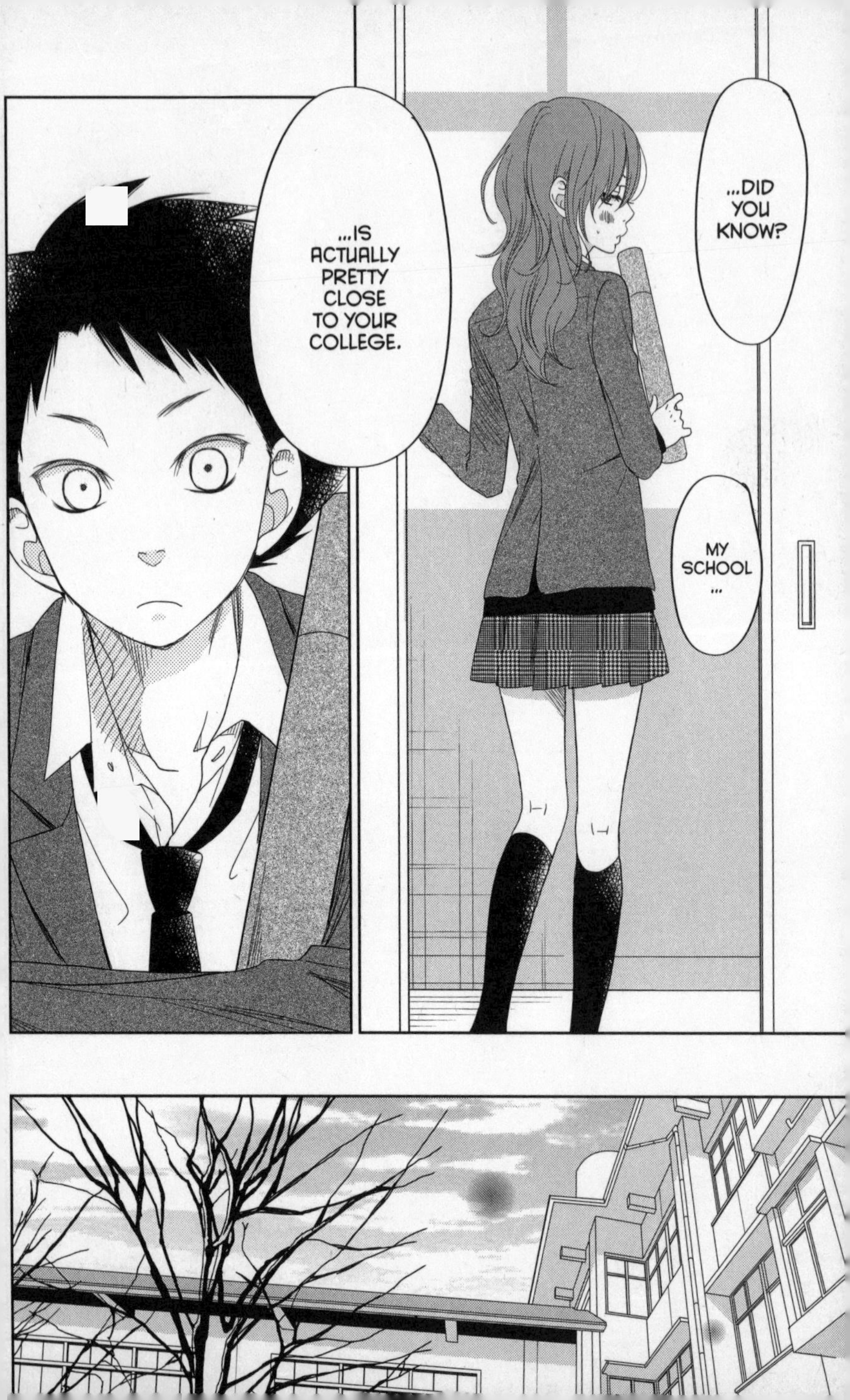
...DID YOU KNOW?
MY SCHOOL ...
...IS ACTUALLY PRETTY CLOSE TO YOUR COLLEGE.

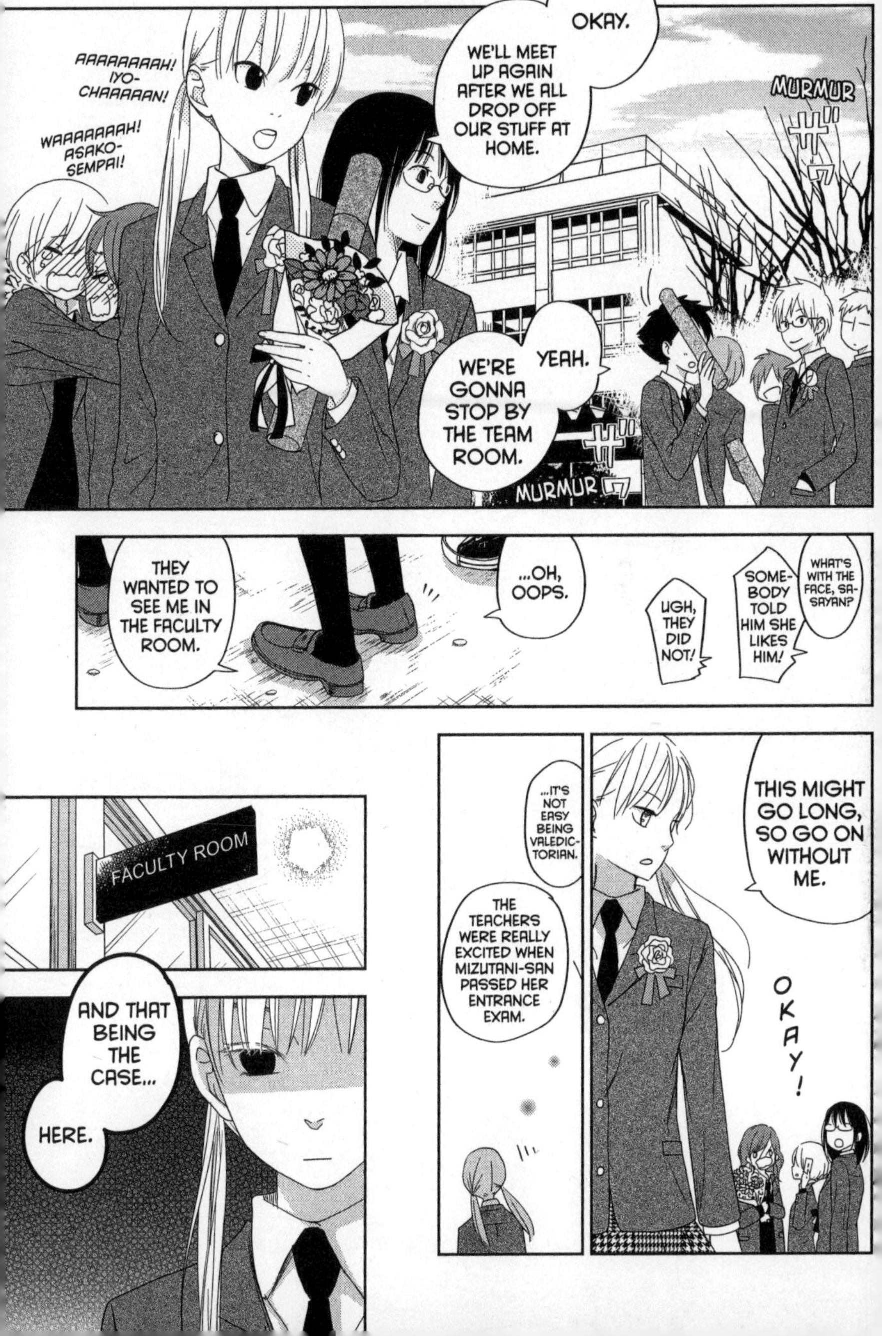
OKAY.
WE'LL MEET UP AGAIN AFTER WE ALL DROP OFF OUR STUFF AT HOME.
MURMUR ザワ
YEAH.
WE'RE GONNA STOP BY THE TEAM ROOM.
MURMUR ザワ
AAAAAAAAH! IYO-CHAAAAAN!
WAAAAAAAH! ASAKO-SEMPAI!
WHAT'S WITH THE FACE, SA-SAYAN?
SOME-BODY TOLD HIM SHE LIKES HIM!
UGH, THEY DID NOT!
...OH, OOPS.
THEY WANTED TO SEE ME IN THE FACULTY ROOM.
THIS MIGHT GO LONG, SO GO ON WITHOUT ME.
OKAY!
...IT'S NOT EASY BEING VALEDIC-TORIAN.
THE TEACHERS WERE REALLY EXCITED WHEN MIZUTANI-SAN PASSED HER ENTRANCE EXAM.
FACULTY ROOM
AND THAT BEING THE CASE...
HERE.

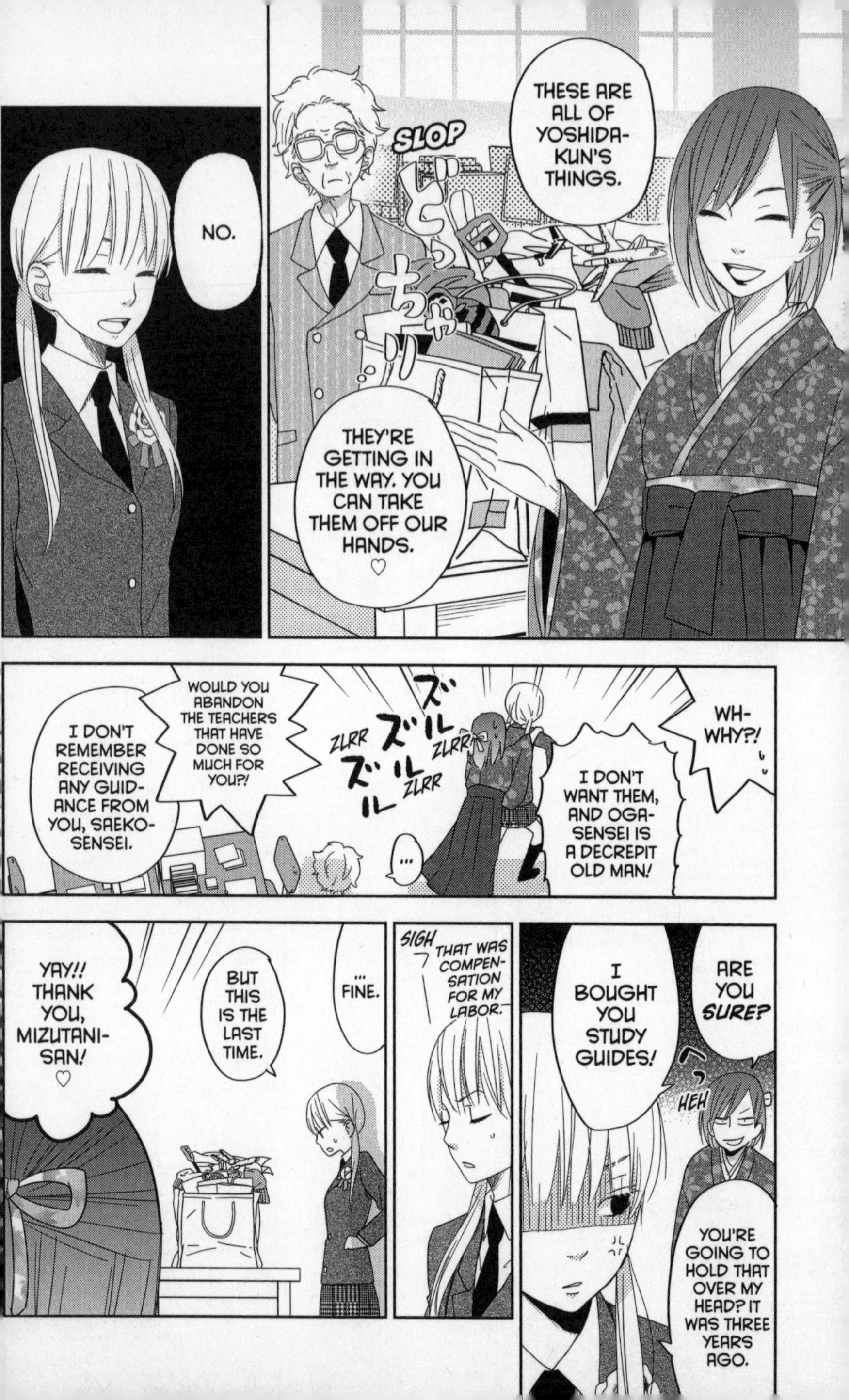
THESE ARE ALL OF YOSHIDA-KUN'S THINGS.
SLOP
THEY'RE GETTING IN THE WAY. YOU CAN TAKE THEM OFF OUR HANDS. ♡
NO.
WH-WHY?!
I DON'T WANT THEM, AND OGA-SENSEI IS A DECREPIT OLD MAN!
ZLRR ZLRR ZLRR
...
WOULD YOU ABANDON THE TEACHERS THAT HAVE DONE SO MUCH FOR YOU?!
I DON'T REMEMBER RECEIVING ANY GUIDANCE FROM YOU, SAEKO-SENSEI.
ARE YOU SURE?
I BOUGHT YOU STUDY GUIDES!
HEH
YOU'RE GOING TO HOLD THAT OVER MY HEAD? IT WAS THREE YEARS AGO.
SIGH
THAT WAS COMPENSATION FOR MY LABOR.
... FINE.
BUT THIS IS THE LAST TIME.
YAY!! THANK YOU, MIZUTANI-SAN! ♡

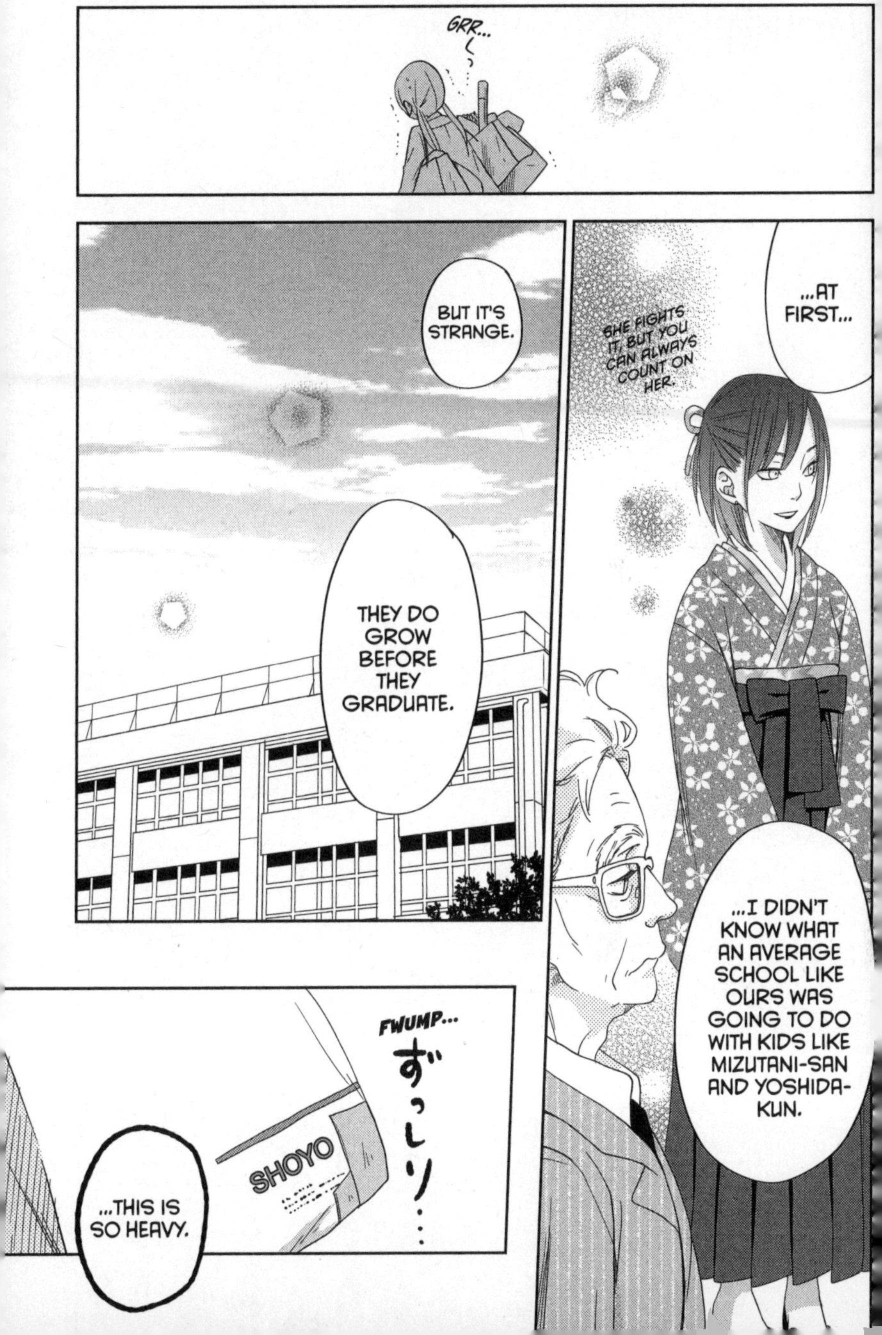
GRR...
...AT FIRST...
SHE FIGHTS IT, BUT YOU CAN ALWAYS COUNT ON HER.
...I DIDN'T KNOW WHAT AN AVERAGE SCHOOL LIKE OURS WAS GOING TO DO WITH KIDS LIKE MIZUTANI-SAN AND YOSHIDA-KUN.
BUT IT'S STRANGE.
THEY DO GROW BEFORE THEY GRADUATE.
FWUMP...
ずっしり…
SHOYO
...THIS IS SO HEAVY.

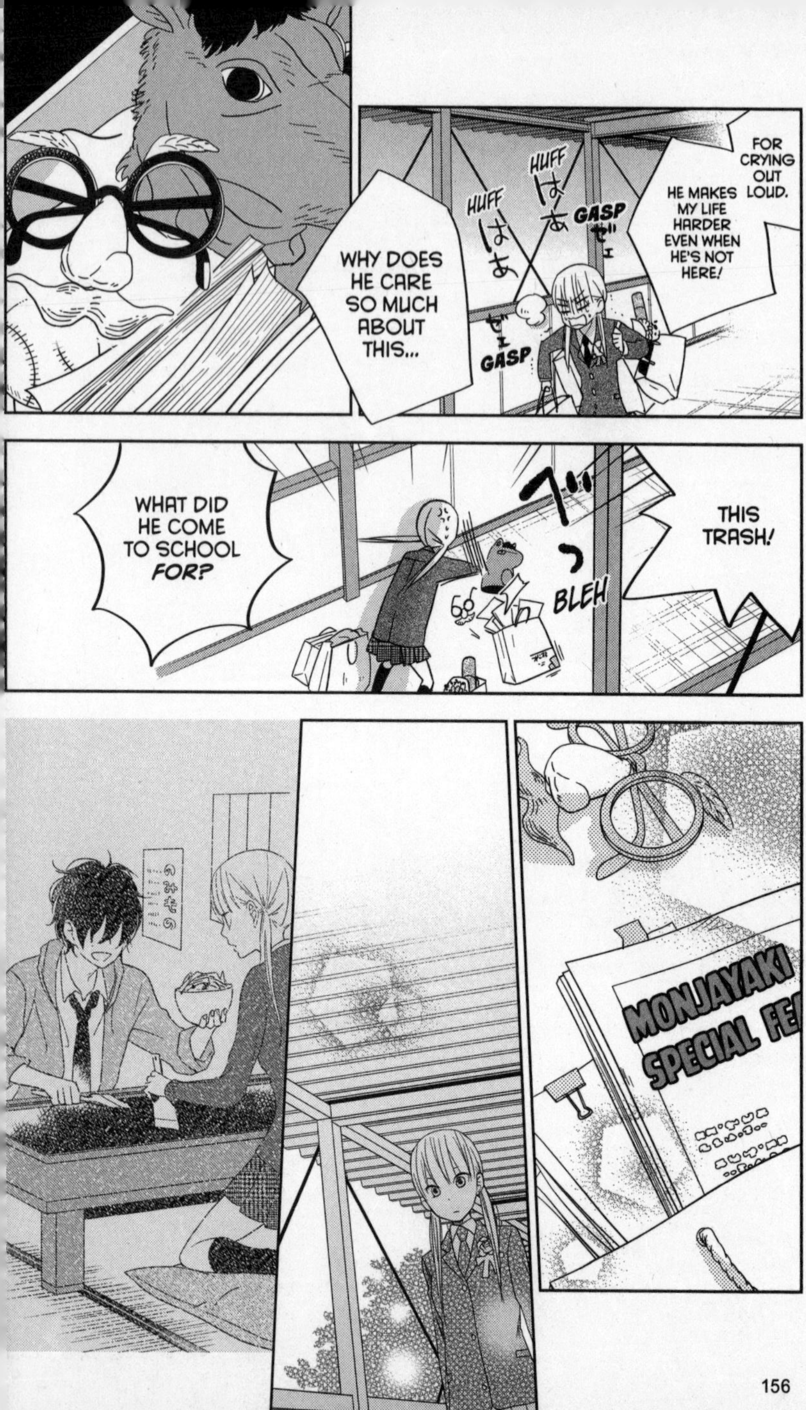
FOR CRYING OUT LOUD.
HE MAKES MY LIFE HARDER EVEN WHEN HE'S NOT HERE!
HUFF はあ
GASP ぜェ
HUFF はあ
GASP ぜェ
WHY DOES HE CARE SO MUCH ABOUT THIS...
THIS TRASH!
BLEH
WHAT DID HE COME TO SCHOOL FOR?
のみもの
MONJAYAKI SPECIAL FEA

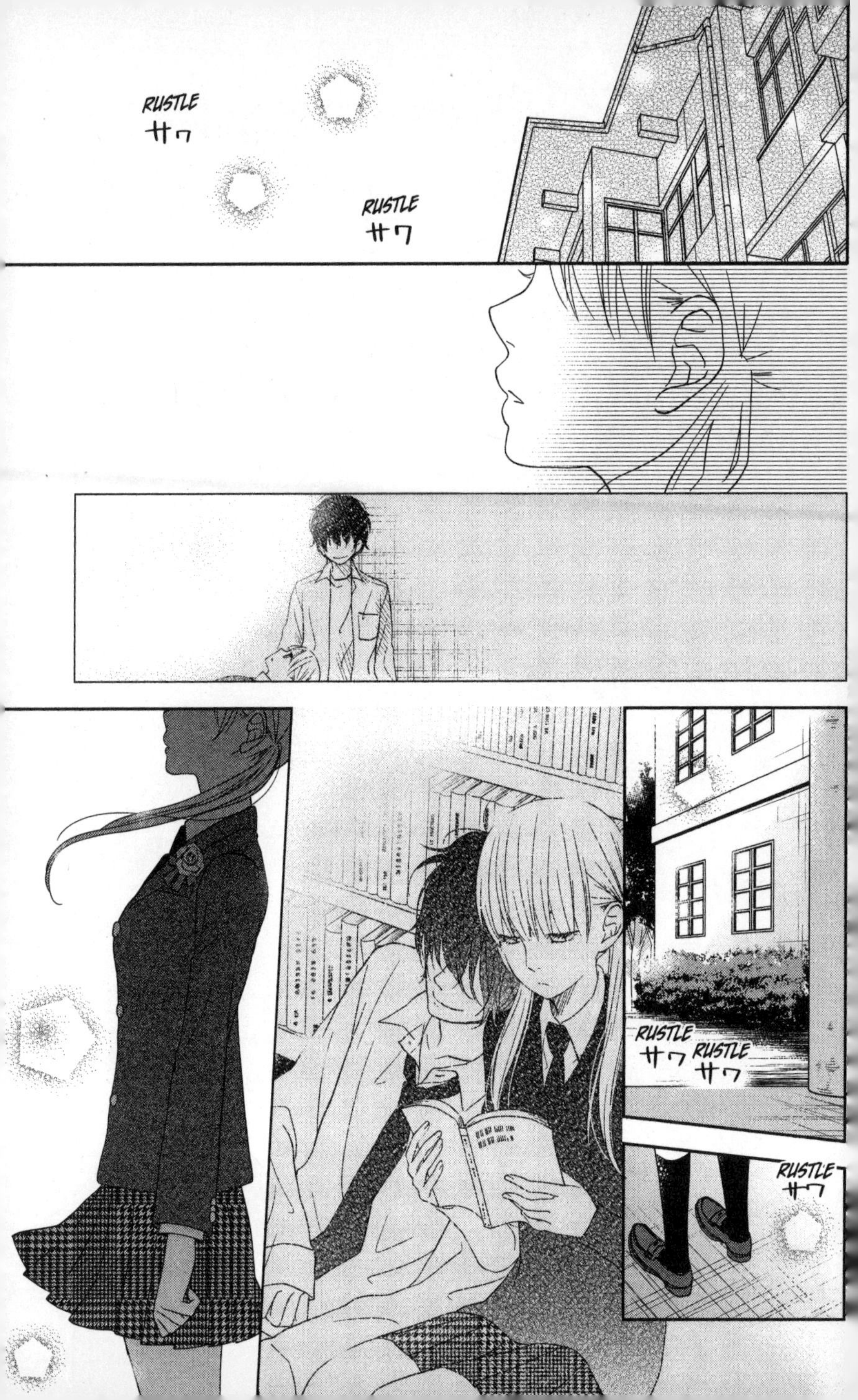
RUSTLE
サワ
RUSTLE
サワ
RUSTLE
サワ
RUSTLE
サワ
RUSTLE
サワ

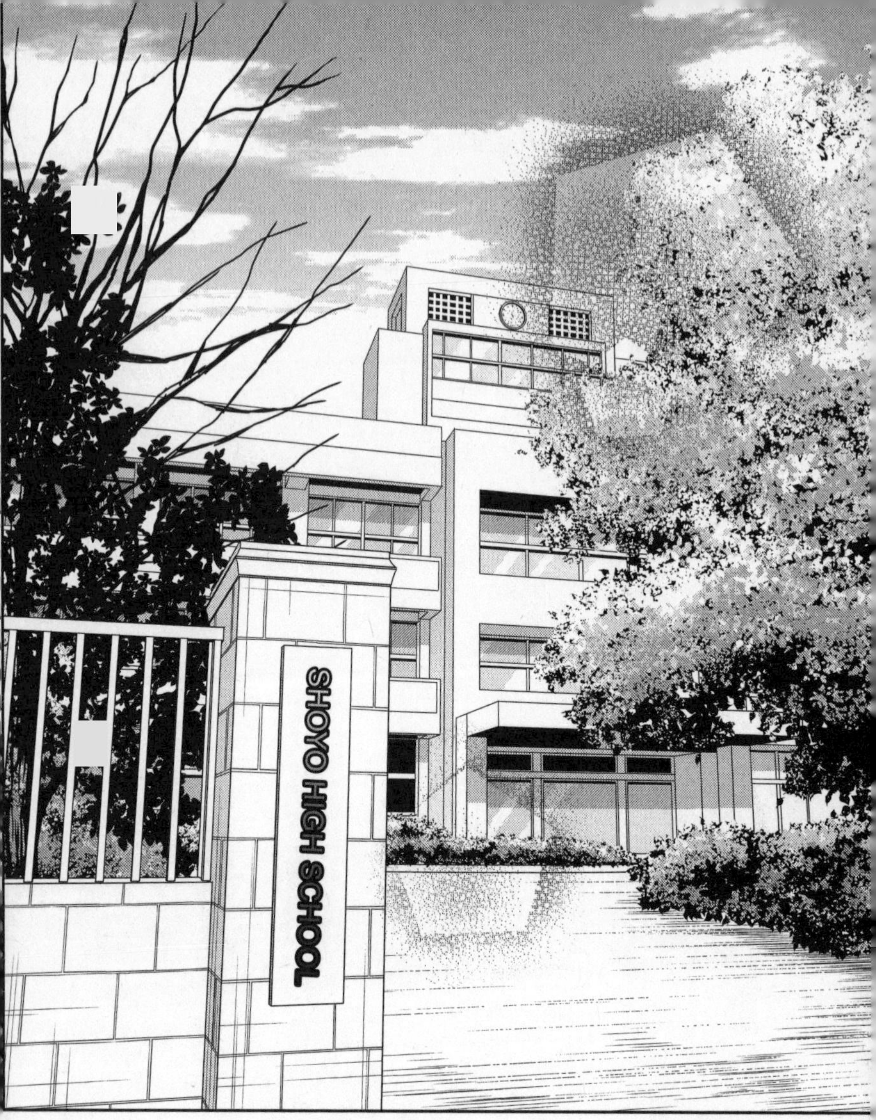
SHOYO HIGH SCHOOL

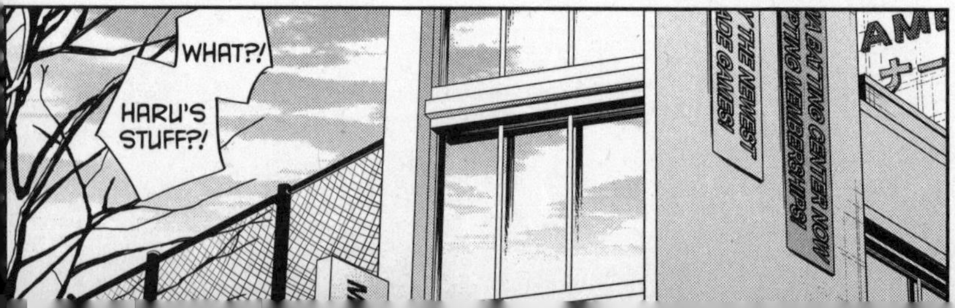
WHAT?!
HARU'S STUFF?!

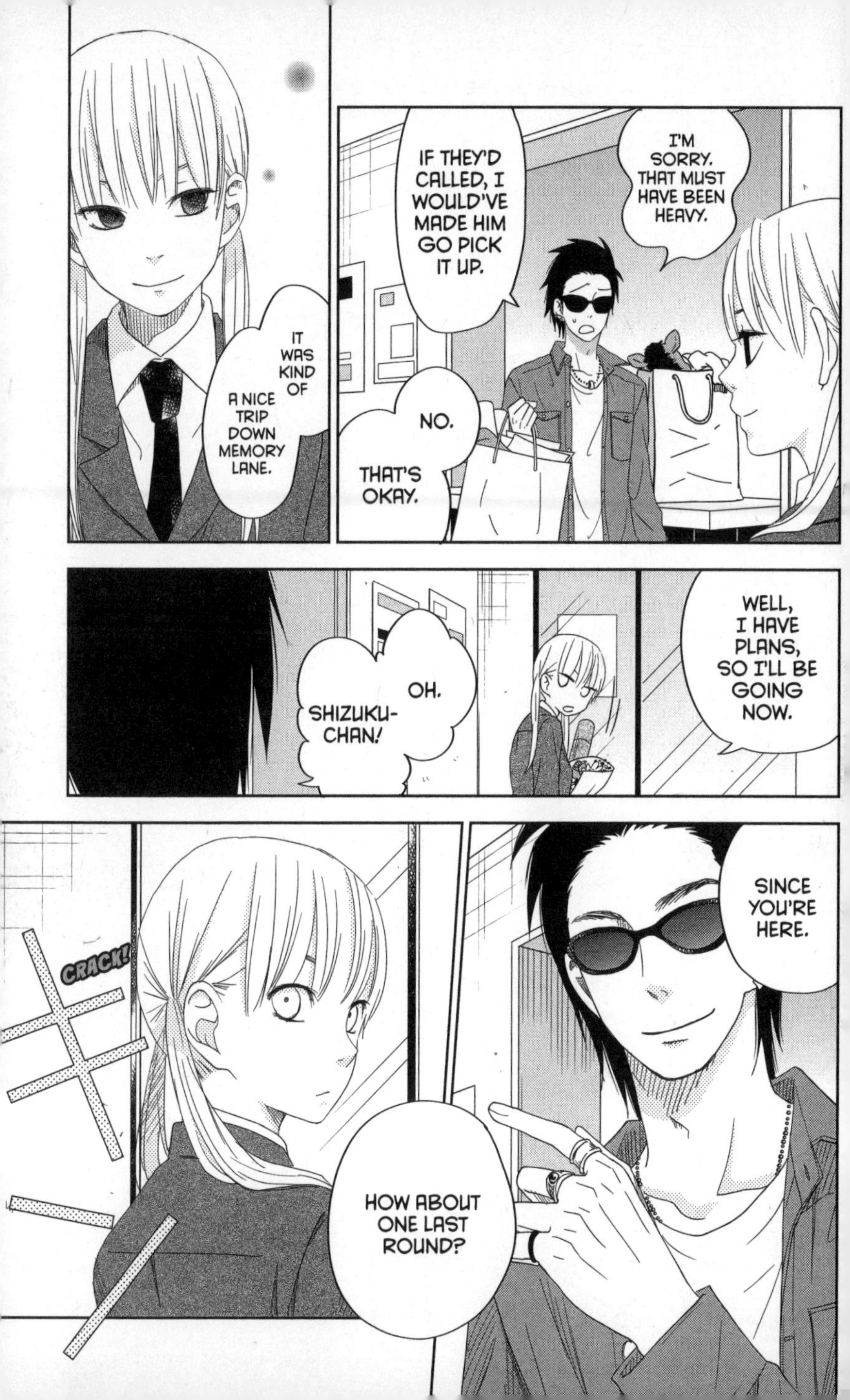
I'M SORRY. THAT MUST HAVE BEEN HEAVY.
IF THEY'D CALLED, I WOULD'VE MADE HIM GO PICK IT UP.
NO.
THAT'S OKAY.
IT WAS KIND OF A NICE TRIP DOWN MEMORY LANE.
WELL, I HAVE PLANS, SO I'LL BE GOING NOW.
OH.
SHIZUKU-CHAN!
SINCE YOU'RE HERE.
HOW ABOUT ONE LAST ROUND?
CRACK!

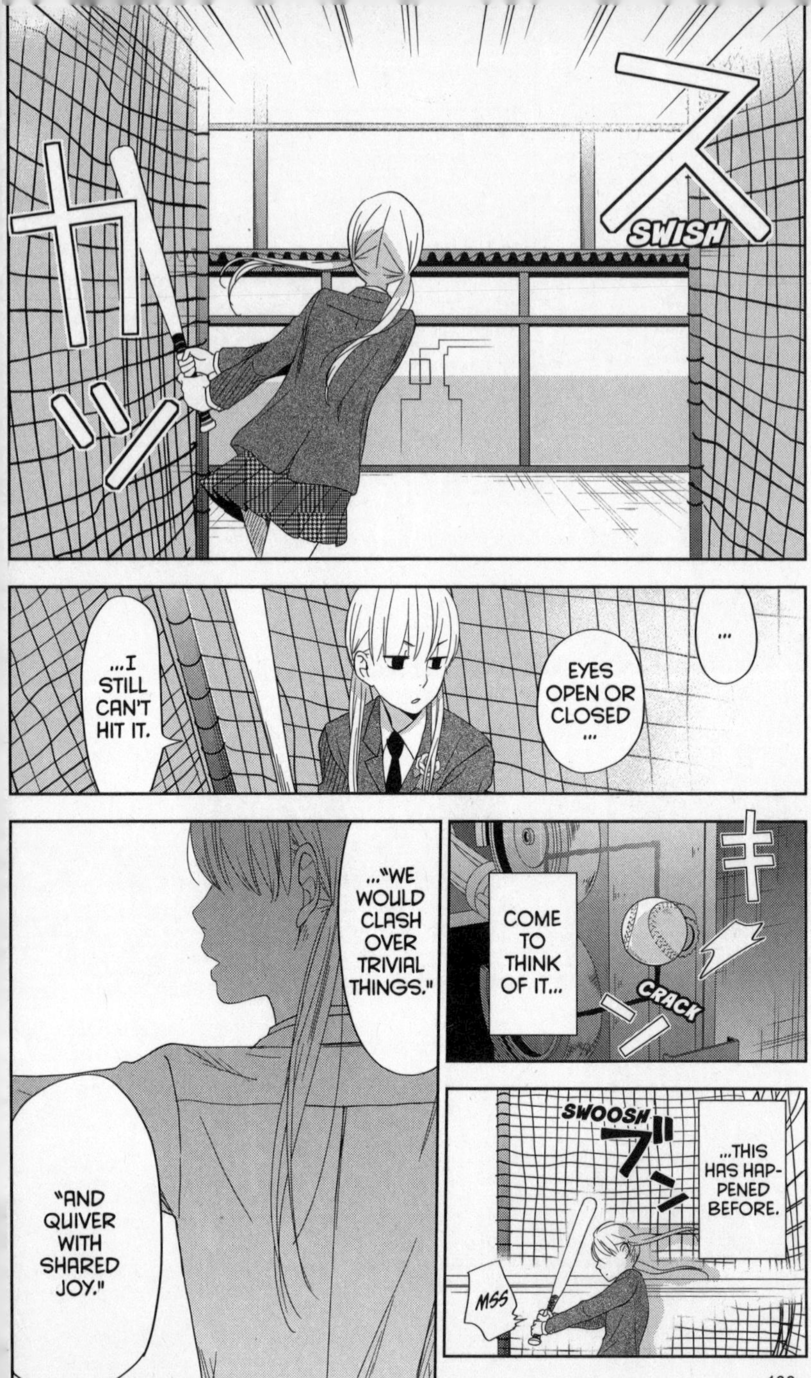
ス
SWISH
カッ
...
EYES OPEN OR CLOSED ...
...I STILL CAN'T HIT IT.
キ
CRACK
COME TO THINK OF IT...
...THIS HAS HAPPENED BEFORE.
SWOOSH
ブン
MSS
..."WE WOULD CLASH OVER TRIVIAL THINGS."
"AND QUIVER WITH SHARED JOY."

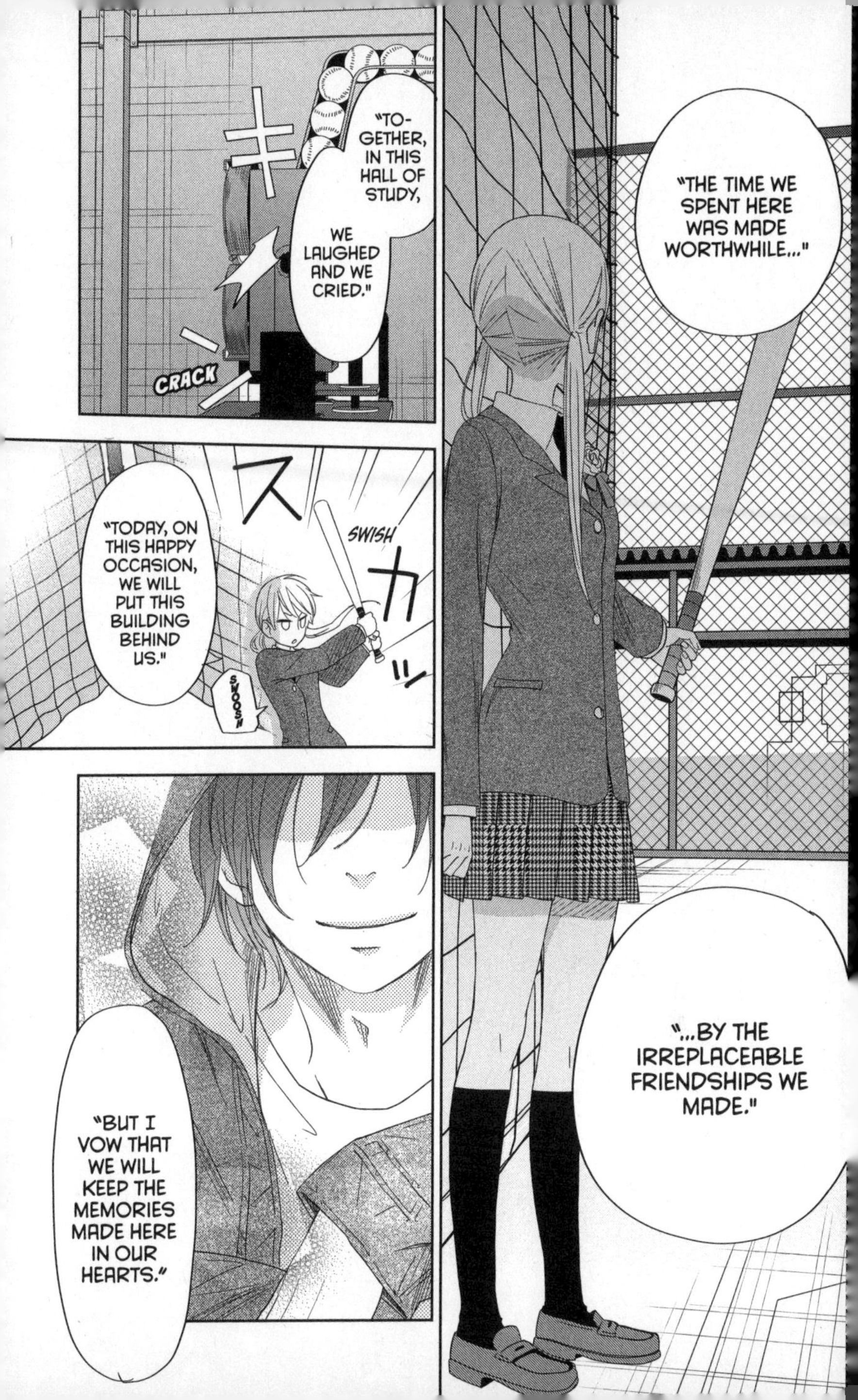
"THE TIME WE SPENT HERE WAS MADE WORTHWHILE..."
"...BY THE IRREPLACEABLE FRIENDSHIPS WE MADE."
"TO-GETHER, IN THIS HALL OF STUDY,
WE LAUGHED AND WE CRIED."
CRACK
"TODAY, ON THIS HAPPY OCCASION, WE WILL PUT THIS BUILDING BEHIND US."
スカッ
SWISH
SWOOSH
"BUT I VOW THAT WE WILL KEEP THE MEMORIES MADE HERE IN OUR HEARTS."

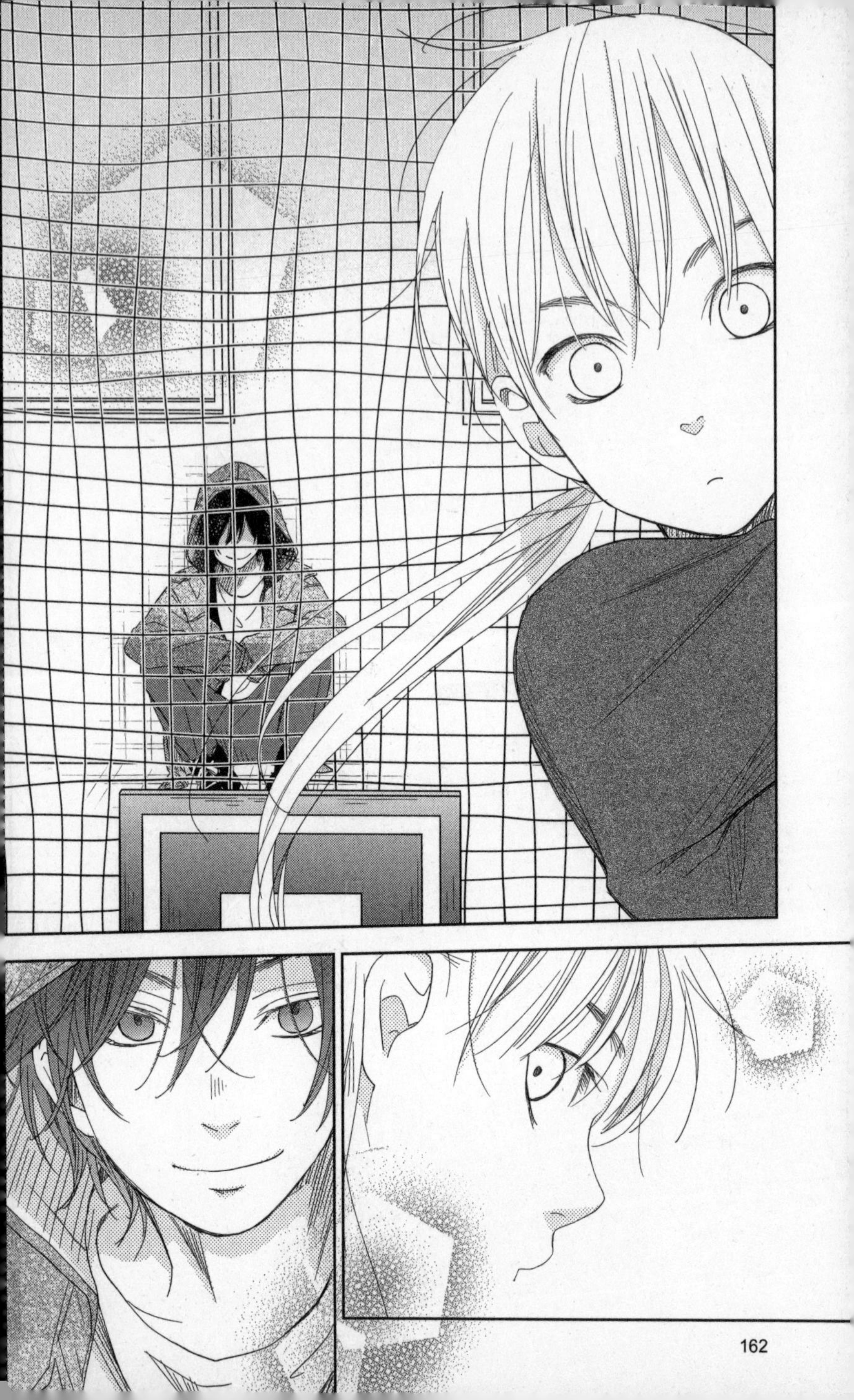

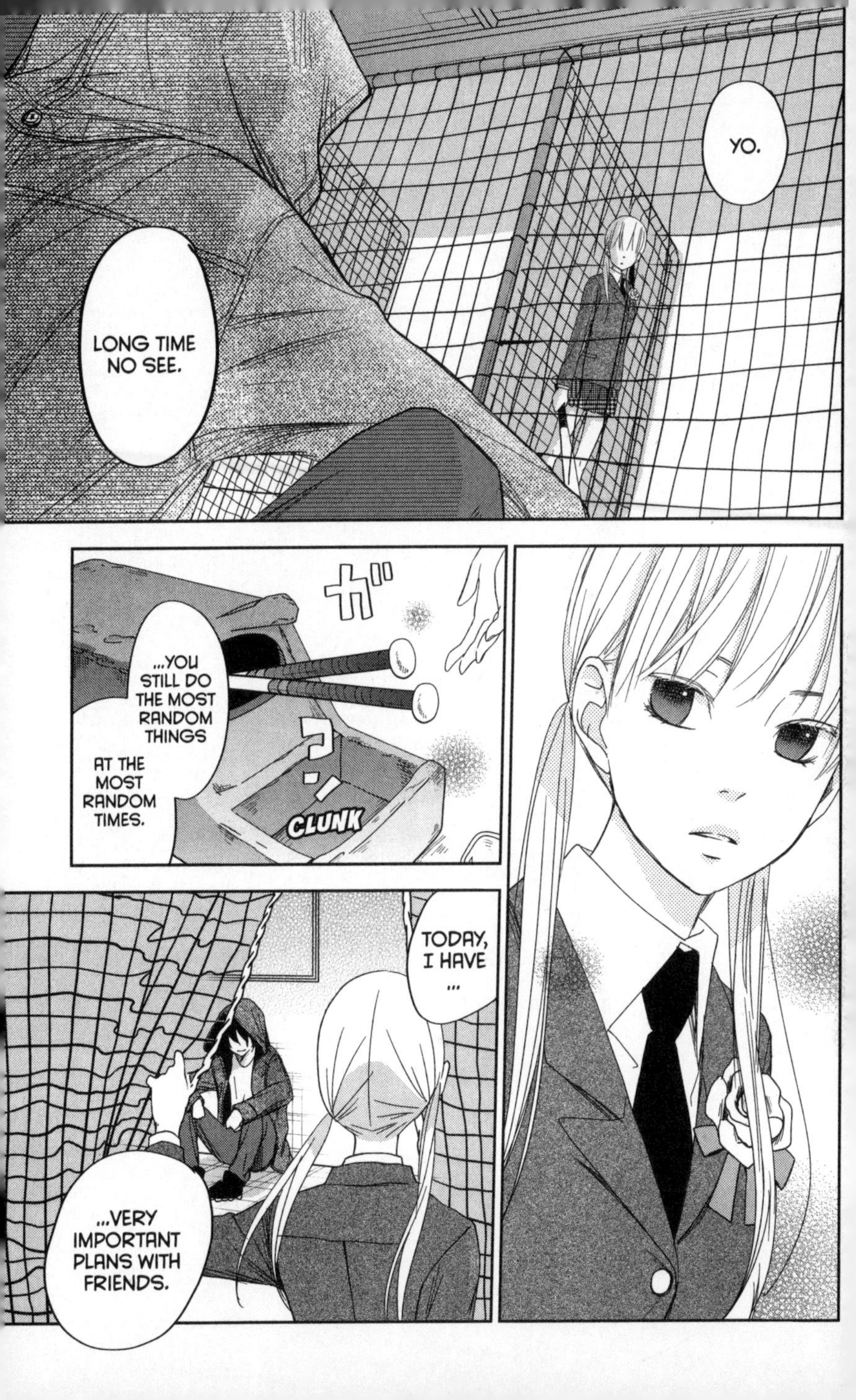
YO.
LONG TIME NO SEE.
ガッ
...YOU STILL DO THE MOST RANDOM THINGS
AT THE MOST RANDOM TIMES.
CLUNK
TODAY, I HAVE ...
...VERY IMPORTANT PLANS WITH FRIENDS.

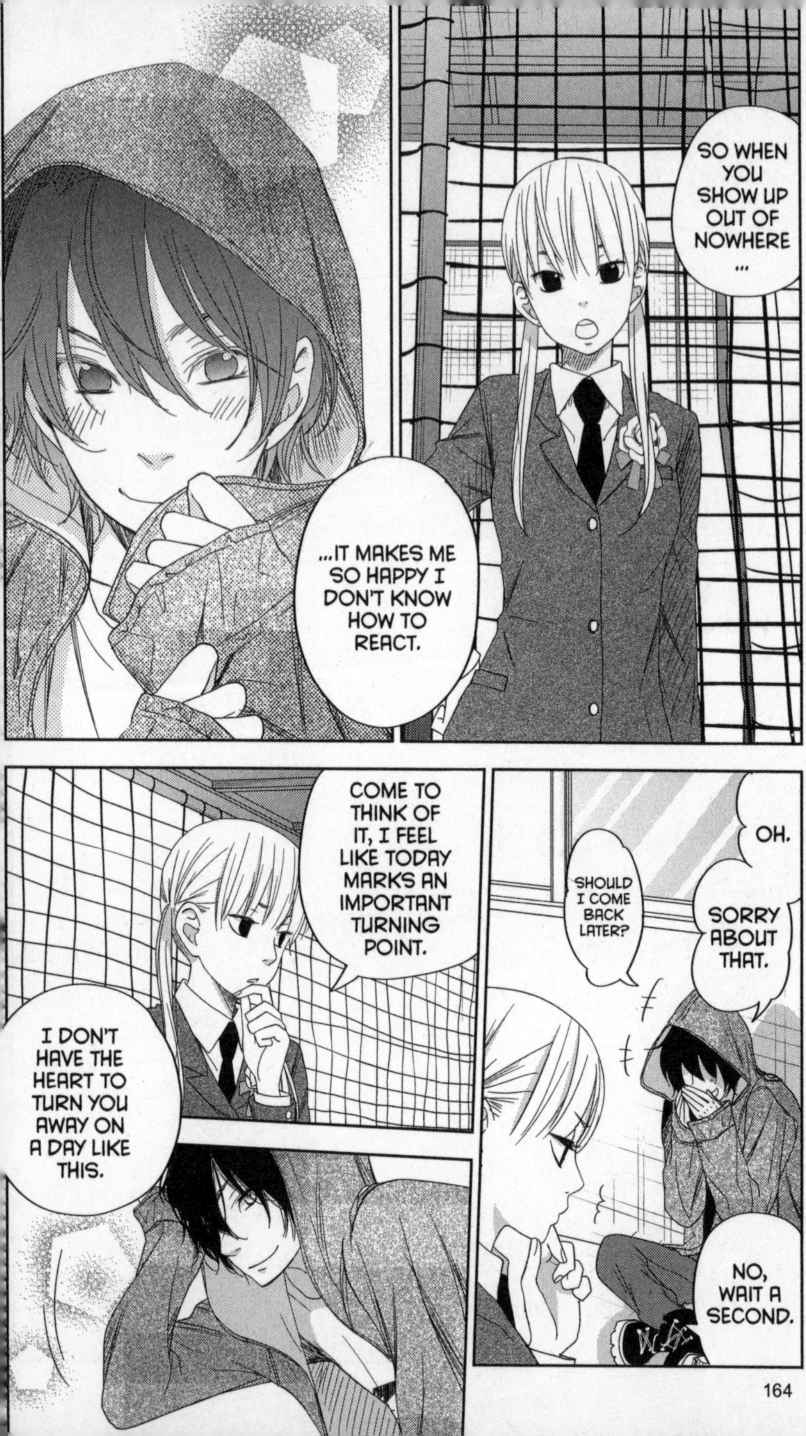
SO WHEN YOU SHOW UP OUT OF NOWHERE ...
...IT MAKES ME SO HAPPY I DON'T KNOW HOW TO REACT.
OH.
SORRY ABOUT THAT.
SHOULD I COME BACK LATER?
NO, WAIT A SECOND.
COME TO THINK OF IT, I FEEL LIKE TODAY MARKS AN IMPORTANT TURNING POINT.
I DON'T HAVE THE HEART TO TURN YOU AWAY ON A DAY LIKE THIS.

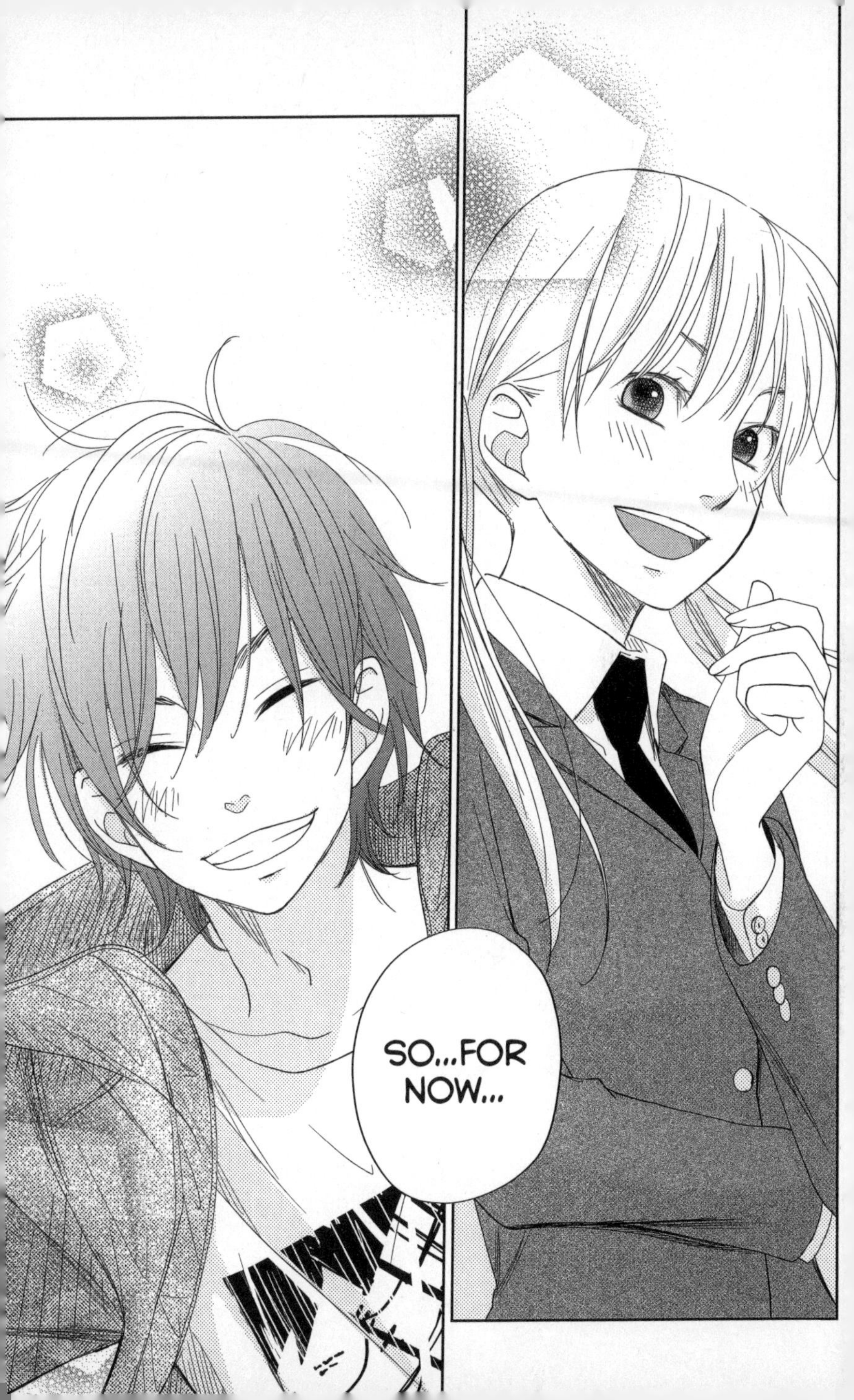
SO...FOR NOW...

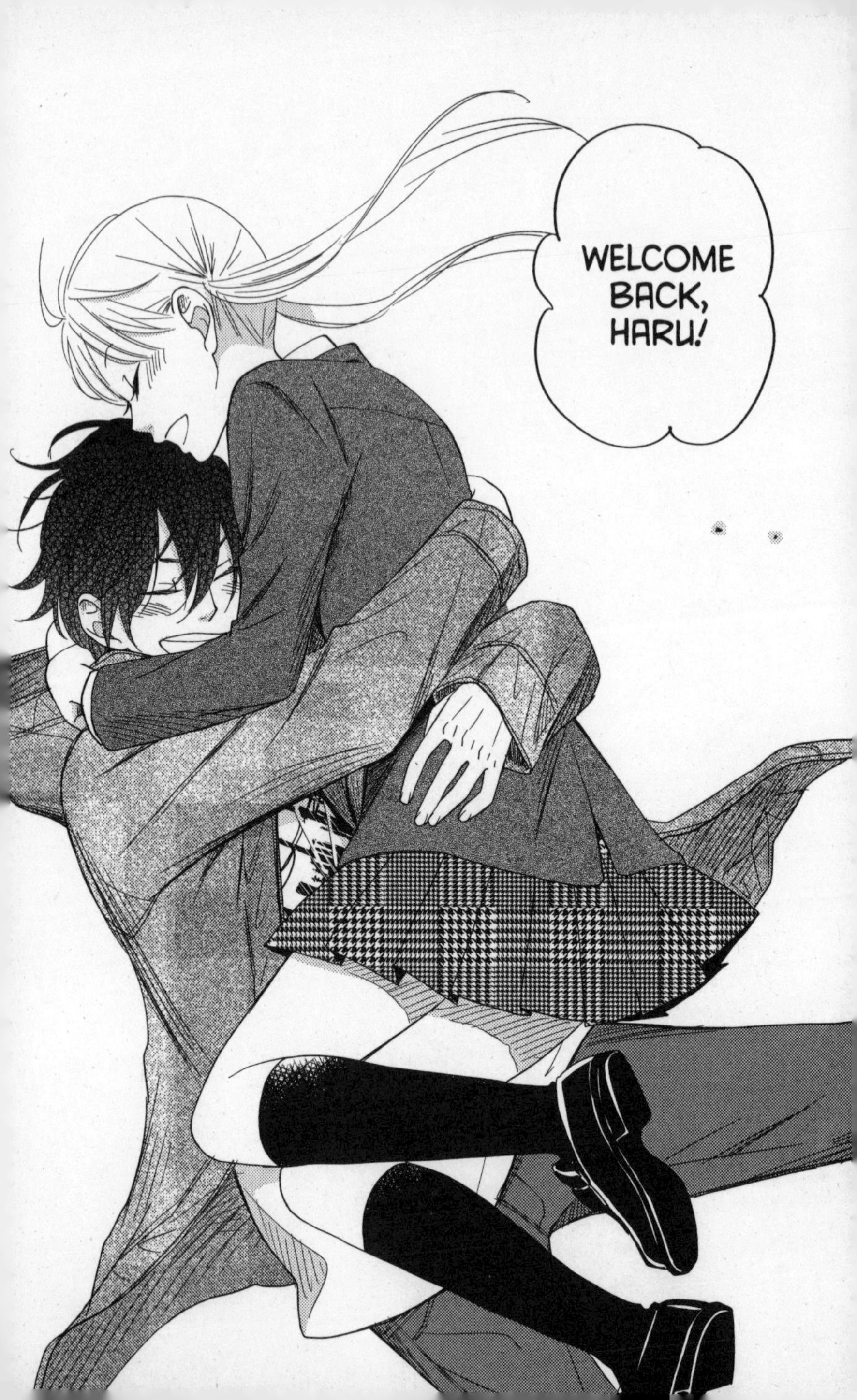
WELCOME BACK, HARU!

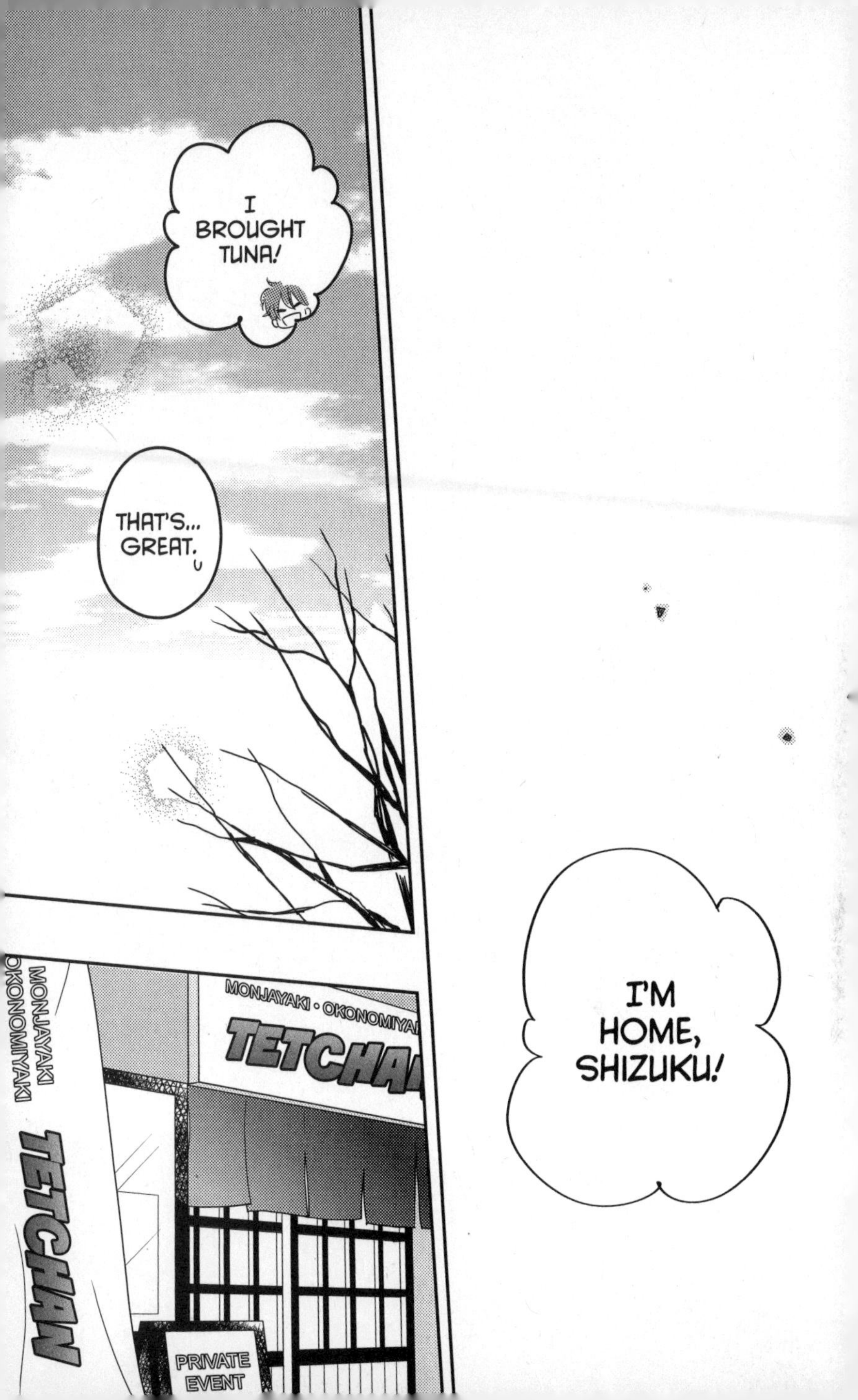
I'M HOME, SHIZUKU!
I BROUGHT TUNA!
THAT'S... GREAT.
MONJAYAKI • OKONOMIYA
TETCHA
MONJAYAKI OKONOMIYAKI
TETCHAN
PRIVATE EVENT

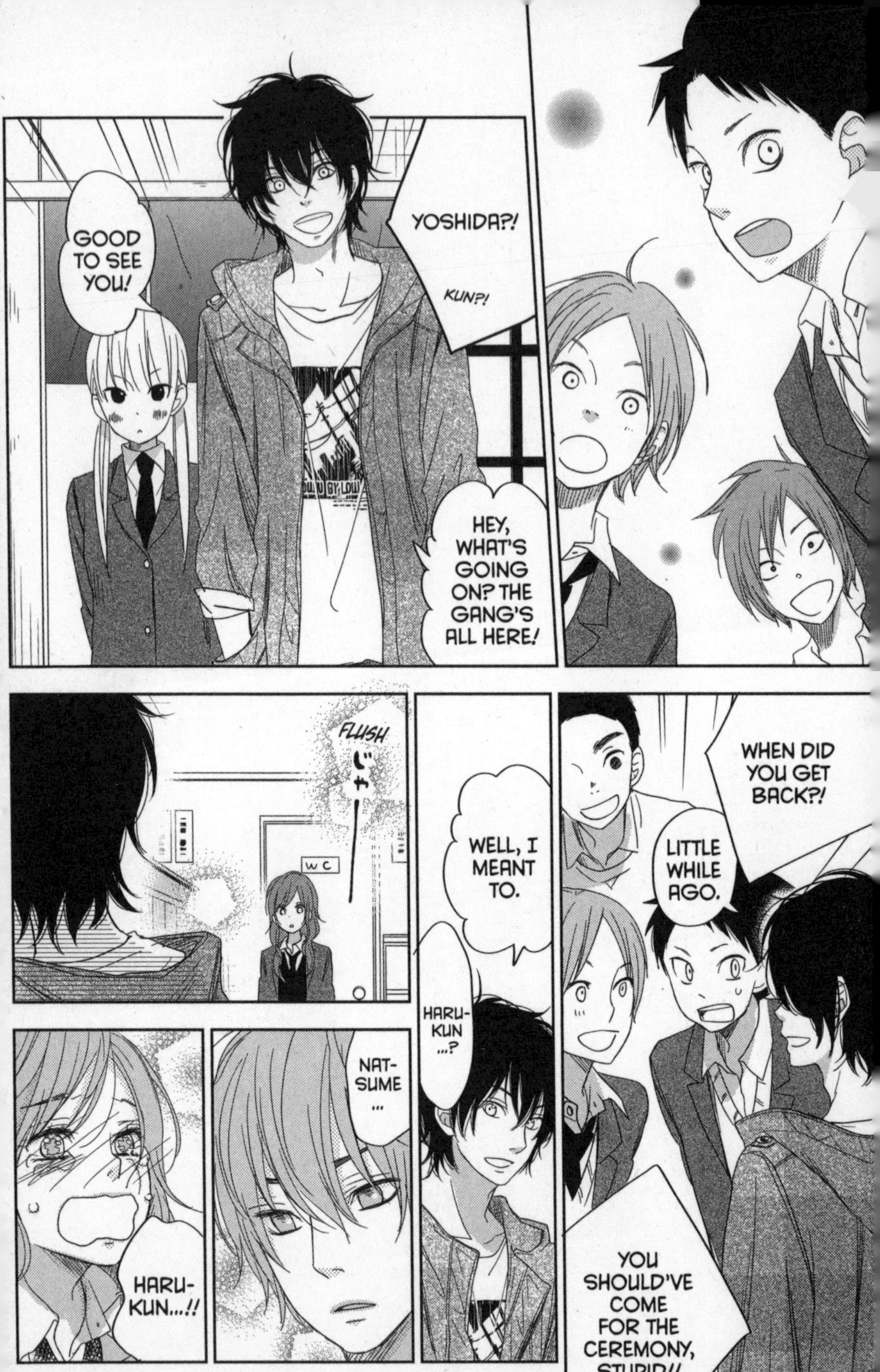
YOSHIDA?!
KUN?!
HEY, WHAT'S GOING ON? THE GANG'S ALL HERE!
GOOD TO SEE YOU!
WHEN DID YOU GET BACK?!
LITTLE WHILE AGO.
YOU SHOULD'VE COME FOR THE CEREMONY, STUPID!!
WELL, I MEANT TO.
FLUSH
じゃー
W C
HARU-KUN...?
NAT-SUME...
HARU-KUN...!!

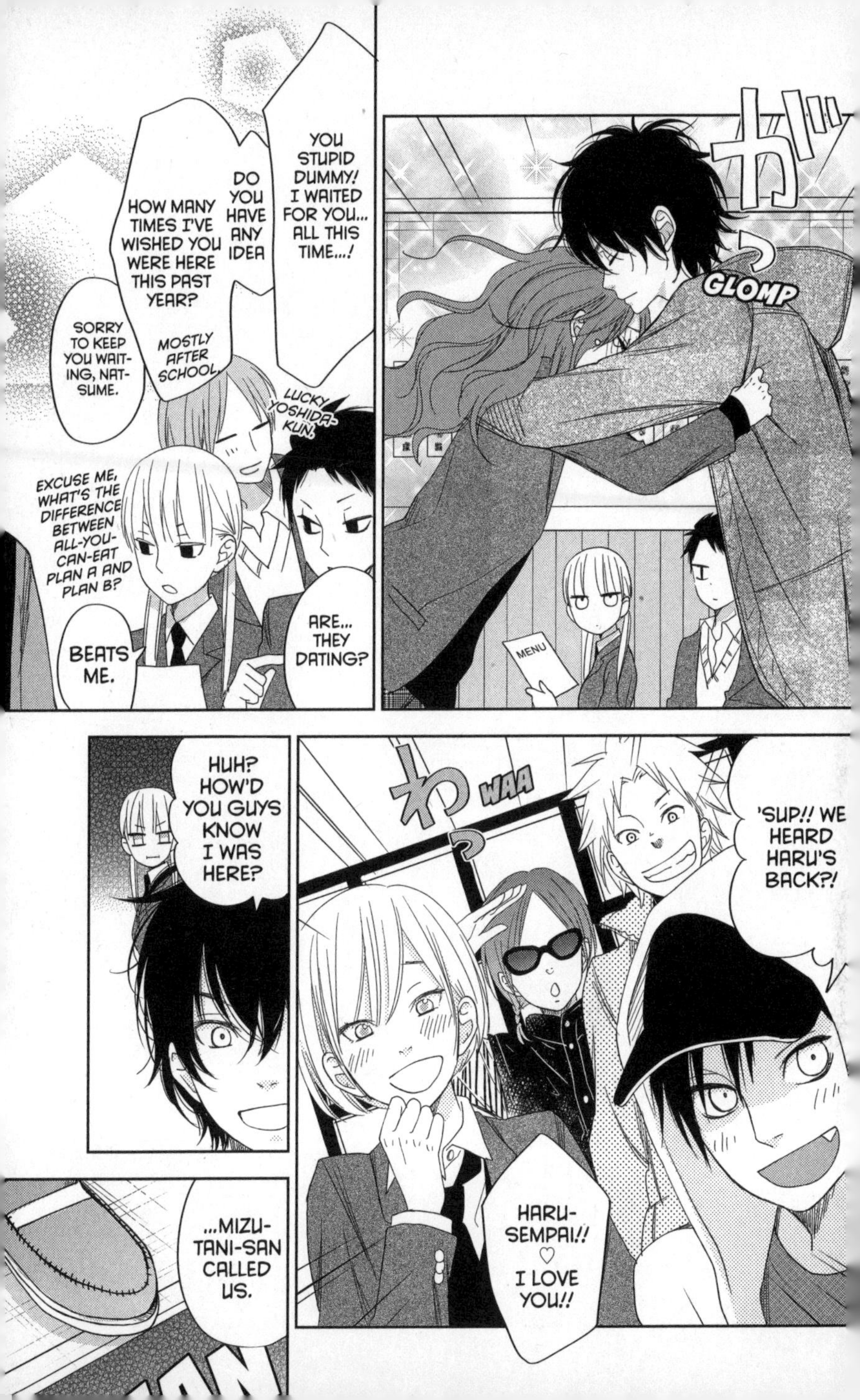

GLOMP
YOU STUPID DUMMY! I WAITED FOR YOU... ALL THIS TIME...!
DO YOU HAVE ANY IDEA
HOW MANY TIMES I'VE WISHED YOU WERE HERE THIS PAST YEAR?
MOSTLY AFTER SCHOOL.
SORRY TO KEEP YOU WAITING, NATSUME.
LUCKY YOSHIDA-KUN.
EXCUSE ME, WHAT'S THE DIFFERENCE BETWEEN ALL-YOU-CAN-EAT PLAN A AND PLAN B?
ARE... THEY DATING?
BEATS ME.
MENU
'SUP!! WE HEARD HARU'S BACK?!
WAA
HARU-SEMPAI!! ♡ I LOVE YOU!!
HUH? HOW'D YOU GUYS KNOW I WAS HERE?
...MIZUTANI-SAN CALLED US.

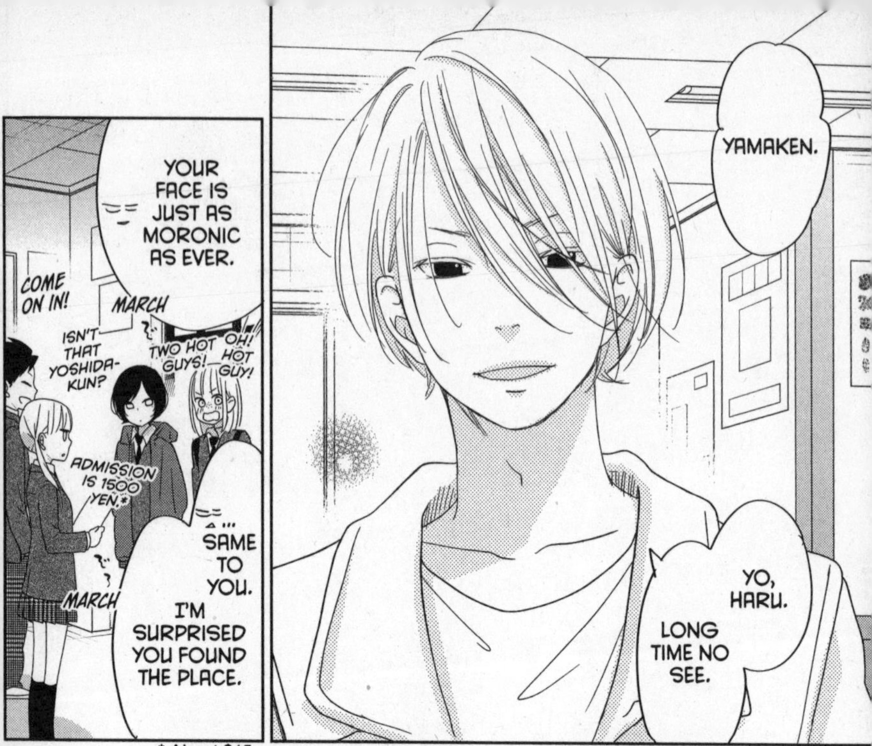
YAMAKEN.
YO, HARU.
LONG TIME NO SEE.
YOUR FACE IS JUST AS MORONIC AS EVER.
MARCH
COME ON IN!
OH! HOT GUY!
TWO HOT GUYS!
ISN'T THAT YOSHIDA-KUN?
ADMISSION IS 1500 YEN.*
...SAME TO YOU.
I'M SURPRISED YOU FOUND THE PLACE.
MARCH

* About $15

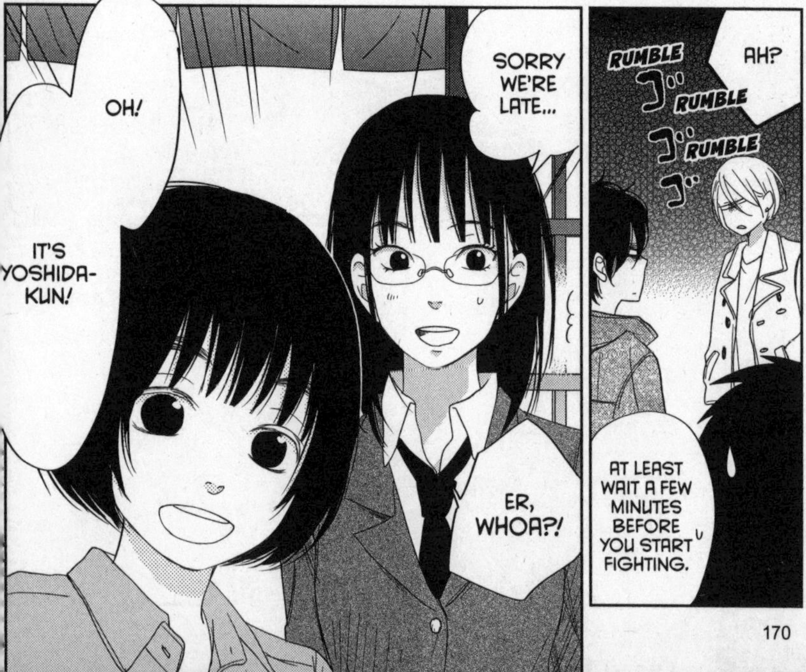
AH?
RUMBLE
RUMBLE
RUMBLE
AT LEAST WAIT A FEW MINUTES BEFORE YOU START FIGHTING.
SORRY WE'RE LATE...
OH!
IT'S YOSHIDA-KUN!
ER, WHOA?!

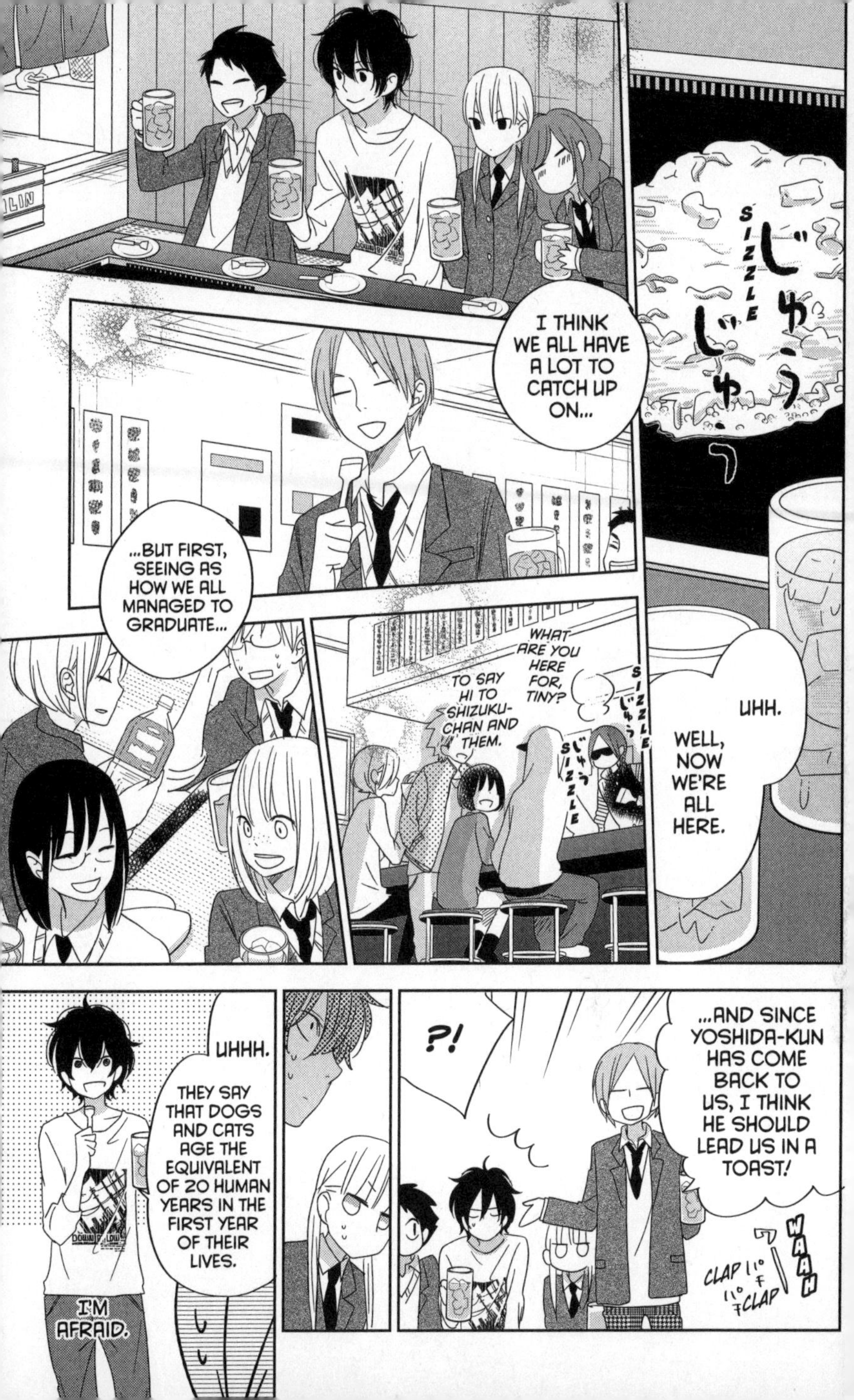

SIZZLE
じゅうじゅう
I THINK WE ALL HAVE A LOT TO CATCH UP ON...
...BUT FIRST, SEEING AS HOW WE ALL MANAGED TO GRADUATE...
UHH.
WELL, NOW WE'RE ALL HERE.
SIZZLE
じゅう
WHAT ARE YOU HERE FOR, TINY?
TO SAY HI TO SHIZUKU-CHAN AND THEM.
じゅう
SIZZLE
...AND SINCE YOSHIDA-KUN HAS COME BACK TO US, I THINK HE SHOULD LEAD US IN A TOAST!
WAAAH
ワ
CLAP パチ
パチ CLAP
?!
UHHH.
THEY SAY THAT DOGS AND CATS AGE THE EQUIVALENT OF 20 HUMAN YEARS IN THE FIRST YEAR OF THEIR LIVES.
I'M AFRAID.

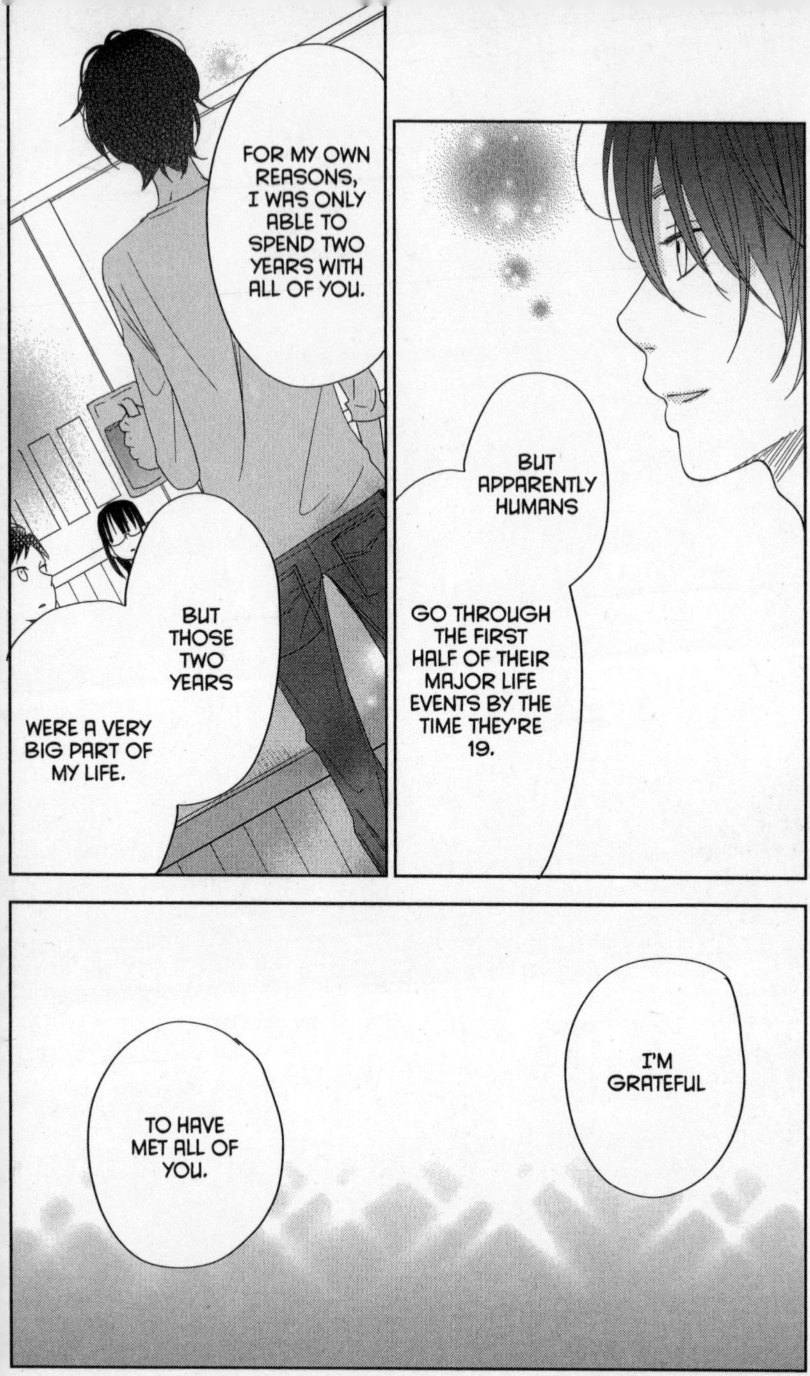
BUT APPARENTLY HUMANS
GO THROUGH THE FIRST HALF OF THEIR MAJOR LIFE EVENTS BY THE TIME THEY'RE 19.
FOR MY OWN REASONS, I WAS ONLY ABLE TO SPEND TWO YEARS WITH ALL OF YOU.
BUT THOSE TWO YEARS
WERE A VERY BIG PART OF MY LIFE.
I'M GRATEFUL
TO HAVE MET ALL OF YOU.

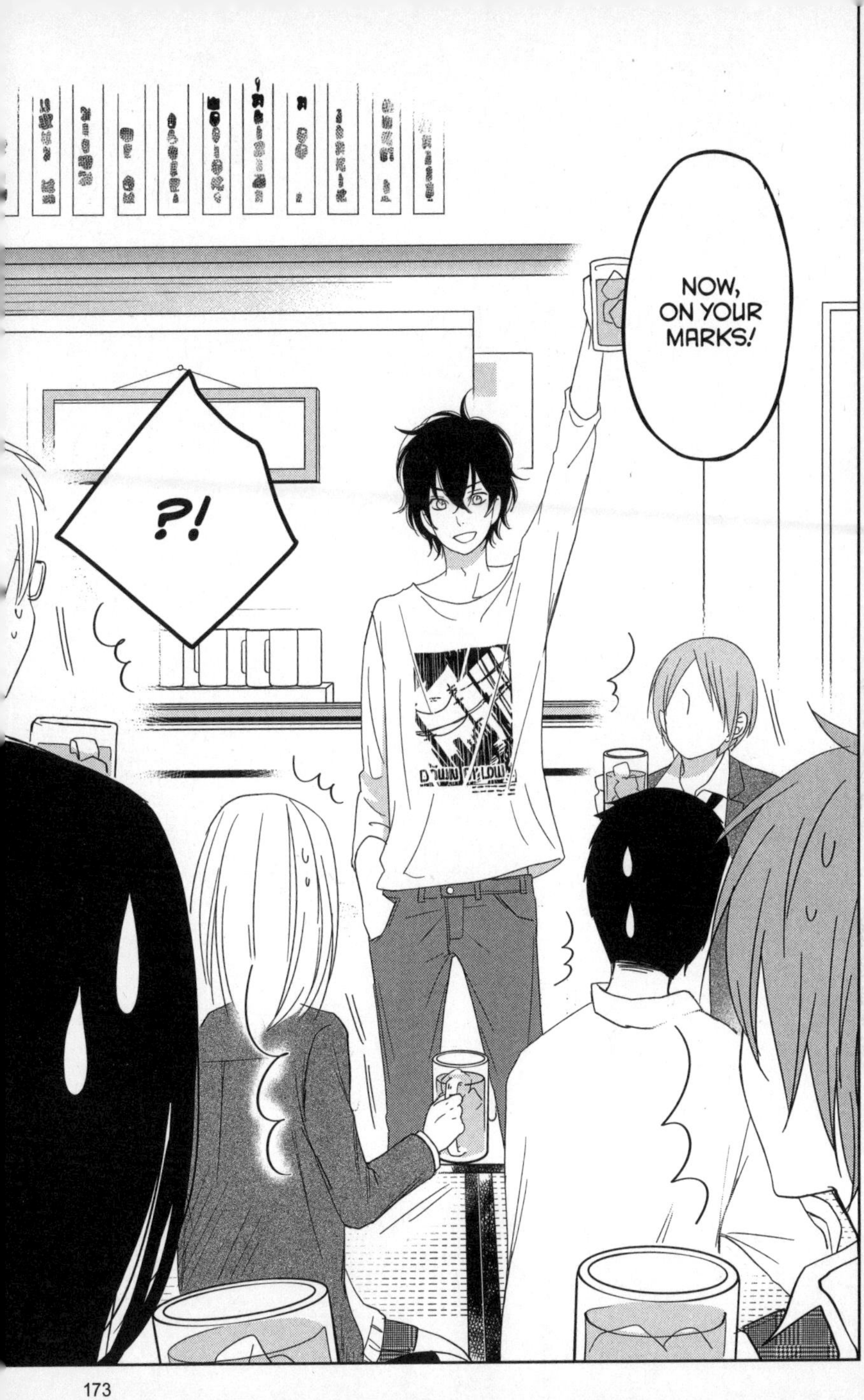
NOW, ON YOUR MARKS!
?!

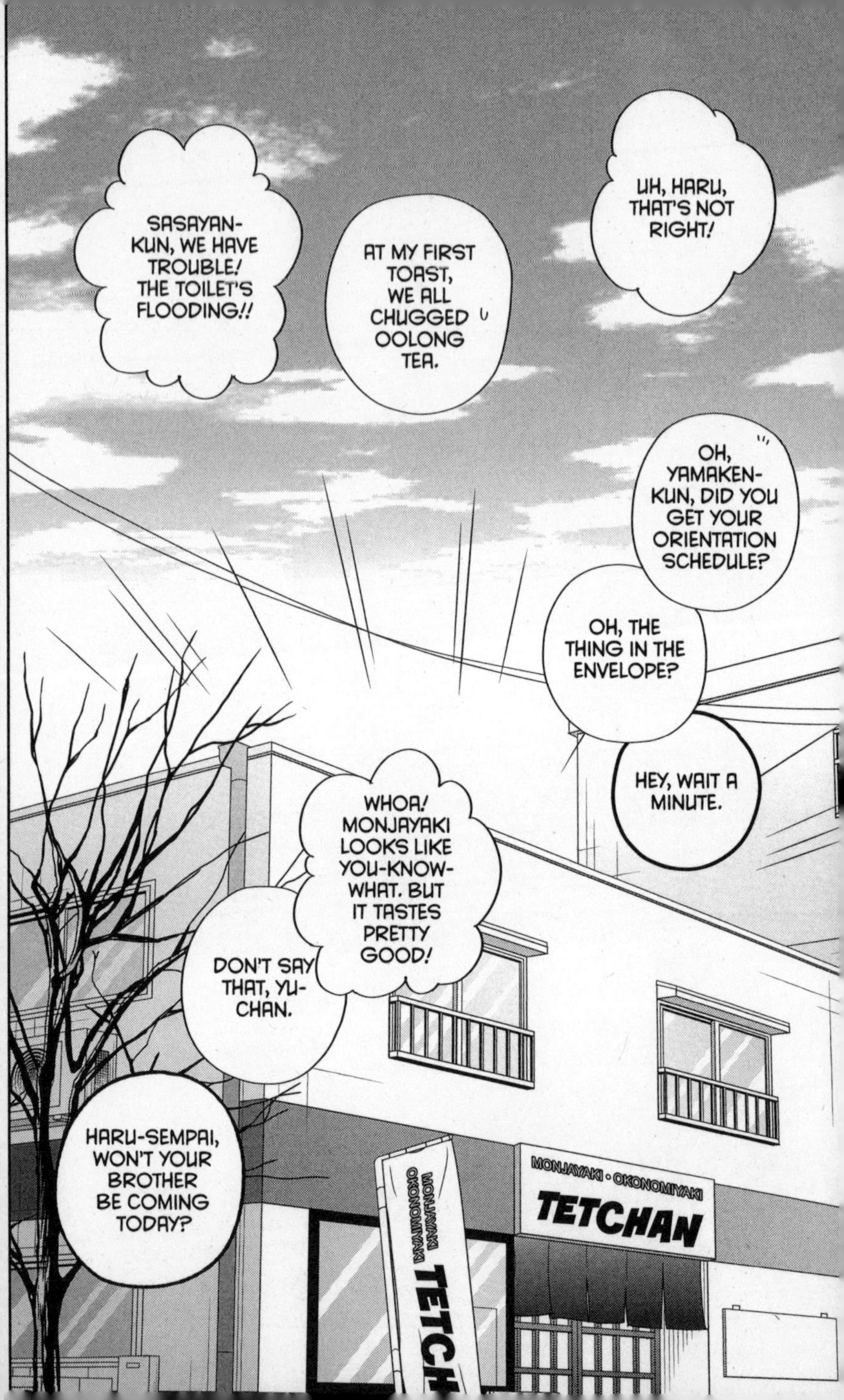
UH, HARU, THAT'S NOT RIGHT!
AT MY FIRST TOAST, WE ALL CHUGGED OOLONG TEA.
SASAYAN-KUN, WE HAVE TROUBLE! THE TOILET'S FLOODING!!
OH, YAMAKEN-KUN, DID YOU GET YOUR ORIENTATION SCHEDULE?
OH, THE THING IN THE ENVELOPE?
HEY, WAIT A MINUTE.
WHOA! MONJAYAKI LOOKS LIKE YOU-KNOW-WHAT. BUT IT TASTES PRETTY GOOD!
DON'T SAY THAT, YU-CHAN.
HARU-SEMPAI, WON'T YOUR BROTHER BE COMING TODAY?
MONJAYAKI • OKONOMIYAKI
TETCHAN
MONJAYAKI OKONOMIYAKI
TETCH

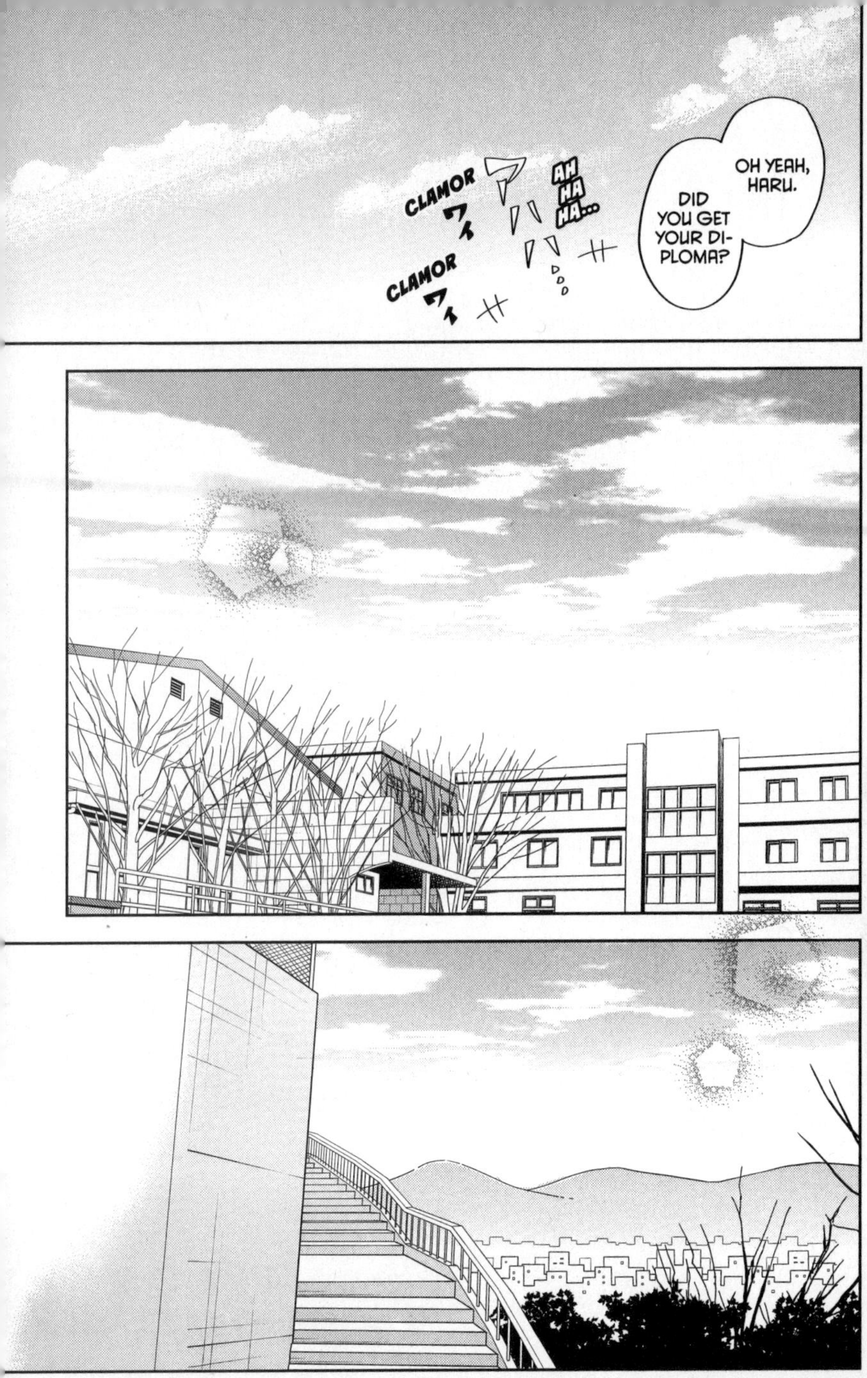
OH YEAH, HARU.
DID YOU GET YOUR DI-PLOMA?
AH HA HA...
CLAMOR
CLAMOR

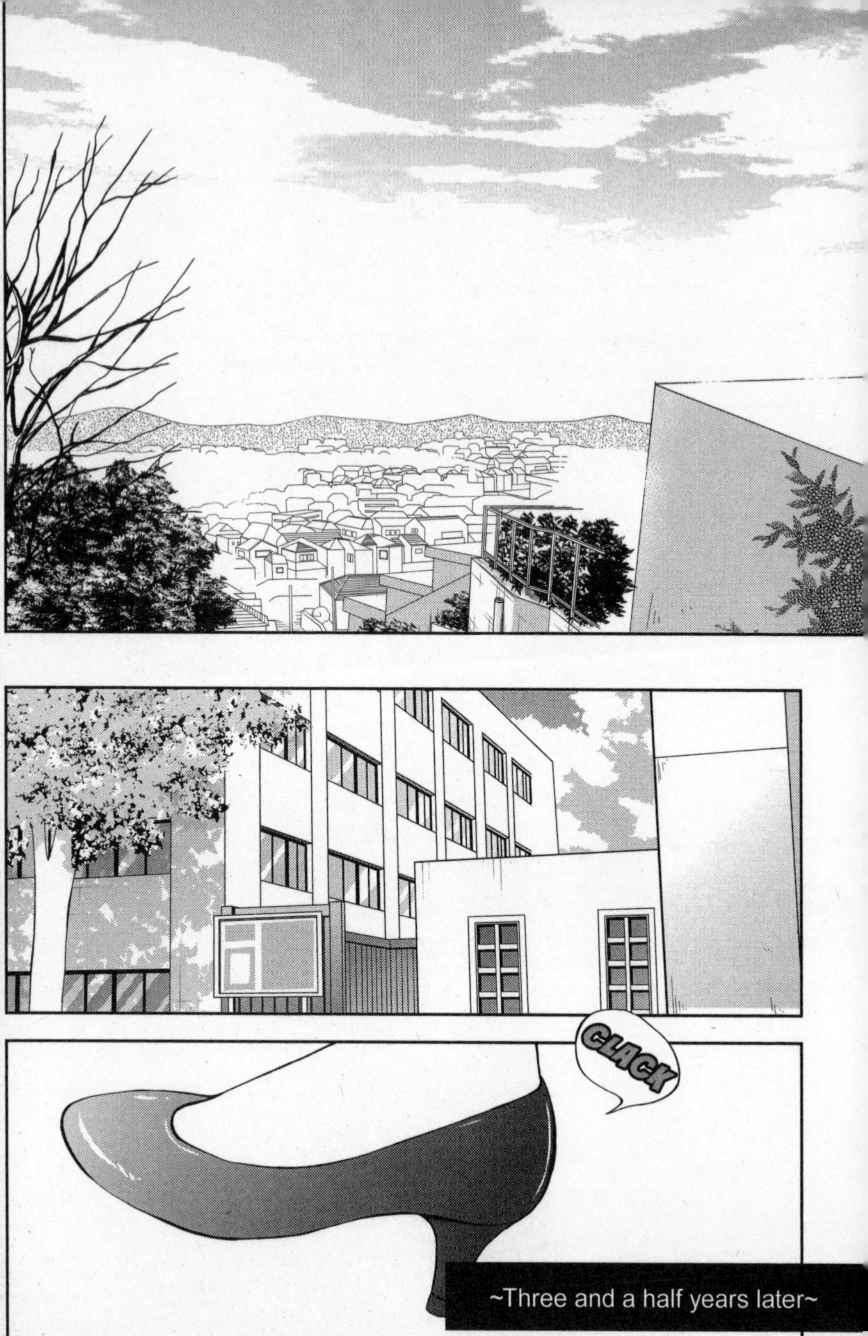
CLACK
~Three and a half years later~

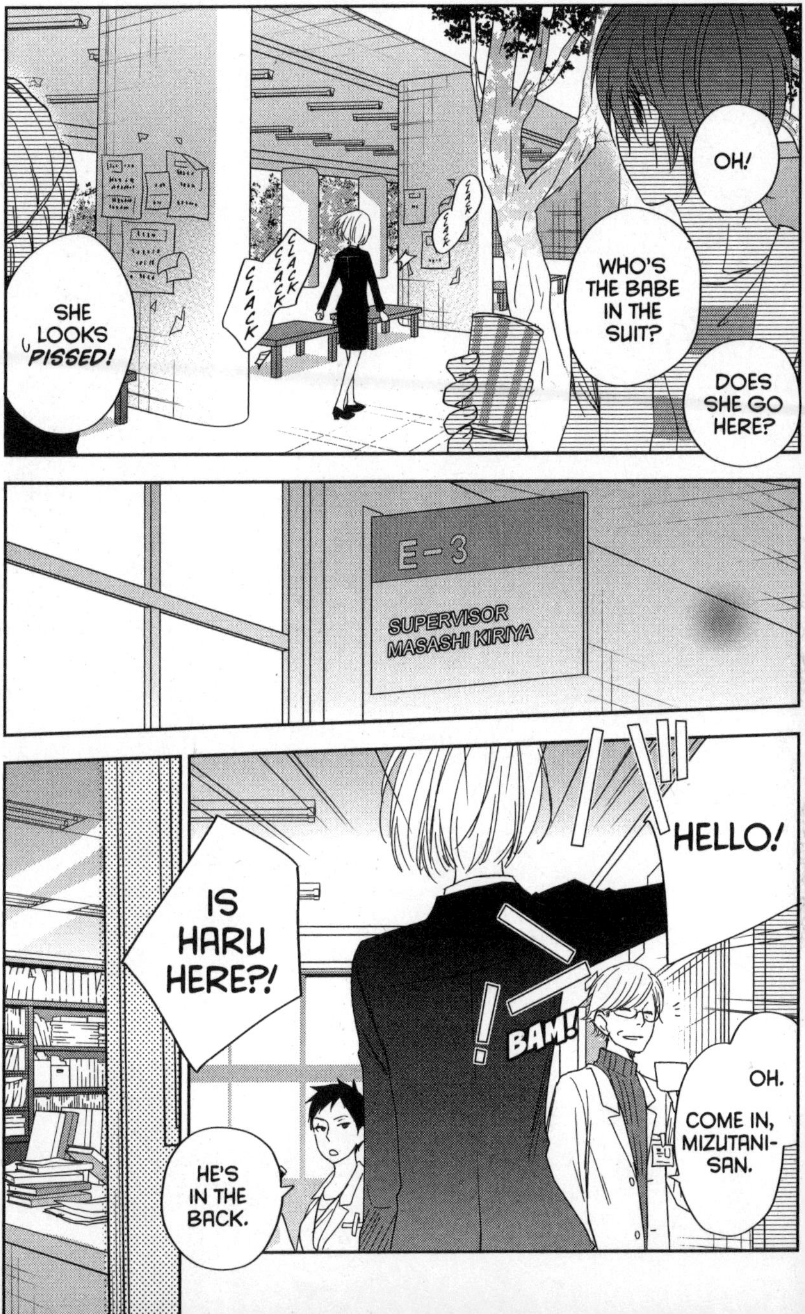
OH!
WHO'S THE BABE IN THE SUIT?
DOES SHE GO HERE?
CLACK CLACK
CLACK CLACK CLACK
SHE LOOKS PISSED!
E-3
SUPERVISOR MASASHI KIRIYA
HELLO!
IS HARU HERE?!
BAM!
OH.
COME IN, MIZUTANI-SAN.
HE'S IN THE BACK.

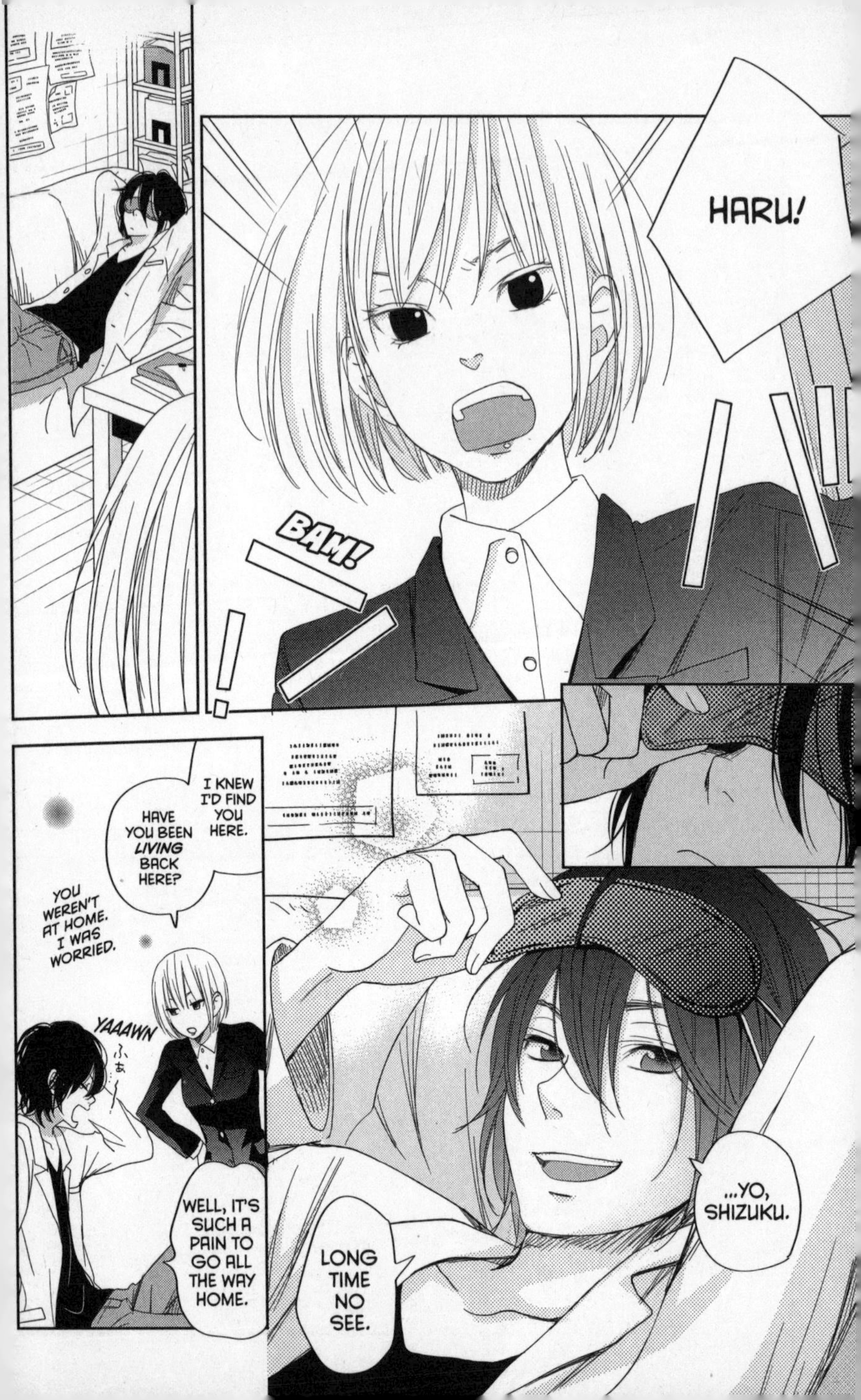
HARU!
BAM!
...YO, SHIZUKU.
LONG TIME NO SEE.
I KNEW I'D FIND YOU HERE.
HAVE YOU BEEN *LIVING* BACK HERE?
YOU WEREN'T AT HOME. I WAS WORRIED.
YAAAWN
ふぁ…
WELL, IT'S SUCH A PAIN TO GO ALL THE WAY HOME.

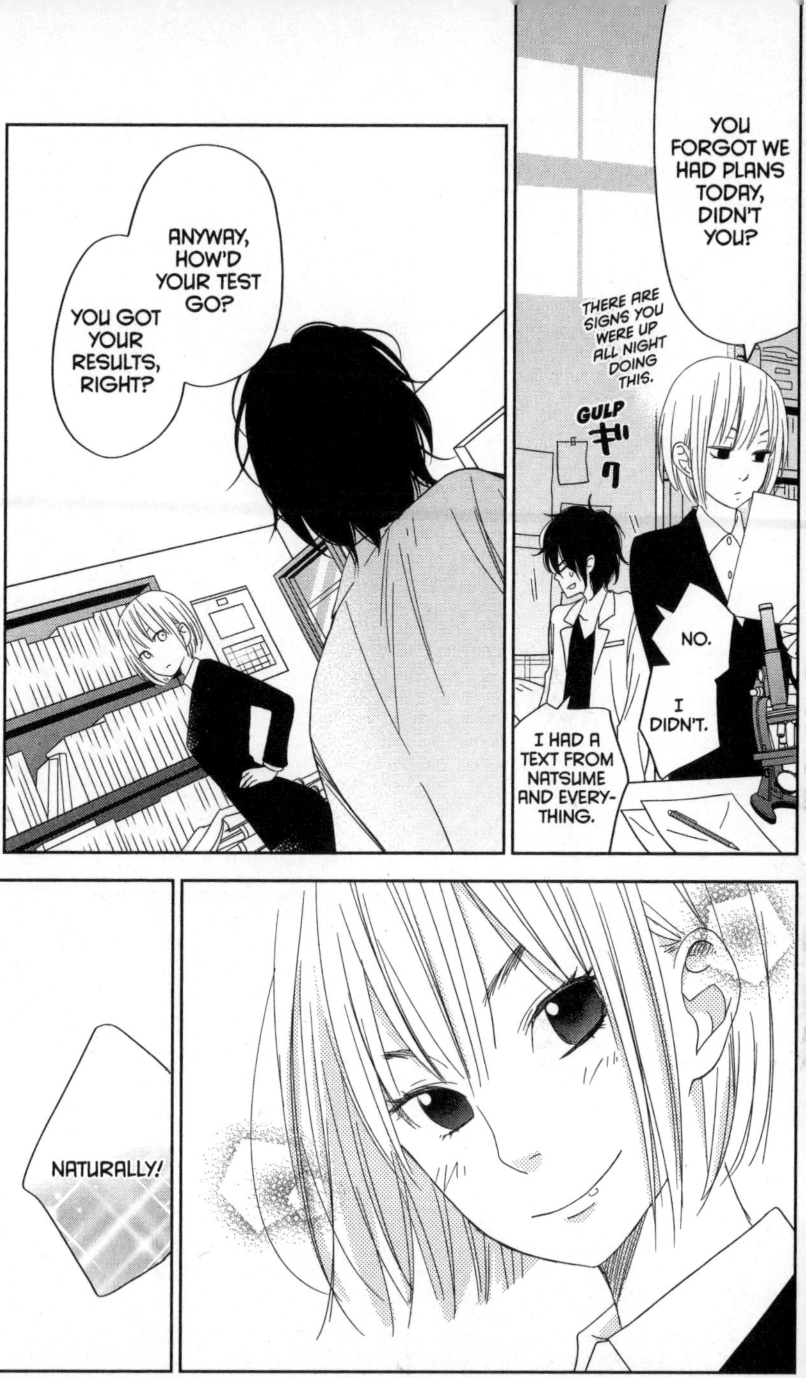
YOU FORGOT WE HAD PLANS TODAY, DIDN'T YOU?
THERE ARE SIGNS YOU WERE UP ALL NIGHT DOING THIS.
GULP
ギク
NO.
I DIDN'T.
I HAD A TEXT FROM NATSUME AND EVERY-THING.
ANYWAY, HOW'D YOUR TEST GO?
YOU GOT YOUR RESULTS, RIGHT?
NATURALLY!

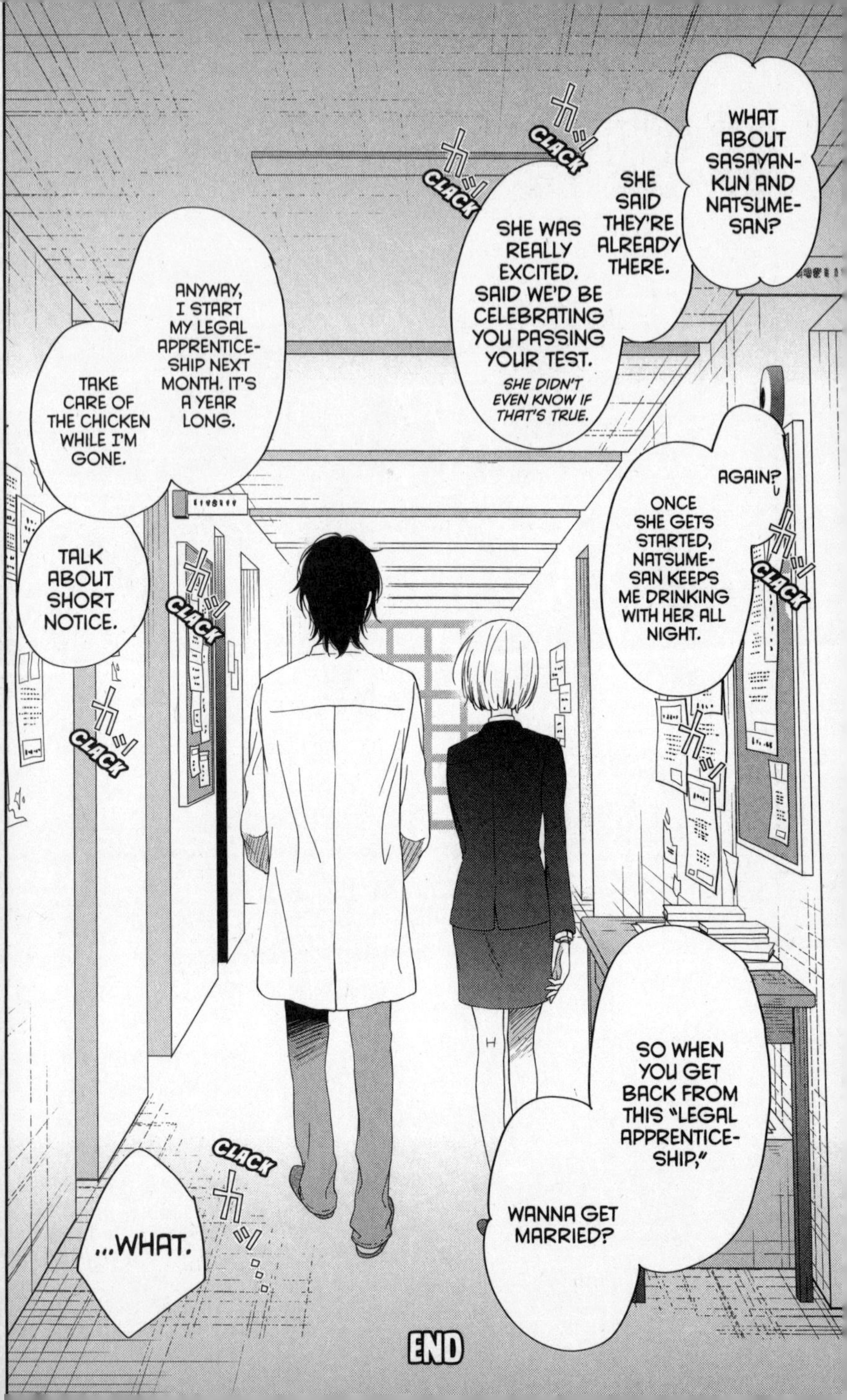
WHAT ABOUT SASAYAN-KUN AND NATSUME-SAN?
SHE SAID THEY'RE ALREADY THERE.
CLACK
CLACK
SHE WAS REALLY EXCITED. SAID WE'D BE CELEBRATING YOU PASSING YOUR TEST.
SHE DIDN'T EVEN KNOW IF THAT'S TRUE.
ONCE SHE GETS STARTED, NATSUME-SAN KEEPS ME DRINKING WITH HER ALL NIGHT.
AGAIN?
CLACK
ANYWAY, I START MY LEGAL APPRENTICESHIP NEXT MONTH. IT'S A YEAR LONG.
TAKE CARE OF THE CHICKEN WHILE I'M GONE.
CLACK
TALK ABOUT SHORT NOTICE.
CLACK
SO WHEN YOU GET BACK FROM THIS "LEGAL APPRENTICESHIP,"
WANNA GET MARRIED?
CLACK
...WHAT.
END

NO TIME LAG

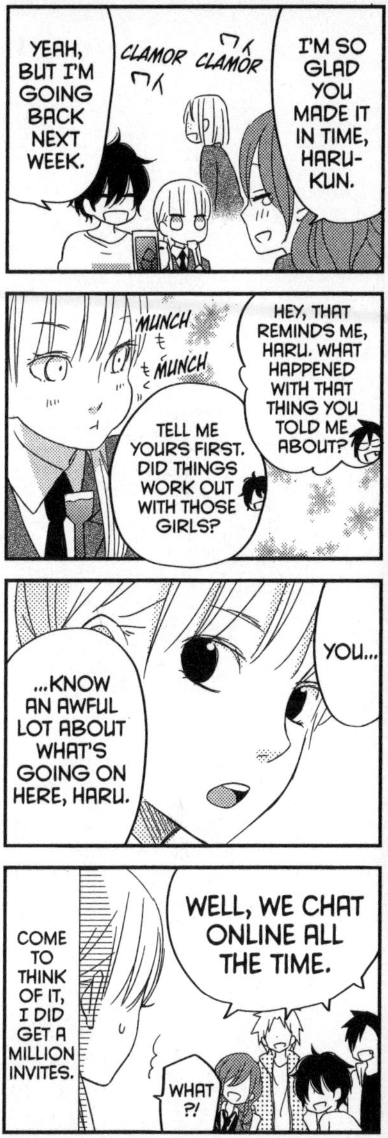
I'M SO GLAD YOU MADE IT IN TIME, HARU-KUN.
CLAMOR CLAMOR
YEAH, BUT I'M GOING BACK NEXT WEEK.
HEY, THAT REMINDS ME, HARU. WHAT HAPPENED WITH THAT THING YOU TOLD ME ABOUT?
MUNCH MUNCH
TELL ME YOURS FIRST. DID THINGS WORK OUT WITH THOSE GIRLS?
YOU...
...KNOW AN AWFUL LOT ABOUT WHAT'S GOING ON HERE, HARU.
WELL, WE CHAT ONLINE ALL THE TIME.
COME TO THINK OF IT, I DID GET A MILLION INVITES.
WHAT?!

TRUTH REVEALED

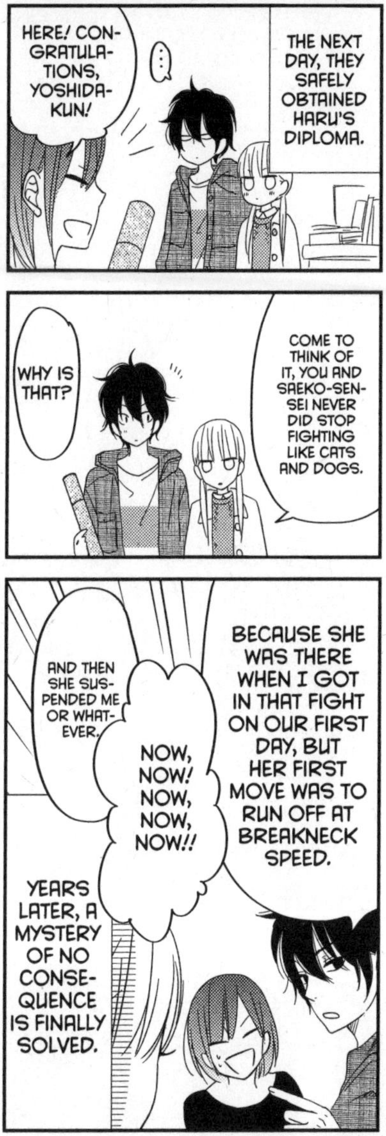
THE NEXT DAY, THEY SAFELY OBTAINED HARU'S DIPLOMA.
...
HERE! CONGRATULATIONS, YOSHIDA-KUN!
COME TO THINK OF IT, YOU AND SAEKO-SENSEI NEVER DID STOP FIGHTING LIKE CATS AND DOGS.
WHY IS THAT?
BECAUSE SHE WAS THERE WHEN I GOT IN THAT FIGHT ON OUR FIRST DAY, BUT HER FIRST MOVE WAS TO RUN OFF AT BREAKNECK SPEED.
AND THEN SHE SUSPENDED ME OR WHATEVER.
NOW, NOW! NOW, NOW, NOW!!
YEARS LATER, A MYSTERY OF NO CONSEQUENCE IS FINALLY SOLVED.

FINAL CHAPTER BONUS "SEQUEL: AFTER HE ASKED"

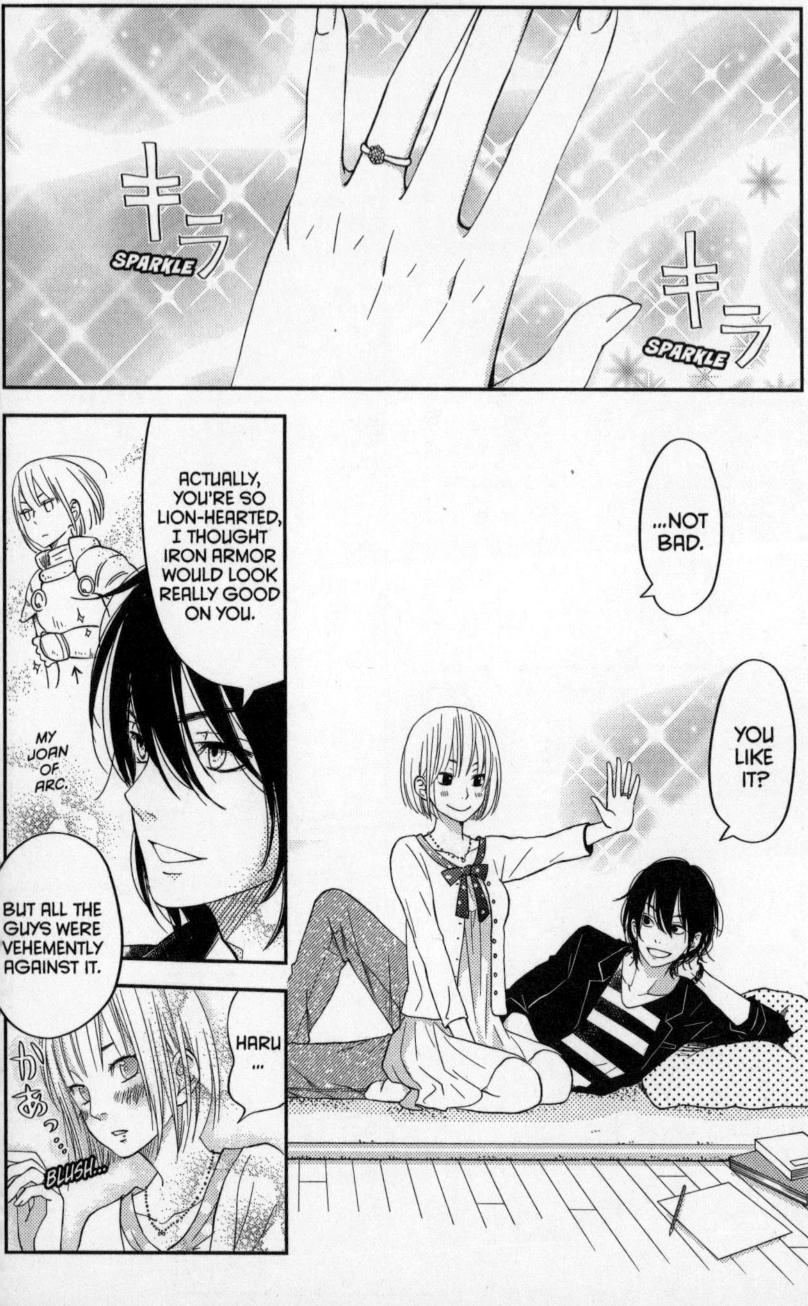
キラ
SPARKLE
キラ
SPARKLE
...NOT BAD.
YOU LIKE IT?
ACTUALLY, YOU'RE SO LION-HEARTED, I THOUGHT IRON ARMOR WOULD LOOK REALLY GOOD ON YOU.
MY JOAN OF ARC.
BUT ALL THE GUYS WERE VEHEMENTLY AGAINST IT.
HARU ...
かあっ...
BLUSH...

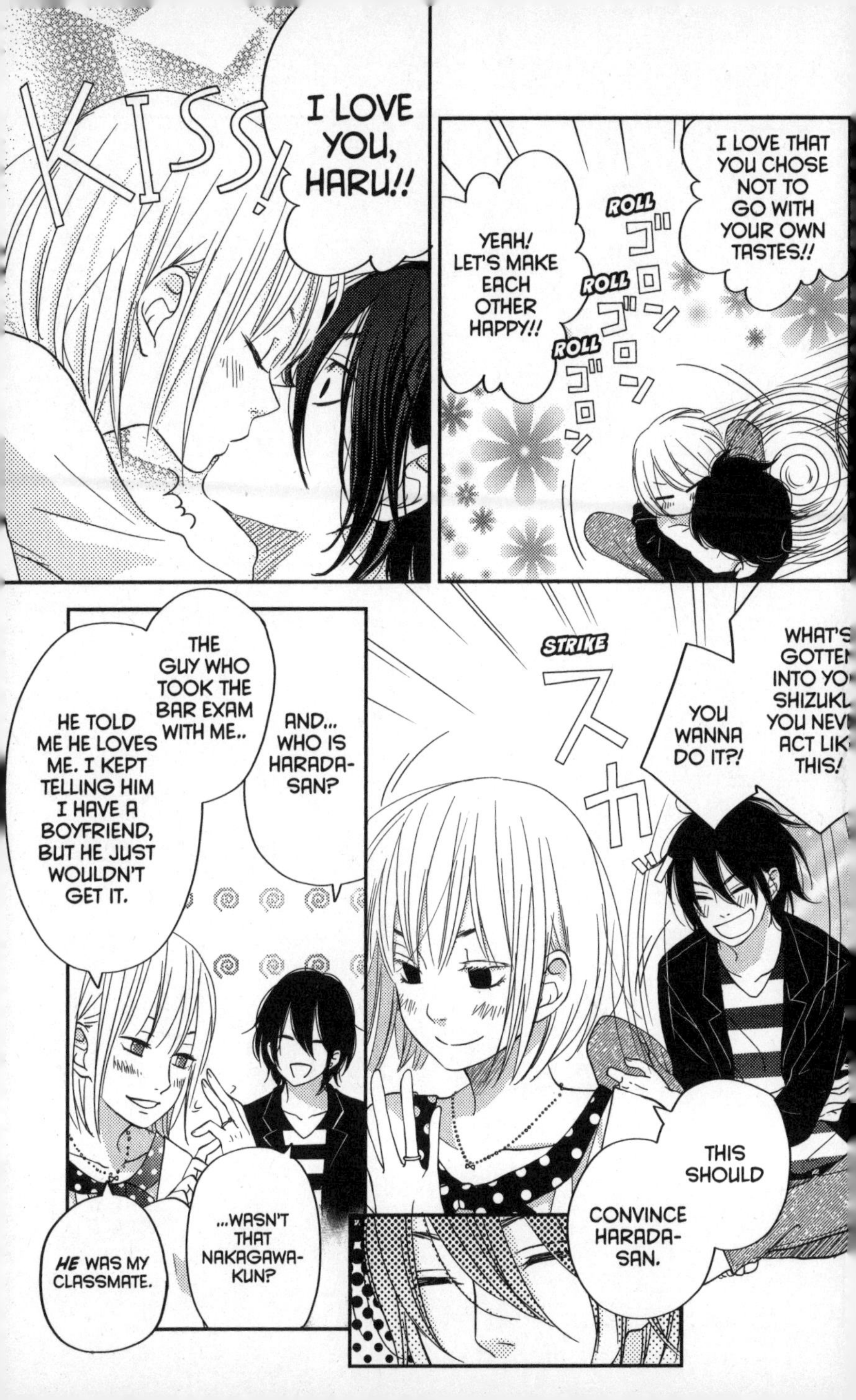
I LOVE THAT YOU CHOSE NOT TO GO WITH YOUR OWN TASTES!!
YEAH! LET'S MAKE EACH OTHER HAPPY!!
ROLL
ゴロッ
ROLL
ゴロッ
ROLL
ゴロッ
KISS!
I LOVE YOU, HARU!!
WHAT'S GOTTEN INTO YO SHIZUK YOU NEV ACT LIK THIS!
YOU WANNA DO IT?!
STRIKE
スカッ
THIS SHOULD
CONVINCE HARADA-SAN.
AND... WHO IS HARADA-SAN?
THE GUY WHO TOOK THE BAR EXAM WITH ME..
HE TOLD ME HE LOVES ME. I KEPT TELLING HIM I HAVE A BOYFRIEND, BUT HE JUST WOULDN'T GET IT.
...WASN'T THAT NAKAGAWA-KUN?
HE WAS MY CLASSMATE.

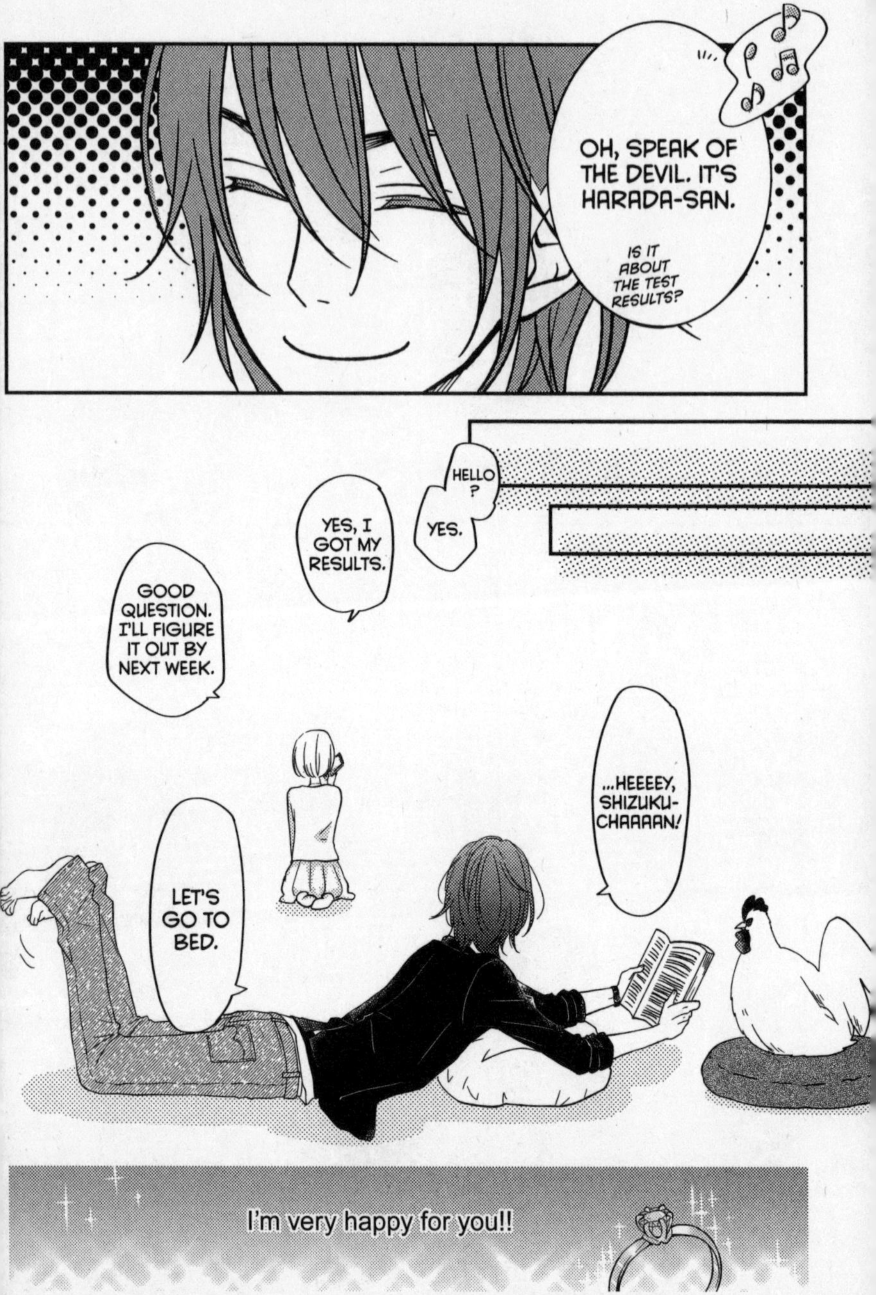
OH, SPEAK OF THE DEVIL. IT'S HARADA-SAN.
IS IT ABOUT THE TEST RESULTS?
HELLO?
YES.
YES, I GOT MY RESULTS.
GOOD QUESTION. I'LL FIGURE IT OUT BY NEXT WEEK.
...HEEEEY, SHIZUKU-CHAAAAN!
LET'S GO TO BED.
I'm very happy for you!!

★END CREDITS★

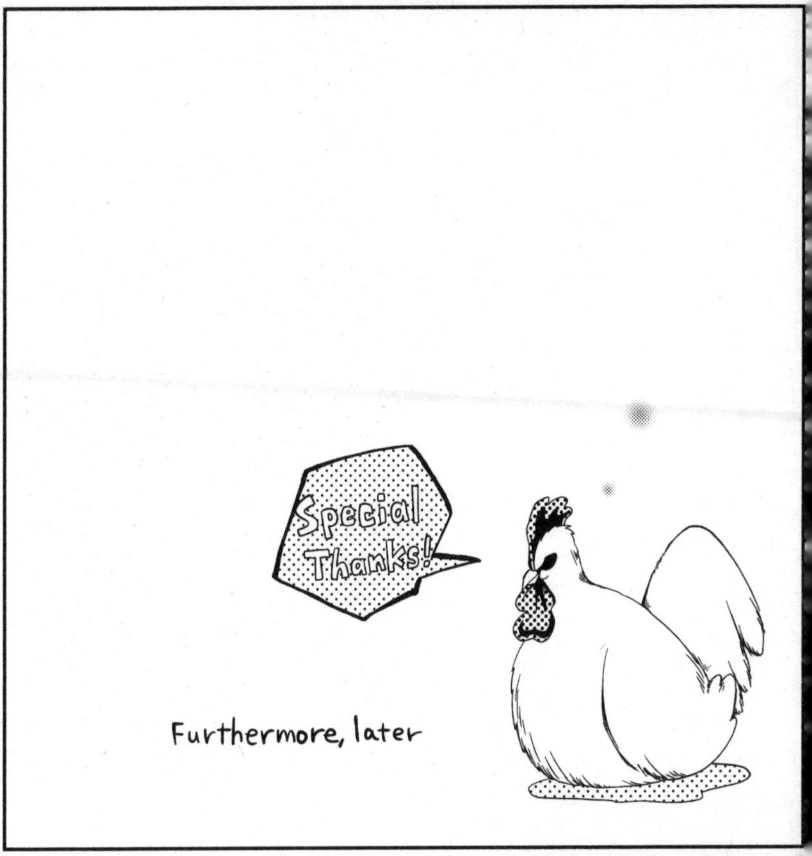
Special Thanks!
Furthermore, later

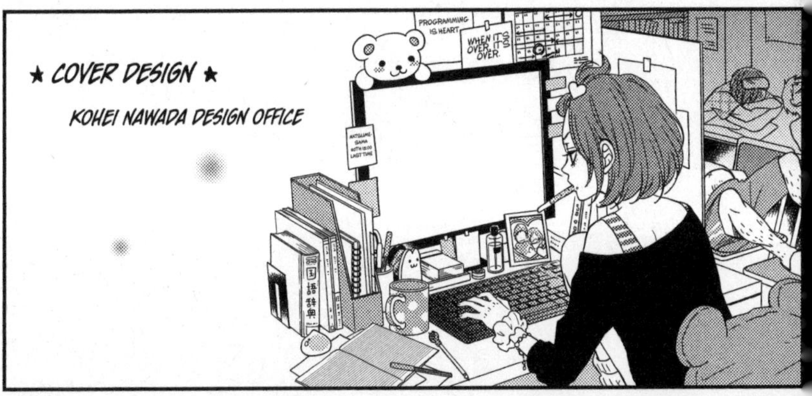
PROGRAMMING IS HEART
WHEN IT'S OVER IT'S OVER.
★ COVER DESIGN ★
KOHEI NAWADA DESIGN OFFICE

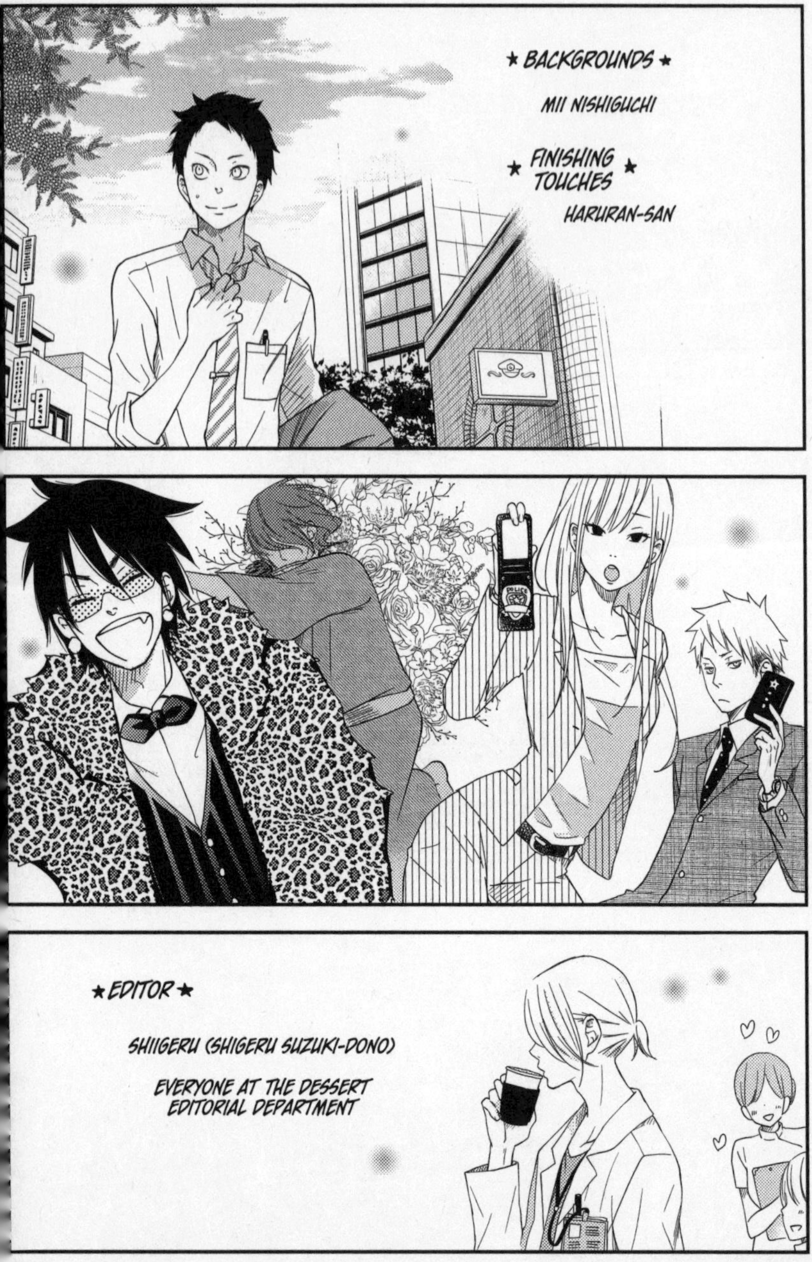
★ BACKGROUNDS ★
MII NISHIGUCHI
★ FINISHING TOUCHES ★
HARURAN-SAN
★ EDITOR ★
SHIIGERU (SHIGERU SUZUKI-DONO)
EVERYONE AT THE DESSERT EDITORIAL DEPARTMENT

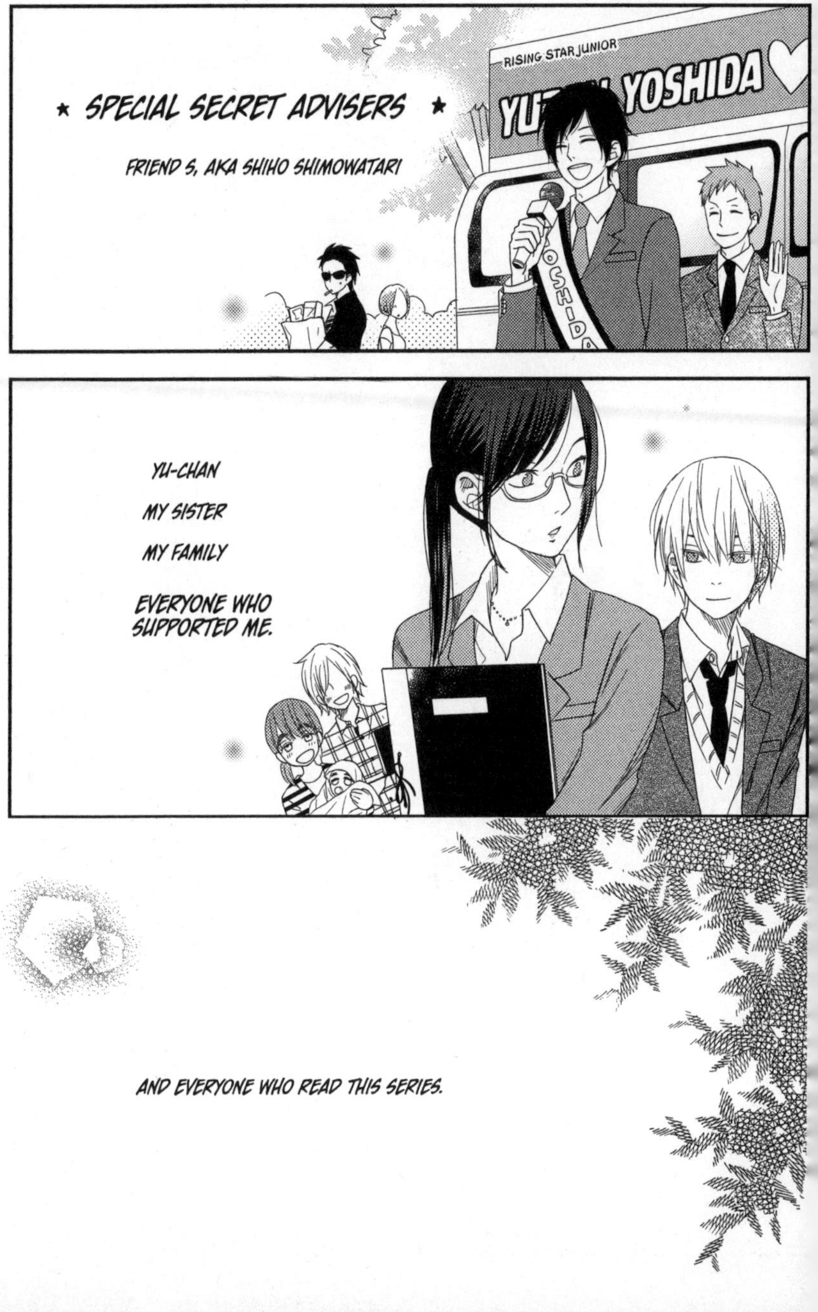
★ SPECIAL SECRET ADVISERS ★
FRIEND S, AKA SHIHO SHIMOWATARI
RISING STAR JUNIOR
YOSHIDA
YU-CHAN
MY SISTER
MY FAMILY
EVERYONE WHO SUPPORTED ME.
AND EVERYONE WHO READ THIS SERIES.

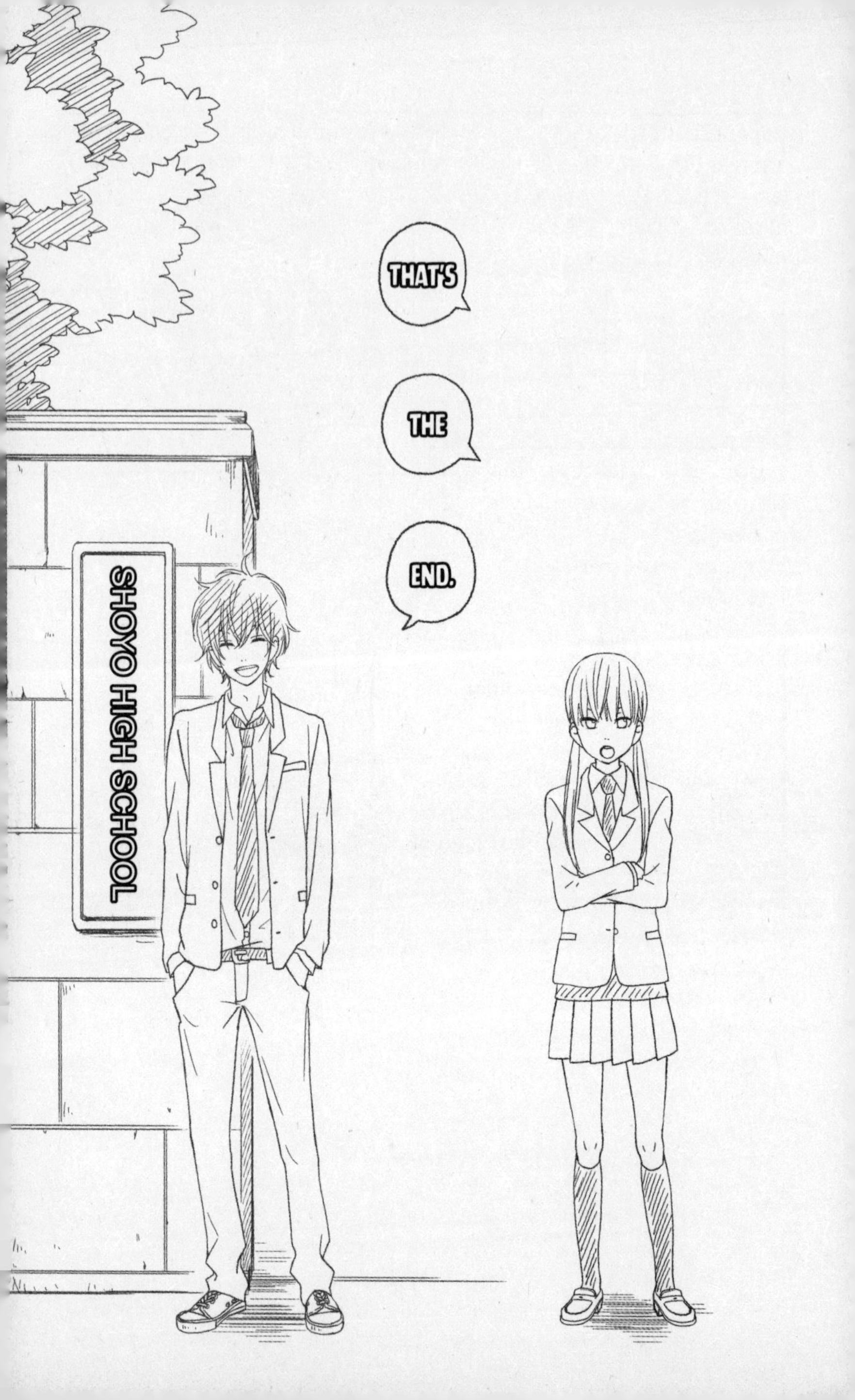
THAT'S
THE
END.
SHOYO HIGH SCHOOL

Translation notes

Japanese is a tricky language for most Westerners, and translation is often more art than science. For your edification and reading pleasure, here are notes on some of the places where we could have gone in a different direction in our translation of the work, or where a Japanese cultural reference is used.

Heattech, page 22

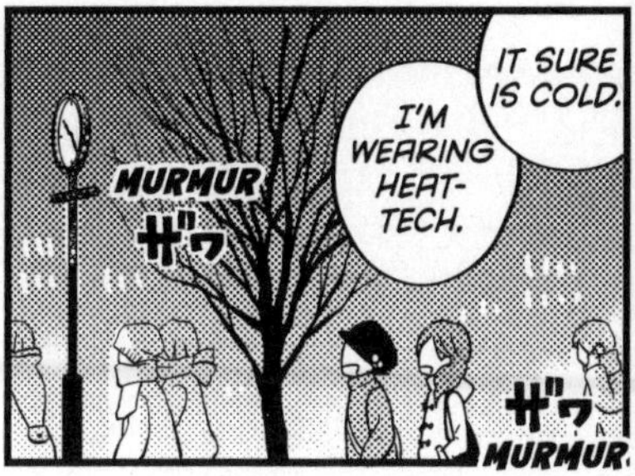
IT SURE IS COLD.
I'M WEARING HEAT-TECH.
MURMUR
ザワ
ザワ
MURMUR

Heattech is clothing designed to keep you warm without bogging you down in lots of bulky layers. It's made from special fabric that supposedly creates heat, so if you're planning to be outside in the middle of the night on New Year's Eve, it would be ideal apparel to stave off hypothermia.

Lucky dreams, page 44

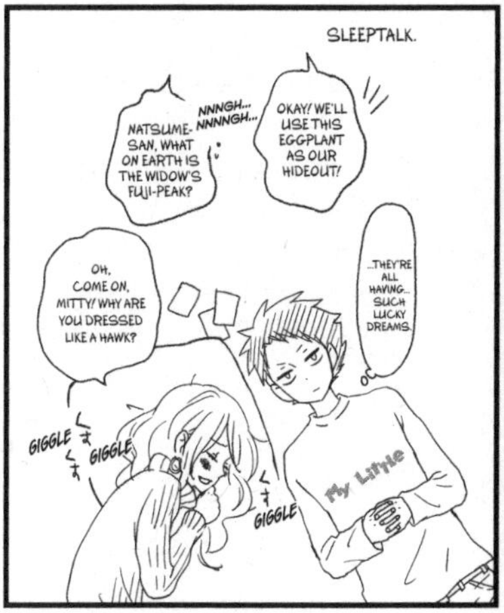
SLEEPTALK.
OKAY! WE'LL USE THIS EGGPLANT AS OUR HIDEOUT!
NNNGH... NNNNGH...
NATSUME-SAN, WHAT ON EARTH IS THE WIDOW'S FUJI-PEAK?
...THEY'RE ALL HAVING... SUCH LUCKY DREAMS.
OH, COME ON, MITTY! WHY ARE YOU DRESSED LIKE A HAWK?
GIGGLE
GIGGLE
GIGGLE
My Little

According to Japanese tradition, the first dream of a new year can predict the dreamer's fortune (or lack thereof) for the rest of the year. The luckiest symbols in New Year's dreams are Mt. Fuji, a hawk, and an eggplant—all of which are being dreamed about, in a way, by Sasayan's friends. As for the meaning of the widow's Fuji-peak, in Japan, a widow's peak (a V-shaped point in the hairline) is called a *fujibitai*, or "Fuji forehead." This is because the shape of the hairline resembles an upside-down Mt. Fuji.

Second death anniversary, page 69

In Japanese Buddhism, there are certain anniversaries of a person's death designated for Buddhist services. One of these is the second anniversary, which is referred to as the *sankaiki*, or "third mourning" (the first two mournings being shortly after the death and on the first anniversary). It is customary to invite extended family to remember the deceased on the more significant anniversaries, the two-year anniversary being one of those.

What to do when visiting a grave, page 70

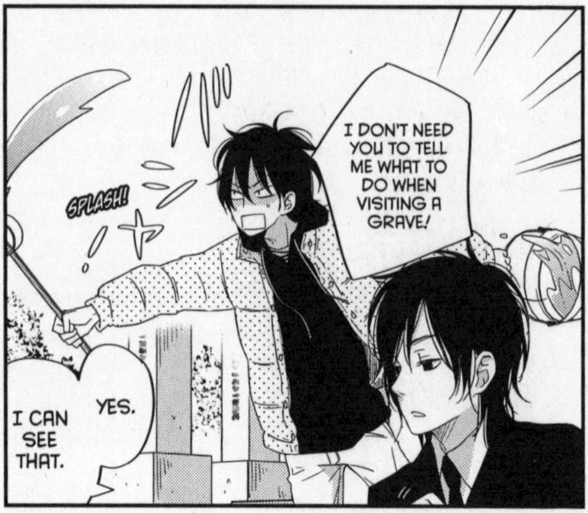
I DON'T NEED YOU TO TELL ME WHAT TO DO WHEN VISITING A GRAVE!
SPLASH!
YES.
I CAN SEE THAT.

There are certain procedures to be followed on a proper visit to a grave in Japan. First, visitors must wash their hands to make sure they are clean. They bring water in a bucket, and after they have paid their respects to the dead, they clean the area around the grave. Part of cleaning the grave involves ladling water over it, as Haru does, and then wiping off dirt, etc. Finally, they burn incense and make their offerings to the deceased.

Feeding the deer, page 100

In the third year of high school, many Japanese students go on a class trip. Shizuku's school chose the more or less common destination of historic Kyoto and Nara. In this picture, the students are at Nara Park, a place inhabited by wild deer. These particular deer have been designated as a national treasure, and you can buy special crackers to feed them.

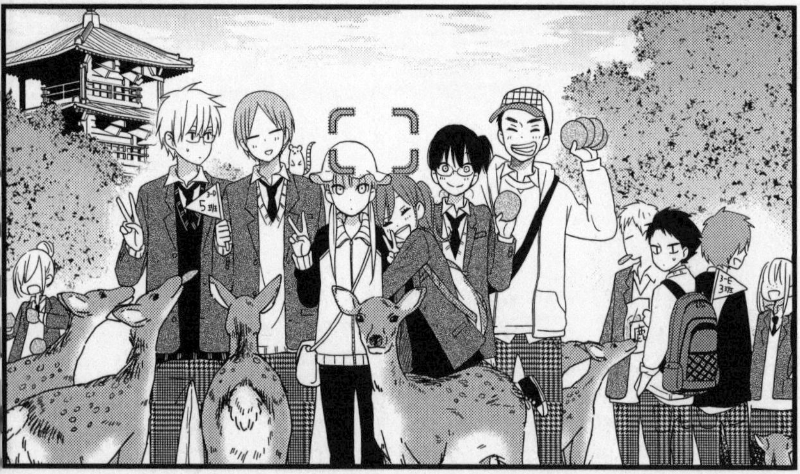

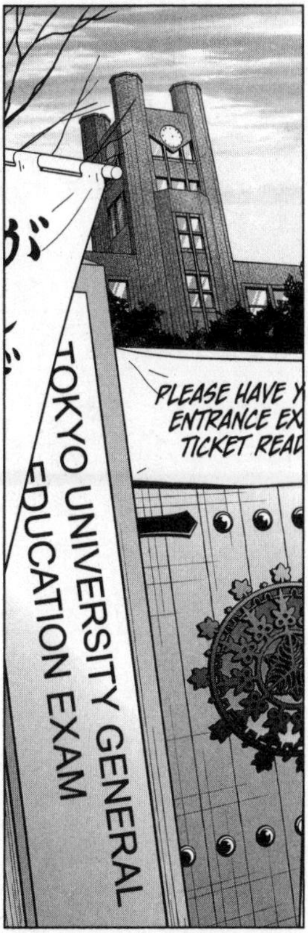
TOKYO UNIVERSITY GENERAL
EDUCATION EXAM
PLEASE HAVE Y
ENTRANCE EX
TICKET REA

Tokyo University, page 113

Tokyo University is the most prestigious university in Japan, and as such, it would be very difficult to get in.

Later, alligator, page 131

The Japanese version of this joke is *bai-baikin,* which is a combination of the English "bye-bye" and the Japanese *baikin*, which means "germ." It's typically used by people who are not as serious as Shizuku.

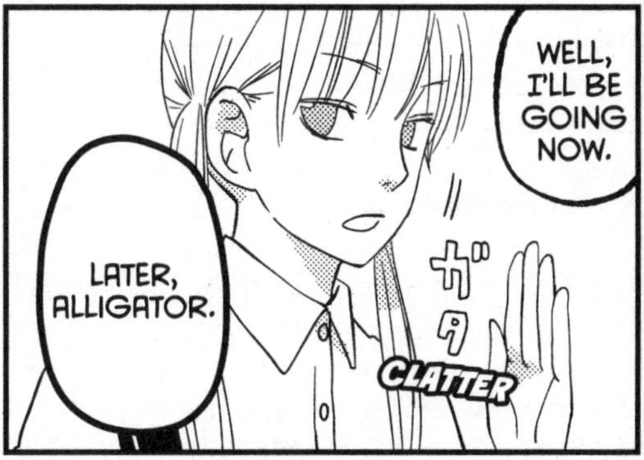
WELL, I'LL BE GOING NOW.
LATER, ALLIGATOR.
ガタ
CLATTER

Covered in white light, page 139

These are a translation of the lyrics to the song *"Tabidachi no Hi ni* (On the Day of Departure)." This song is a standard song sung at graduation ceremonies in Japan. The song is about saying good-bye and setting off for a new future, full of hope and dreams.

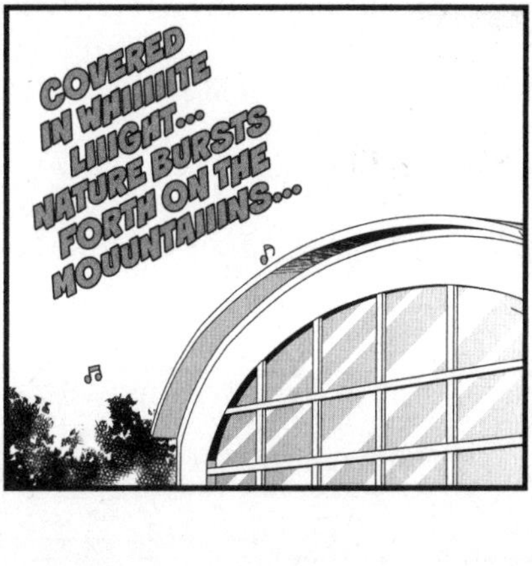
COVERED IN WHIIIIITE LIIIGHT... NATURE BURSTS FORTH ON THE MOUUNTAIIINS...

A Kodansha Comics Trade Paperback Original.

My Little Monster volume 12 copyright © 2013 Robico
English translation copyright © 2016 Robico

All rights reserved.

Published in the United States by Kodansha Comics, an imprint of Kodansha USA Publishing, LLC, New York.

Publication rights for this English edition arranged through Kodansha Ltd., Tokyo.

First published in Japan in 2013 by Kodansha Ltd., Tokyo, as *Tonari no Kaibutsu-kun*, volume 12.

ISBN 978-1-63236-127-1

Printed in the United States of America.

www.kodanshacomics.com

9 8 7 6 5 4 3 2 1

Editing: Lauren Scanlan
Translator: Alethea Nibley & Athena Nibley
Lettering: Paige Pumphrey